THE LOEB CLASSICAL LIBRARY

FOUNDED BY JAMES LOEB, LL.D.

EDITED BY
G. P. GOOLD, PH.D.

MENANDER
I

132

MENANDER

EDITED
WITH AN ENGLISH TRANSLATION BY

W. G. ARNOTT

UNIVERSITY OF LEEDS

IN THREE VOLUMES

I

ASPIS TO EPITREPONTES

CAMBRIDGE, MASSACHUSETTS
HARVARD UNIVERSITY PRESS
LONDON
WILLIAM HEINEMANN LTD
MCMLXXIX

© The President and Fellows of
Harvard College 1979

American ISBN 0–674–99147–8
British ISBN 0 434 99132 5

*Printed in Great Britain by
Fletcher & Son Ltd, Norwich*

To my mother and my wife

CONTENTS

PREFACE

Francis G. Allinson published his edition of Menander for the Loeb Classical Library in 1921 (revised 1930). It was a valuable work in its day, but the large accretions of new papyri since the Second World War have greatly diminished its usefulness, and this new edition in three volumes is intended to replace it. The surviving remains of Menander are presented here (as in F. H. Sandbach's Oxford Text of 1972) in alphabetical order of play titles. Volume I contains *Aspis* to *Epitrepontes*, Volume II *Heros* to *Perinthia*, and Volume III *Samia* to *Phasma* together with those papyri certainly or plausibly assigned to unidentified plays of Menander, and the more important fragments quoted in ancient authors. In Volume I the scanty remains of *Encheiridion* (omitted by Sandbach) will be found, but nothing from *Kekryphalos* will appear in Volume II (the attribution of *P. Hamburg* 656 to the play seems too dubious).

The publication of any Greek text of Menander poses severe problems. Many of the papyri are severely mutilated, with portions of text torn off or abraded into nothingness. How far gaps should be supplemented is a matter of dispute, and there is no obviously correct answer. This edition normally prints supplements only where they are certain or highly plausible, but occasionally with the better preserved texts (such as *Dyskolos* and large stretches of *Aspis* and *Epitrepontes*) a supplement is printed *exempli gratia*, in order that an otherwise complete passage of Greek may not be disfigured by a disjunctive gap. Some inconsistency here is probably unavoidable. All supplements, however, even if they consist of only one letter, are marked by square brackets.

Greek papyri vary considerably in their indications of part-division in dramatic texts. The Bodmer papyrus of the third century A.D. and the Cairo papyrus of the fifth use a reasonably satisfactory system of *dicola* (:) to mark off each speech, with *paragraphi* (sublinear dashes extending into the left-hand margins) under the beginning of each line where a part-division occurs. Marginal abbreviations of speakers' names sometimes accompany the other indications, but not always systematically. Earlier papyri, like the Sorbonne roll of the *Sikyonioi*, which dates from the third century B.C., are very much less helpful over part-division. Occasionally but not consistently they leave small spaces to mark off intra-linear changes of speaker, a system which is wholly useless when the change comes at the end of a line. Departures from the papyri over part-division or the assignment of single speeches are indicated in the critical apparatus but not in the text.

This critical apparatus registers all manuscript readings which differ from the printed text, except for those minor misspellings or vowel confusions (e.g. $\epsilon/\alpha\iota$, $\epsilon\iota/\iota$, θ'/τ', $o/ov/\omega$) which are endemic in papyri. Conjectures are cited only when they have been

PREFACE

adopted in the text. Where more than two scholars hit on the same emendation at about the same time their names are replaced in the apparatus by the space-saving word ' several '.

The line-numberings in each play agree almost entirely with those of Sandbach's Oxford Text. For fifty years there has been confusion in referring to the line-numbers of such plays as the *Epitrepontes*, where different systems were operated by different scholars. It is hoped that acceptance of Sandbach's numberings will end such confusions. Unfortunately, in two places total adhesion to Sandbach has not been possible. *Epitrepontes* 1000–58 Sandbach is the mutilated text of two fragments of the Cairo codex (β, U). It appears to me that Sandbach misplaces these two fragments slightly,[1] and I have accordingly adjusted the line-numberings a little as follows:

Sandbach	*Arnott*
1003–17	1000–14
1037–51	1035–49

The other place is the *Misoumenos*, where new discoveries have thrown all current systems into a messy confusion. Here I have attempted a systematic renumbering to avoid the use of letters as well as numbers for the lines of the prologue.

The text and apparatus are based on a study of good photographs of the papyri whenever possible. I have supplemented published photographs with new ones of the Cairo codex and of the Geneva fragments of the *Georgos*. Unpublished photographs of

---

[1] The case is argued in my paper in the *Actes du XVe Congrès International de Papyrologie*, Brussels, III, 31 ff.

the Florence and London fragments of the *Georgos* and
of the Florence fragment of the *Encheiridion* have
been supplied to me; acknowledgements are made
below. No photograph has ever been published of
lines 159–77 of the *Epitrepontes* in the Leningrad frag-
ment, and here I have had to be satisfied with V.
Jernstedt's drawing (see the introduction to this play).

The translation perhaps foolishly attempts the im-
possible. Menander's plays are written in a style
that appears to grade from the colloquialism of con-
temporary Attic to the formality of tragic parody.
They use verse, basically the iambic trimeter with
occasional scenes in trochaic or iambic tetrameters,
and very rare ventures into other metres. For
Menander's trimeters I have used English blank
verse, basically a lightly-stressed ten-syllabled line
that occasionally stretches to eleven or twelve syl-
lables. The reason for these anomalies is not in-
sensitivity to metrical rules or innumeracy, but the
duress of translating one line of Greek normally by
one line of English. Menander's tetrameters are
rendered into the corresponding English metres. The
structure of the two languages forbids absolute
correspondence of lines between original and transla-
tion, but at any given point the line-numbering of the
two should not differ by more than one line. The
translation aims to be accurate rather than literal,
colloquial but not slangy, and speakable. Whether
it can be acted I must leave others to decide. Sup-
plements to Menander's text appear in square
brackets also in the translation; where they are in
any way doubtful, they are accompanied by a
bracketed question mark.

In preparing this edition, I have been helped by

PREFACE

more people and institutions than I can possibly mention in the brief space of a preface. For twenty years I have discussed problems connected with Menander orally and by post with a host of scholars, many of whom have become friends as well as colleagues. The living will know whom I mean; E. Fraenkel, L. A. Post and T. B. L. Webster, all still sadly mourned, have given me unstintingly of their knowledge and their time. For the loan or supply of photographs I should like to thank C. Austin (the Berlin fragment of the *Kitharistes*), the British Museum (the *Georgos* fragment), R. A. Coles and L. Koenen with the International Photographic Archive of the *Association Internationale de Papyrologues* and the authorities of the Cairo Museum (the Cairo codex), the Library of the City and University of Geneva (the *Georgos* papyrus), M. Manfredi (the *Encheiridion* and *Georgos* fragments), and F. H. Sandbach (the Cairo codex of the *Samia* by infra-red photography). E. W. Handley and E. G. Turner have, in addition to other valuable help, supplied me with information about yet unpublished papyri, such as the Oxyrhynchus fragment of lines 47–63 and 89–90 of the *Dis Exapaton*; I gratefully give them my thanks. I should like also to acknowledge my gratitude to the Institute for Advanced Study, Princeton, and to the National Endowment for the Humanities in the U.S.A. (Grant H5426) for their aid and facilities which made my stay at Princeton in 1973, when this edition was first begun, so rewarding. The photographic section of my own University of Leeds has helped me greatly with enlargements and copies of photographs. I wish to thank the Oxford University Press for permission to incorporate material from my

PREFACE

Menander, Plautus, Terence (*Greece & Rome, New Surveys in the Classics* 9, Oxford 1975) in my introduction. Mrs Philippa Goold has checked my manuscript and given unstintingly of her time and experience in the laborious task of seeing this volume through the press. F. J. Williams has helped with the proofs. Their generous, time-consuming assistance is gratefully acknowledged. Finally, but not least, I should like to thank my wife and children for their patient tolerance of an editor's unsociability during these last four years.

University of Leeds   W. Geoffrey Arnott
November 1977

INTRODUCTION

Life

Menander's family came from Cephisia, a large deme which still retains its name today, on the western slopes of Mount Pentelicon about eight miles north-east of the centre of Athens. The family was both distinguished and wealthy, according to an anonymous ancient tract on comedy (G. Kaibel, *Comicorum Graecorum Fragmenta*, I p. 9, section 17 = *Testimonium* 2 in volume II of the Teubner edition of Menander, edited by A. Körte and A. Thierfelder), although none of its members is known to have performed a liturgy. Menander's father was Diopeithes, born apparently in the year 385/4 B.C., since his name appears on the list of public arbitrators for Athens in the year 325/4 (*IG* ii² 1926. 19 = *Test.* 4) [1]; his mother was called Hegestrate. The dates of Menander's own birth and death are impossible to establish with absolute precision, because the ancient records are confused and contradictory. He is said to have been born when Sosigenes was archon (342/1: *IG* xiv 1184 = *Test.* 3), and to have died at the age of

[1] This is all that we know about him, unless it was he who acted as χορηγός for the winning comedy at the Dionysia in 333/2 B.C. (*IG* ii² 2318. 325–7).

52 (*Test.* 3; the Athenian scholar Apollodorus in Aulus Gellius 17. 4. 4 = *Test.* 14) or 57 (*Test.* 2, according to the ms.) when Philippos was archon (almost certainly 292/1 [1]), in the 32nd year of the reign of Ptolemy Soter (also 292/1: *Test.* 3). Other writers give 293/2 (Eusebius, *Chronica* 5. 198 Karst = *Test.* 15b), 292 (Aulus Gellius 17. 21. 42 = *Test.* 16) or 292/1 (Jerome, *Chronicle* = *Test.* 15a) as the year of his death. Errors are perhaps more likely to have been made about the date of a man's birth than about that of his death or his age at death, and so the statement that Menander died between 293 and 291, most probably in the Athenian year that lasted from June 292 to June 291, at the age of 52, is probably the one most worthy of credence. He was drowned apparently while swimming at the Piraeus (Ovid, *Ibis* 591 f. and the scholiast *ad loc.*: = *Test.* 17), and his tomb was to be found on the road leading from that port to Athens (Pausanias 1. 2. 2 = *Test.* 18).

The few facts recorded about Menander's life are also riddled with contradictions and uncertainties. He is said to have been taught philosophy by Theophrastus (Diogenes Laertius 5. 36 = *Test.* 7) and play-writing by Alexis, a comic poet of an older generation (*Test.* 2; the *Suda* Lexicon, s.v. Ἄλεξις, = *Test.* 5, falsifies this relationship into one of blood). Both statements are plausible; a promising son in a wealthy family is likely to have secured distinguished teachers. The date when Menander produced his

---

[1] This is now the accepted dating: cf. especially W. B. Dinsmoor, *The Archons of Athens*, Cambridge U.S.A. 1931, 30 and 37 ff.; W. S. Ferguson, *Athenian Tribal Cycles in the Hellenistic Age*, Cambridge U.S.A. 1932, 66 ff.; and B. D. Meritt, *Hesperia* 26 (1957), 53 f.

first play, the *Orge* (*Anger*), is disputed. Different sources give 323/2 (Eusebius, *Chronica* 5. 198 Karst = *Test.* 23c), 321/0 (Jerome = *Test.* 23a), and the period when he was an ephebe, in the nineteenth and twentieth years of his age, possibly when Anticles was archon (325/4: *Test.* 2).[1] Some chroniclers (*Test.* 23a–c) allege that the *Orge* won first prize in its dramatic competition; the *Marmor Parium* dates Menander's first victory in Athens to 316/5 (*Test.* 24); the didascalic notice prefixed to the Bodmer papyrus of the *Dyskolos*, however, affirms that this play won first prize at the Lenaea, one of the two major Athenian dramatic festivals, in 317/6. It is possible[2] to reconcile these three statements by assuming that the *Orge* won its prize either at the Lenaea or at a competition held outside Athens, and that the *Marmor Parium* here is distorting an original record which gave to Menander his first victory at the other major Athenian dramatic festival, the City Dionysia, in 316/5. In a relatively short career of about 30 years Menander wrote over 100 plays; 108 is the commonly recorded figure (the *Suda* entry on Μένανδρος = *Test.* 1; *Test.* 2 and 14), but 109 and 105 are also given (*Test.* 14). Some 97 titles are still known, but a few of these may be ghosts, alternative titles attached to plays at a second or later performance. Not all of Menander's plays could have been produced

---

[1] The manuscript of the anonymous tract on comedy names the archon ' Diocles ', which must be corrupt (there was no eponymous archon of this name in the relevant period) for either Anticles (325/4) or Philocles (322/1). Dinsmoor (*loc. cit.* in the preceding note) provides good arguments for preferring the former correction.

[2] But not necessarily advisable: the statement that the *Orge* won first prize, for instance, may be a fabrication.

at the two major Athenian festivals, where Menander was in fact remarkably unsuccessful. He won there only eight victories (Apollodorus in Aulus Gellius 17. 4. 4 = *Test.* 14): between two and four at the Lenaea, according to the mutilated didascalic records (*IG* ii ² 2325. 160 = *Test.* 25), and the remainder at the Dionysia. As the Roman epigrammatist Martial wrote later (5. 10. 9 = *Test.* 26), ' Rarely cheered the theatres a victor's garland for Menander.'

Several anecdotes are recorded about his personal life, but none of them is of unimpeachable authenticity. Menander's ephebe service coincided apparently with that of Epicurus (Strabo 14. 638 = *Test.* 6), and Alciphron alleges that Menander was a personal friend of this philosopher as well as of Theophrastus, his teacher. This latter allegation, however, comes in a pair of letters (4. 18, 19) ¹ whose contents ought perhaps to be regarded as an unverifiable blending of imaginative fiction and historical fact. Alciphron here imagines an exchange of letters between Menander and a dearly loved mistress, a *hetaira* named Glykera, in which the two discuss an invitation to visit Egypt which Menander and his comic rival Philemon have received from King Ptolemy. Menander, in ill health, turns down this invitation because he cannot bear to be separated from Glykera and Athens. The invitation to Ptolemy's court may well have had some basis in

---

¹ Cf. especially A. Körte, *Hermes* 54 (1919), 87 ff., together with his article in *RE* s.v. *Menandros* 9, 712; J. J. Bungarten, *Menanders und Glykeras Brief bei Alkiphron*, Diss. Bonn 1967; P. M. Fraser, *Ptolemaic Alexandria*, Oxford 1972, II, 873 n. 11; and K. Treu, *Schriften zur Geschichte und Kultur der Antike* 6 (1973), 207 ff.

historical fact. It is mentioned also by the elder
Pliny (*HN* 7. 111 = *Test.* 10), and is in itself plausible
enough; the early Ptolemies tried very hard to
attract the leading literary figures to Alexandria.
The love affair with Glykera, on the other hand,
although described as 'common knowledge' by a
rough contemporary of Alciphron (Athenaeus
15. 594d = *Test.* 12),[1] is almost certainly an invention
of later writers, who had been misled by the coinci-
dence that a real-life *hetaira* named Glykera existed
in fourth-century Athens (but in the decade before
Menander began writing) and that Menander chose
this name for several *hetairai* in his plays (*Glykera*,
Misogynes, *Perikeiromene*). A similar tradition (cf.
Martial 14. 187 = *Test.* 13) linked Menander also
with another *hetaira* named Thais. An Athenian
hetaira of this name had been the mistress of Alex-
ander the Great and Ptolemy Soter (cf. Athenaeus
13. 576d–e), and Menander had written a play called
Thais whose heroine was a *hetaira*. The story of a
real-life affair involving Menander was clearly
fabricated afterwards out of this concurrence.
Menander may have been a womaniser, as the potted
biography in the *Suda* alleges ('sharp in intellect and
absolutely mad about women', *Test.* 1), but alter-
natively all these allegations may have been false
assumptions based on the sympathetic portrayal of
characters like Habrotonon in the *Epitrepontes* and
Glykera in the *Perikeiromene*.

Two other stories about Menander sound rather
more credible. According to Diogenes Laertius
(5. 79 = *Test.* 8) the comic poet 'came within an ace

---

[1] Cf. also Philostratus, *Epist.* 38.

of conviction in the law-courts for no other reason than that he was a friend of Demetrius of Phalerum. He got off, however, through the intercession of Telesphorus, Demetrius' cousin.' This Demetrius, who governed Athens as a pro-Macedonian regent between 317 and 307, was himself a Peripatetic philosopher like Theophrastus, and there is no intrinsic implausibility in the story of his friendship with Menander, although some details about its initiation which appear in a fable by Phaedrus (5. 1 = *Test.* 9) look like sheer embroidery. Demetrius' expulsion in 307 was followed by trials of his supporters, and Menander may have been among the victims. His rescuer Telesphorus, however, is misidentified by Diogenes; he was the cousin of Demetrius Poliorcetes, not of Demetrius of Phalerum.[1]

The other anecdote is the only one that impinges on Menander's relation to his art. It is preserved by Plutarch (*De Gloria Atheniensium* 4 = *Moralia* 347f = *Test.* 11): ' the story goes that one of Menander's friends asked him, " The Dionysia are coming, Menander—haven't you composed your comedy ? " He replied, " I have indeed composed it—the plot's worked out, but I've still got to add the lines." ' The anecdote may be apocryphal, but it has a plausible ring. The most cursory study of Menander's plays shows that the careful and complex structuring of plots takes precedence over other things such as characterisation, however brilliant and individualistic his characterisation may be.

About Menander's personal appearance one credible and two doubtful statements survive. Athenaeus

---

[1] Cf. W. S. Ferguson, *The Hellenistic City of Athens*, London 1911, 101 and n. 4.

twice calls the poet καλός (6. 248d, 8. 364d), and this adjective could as well mean physically ' handsome ' as artistically ' fine '. In the fable of Phaedrus discussed above (5. 1 = *Test.* 9) Menander is described as looking like a beautiful homosexual: ' Perfumed, in dress effeminate, / He walked with mincing lazy steps.' The description may owe more to Phaedrus' imaginative embroidery or to inaccurate traditions than to truth. The one credible statement comes in the *Suda* biography (*Test.* 1), which says that Menander had a squint. There seems to be no reason why such a statement should be invented, and it has recently received support from the world of art. A large number of busts and medallions of Menander have now been identified,[1] revealing a conventionally handsome man with wavy hair, deep-set eyes, a long and sensitive nose and full lips. Two representations, however—a mosaic in the so-called ' House of Menander ' at Mytilene and a miniature bronze bust now in the J. Paul Getty Museum in Malibu—do not idealise the face but include a pronounced squint.

After Menander's Death

Menander's lack of success apparently ended with his death. ' Some people, like Menander, have won a more just appraisal from posterity than from their

---

[1] The best survey is now Gisela M. A. Richter, *The Portraits of the Greeks*, II, London 1965, 224 ff. and figs. 1514–1643; on the Menander mosaic at Mytilene, however, see also Lily Kahil and others, *Les Mosaïques de la Maison du Ménandre à Mytilène* (*Antike Kunst, Beiheft* 6, Berne 1970), 27 ff. and colour plate 2; and on the Malibu bronze see B. Ashmole, *AJA* 77 (1973), 61 and pls. 11–12.

own time,' wrote Quintilian (*Inst. Orat.* 3. 7. 18 = *Test.* 37). For more than 800 years, while at least a selection of his works survived, Menander's name was lionised. A statue was erected to him in the Theatre of Dionysus at Athens (Pausanias 1. 21. 1; *IG* ii² 3777 = *Test.* 19). His plays were frequently staged, and our scanty records of official Athenian productions (*IG* ii² 2323, lines 160, 387 f.[1]; B. D. Meritt, *Hesperia* 7 [1938], 116 ff. no. 22, line 10; *Test.* 29–31) inform us that the *Phasma* was performed, perhaps at the Lenaea,[2] in 255/4 B.C. and at the Dionysia in 168/7 B.C., and the *Misogynes* at the Dionysia in ?196/5 B.C. Portraits and sculptures of him must have been popular possessions, for at least 40 heads, five busts, five herms, three mosaic portraits, and one painting still survive. Scenes in mosaic from eleven of Menander's plays formed the main decoration of a third-century A.D. house in Mytilene. Similar scenes in mosaic or on frescoes occur in other houses as far apart as Ulpia Oescus in modern Bulgaria (Menander's *Achaioi*), Ephesus (*Perikeiromene, Sikyonioi*), and Pompeii (*Theophoroumene, Synaristosai*).[3]

The number of papyrus texts and fragments clearly indicates the extent of Menander's popularity in Egypt from Hellenistic times until the Moorish invasions in the middle of the seventh century A.D. In the number of texts found, he is surpassed only by Homer and Euripides. Many ancient scholars wrote

---

[1] Cf. C. A. P. Ruck, *IG II² 2323: The List of the Victors in Comedies at the Dionysia*, Leiden 1967.

[2] So Meritt, but see A. Pickard-Cambridge, *The Dramatic Festivals of Athens* ² (Oxford 1968: revised by J. Gould and D. M. Lewis), 41 n. 11.

[3] Cf. the volume by Lily Kahil and others, cited above (p. xix, n. 1).

about him, beginning with Lynceus of Samos, a contemporary (Athenaeus 6. 242b = *Test.* 50). Didymus of Alexandria and Soteridas wrote general commentaries about him (the *Etymologicum Gudianum* s.v. Κορύβαντες, the Suda s.v. Σωτηρίδας : = *Test.* 53, 54), Timachidas of Rhodes annotated the *Kolax* (J. A. Cramer, *Anecdota Graeca e codd. MSS. Paris.* iv. 25 = *Test.* 52), and Nicadius the *Theophoroumene* (fr. 8 of that play = *Test.* 57). One Latinus wrote a dissertation in six books on Menander's plagiarisms (Eusebius, *Praeparatio Evangelica* 10. 3. 12 = *Test.* 51). And a Sellius wrote prose summaries of Menander's plots, some of which may survive in fragments on papyrus (the *Suda* s.v. Ὅμηρος Σέλλιος and Σέλλιος; *P. Oxyrhynchus* 1235 and 2534, edited by A. Hunt, *The Oxyrhynchus Papyri* 10 [1914], 81 ff., and J. Barns and R. A. Coles, 31 [1966], 12 f.: = *Test.* 56). An epitome of Plutarch's essay comparing Philemon and Menander survives in the manuscripts of the *Moralia* (853a–854d).

The man who led the Menandrean panegyrists appears to have been the Alexandrian critic Aristophanes of Byzantium. He apparently ranked Menander second only to Homer among the poets of Greece (*IG* xiv 1183 = *Test.* 61), singling out Menander's realism for praise in a celebrated apostrophe: ' O Menander and life, which of you copied the other ? ' (Syrianus' commentary on Hermogenes, II p. 23 Rabe = *Test.* 32). Such extravagant compliments became the fashion; Menander was ' the star of New Comedy ' (an unknown poet quoted by a scholiast on Dionysius Thrax, 20. 5 Hilgard = *Comicorum Graecorum Fragmenta* p. 15. 75 Kaibel = *Test.* 49), ' Love's companion and the siren of the theatres '

(*Test.* 61), and a writer whose comedies were filled with ' wit's holy salt, as if born from the very sea which produced Aphrodite ' (the epitome of Plutarch's *Comparison*, 854d = *Test.* 41). Dissentient voices were few, and confined to those grammarians like Phrynichus who were offended by a lack of classical Attic purity in Menander's vocabulary (*Eclogae* 393, 400 and *passim*: *Test.* 46).

In Rome and the Latin West Menander shared the same posthumous glory. Many of his plays were adapted with varying degrees of freedom for the Roman stage in the third and second centuries B.C. Plautus' *Bacchides*, *Cistellaria* and *Stichus* recreate Menander's *Dis Exapaton*, *Synaristosai* and first *Adelphoi* respectively, and his *Aulularia* probably derives from another Menandrean original, possibly the *Apistos*.[1] Four of Terence's plays, the *Adelphoe*, *Andria*, *Eunuchus* and *Heauton Timorumenos*, seem to be fairly close adaptations of their Menandrean homonyms, the Greek *Adelphoi* being in this case a second play with the title and different from the one adapted for Plautus' *Stichus*. These Roman plays survive; others, taken from Menandrean models by dramatists like Caecilius, Luscius Lanuvinus and Turpilius, have been lost along with their sources. Even after the decline of the Roman *palliata*, however, Latin authors were as eager as their Greek counterparts to idolise Menander. Manilius (*Astronomica* 5. 476 f. = *Test.* 36) and Quintilian (*Inst. Orat.* 10. 1. 69 = *Test.* 38) praised the dramatist's realism.

---

[1] Compare K. Gaiser, *Wiener Studien* 79 (1966), 191 ff., F. H. Sandbach, *Entretiens Hardt* 16 (1970), 97 f., and my own *Menander, Plautus, Terence* (*G & R New Surveys in the Classics* 9, Oxford 1975), 40 f.

INTRODUCTION

The fourth-century poet Ausonius in a verse letter
(*Epist.* 22. 45 ff. = *Test.* 48) advised his grandson to

> Read all that's precious.   First I urge you to
> Unfold the *Iliad*'s composer, and
> The works of lovable Menander . . .

And Ovid claimed immortality for the plays (*Amores*
1. 15. 17 f. = *Test.* 34):

> While tricky slaves, stern fathers, shameless bawds
> And charming whores exist, Menander's safe!

But Ovid was wrong.   The vogue for Menander
came to an end with the collapse of the Roman empire
in the west and the Moorish conquest of Egypt.[1]
Towards the end of the fifth century in Gaul Sidonius
Apollinaris was still reading the *Épitrepontes* in the
original Greek (*Epistulae* 4. 12. 1, cf. *Carm.* 9), and in
Byzantium apparently the Greek epistolographer
who goes by the name of Aristaenetus was filching
memorable words and phrases from several plays to
adorn his tired prose.[2]   At the beginning of the sixth
century Choricius of Gaza may still have known some
complete plays (cf. *Apologia Mimorum* 9. 3 = *Rev.
Phil.* 1 [1877], 228 f.), and in the seventh the historian
Theophylactus Simocatta adorned his letters (*Epist.* 27,
29, 61, 77, perhaps also 4, 15 and 24) with phrases and
themes culled from Menander.   The plays were not
read or studied in Byzantine schools, however.
Menander's exclusion from the curriculum owed more

---

[1] On the fate of Menander subsequent to this period see
especially A. Dain, *Maia* 15 (1963), 278 ff.
[2] Cf. *GRBS* 14 (1973), 197 ff.

in all probability to his linguistic offences against the canons of pure Attic which had already been stigmatised by Phrynichus, than to any immoral features in his plots. Consequently, any surviving texts on old papyrus were not copied on to vellum in the ninth and succeeding centuries, and Menander never became part of the mediaeval tradition.[1]

Even so, Menander was not totally lost to the Renaissance and subsequent centuries. The Latin adaptations by Plautus and Terence were always familiar, but some knowledge of Menander's own style and imaginative language was preserved in quotations, several of a dozen lines or more in extent, made for various purposes throughout antiquity. At the end of the second century, for example, Athenaeus of Naucratis wrote his *Deipnosophistai* (' *The Dinner Scholars* '), a rambling and often pedantic series of dinner-table discussions on a large number of topics, the majority of which are concerned with food and such related pleasures as music and courtesans. Among the numerous illustrative citations are over 80 fragments of Menander. In the fifth century John Stobaeus made, for his son's edification in the first instance, a large anthology of quotations, mainly

---

[1] Sixteenth-century references to two lost manuscripts, one allegedly from Constantinople containing 24 plays, and the other from Rhaedestus (= the modern Tekirdag), are unreliable and very probably impostures (cf. P. Maas, *Byz. Zeits.* 98 [1938], 409 ff.; A. Körte, *Philol. Woch.* 59 [1938], 114 ff.). In the twelfth century Guillaume de Blois wrote in Latin elegiac couplets a comedy with the title *Alda* which was allegedly derived from Menander's *Androgynos*, but Guillaume's source was not the Greek play itself but a Latin prose summary (lines 13–16 of the *Alda*; cf. G. Neumann, *Hermes* 81 [1953], 491 ff.).

INTRODUCTION

ethical in content and arranged neatly under head-
ings. About 300 of these come from Menander, and
they include some of the poet's most memorable lines
(e.g. fr. 416 Körte-Thierfelder). The rest of these
Menandrean fragments preserved as quotations,
which number over a thousand *in toto*, come from a
wide variety of sources—grammarians and lexico-
graphers illustrating a word or usage, scholiasts
explaining their own authors' texts by a citation from
Menander, (paroemiographers) exemplifying the use
of a proverb, and very occasionally scholars interested
in the ways that the Roman dramatists adapted their
Greek models. Throughout later antiquity col-
lections were made of those individual lines from
Menander's plays which could stand on their own as
aphorisms. In the course of time the text of many of
these now contextless lines became badly garbled,
and the genuinely Menandrean material was aug-
mented with much that was spurious. Several col-
lections of these ' monostichs ', as they are called,
survive in mediaeval manuscripts, but few of their
lines can now be positively identified as Menandrean.[1]

Up to the nineteenth century Menander's worth
was assessed on the evidence of these contextless
fragments alone, while the loss of complete plays was
often mourned. ' We are deprived of a great stock
of wit in the loss of Menander among the Greek
poets,' wrote Dryden in his *Essay of Dramatic Poesy*,
first published in 1668.[2] A century later Winckel-
mann was even more enthusiastic: ' With the most

[1] Cf. S. Jäkel's edition, *Menandri Sententiae*, Leipzig 1964.
[2] P. 20 of volume XVII (edited by S. H. Monk, 1971) of the
standard modern edition of John Dryden's works, published by
the University of California Press.

exquisite words, with the most calculated and harmonious proportion, . . . with a fine Attic wit Menander appeared on the stage as the first man to whom the graceful charm of comedy has been revealed in its liveliest beauty.' [1]

The Rebirth of Menander

Today the situation is different. The assessment of Menander's quality no longer depends on isolated quotations in ancient authors. Texts of his plays, although often admittedly in a mutilated and fragmentary condition, have been one of the major rewards of excavations from Hellenistic and Roman houses in Egypt. The major discoveries were prefaced by Konstantin Tischendorf's visit to the library of St. Catherine's monastery on Mt. Sinai in 1844. There he found three small fragments of a Menander manuscript glued into the binding of another manuscript. These fragments were identified as belonging to the *Epitrepontes* and the *Phasma*. In 1905 the French archaeologist Gustave Lefebvre was investigating the remains of the house of one Flavius Dioscorus, a Romanised native official who had led a cultivated life as lawyer and poet in sixth-century Aphrodito (Kom Ishqâw). On top of and around a jar stuffed with papyri he discovered the remains of the fifth-century Cairo codex, which may originally have contained five complete plays on some 160 pages. Only a third of the codex has been preserved, including over half of the *Epitrepontes*, two-fifths of the *Perikeiromene* and *Samia*, and shorter fragments of

---

[1] Quoted by U. von Wilamowitz, *Neue Jahrbücher* 21 (1908), 62 = *Kleine Schriften*, I (Berlin 1935), 270.

INTRODUCTION

the *Heros* and an unidentified play.[1] After the Second World War the Genevan industrialist and collector Martin Bodmer acquired the remains of another Menander codex which had once belonged to a monastic library in Egypt. This codex originally contained on its 64 pages the text of three plays: the *Samia, Dyskolos* and *Aspis*. The first four leaves of the *Samia* are badly mutilated, and the last five of the *Aspis* are either lost or fragmentary, but the rest of the codex is only slightly damaged, and its text of the *Dyskolos* is virtually complete.[2]

To these large-scale finds many others of lesser extent but not always of comparably lesser importance may be added. 1964, for example, saw the successful conclusion of the work of two papyrologists at the Sorbonne, A. Blanchard and R. Bataille.[3] Some Egyptian mummies of the Ptolemaic period were preserved there in cartonnage made from sheets of second-hand papyrus cut up and glued together. Laboratory tests revealed that the discarded papyrus came from a roll of the third century B.C. that originally contained the text of the *Sikyonioi*. 1968 is another notable date. The excavations at Oxyrhynchus (the modern Behnesa) from 1896 to 1907 yielded a large number of Menandrean papyri, mainly very mutilated and fragmentary.[4] Of the 17 now published the most interesting is the scrap of a hundred or so verses of the *Dis Exapaton* which E. W.

---

[1] Cf. Gomme and Sandbach, *Menander: A Commentary*, Oxford 1973, 42 ff., with bibliography.

[2] Cf. Sandbach, *Commentary*, 47 ff., with bibliography; R. Kasser, *Scriptorium* 25 (1971), 46 ff.

[3] *Recherches de Papyrologie* 3 (1964), 103 ff.

[4] Cf. E. G. Turner, *Greek Papyri*, Oxford 1968, 27 ff.

Handley published provisionally in 1968.[1] These verses provided scholars for the first time with a portion of continuous text from a Greek play that had later been adapted for the Roman theatre in an extant play (the *Bacchides*) by Plautus.

The catalogue of discoveries is now extensive. The following papyri and other manuscripts can be assigned certainly to named plays:

Aspis: P. Bodmer 26, P. Cologne 904, PSI 126.

Georgos: P. Berlin 21106, P. British Museum 2823a, P. Geneva 155, PSI 100.

Dis Exapaton: an unnumbered Oxyrhynchus papyrus. (? P. Antinoopolis 122.)

Dyskolos: P. Berlin 21199, P. Bodmer 4, P. Oslo 168, P. Oxyrhynchus 2467, Membr. Hermupolitana (Bodleian Library, Oxford, Gr. Class. g. 50 [P]).

Encheiridion: PSI 99.

Epitrepontes: P. Cairo 43227, P. Oxyrhynchus 1236, 2829, Membr. Petropolitana 388. (? P. Berlin 21142.)

Heros: P. Cairo 43227.

Theophoroumene: PSI 1280 and an unnumbered Florence papyrus.

Karchedonios: P. Oxyrhynchus 2654. (? P. Oxyrhynchus 866, P. Cologne 5031.)

Kitharistes: P. Berlin 9767.

Kolax: P. Oxyrhynchus 409, 1237, 2655.

Koneiazomenai: P. Russia/Georgia 10.

---

[1] *Menander and Plautus: A Study in Comparisons* (Inaugural lecture, University College, London, 1968), reprinted in German translation by E. Lefèvre, *Die römische Komödie*, Darmstadt 1973, 249 ff.

Misoumenos: P. *Berlin* 13281, 13932, *P.IFAO* 89,
P. *Oxyrhynchus* 1013, 1605, 2656, 2657, and an
unnumbered Oxyrhynchus papyrus.

Perikeiromene: P. *Cairo* 43227, P. *Heidelberg* 219,
P. *Leipzig* 613, P. *Oxyrhynchus* 211, 2830.

Perinthia: P. *Oxyrhynchus* 855.

Samia: P. *Barcelona* 45, P. *Bodmer* 25, P. *Cairo*
43227, P. *Oxyrhynchus* 2831, 2943.

Sikyonioi: P. *Oxyrhynchus* 1238, P. *Sorbonne* 72,
2272, 2273.

Phasma: P. *Oxyrhynchus* 2825, *Membr. Petropolitana*
388.

In addition to these assigned papyri, there are a few
others which are recognised to be Menandrean but
from unidentified plays (*P. Berlin* 9772, the fragments
of the *Fabula Incerta* in *P. Cairo* 43227, *P. Oxyrhynchus*
2534), and several more whose style makes an attribu-
tion to Menander highly plausible (e.g. *P. Antinoopolis*
15, *P. Didot* II, *P. Hamburg* 656). This leaves an
enormous residue of papyrus fragments [1] whose
metre, style and subject matter clearly ascribe them
to the genre of New Comedy, without providing
enough information for their assignment to a named
author. Since Menander was the favourite author of
New Comedy at the times when these papyri were
written, many (perhaps the vast majority) of these
fragments must derive from his plays. As new
papyri continue to be discovered and published, there
are hopes that some at least of these homeless
waifs will, with the help of the new discoveries, be

[1] They are collected most conveniently by C. Austin, *Comi-
corum Graecorum Fragmenta*, Berlin 1973, 239 ff. (nos. 239–
319).

identified at last and restored to their original titles
like some of the heroines themselves in Menander's
plays.

Menander's Achievement: Oasis or Desert?

Fractured and fractional as the papyrus recoveries
have been (we still possess less than eight per cent of
Menander's work, and only one play complete out of
more than a hundred), enough has now been rescued
to tempt readers into assessing the quality of Menan-
der's achievement. Modern critics do not all share
the adulatory enthusiasm of the ancients. ' It is
usual to praise him without stint,' writes one dis-
tinguished specialist in the Hellenistic period,[1] '. . .
but to the writer he and his imitators seem about the
dreariest desert in literature. Life is not entirely
composed of seductions and unwanted children, co-
incidence and recognitions of long-lost daughters,
irate fathers and impertinent slaves.'

Judgments of this kind are not rare among those
American and British scholars who fail to penetrate
beneath the veneers of Menander's comedy. The
flaws in his plots are all on the surface: an excessive
reliance on coincidence, and the complaisant accept-
ance of hackneyed motifs.[2] Coincidence does play a
larger part in Menander than in real life; the odds
would be very high against a real-life Kleostratos
arriving home at the very moment when he can foil
Smikrines' plans, as he appears to have done in the

---

[1] Sir William Tarn, *Hellenistic Civilisation* (3rd edition,
revised with the help of G. T. Griffith, London 1952), 273.
[2] Cf. my earlier essay in *Menander, Plautus, Terence* (*G & R
New Surveys in the Classics* 9, Oxford 1975), 19 ff.

INTRODUCTION

Aspis, and against a real-life Demeas chancing to lodge next door to his long-lost daughter, as in the *Misoumenos*. It is equally true that Menander's plots permutate a limited number of human experiences, of which some at least—rapes at night festivals and identifications of long-separated relatives by means of keepsakes, for instance—must have been less common in real life. In every play one or two love affairs come through obstacles to a happy conclusion. The obstacles are always the same: differences of class or background, shortage of cash, parental opposition. The expedients by which the conclusion is achieved have a similarly small range— identification of a raper, family reunion, a confidence trick devised usually by a slave of the house. These may all be flaws, but they affect the surface only, the mechanical framework of the plot that an audience readily forgets. What it remembers is Menander's effective highlighting, in scene after scene, of vivid, realistic and significant detail, economically described or presented in imaginative language which implies far more than it actually says.[1] Each reader must make his own selection: the corpses with bloated faces on a Lycian battlefield (*Aspis* 70 ff.), Polemon's obsession with the beauty of Glykera's wardrobe, which reveals the depth of his infatuation (*Perikeiromene* 516 ff. Sandbach), a neglected baby crying amid the bustle of wedding preparations (*Samia* 239), Habrotonon's total absorption with the baby for a few moments while Onesimos is trying to draw her atten-

---

[1] Cf. Camille Préaux, *Chronique d'Égypte* 32 (1957), 84 ff.; T. B. L. Webster, *Bulletin of the John Rylands Library* 45 (1962), 240 f.; D. Del Corno, *Maia* 22 (1970), 336 ff.; and E. W. Handley, *Entretiens Hardt* 16 (1970), 5 f., 20.

tion to the ring (*Epitrepontes* 464 ff.), or Kichesias'
anguished question about his nubile daughter
' Dromon, is she decently / Safe, or just safe ? '
(*Sikyonioi* 371 f.), for example. Each of these is
functionally necessary to the mechanics of the plot at
its particular point, but each is memorable because
the detail imaginatively captures and universalises
the reality of human experience, producing ' a novel
in a single gesture, a joy in a breath.' [1]

In one crucial respect Menander's approach to
characterisation parallels his approach to plot-
construction. It aims at the same controlled tension
between the familiar and unfamiliar, convention and
reality, the typical and the exceptional. Due weight
of course needs to be given to the limitations put on
Menander's character-drawing by his genre and his
time. A play of a thousand or fewer lines cannot
burrow as deeply into the complexities of character as
a Dostoievsky novel of a thousand pages. Secondly,
in the comedy of Menander's period, just as in fifth-
century Athenian tragedy, plot takes precedence
over character. Finally, the ancient attitude to
characterisation differs to some extent from that of
some modern novelists. Playwrights like Menander
saw ' character ' as the sum of a person's idiosyncra-
sies in speech and in behaviour, an externally viewed
set of matching characteristics that slot into a con-
ventional pattern like the tesserae of a mosaic.[2]

Menander's first individual touch is revealed by the
way in which he makes a character react and clash

---

[1] So Arnold Schoenberg (on Webern's six *Bagatelles for
String Quartet*).

[2] Cf. Eva Keuls, *Proceedings of the XIV International Con-
gress of Papyrologists*, London 1975, 195 ff.

startlingly against the type.[1] He apparently in-
herited a drama of conventional type-figures—brag-
gart soldier, greedy parasite, garrulous cook, spineless
lover, choleric father, selfish courtesan and the like—
immediately identifiable by the audience from the
masks these characters wore and the names they
were given. These enabled an experienced member
of the audience to predict the total personality of a
character on his first entrance, provided the play-
wright had made it conform to type.

A warlike name like Polemon and a soldier's mask
would thus normally lead one to expect certain con-
ventional characteristics: a garrulous conceit about
imaginary exploits on the battlefield and in the
boudoir, allied to basic cowardice, lustfulness, stupid-
ity and a quick temper. These at any rate are the
traits of those Plautine soldiers derived from non-
Menandrean sources. What Menander does is to
take over the skeletal role, and then to add a series of
characteristics which are either wholly unexpected,
being outside the conventional gamut, or only half
surprising, because they refine the grossness out of
the conventional traits and so turn them inside out.
Virtually all the typical characteristics can be de-
tected in Polemon at one point or other of the *Peri-
keiromene*, but mainly in a refined or everted form.
The plot requires this soldier to be hot-tempered, but
Menander adds a weighting of infatuated jealousy, in
order to make the story's starting-point more plaus-
ible, when Polemon cut off Glykera's hair after seeing
her in the arms of a strange young man. Polemon is
not exactly stupid, but he needs to have the legal

---

[1] Cf. E. W. Handley, *Entretiens Hardt* 16 (1970), **3** ff.

implications of his liaison with Glykera and her desertion clearly and simply spelled out (488 ff. Sandbach). He is not exactly a coward, but he lacks the confidence to face Glykera and plead with her (504 ff.). He is not conceited, but he brags about Glykera's clothes (516 ff.). And the traditional soldier's lechery is transformed into a serious love which turns the stereotype upside down.[1]

Parallel points might be made for many of Menander's major characters. The combination in each one of something conventional with something unusual produces a lively and sometimes astringent freshness. The young rustic Gorgias in the *Dyskolos* tries to talk like a philosopher (271 ff.), the charcoal-burner Syros in the *Epitrepontes* is proud of his knowledge of Attic tragedy (325 ff.), and the *hetaira* Habrotonon in the same play combines the opportunism typical of her class (cf. 541, 548) with a suppressed maternal instinct (contrast 464 ff., where Habrotonon is absorbed in the baby, with 547 ff.) and an inventive flair that turns her very unexpectedly into a planning slave. [Cleverness and the devising of stratagems in Greco-Roman comedy and its derivatives are normally the perquisites of the male servant, who typically takes control of a difficult situation, describes his stratagem to one or more colleagues who are mystified at first but generally come to grasp his intentions; the stratagem usually involves personation.] In the *Epitrepontes* Habrotonon adds this role to her other, more feminine characteristics, taking control of the situation when Onesimos is helpless (511), describing her stratagem to an initially puzzled Onesimos (515 f.),

---

[1] Cf. W. T. MacCary, *AJP* 93 (1972), 281 ff.

INTRODUCTION

and masquerading as Charisios' victim and the baby's mother (517 ff.).[1]

Two other techniques used by Menander with the aim of individualising and enlivening his characters call for attention. One is rooted in their language. Women and men, slaves and free, rich and poor, educated and uneducated alike, all speak the same dialect, a largely colloquial, grammatically accurate late Attic, with some infusions of the *koine*. Yet a good number of the characters in Menander's plays have distinctive modes or habits of speech.[2] A few examples will suffice. The cook Sikon in the *Dyskolos* colours his speech with flamboyant metaphors. In the *Samia* Nikeratos prefers short asyndetic sentences while Demeas emphasises his remarks with a subjoined ' tell me ' ($\epsilon i \pi \acute{\epsilon} \mu o \iota$) or by repetition (326 f., 470 f.). In the arbitration scene of the *Epitrepontes* Daos prefers simple short clauses, repeats his words and ideas, and employs a limited vocabulary, while his opponent Syros affects more complex structures, introduces gnomes and vividly coined phrases, and is not averse to abstract nouns. And finally in the *Dyskolos* Knemon, who reduces every issue to simple blacks and whites without intervening shades of grey, is overfond of words like ' all ' and ' nobody ' or ' nothing '. These verbal mannerisms, however, are never overdone. Menander never floods a role with idiosyncrasies either of speech or of behaviour. By

---

[1] I have discussed this example at greater length in ' Time, Plot and Character in Menander ', *Papers of the Liverpool Latin Seminar* 2 (1979), 343 ff.

[2] Cf. F. H. Sandbach, *Entretiens Hardt* 16 (1970), 111 ff.; D. Del Corno, *Studi Classici e Orientali* 24 (1975), 13 ff.; and my papers in *G & R* 17 (1970), 32 ff., and 22 (1975), 146 ff.

this means he avoids caricature, just as by the other technique analysed above he avoids conventional typology.

The final technique of characterisation is a mark of talent in any playwright—that of using hints in a person's words rather than direct statement to establish his or another's character. When in the *Perikeiromene* Polemon discusses with Pataikos Glykera's desertion of him, he never *says* that he is in love with her, but the way that he goes on about her wardrobe (516 ff. Sandbach) leaves a sensitive spectator or reader in no doubt. At the beginning of the *Aspis* Daos ends two successive remarks with words (κληρονόμε ' for you to inherit ' 85, οἰκεῖον ' all yours ' 89) that hint at Smikrines' avarice well before the prologue divinity spells it out clearly for the less discerning (138 ff.).

All these techniques are unobtrusively welded together by Menander to produce characters that are nearer to individuals than to types, and when they are reinforced by the effective highlighting of significant details of action or behaviour, these characters become not only individual but also memorable. With the loss of every comedy written between Aristophanes' *Plutus* in 388 B.C. and Menander's *Dyskolos* in 316, it is impossible now to know how far Menander patented or developed any of these characterising techniques himself. Our ignorance here, however, is comparatively unimportant. What matters is that Menander employed them in such a way that they produce a vivid illusion of realism even when set against the unrealities of coincidence and the absurdities of stereotyped plots.

One further detail of Menander's art, however, is

INTRODUCTION

most appropriately mentioned here, because it links
characterisation to plot-construction and helps to
explain why the critic is so very rarely forced to con-
sider the question of priorities between plot and
character in these comedies. Menander had the
ability to make a vivid incident, short speech or
snatch of dialogue serve several purposes at once.
His skill here has been aptly compared to that of a
juggler manipulating several balls in the air at once.[1]
Sostratos' monologue at *Dyskolos* 259 ff., for example,
gives a plausible reason for the speaker's early return
to the stage alone, it prepares for the later entry of
the slave Getas at 402 and for the sacrifice to Pan
which links so many of the play's separate incidents,
it illustrates the fussy pietism of Sostratos' mother, it
reveals with some subtlety several facets of the
speaker's own character—his slight contempt for his
mother's activities, the petulant self-centredness of a
spoiled teenager, a decisive directness—and it does
all these things humorously (261 ff.) and graphically
(264 ff.).[2] At 860 ff. Sostratos has another short
speech which is similarly multivalent. When he says
here that ' In one day I have achieved / A marriage '
he is clearly emphasising the time-scale of New-
Comedy plots, which largely conform to that of Greek
tragedy as described by Aristotle (*Poetics* 1459[b] 12)
and to that of seventeenth-century drama as de-
scribed by Castelvetro.[3] But the speech also adds an
ironic twist to the portrait of Sostratos, here so

---

[1] L. A. Post, *AJP* 80 (1959), 410. The idea is developed by
E. W. Handley, *Entretiens Hardt* 16 (1970), 8 ff.

[2] Cf. my paper in *Phoenix* 18 (1964), 110 ff.

[3] For a fuller account of Menander's attitude to the Unity of
Time see the paper cited on p. xxxv, n. 1.

confident about the success of his ' care and work '. Sostratos has now achieved his heart's desire by winning the hand of the girl he loves, but his success owed very little to his own efforts, and much more to Gorgias' heroic and altruistic rescue of Knemon from the well (753 ff.), to the indulgent complaisance of Sostratos's father, and to Pan's wish to reward a girl's piety by giving her a rich husband (35 ff.). The irony here is of a kind particularly Menandrean, where the speaker sincerely believes what he is saying, but misinterprets key facts which the audience have been taught to interpret more accurately. The teaching is never obtrusive or crudely underscored, and may well have passed by those members of Menander's audience unprepared for the cleverness of a Hellenistic poet.

The Cleverness of the Hellenistic Poet

Menander's plays were written barely one generation before Callimachus, Theocritus and other Alexandrian poets set a premium on cleverness in both form and content. It is not surprising to see signs of the new Hellenistic age in Menander also, although his tricks and sleights of hand often contribute valuably to the plays in which they occur. Some of these have already been discussed in the previous section, but a further series of tricks shares with some Hellenistic poetry an obsession with cleverness for its own sake which delights some critics and infuriates others. Four types of formal and verbal trickery, it seems to me, best merit discussion: the preoccupation with parallelism, the secularisation of familiar tragic scenes, the use of link devices, and a fondness for word games.

INTRODUCTION

Several of Menander's plays reveal the same pre-
occupation with parallelism and balanced structures
as a Theocritean idyll. Scenes, for example, may
echo each other. At 464 ff. of the *Dyskolos* Getas
knocks on Knemon's door and tries to borrow a stew-
pot. He fails. Directly afterwards, Sikon jeers at
Getas' failure, knocks on Knemon's door and tries to
borrow the pot. He too fails. Of course the paral-
lelism here has a comic purpose. After witnessing
Getas' discomfiture, the audience can predict even
worse treatment for Sikon at the hands of Knemon.
But the parallelism also acts as preparation for the
ragging scene in the last act which involves the same
three characters. At 911 ff. Getas and Sikon torment
the now helpless Knemon by repeating in mimicry,
one after the other with balanced phrases, the earlier
rat-a-tat on Knemon's door and the request for a
loan.[1]

Another kind of parallelism exploited by Menander
is that of situation. Two different groups of charac-
ters experience or appear to experience parallel fates.

---

[1] This technique is so characteristic of Menander that it can
be followed even in the Roman adaptations of his plays and
interpreted as evidence of fidelity to the original. In Plautus'
Stichus, which is derived from Menander's first *Adelphoi*, for
example, the parasite Gelasimus is rejected by the two
brothers, Epignomus and Pamphilippus, in a pair of balanced
scenes marked by echoes of phraseology; each brother in turn
is described by Gelasimus as his ' life ' (372, 583 f.), each brother
in turn answers the parasite's polite enquiry about his health
with a confident *sustentatumst sedulo*, ' got on splendidly '
(467, 586). As with the paired scenes in the *Dyskolos*, one aim
of the repetition in the *Stichus* is ironic humour; the audience
is carefully instructed that what Gelasimus suffered from the
one brother he will also suffer from the other. Cf. my paper
in *BICS* 19 (1972), 68 f.

INTRODUCTION

In the *Aspis* all the human characters believe that Kleostratos is dead in Lycia until he comes on to the stage in the fourth act (491) quite definitely alive. His appearance is ironically foreshadowed by two of Smikrines' remarks, ' If only *he* had lived! ' (89) and ' He *should* have lived ' (168 f.). The parallel comes in Daos' stratagem, where Smikrines is persuaded that his brother Chairestratos has died, until his corpse too rises from the dead in the fifth act. Chairestratos' pretended death is ironically foreshadowed by several remarks that he himself makes (282 f., 299 f., 305 f., 314 f.).[1] In the *Heros* the parallel is between two different generations. Eighteen years or so before the staged action of the play begins, Laches had raped Myrrhine, who bore twins in consequence. The twins were brought up by Tibeios, a shepherd, who was believed to be their father. Laches later married Myrrhine, his victim. In the new generation of the dramatic present Pheidias has raped Plangon, one of these twins who has now grown up. At the end of the play this young man too marries his victim, but before that another slave, Daos, wishes to marry Plangon and to represent himself as the baby's father. Much of the plot of the *Kitharistes* is now lost, but it is at least worth considering whether this play exploited parallelism between incidents of the present and the preceding generations in the same way.[2] Moschion has just visited

---

[1] Cf. D. B. Lombard, *Acta Classica* 14 (1971), 123 ff.; N. Bozanic, *Structure, Language and Action in the Comedies of Menander*, Diss. London 1977, 119 ff.

[2] Cf. U. von Wilamowitz, *Berliner Klassikertexte, V: Griechische Dichterfragmente, ii: Lyrische und Dramatische Fragmente*, Berlin 1907, 121; and my introduction to the play.

Ephesus and there apparently raped Phanias'
daughter. She is probably pregnant as a result,
bears a child, and marries Moschion at the end of
the play. Had Phanias himself many years before
also visited Ephesus, raped a woman there who
had borne a daughter, and then later married the
victim? This seems to me to be the one theory that
makes sense of the scattered hints in the play frag-
ments.

One obvious function of such parallelisms is to link
parents and their grown-up children by showing that
when young both generations behave exactly alike.
Another function is structural, to achieve a satisfying
unity out of a series of events imagined to span
eighteen years or so. There may also be a slightly
self-indulgent interest in structural patterns for their
own sake.

The purpose of the second type of Menandrean
cleverness, which I have labelled the secularisation of
familiar tragic scenes, is far harder to understand.
Only one example is yet known for certain, although
others may be suspected.[1] The certain example,
which occurs in Menander's *Sikyonioi*, secularises a
scene from Euripides' *Orestes*.[2] In the tragedy, after
the messenger has described himself as a supporter of

---

[1] For example, the arbitration scene in the *Epitrepontes* may
be partly inspired by a lost scene from Euripides' *Alope* (cf.
F. H. Sandbach, *Commentary* on *Epit.* 218–375), and some
events in the *Heros* may have been influenced by parallel
events in Euripides' *Auge* (cf. my translation of *Heros*, on
fr. θη).

[2] Cf. E. W. Handley, *BICS* 12 (1965), 47 ff. and *Entretiens
Hardt* 16 (1970), 22 f.; R. Kassel, *Eranos* 63 (1965), 8 f.;
H. Lloyd-Jones, *GRBS* 7 (1966), 140 f.; my paper in *G & R* 19
(1972), 74 f.; and F. H. Sandbach, *Commentary*, *ad loc.*

the royal house (868 f.), he launches into a vivid description of the assembly at Argos which condemned Orestes and Electra to death. Menander's plot substitutes a fugitive girl and a male slave for the royal pair, Eleusis for Argos, and a debate about the girl's legal position for the murder trial, but the parallels are clearly, if discreetly, drawn. Menander's narrator, a convinced democrat, also begins by affirming his political interest, thus enabling the audience to allow for his partiality. His speech parallels that of the tragic messenger not only in its general subject-matter, but also in its structure; it too is very long (103 or 104 lines as against 87 in the *Orestes*), and combines verbal quotations of the speeches made by the participants in the debate with graphic sketches of their appearance and characters. To substantiate the source of his inspiration, Menander deliberately echoes phraseology from the Euripidean scene (*Or.* 866, 920) at key points in his narrative (*Sik.* 176, 182). The technique is clear, but what was Menander's purpose? It is hard to be certain. The comedy speech is remarkably long by the standards of its genre, and the clever references to an almost equally long speech on a parallel subject in a tragedy well-known to fourth-century audiences may have been intended as an implied defence of its length. And just as Euripides deglamorised the incidents and characters of myth by presenting them as if they were contemporary with his own age, so also Menander may have wished to carry the experiment further by removing altogether the patina of mythical names and traditional stories. Yet there must also have been an element of sheer self-indulgent virtuosity in making this transformation, since few of Menander's audience at the play's first production could have been expected to appreciate all these refinements.

The third type of Hellenistic cleverness, the use of link devices, has a clear dramatic function. Disparate scenes are connected by verbal echoes and a feeling of continuity results. At *Dyskolos* 521, for example, Sikon leaves the stage at the end of one scene in resigned discomfiture; he is short of a cooking-pot, accepts that he'll have to make do with what he has there, and disappears with a ' Farewell to Phyle! ' He is replaced on the empty stage by Sostratos, whose opening remark is ' If anybody's short of troubles, Let / Him come to Phyle for the hunting '. Thus two different scenes are linked together verbally, not only by the obvious repetition of the place name, but also more subtly by the way Sostratos' phrase ' If anybody's short of troubles ' implicitly echoes the burden of Sikon's complaint about his troubles caused by the shortage of a cooking-pot.[1]

A variation of this technique occurs when two characters have been on stage at the same time, but express their parallel emotions not to each other but in juxtaposed exclamations. Towards the end of the first act of the *Dyskolos*, Sostratos offers to fill the jar of Knemon's daughter from the spring in Pan's shrine, and she agrees. As he leaves the stage to get the water he bewails his enslavement in line 202 f.: ' O [honoured] gods, what power could save me now ? ' Knemon's daughter, now alone, hears a door rattling and is terrified of being caught out of doors. Her first words (203) are τάλαιν᾽ ἐγώ, literally ' Woe is

[1] Other examples of this technique are discussed in my paper, *G & R* 22 (1975), 140 ff.

me!' There is a pleasant irony in the tonal echo here. Two young people, whose marriage will end the play, bewail their separate miseries in a deliberate juxtaposition of balancing exclamations.

And finally, Menander's word games. These have more in common, it seems to me, with Callimachus' logodaedaly in his *Hymns* than with the comic tradition of verbal humour. They often display an attractive verbal wit, but one whose appeal must largely have been confined to an intellectually acute minority. For instance, Menander often plays on the difference between a word's etymological and everyday significance.[1] There is the sheep (πρόβατον, literally ' front-goer ') that won't ' budge ' forward (οὐ προέρχεται) in *Dyskolos* 393, the slave who is addressed as ἱερόσυλε (literally ' temple-robber ', but used in Menander's time as a generalised insult) just because he has *not* robbed his employer in *Aspis* 227, and the cook who plays on the double meaning of οἴχομαι (' I go / come ' and ' I am ruined ') when he complains that his contract has been cancelled and so he must go off a ruined man (ἀλλ' οἴχομαι / ἀπιὼν ἐγώ) at *Aspis* 219 f. Two of these examples gain their effects by juxtaposing words of apparently related meanings; partly but not wholly parallel is *Dyskolos* 609, where Getas sees Sostratos approaching with Gorgias and Daos and exclaims that Sostratos' companions are workmen from the neighbourhood (τόπου, literally ' place '), which is an extraordinary happening (ἀτοπίας, literally a situation that is ' out of place ').

Occasionally Menander extends these double

[1] Cf. L. A. Post, *AJP* 80 (1959), 404; and my papers in *Phoenix* 18 (1964), 123 and *G & R* 22 (1975), 149 ff.

meanings cleverly over a whole phrase. At *Dyskolos* 965 f. the speaker asks the audience to applaud if they've enjoyed κατηγωνισμένοις / ἡμῖν τὸν ἐργώδη γέροντα, ' our victory with this old nuisance '. The words partly refer to Getas and Sikon's successful taming of Knemon in the last act, but they also bear a second meaning, ' our acting the *Dyskolos* to the end.' [1] At *Aspis* 329 f. Daos introduces his stratagem for hoodwinking Smikrines with the words δεῖ τραγῳδῆσαι πάθος / ἀλλοῖον ὑμᾶς, 'You must perform / A sombre tragedy.' The uppermost reference here is to the charade of Chairestratos' pretended death and the mourning round the corpse. But the more I read this scene, the more convinced I am that here Menander is also subsuming a reference to the scene in which Daos hurls his volley of tragic quotations to the bemused Smikrines. Menander's phrase at 329 f. is capable also of the meaning ' You must surround / A sad event with tragic language.'

For some of the examples of cleverness discussed in this section parallels can of course be cited from Menander's predecessors. Euripides' *Hippolytus*, for instance, is a very successful exercise in formal symmetry, and Aristophanes from time to time makes jokes out of a word's etymology. Menander probably invented few if any of the techniques analysed here. More important, however, is the cumulative effect of their various exploitations in the plays and fragments that survive. It is this that makes us realise that Menander's plays are on the threshold of a new age, when classical Athens gave way to Hellenistic Alexandria.

[1] Cf. the commentaries of E. W. Handley and F. Stoessl, *ad loc.*

A Bibliography of Editions and Bibliographies

Work on Menander has increased so enormously since the *Dyskolos* was first published in 1958 that a full bibliography such as adorned Allinson's 1921 Loeb edition would fill a sizeable volume by itself. Fortunately, the easy availability of the annual issues of *Année Philologique* makes the provision of such a bibliography less necessary. Here I restrict myself to a list of (a) editions of the text of Menander (omitting publications in purely papyrological series or periodicals), and (b) bibliographies devoted to Menander. These are as complete as I can make them, but doubtless some fish will have escaped the net.

Editions

(a) The fragments known in antiquity.[1] *G. Morel, *Ex veterum comicorum fabulis . . . sententiae* (Paris 1553–54). *J. Hertel, *Vetustissimorum et sapientiss. comicorum quinquaginta sententiae* (Basel 1560: largely a copy of Morel). *H. Grotius, *Excerpta ex tragoediis et comoediis graecis* (Paris 1626). J. Clericus, *Menandri et Philemonis Reliquiae cum notis H. Grotii et J. Clerici* (Amsterdam 1709). J. A. F. A. Meineke, *Menandri et Philemonis*

---

[1] Volumes with selections only are asterisked.

BIBLIOGRAPHY

Reliquiae (Berlin 1823); *Fragmenta Comicorum Graecorum*, IV (Berlin 1841), 69–374 and *Fr. Com. Gr., editio minor* (Berlin 1847), 867–1066. *J. Bailey, *Comicorum Graecorum Fragmenta* (Cambridge 1840), 116–54. F. Dübner in W. Dindorf's edition of Aristophanes (Paris 1842), 1–106. T. Kock, *Comicorum Atticorum Fragmenta*, III (Leipzig 1888), 3–272. *F. A. Paley, *Fragments of the Greek Comic Poets* (London 1892), 108–29. *A. W. Pickard-Cambridge, *Select Fragments of the Greek Comic Poets* (Oxford 1900), 122–151. J. Demiańczuk, *Supplementum Comicum* (Krakow 1912), 54–63 (a supplement to Kock). A. Körte, *Menandri quae supersunt*, II (Leipzig, 1st edition 1953, 2nd 1959: with addenda by A. Thierfelder).

(b) The monostichs. A bibliography (not well arranged) will be found in the standard edition of S. Jäkel (Leipzig 1964, after a Hamburg dissertation of 1958). Corrections and additions to Jäkel's edition will be found in D. Hagedorn and M. Weber, *ZPE* 3 (1968), 15–50.

(c) Complete editions of the papyri as known before 1958. G. Lefebvre (Cairo, 1st edition 1907, 2nd 1911). J. van Leeuwen (Leiden, 1st and 2nd 1908, 3rd 1919). C. Robert (Berlin 1908). Viscount Harberton (' Unus Multorum ': Oxford 1st and 2nd 1909). S. Sudhaus (Bonn 1st 1909, 2nd 1914). A. Körte (Leipzig 1st edition major and minor 1910, 2nd major and minor 1912, 3rd 1938, 3rd with addenda 1955). E. Capps (Boston 1910). L. N. de Olwer (Barcelona 1911). F. G. Allinson (London and New York 1st 1921, 2nd 1930). G. Coppola (Turin 1st 1927, 2nd 1938).

BIBLIOGRAPHY

C. Jensen (Berlin 1929). J. M. Edmonds, *The Fragments of Attic Comedy*, IIIB (Leiden 1961).[1] D. Del Corno (Milan 1966).

(d) Complete editions of the papyri known today. F. H. Sandbach (text: Oxford 1972; commentary, with A. W. Gomme: Oxford 1973).

(e) Selections from the papyri. L. Bodin and P. Mazon (Paris 1908: parts of *Epit.*, *Sam.*). W. G. Waddell (Oxford 1927: parts of the Cairo plays, of *Georgos*, some ancient fragments). G. Zuntz (Paderborn 1st before 1937, reprint 1953: *Epit.*, *Sam.*, some ancient fragments). D. L. Page, *Greek Literary Papyri* (Cambridge, U.S.A. and London 1941: parts of *Theoph.*, *Mis.*, *Aspis* [then known as ' *Comoedia Florentina* '], *P. Didot II*). C. Austin, *Comicorum Graecorum Fragmenta in Papyris Reperta* (Berlin 1973: *Encheir.*, *Karch.*, *Kol.*, *Mis.*, and newly discovered papyri of some other plays).

(f) Single plays.
Aspis: R. Kasser and C. Austin (Geneva 1969). C. Austin (Berlin 1969–70, *I: Textus* and *II: Subsidia Interpretationis*; with *Sam.*). F. Sbordone (Naples 1969). F. Sisti (Rome 1971). A. Borgogno (Milan 1972).

Georgos: J. Nicole (Basle and Geneva 1897–98). B. P. Grenfell and A. Hunt (Oxford 1898).

Dis Exapaton: E. W. Handley, *Menander and*

---

[1] This edition, which includes the fragments known from antiquity, is vitiated by a series of delusions about what the editor imagined he could decipher on infra-red photographs of the Cairo codex.

BIBLIOGRAPHY

Plautus: A Study in Comparison (London 1958, reprinted in a German translation in E. Lefèvre, *Die römische Komödie*, Darmstadt 1973, 249–76). D. Del Corno (Milan 1973). The Greek text is reprinted by V. Pöschl, *Die neuen Menanderpapyri und die Originalität des Plautus* (*SB Heidelberg* 1973, *Abh.* 4), and as an appendix to C. Questa's second edition of Plautus' *Bacchides* (Florence 1975).

Dyskolos: V. Martin (Geneva 1958). C. Diano (Padua 1st 1959, 2nd 1968). C. Gallavotti (Naples 1959). B. Marzullo (Turin 1959). N. B. Sphyroeras (Athens 1959/60). J. Bingen (Brussels 1st 1960, 2nd 1964). O. Foss (Copenhagen 1960). B. A. van Groningen (Amsterdam 1960). W. Kraus (Vienna 1960, Zürich 1960). J. Lanowski (Wroclaw 1960). H. Lloyd-Jones (Oxford 1960). H. J. Mette (Göttingen 1st 1960, 2nd 1961). M. Treu (Munich 1960). J. Martin (Paris 1st 1961, 2nd 1972). F. Stoessl (Paderborn, Text 1961 and Commentary 1965). J. M. Jacques (Paris 1st 1963, 2nd 1976). E. W. Handley (London 1965). D. C. de Pozzi (Buenos Aires 1965). W. E. Blake (New York 1966). P. Lekatsas (Athens, date unknown).

Epitrepontes: M. Croiset (Paris 1908). U. von Wilamowitz (Berlin 1925, reprint 1958). H. Wachtler (Leipzig and Berlin 1931). V. de Falco (Naples 1st 1945, 2nd 1949, 3rd 1961). H. Oppermann (Frankfurt 1953).

Misoumenos: E. G. Turner (Supplement 7 to *BICS*, London 1965).

Samia: J. M. Edmonds (Cambridge 1931, reprinted in *The Fragments of Attic Comedy*, IIIB:

BIBLIOGRAPHY

Leiden 1961; see p. xlix, n. 1). C. Dedoussi (Athens 1965). R. Kasser and C. Austin (Geneva 1969). C. Austin (see above, on *Aspis*). J. M. Jacques (Paris 1st 1971, 2nd 1976). F. Sisti (Rome 1974).

Sikyonioi: C. Gallavotti (Rome 1st and 2nd 1965). R. Kassel (Berlin 1965).

Bibliographies

(a) Before 1958. See especially E. Wüst in *Jahresbericht*, as follows: 174 (1919), 186–233 (for the years 1902–14); 195 (1923/24), 173–85 (for the years 1914–21); 207 (1926), 116–20 (for the years 1921–25); 234 (1932), 153–65 (for the years 1925–31); 263 (1939), 76–91 (for the years 1931–37). The editions (see under (c) above) of Capps, Allinson, Jensen and Del Corno also include useful bibliographies. A. Körte, *RE* xv (1931), 707–62.

(b) After 1958.
   (i) *Dyskolos.* I. I. Skardasis, *Platon* 11 (1959), 460–64 and 12 (1960), 260–64. G. Barabino, *Menandrea: Miscellanea Philologica* (Genoa 1960), 203–219, and *Lanx Satura: Miscellanea N. Terzaghi Oblata* (Genoa 1963), 37–76. J. T. McDonough, *CW* 53 (1960), 277–80 and 296–98, and (with L. A. Post) 54 (1961), 173–75. D. C. de Pozzi, *Anales de Filologia Clásica* 8 (1961/64), 137–77. C. Corbato, *Dioniso* 37 (1963), 157–221 and 38 (1964), 182–202. See also A. Schäfer, *Menanders Dyskolos: Untersuchungen zur dramatischen Technik*, Meisenheim 1965, 11–23.

BIBLIOGRAPHY

(ii) Other papyri. H. J. Mette in *Lustrum*, as follows: 10 (1965), 5–211; 11 (1966), 139–43; 13 (1968), 535–68; 16 (1971/72), 5–8. Cf. also the same author in *RE Suppl.* xii (1970), 854–64. W. G. Arnott, *Arethusa* 3 (1970), 49–70.

(iii) General surveys. W. Kraus, *Anzeiger für die Altertumswissenschaft* 26 (1973), 31–56. W. G. Arnott, *Menander, Plautus, Terence* (*G & R New Surveys in the Classics* 9, Oxford 1975), 5–27.

ABBREVIATIONS

AHRC	*Australian Humanities Research Council*
AJA	*American Journal of Archaeology*
AJP	*American Journal of Philology*
BICS	*Bulletin of the Institute of Classical Studies*, London
Byz. Zeits.	*Byzantinische Zeitschrift*
C.A.G.	*Commentaria in Aristotelem Graeca*
corr.	corrected (by)
CQ	*Classical Quarterly*
Diss.	Dissertation (followed by the name of the university)
ed. pr.	*editio princeps* (with particular reference here to the name of the editor who made corrections and supplements in the first edition of a papyrus text)
Entretiens Hardt	*Entretiens sur l'antiquité classique, Fondation Hardt*, Vandoeuvres-Geneva
G & R	*Greece and Rome*
GRBS	*Greek, Roman and Byzantine Studies*
IG	*Inscriptiones Graecae*
JEA	*Journal of Egyptian Archaeology*
Les Mosaïques	*Les Mosaïques de la Maison du Ménandre à Mytilène* (*Antike Kunst, Beiheft* 6, Berne 1970)

ABBREVIATIONS

Membr.	*Membrana* (Parchment)
Migne, *P.G.*	Migne, *Patrologiae Cursus, series Graeca*
monost.	monostich (with particular reference to the collections made in classical and Byzantine times of allegedly Menandrean monostichs; see especially S. Jäkel, *Menandri Sententiae*, Leipzig 1964)
Mus. Helv.	*Museum Helveticum*
om.	omitted (by)
P.	Papyrus (followed usually by the name of the place or the collection with which it is associated)
Philol. Woch.	*Philologische Wochenschrift*
P.IFAO	*Papyrus de l'Institut Français d'Archéologie Orientale du Caire*
P. Oxy.	Oxyrhynchus papyrus (followed by the number assigned to the papyrus on publication)
PSI	*Papiri Greci e Latini. Pubblicazioni della Società italiana per la ricerca dei papiri greci e latini in Egitto* (followed by the number assigned to the papyrus from this collection on publication)
RE	A. Pauly, G. Wissowa and W. Kroll, *Real-Encyclopädie der classischen Altertumswissenschaft*
Rev. Phil.	*Revue de philologie*
Rh. Mus.	*Rheinisches Museum für Philologie*
Sandbach, *Commentary*	A. W. Gomme and F. H. Sandbach, *Menander: A Commentary* (Oxford 1973)

ABBREVIATIONS

SB	*Sitzungsberichte* (followed by the name of the Academy or Society)
suppl.	supplied or supplemented (by)
Supp. Vol.	Supplementary Volume
TAPA	*Transactions of the American Philological Association*
ZPE	*Zeitschrift für Papyrologie und Epigraphik*

ASPIS

(The Shield)

ASPIS (The Shield)

Manuscripts[1]

B = *P. Bodmer* 26, the third play (after *Samia* and *Dyskolos*) in a papyrus codex of the third century A.D. It contains lines 1–146, 149–400, 405–82, 497–520, 535–44. First edition: R. Kasser and C. Austin, *Papyrus Bodmer XXVI. Ménandre: Le Bouclier* (Cologny-Geneva 1969), with photographs of *P. Bodmer* 26 and also (see below) of *P. Cologne* 904.

B = also *P. Cologne* 904, part of folio 31 of *P. Bodmer* 26, detached from its original position. It contains lines 482–97, 520–35. First edition: R. Merkelbach, *ZPE* 1 (1967), 103.

F = *PSI* 126, a fragment of papyrus of the fifth century A.D. It contains lines 120–35, 145–60, 378–408, 410–29. First edition: G. Vitelli, *PSI* 2 (1913), 27 ff., with photographs. This fragment was generally known as the *Comoedia Florentina* (*The Florence*

---

[1] I do not include here several scraps from an Oxyrhynchus papyrus [inv. 16 2B52/E(a) and A 2B48/(a)] provisionally published by E. W. Handley, *Proceedings of the XIV International Congress of Papyrologists*, London 1975, 133 ff., with photographs. Handley's tentative suggestion that these scraps may derive from the *Aspis* seems to me mistaken: see pp. 7 ff. below.

Comedy) before the discovery of *P. Bodmer* 26 made possible its identification as part of the *Aspis*.

Fragments 1–5b are scraps or quotations from a variety of sources. See Introduction, pp. xxiv f.

*   *   *

The *Aspis* is only partially preserved. The first two acts and the opening 46 lines of the third are virtually intact, but from the second half of the play hardly more than a hundred fragmentary lines survive. From calculations based on the format of the Bodmer papyrus it appears that the play's original length was between 818 and 883 lines, with the balance of probability in favour of 860 to 870 (cf. J. C. B. Lowe, *BICS* 20 [1973], 94 f.).

The line-numbering of this edition agrees with that in the *editio princeps* of Kasser and Austin, in Austin's *Kleine Texte* (*Menandri Aspis et Samia, I: Textus*, Berlin 1969), and in Sandbach's Oxford Text (*Menandri Reliquiae Selectae*, Oxford 1972). On the right-hand margin of the Greek text is added, in brackets, the original numbering of the Florence fragment as it is given, for example, in Körte's third Teubner edition (*Menandri quae supersunt*, I, Leipzig 1945).

No hypothesis, didascalic notice, or cast-list is preserved on the papyri. The production date of the play is consequently unknown. Attempts have been made, however, to date the play on internal evidence.[1]

---

[1] E.g. T. B. L. Webster, *Studies in Menander* (2nd edition, Manchester 1960), 103; R. K. Sherk, *AJP* 94 (1973), 94 f.; Ursula Treu, *Antiquité Classique* 45 (1976), 606 f.

INTRODUCTION

At lines 23 ff., Daos describes how his master Kleostratos had taken part as a mercenary soldier in a Greek freebooting expedition to Lycia on the south coast of Asia Minor; at first there had been easy success and abundant booty, but later, in a battle against the natives fought by the River Xanthos, Kleostratos seemingly had lost his life. Could Menander have based his description here on a real event of contemporary or recent history? Very possibly: but it is impracticable now to attempt to identify it. As Treuber wrote nearly a century ago (*Geschichte der Lykier*, Stuttgart 1887, 140), the operations of Alexander the Great's generals after his death cost Lycia great sacrifices of money and blood. Land and sea armies frequently swarmed over the coastal areas. What we know today from the historians may well represent just the visible tip of a large iceberg: Eumenes' enrolment of mercenaries in Lycia in 318 B.C. (Diodorus Siculus, 18. 61. 4), for example, or Ptolemy's storming of the city of Xanthos in 309 (id. 20. 27).[1] Then fr. 1 of the play contains a reference to the wretched life of ' Those/Who guard the forts, who hold the citadels ' and to the dangers that they face of assassination by the dagger. It is just as impracticable, however, to associate this reference precisely with any recent

---

[1] And the inspiration behind Menander's exciting account need not have been confined to these Lycian incursions. Dr. Treu (*loc. cit.* in the previous note) has perceptively observed that an attack made by one of Antigonus' generals on the Nabataean stronghold of Petra in 312 B.C. (Diodorus, 19. 94 ff.) appears to have had some striking points of similarity to Menander's narrative: early success and rich booty, followed by carelessness in posting guards at night and a consequent severe defeat.

historical incident as it was to identify the reality
behind the description of the Lycian incursion. In
the fragment (see n. 1, *ad loc.*) Menander could
simply have been recalling in a hackneyed fashion the
legend of the tyrannicides of 514 B.C., or alternatively
he could have based his remarks on one of the many
political assassinations that occurred during his
dramatic career. Allegedly historical references in
the play text are unsatisfactory guides for dating the
Aspis.

Certain dramatic weaknesses are particularly
noticeable when the play is contrasted with the rest
of the Menandrean corpus. Sandbach (in his
Commentary, 62 f.) calls attention to a lack of breadth
in some of the main characters; Smikrines is wholly
bad in the preserved portion of the play (whether his
villainy was redeemed in the lost second half by any
compensating virtue, we cannot of course now know),
and Daos by comparison seems rather too faultless.
A second dramatic weakness is revealed in
Menander's handling of dialogue when three charac-
ters are on stage together. In all the other plays,
including the relatively early *Dyskolos* of 316 B.C.,
Menander handles his third actor without any sign
of strain; tripartite dialogue proceeds with a natural
fluency. The extant scenes of the *Aspis*, on the other
hand, are played mainly by one or two characters,
and the two attempts at tripartite dialogue seem
relatively clumsy. At 430 Chaireas and the false
doctor enter onto a stage already occupied by Daos
and Smikrines. Daos addresses the newcomers, he
receives a brief reply from one of them (the other
would here be played by a mute), and then im-
mediately the two newcomers disappear into Chaire-

stratos' house. This hasty passage onto and off stage can be defended dramatically, for Chairestratos is allegedly dying and the doctor's examination of his patient must not be delayed; nevertheless, the brevity of the third character's intervention in the dialogue here is unusual for Menander. At 250 ff. Smikrines, Chairestratos and Chaireas are on stage together, but the handling of Chaireas' part here is less assured than we normally expect from Menander. While Smikrines and Chairestratos converse, Chaireas remains largely silent. We are obliged to assume that he entered with Smikrines and Chairestratos at the beginning of the scene from the casual reference to his presence there at 262, but Chaireas does not open his mouth until the other two have departed at 284. He now delivers a monologue 15 lines long. During the next scene, which is dominated by Daos and Chairestratos, he remains on stage, before departing at 380 to fetch the false doctor. In the 82 lines before his departure, however, his spoken interventions are confined to five words in 347, five words in 375, and 376–79.

We still possess too little of Menander's dramatic output, however, to argue that such treatment of tripartite dialogue (in one case perhaps dramatically justified) ought to be ascribed to dramatic inexperience. An anecdote of Plutarch's (*Mor.* 347F; *testimonium* 11 Körte) implies that Menander wrote very quickly, and even if carelessness over the handling of a minor character is uncharacteristic, it is not in itself a sign of immaturity.

Balanced against these weaknesses are some dramatic virtues of considerable subtlety. In addition to Menander's typically careful and ingenious plot-construction, imaginative writing at its best in Daos' vivid but economical description of the Lycian campaign (23 ff.), and the maintenance of interest by precisely calculated frustrations and surprises, the hand of a master is revealed in a number of subtle or ironic details. The theatrically effective repartee of Daos' κληρονόμε (85) and οἰκεῖον (89), stinging last words appended to otherwise innocuous remarks; the paradoxical application of ἱερόσυλε (227) to a man who is in fact honest in a situation that conventionally invites thieving; the way in which Daos' flood of tragic quotations at the beginning of Act III puts an ironic and unexpected gloss on this character's earlier remark (329 f.) 'You must perform/A sombre tragedy' (cf. *Greece and Rome* 22 [1975], 144 f., 149, 150 f.)—such details suggest the sensitive touch of an experienced playwright, not an apprentice. The question of the play's dating must accordingly be left open.

*   *   *

In a fascinating paper (*Proceedings of the XIV International Congress of Papyrologists*, London 1975, 133 ff.), E. W. Handley provisionally published some fragments from an Oxyrhynchus papyrus roll [inv. 16 2B52/E(a) + A 2B48/(a)] dating from the end of the second or the beginning of the third century A.D. These fragments contain the mutilated remains of three columns of text from a play of later Greek comedy, and Handley 'suggests, but does not claim,' that this play was Menander's *Aspis*.

At first sight the argument for attribution seems very seductive. The new Oxyrhynchus fragments

come from a dialogue between an ' angry enquirer '
and a slave, and one of the subjects of their con-
versation is an inventory of possessions (A14 f.). In
the *Aspis* Smikrines makes several enquiries from
the slave Daos about Kleostratos' possessions (82 ff.)
and later complains angrily that Daos has not pro-
vided him with an inventory of these possessions
(391 ff.). Could the new fragments, Handley asks,
have belonged to a scene between Smikrines and
Daos which originally slotted into the big lacuna
after line 468?

Handley's theory, unfortunately, is not cor-
roborated by further coincidences of detail. The
names Smikrines and Daos do not appear in the new
Oxyrhynchus fragments, nor are there any verbal
ties with any known fragments of the *Aspis*. These
facts alone must sound a warning against too ready an
acceptance of the attribution, especially when one
takes into consideration the number of Greek
comedies whose plots focused on possessions and
inheritances. Furthermore, three details in the
Oxyrhynchus fragments appear not to tally exactly
with the specifications of the *Aspis'* plot.

(i) The inventory mentioned in the new fragments
is to include ' in detail/[All that's] inside, and [all]
we've loaned to people ' (A14–15). If the subject
of the inventory were Kleostratos' property, this
reference to ' loans ' would tie up well enough with
Daos' references to ' seals on goods ' and ' contracts '
when he was talking about Kleostratos in an early
scene of the *Aspis* (195). But in the gap after line
468 of that play Smikrines' interests will suddenly
have switched away from Kleostratos' property to
that of Chairestratos, and any reference by Daos in

these new circumstances to ' [all] we've loaned to people ' becomes less easy to explain. As Kleostratos' devoted slave he could readily associate himself with his lost master in references to Kleostratos' property; he was not Chairestratos' slave, and so could hardly use the first person plural in reference to loans which Chairestratos had made.

(ii) Another scrap of the Oxyrhynchus fragments (C1) appears to mention the *archon polemarchos*. In Menander's time this official's legal duties were particularly attached to disputes about inheritance involving metics (Aristotle, *Ath. Pol.* 58).[1] This suggests that the plot of the play in the Oxyrhynchus fragments revolved around a disputed inheritance involving a person or persons of non-Athenian citizenship. The characters at the centre of the dispute in the *Aspis*, however, are of pure Athenian blood. An Iberian girl, it is true, is mentioned in an ancient citation from this play (fr. 2), but it is unlikely that she played any functional role in its plot; most probably she was merely given a passing mention as (for instance) one of the slave girls in Kleostratos' booty.

(iii) An obscure and partly indecipherable note in the margin of one of the Oxyrhynchus fragments (B18) refers to somebody called Kallias. This name is perhaps most plausibly interpreted as that of a character in the play (cf. e.g. *Encheiridion* 8). There is, however, no Kallias in Menander's *Aspis*.

When everything is taken into account, the balance of the evidence seems to be tilted against

---

[1] Cf. A. R. W. Harrison, *The Law of Athens, I: The Family and Property*, Oxford 1968, 193 ff.

INTRODUCTION

Handley's attribution of the new Oxyrhynchus fragments to Menander's *Aspis*. Accordingly, they are not printed here. Further illumination is needed.[2]

*   *   *

Dramatis personae, in order of speaking, so far as is known:

Daos, an elderly slave, former tutor of Kleostratos
Smikrines, Kleostratos' uncle
The goddess Chance (Τύχη), speaker of the prologue
A cook (see p. 38, n. 2)
A waiter
Chairestratos, Smikrines' younger brother
Chaireas, Chairestratos' stepson
A friend of Chaireas, disguised as a doctor
Kleostratos, son of an unnamed dead brother of Smikrines and Chairestratos

Mute characters include a group of Lycian captives with pack animals, Spinther the cook's assistant, slaves of Chairestratos, and possibly Kleostratos' sister and Chairestratos' daughter. There is a conventional chorus of tipsy revellers, to perform the entr'actes.

[2] Cf. M. Rossi, *Prometheus* 3 (1977), 43 ff.; E. W. Handley, *BICS* 24 (1977), 132 ff.

ΑΣΠΙΣ

(SCENE: Athens. A city street, with two adjoining houses. One belongs to Smikrines, the other to his younger brother Chairestratos.)

(At the beginning of the play Daos, formerly Kleostratos' tutor, enters carrying a badly buckled shield. He is preceded by a mournful group of Lycian captives with pack-animals carrying booty: gold coins, silver cups,

ΔΑΟΣ

>] ἡμέραν ἄγω,
> ὦ τρόφιμε, τὴν [νῦν,] οὐδὲ διαλογίζομ[αι
> παραπλήσι᾽ ὡς τό[τ᾽ ἤλ]πισ᾽ ἐξορμώμεν[ος.
> ᾤμην γὰρ εὐδο[ξο]ῦντα καὶ σωθέντα σ[ε
> 5 ἀπὸ στρατείας ἐν βίῳ τ᾽ εὐσχήμονι
> ἤδη τὸ λοιπὸν καταβιώσεσθαί τινι,
> στρατηγὸν ἢ σ[ύμ]β[ο]υλον ὠνομασμένον,
> καὶ τὴν ἀδελφήν, ἧσπερ ἐξώρμας τότε
> ἕνεκα, σεαυτοῦ νυμφίῳ καταξίῳ
> 10 συνοικιεῖν ποθεινὸν ἥκοντ᾽ οἴκαδε,

In the apparatus to this play, those corrections and supplements whose author is not named were made by C. Austin, *Menandri Aspis et Samia, I: Textus* and *II: Subsidia Interpretationis* (*Kleine Texte* 188a, 188b, Berlin 1969–70). 1 The opening part of the line, a length of about 16 letters, is torn off

ASPIS
(The Shield)

clothes of rich fabric. Daos' opening speech apostro-
phises Kleostratos, the master he loved and left apparently
dead on the battlefield, but his words are overheard by
Smikrines, who must therefore have either already entered
the stage from his house at the time of Daos' arrival, or
come on stage in company with Daos and his party.)

DAOS
Today's [as sad a] day [as] I have spent,
Master, and all the thoughts that cloud my brain
Aren't what I hoped they'd be when we set off.
I thought you'd come back safe and rich in honour
From your campaign, and afterwards you'd live   5
Your future years in style.   You'd have the title
Of General or Counsellor of State,
And see your sister, for whose sake you went
Campaigning,[1] married to a man you felt
Was right, upon your glad arrival home.   10

[1] His aim was to win some booty, which would help to pro-
vide his sister with a dowry.

---

in B. 2 Suppl. ed. pr. 3 [ἤλ]πισ' Lloyd-Jones. 4 εὐδο[ξο]ῦντα
Sandbach. σωθουντα B. 7 Suppl. ed. pr. 8 ηνπερ B.

ἐμοί τ᾽ ἔσεσθαι τῶν μακρῶν πόνων τινὰ
ἀνάπαυσιν εἰς τὸ γῆρας εὐνοίας χάριν.
νῦν δὲ σὺ μὲν οἴχει παραλόγως τ᾽ ἀνήρπασαι,
ἐγὼ δ᾽ ὁ παιδαγωγός, ὦ Κλεόστρατε,
15 τὴν οὐχὶ σώσασάν σε τήνδ᾽ ἐλήλυθα
ἀσπίδα κομίζων ὑπὸ δὲ σοῦ σεσωσμένην
πολλάκις· ἀνὴρ γὰρ ἦσθα τὴν ψυχὴν μέγας,
εἰ καί τις ἄλλος.

ΣΜΙΚΡΙΝΗΣ
τῆς ἀνελπίστου τύχης,
ὦ Δᾶε.

ΔΑΟΣ
δεινῆς.

ΣΜΙΚΡΙΝΗΣ
πῶς δ᾽ ἀπώλετ᾽ ἢ τίνι
20 τρόπῳ;

ΔΑΟΣ
(KT fr. 70)   στρατιώτῃ, Σμικρίνη, σωτηρίας
ἔστ᾽ ἔργον εὑρεῖν πρόφασιν, ὀλέθρου δ᾽ εὔπορον.

ΣΜΙΚΡΙΝΗΣ
ὅμως διήγησαι τὸ πρᾶγμα, Δᾶε, μοί.

ΔΑΟΣ
ποταμός τίς ἐστι τῆς Λυκίας καλούμενος
Ξάνθος, πρὸς ᾧ τότ᾽ ἦμεν ἐπιεικῶς μάχαις

11 μακαρων B.   14 ὦ om. B.   15 σασαν B.   17 της B.   20 Corr.
Edmonds, Austin: στρατιωτης B, -την mss. of Stobaeus, *Ecl.* 4.
12. 6.   22 διηγησασθαι B.   23 Corr. several: καλουμενης B.

And for me too, as I grew old, I hoped
There'd be a rest from these long labours, after all
I'd done for you.   But now you're dead, snatched off
Against all reason, and, Kleostratos,
It's I who've come—your tutor, bringing back   15
This shield which didn't protect you, though you often
Protected it.   You always showed fine spirit,
Second to none.

          SMIKRINES (*coming forward*)
               Oh Daos, what a tragedy!
So unexpected!

          DAOS
          Terrible.

          SMIKRINES
              How did he die?
What way?

          DAOS
            If you're a soldier, Smikrines,   20
It's hard to find good reasons for survival;
For death though, easy.

          SMIKRINES
              But what happened?   Tell me,
Daos.

          DAOS
     In Lycia there's a river called
The Xanthos.[1]   There we saw some action, quite a lot,

  [1] Its modern name is the Eşen Çaï, which flows into the sea
on the south coast of Turkey, about 95 miles south-west of
Antalya.

MENANDER

25 πολλαῖς διευτυχοῦντες, οἵ τε βάρβαροι
ἐπεφεύγεσαν τὸ πεδίον ἐκλελοιπότες.
ἦν δ' ὡς ἔοικε καὶ τὸ μὴ πάντ' εὐτυχεῖν
χρήσιμον· ὁ γὰρ πταίσας τι καὶ φυλάττεται.

(KT
fr. 71)

29 ἡμᾶς δ' ἀτάκτους πρὸς τὸ μέλλον ἤγαγε
τὸ καταφρονεῖν· πολλοὶ γὰρ ἐκλελοιπότες
τὸν χάρακα τὰς κώμας ἐπόρθουν, τοὺς ἀγροὺς
ἔκοπτον, αἰχμάλωτ' ἐπώλουν, χρήματα
ἕκαστος ε[ἶ]χε πόλλ' ἀπελθών.

ΣΜΙΚΡΙΝΗΣ

ὡς καλόν.

ΔΑΟΣ

αὐτὸς δ'] ὁ τρόφιμος συναγαγὼν χρυσοῦς τινας
35 ἐξακοσί]ους, ποτήρι' ἐπιεικῶς συχνά,
τῶν τ' αἰχ]μαλώτων τοῦτον ὃν ὁρᾷς πλησίον
ὄχλον, δια]πέμπει μ' εἰς Ῥόδον καί τῳ ξένῳ
φράζει κ]αταλιπόντ' αὐτὰ πρὸς ἑαυτὸν πάλιν
τάχιστ' ἀ]ναστρέφειν.

ΣΜΙΚΡΙΝΗΣ

τί οὖν δὴ γίνεται;

ΔΑΟΣ

40 ἐγὼ μὲν ἐξώρμων ἔωθεν· ἦ δ' ἐγὼ
ἀπῆρον ἡμέρᾳ λαθόντες τοὺς σκοποὺς

---

31 τονκαταχαρασκωμας B.   33 απελθειν B.   34 Suppl. Jacques.
συναγων B.   35, 36 Suppl. ed. pr.   37 ὄχλον suppl. ed. pr.
δια]πέμπει suppl. Arnott, Jacques.   38 φράζει suppl. Kassel.
κ]αταλιπόντ' αὐτὰ Pieters:]αταλιπεινταυτα B.

And we'd been lucky all the time. The natives   25
Had taken to their heels and left the plain.
It looks as if *not* winning everything
Is an advantage. When you've had a fall
You take care. Over-confidence led us
Undisciplined towards the morrow. Many   30
Were out of camp, looting the villages,
Destroying crops, selling their booty. Everyone
Came back with loads of money.

SMIKRINES
         Excellent!

DAOS
My master had [himself] collected some
[Six hundred] gold staters,[1] and quite a number   35
Of cups, and all this [crowd] of slaves you see
Around you. Well, he sent me over to Rhodes
And [told] me to leave them there with a friend,
And hurry back again to him.

SMIKRINES
        What happened then?

DAOS
I planned to start at dawn, but on the day   40
When I was setting out, without our scouts

---

[1] At the time of this play, a gold stater (χρυσοῦς) was worth
20 silver drachmas in Athens. 600 gold staters, therefore,
were the equivalent of 12,000 drachmas or two talents, a suit-
able figure for a dowry on the comic stage (cf. *Aspis* 135 f.,
268 f., and Handley's edition of the *Dyskolos*, on lines 842–44).

MENANDER

τοὺς ἡμετέρους οἱ βάρβαροι λόφον τινὰ
ἐπίπροσθ' ἔχοντες ἔμενον, αὐτομόλων τινῶν
πεπυσμένοι τὴν δύναμιν ἐσκεδασμένην.
45 ὡς δ' ἐγένεθ' ἑσπέρα κατὰ σκηνάς θ' ἅπαν
ἦν τὸ στρατόπεδον ἔκ τε χώρας ἄφθονα
ἅπαντ' ἐχούσης, οἷον εἰκὸς γίνεται·
(KT fr. 74?) ἐβρύαζον οἱ πλεῖστοι.

ΣΜΙΚΡΙΝΗΣ

πονηρόν γε σφόδρα.

ΔΑΟΣ

ἄφνω γὰρ ἐπιπίπτουσιν αὐτοῖς μοι δοκεῖ.

ΣΜΙΚΡΙΝΗΣ

50 . .] . . . . .[. . .] . . . .νσ . . φα . .[. .] .[

(Lacuna of one line)

ΔΑΟΣ

] . .[. . . .] .εγω
]τα περὶ μέσας δ' ἴσως
νύκτας φυλακ]ὴν τῶν χρημάτων ποούμενος
55 τῶ]ν τ' ἀνδραποδίων περιπατ[ῶ]ν ἔμπροσθε τῆς
σκηνῆς ἀκούω θόρυβον οἰμω[γ]ὴν δρόμον
ὀδυρμόν, ἀνακαλοῦντας αὐτοὺς ὀνόματι,
ὧν καὶ τὸ πρᾶγμ' ἤκουον· εὐτυχῶς δέ τι
λοφίδιον ἦν ἐνταῦθ' ὀχυρόν· πρὸς τοῦτ' ἄνω
60 ἠθροιζόμεσθα πάντες, οἱ δ' ἐπέρρεον
ἱππεῖς ὑπασπισταὶ στρατιῶται τραύματα
ἔχοντες.

48 βρυαζον B.   54 Suppl. Kassel.   55 τ' Kassel: δ' B.   55, 56
Suppl. ed. pr.   58 εκτυχως B.

18

ASPIS

Spotting a trace of movement, the natives seized
A hill above us, and lay low. They'd learnt
How scattered our force was from some deserters.
When evening fell, and all the troops were back   45
From scouring a land of plenty, and in their tents,
What happened next was natural: most of our
Men were carousing.

SMIKRINES
That's quite scandalous!

DAOS
Yes. I think there was a surprise attack.   49

(*Lines 50 and 51, coming at the bottom of one folio and
the top of the next, have been torn off the papyrus, and
lines 52 and 53 are badly mutilated. In this gap
Smikrines comments or asks a question, and then Daos
goes on with his story. Presumably he described how he
had travelled on his mission for just one day, and then
encamped.*)

DAOS
. . . .] I suspect it was about   53
Mid[night], and I was standing guard over the slaves
And booty, walking up and down in front of   55
The tent, when I heard noises, cries of grief,
Men running, wailing, shouting each other's names.
From them I heard the news. Now, luckily
There was a knoll, a strong point on the ridge;
Up to it we all crowded, then in waves   60
Our wounded flowed in—cavalry, guards, infantry.

MENANDER

ΣΜΙΚΡΙΝΗΣ

ὡς ὤνησ' ἀποσταλεὶς τότε.

ΔΑΟΣ

αὐτοῦ δ' ἕωθεν χάρακα βαλόμενοί τινα
ἐμένομεν, οἱ δὲ τότε διεσκεδασμένοι
65 ἐν ταῖς προνομαῖς αἷς εἶπον ἐπεγίνοντ' ἀεὶ
ἡμῖν· τετάρτῃ δ' ἡμέρᾳ προήγομεν
πάλιν, πυθόμενοι τοὺς Λυκίους εἰς τὰς ἄνω
κώμας ἄγειν οὓς ἔλαβον.

ΣΜΙΚΡΙΝΗΣ

ἐν δὲ τοῖς νεκροῖς
πεπτωκότ' εἶδες τοῦτον;

ΔΑΟΣ

αὐτὸν μὲν σαφῶς
70 οὐκ ἦν ἐπιγνῶναι· τετάρτην ἡμέραν
ἐρριμμένοι γὰρ ἦσαν ἐξῳδηκότες
τὰ πρόσωπα.

ΣΜΙΚΡΙΝΗΣ

πῶς οὖν οἶσθ';

ΔΑΟΣ

ἔχων τὴν ἀσπίδα
ἔκειτο· συντετριμμένην δέ μοι δοκεῖ
οὐκ ἔλαβεν αὐτὴν οὐδὲ εἷς τῶν βαρβάρων.
75 ὁ δ' ἡγεμὼν ἡμῶν ὁ χρηστὸς καθ' ἕνα μὲν
κάειν ἐκώλυσεν, διατριβὴν ἐσομένην

62 Speech-division thus indicated by Austin (εχοντεσωσωνησ:
αποσταλεις B). 63 Reeve: βαλλομενοι B. 64 διεσκεδασμενοι
Kassel: εσκεδασμενοι B. 65 Corr. Sandbach: επαιτιμοντ' B.

20

ASPIS

SMIKRINES

How fortunate you'd just been sent away!

DAOS

At dawn we built a palisade, and there
We stayed.   Those who'd got scattered in the raids
I mentioned now came streaming back to join   65
Us.   Three days later we could move again.
The Lycians, so we'd heard, were taking off
Their prisoners to their highland villages.

SMIKRINES

And did you see him lying there among the dead?

DAOS

His body I couldn't identify for sure.   70
They'd been out in the sun three days, their faces were
Bloated.

SMIKRINES
Then how could you be certain?

DAOS
                                        There
He lay, with his shield.   Buckled and bent—that's
    why
None of the natives took it, I suppose.
Our fine commander banned all separate   75
Cremations, for he realised how much time

---

66 θ' B.   Corr. Sandbach: προσηγομεν B.   68 οις B.   73 δέ μοι
Sandbach after Handley: διεμοι B.   74 ουκ corrected to ουδ'
in B.   75 Corr. Kassel: ουδ' B.   76 Corr. Kassel: κλαιειν B.

ὁρῶν ἑκάστοις ὀστολογῆσαι, συναγαγὼν
πάντας δ' ἀθρόους ἔκαυσε· καὶ σπουδῇ πάνυ
θάψας ἀνέζευξ' εὐθύς· ἡμεῖς τ' εἰς Ῥόδον
80 διεπίπτομεν τὸ πρῶτον, εἶτ' ἐκεῖ τινας
μείναντες ἡμέρας ἐπλέομεν ἐνθάδε.
ἀκήκοάς μου πάντα.

ΣΜΙΚΡΙΝΗΣ
χρυσοῦς φὴς ἄγειν
ἑξακοσίους;

ΔΑΟΣ
ἔγωγε.

ΣΜΙΚΡΙΝΗΣ
καὶ ποτήρια;

ΔΑΟΣ
ὁλκὴν ἴσως μνῶν τετταράκοντ', οὐ πλείονος,
85 κληρονόμε.

ΣΜΙΚΡΙΝΗΣ
πῶς; οἴει μ' ἐρωτᾶν, εἰπέ μοι,
διὰ τοῦτ'; Ἄπολλον· τἄλλα δ' ἡρπάσθη;

85 μ' omitted by B.

---

[1] About 18·3 kilogrammes. At that time in Athens a mina
weighed 457·8 grammes (cf. M. Lang and M. Crosby, *Weights
and Measures and Tokens* [*The Athenian Agora*, volume X:
Princeton 1964]).

Would be required for gathering, man by man,
The ashes; all the dead were heaped together
And burnt, then buried with all speed. Immediately
He broke up camp, and we slipped off to Rhodes   80
First, where we stayed some days, and then sailed
  here.
Now you've heard all my story.

SMIKRINES

Do you say you've brought
Six hundred gold staters?

DAOS

Yes.

SMIKRINES

Silver cups as well?

DAOS

Weighing some forty minas,[1] hardly more—
For *you* to inherit.[2]

SMIKRINES

What? Tell me, do you think   85
That's why I ask? Apollo! And the rest
Were seized?

[2] In hitting at Smikrines' cupidity, Daos exaggerates. By
Athenian law, on Kleostratos' death his property would have
passed to his unmarried sister. She would thus become an
heiress whose disposal in marriage was now limited by strict
legal provisions designed to keep the property in the family.
Here Smikrines, as head of the family to which Kleostratos
belonged, was in a controlling position, as the course of the
plot reveals (cf. A. R. W. Harrison, *The Law of Athens*, I,
Oxford 1968, 122 ff.).

MENANDER

ΔΑΟΣ

σχεδὸν
τὰ πλεῖστα, πλὴν ὧν ἔλαβον ἐξ ἀρχῆς ἐγώ.
ἱμάτι᾽ ἔνεστ᾽ ἐνταῦθα, χλαμύδες· τουτονὶ
τὸν ὄχλον ὁρᾷς οἰκεῖον.

ΣΜΙΚΡΙΝΗΣ

οὐθέν μοι μέλει
90 τούτων· ἐκεῖνος ὤφελε ζῆν.

ΔΑΟΣ

ὤφελε.
παράγωμεν εἴσω τὸν ταλαίπωρον λόγον
ἀπαγγελοῦντες τοῦτον οἷς ἥκιστ᾽ ἐχρῆν.

ΣΜΙΚΡΙΝΗΣ

εἶτ᾽ ἐντυχεῖν βουλήσομαί τι, Δᾶε, σοὶ
κατὰ σχολήν· νυνὶ δὲ καὐτός μοι δοκῶ
95 εἴσω παριέναι σκεψόμενος τίν᾽ ἂν τρόπον
τούτοις προσενεχθείη τις ἡμερώτατα.

ΤΥΧΗ

ἀλλ᾽ εἰ μὲν ἦν τούτοις τι γεγονὸς δυσχερές,
θεὸν οὖσαν οὐκ ἦν εἰκὸς ἀκολουθεῖν ἐμέ.

89 Change of speaker indicated by Kassel (οικειον· B). 92 χρη
B: χρῆν V. Schmidt, but in this idiom ἐχρῆν is the normal
orthography (cf. C. Austin, *Menandri Aspis et Samia*, II, 12).
93 συ B. In the right-hand margin B has ησυχη, referring
presumably to the tone of delivery of 94b–96. 94 Corr.
Kassel: δοκει B. 97 γεγονοσο B.

ASPIS

DAOS (*as Smikrines pries into the baggage*)
>About the biggest part, except for what
I got at first.   In there we've clothes and cloaks.
There's this crowd you see here—all *yours*!

SMIKRINES
>>I don't
Care about that.   If only *he* had lived!　　　　　90

DAOS
Yes, if only—but let's go inside to tell
This sorry tale to those who'd least deserved such news.

(*Here Daos begins his exit into Chairestratos' house, accompanied by the slaves and the baggage-animals.*)

SMIKRINES
(*To the departing Daos*) And afterwards I'd like a talk
　with you,
Daos.   No hurry.   (*To himself, on an empty stage*)
　But now I'll go in
Myself as well, I think, to puzzle out　　　　　95
The gentlest mode of dealing with these people.

(*Exit Smikrines into his house.   After a short pause the goddess Chance appears, to deliver her prologue to the audience.*)

CHANCE
If a real tragedy had struck these people,
A goddess like me couldn't come on next.[1]

---

[1] It was believed that the ancient Greek divinities (and their temples) must be kept free of the pollution caused by contact with dying and dead people (cf. Barrett's note on Euripides, *Hippolytus* 1437–39).

MENANDER

νῦν δ᾽ ἀγνοοῦσι καὶ πλανῶνται· τοῦτο δ[ὲ
100   ὁ προσέ]χων μαθήσετα[ι
. .]ν . . . . [.] . [. .] . [
ξ]ένος ἄλλος ωσ . [. . .]τοκαι[
ἥ τ᾽ ἐπίθεσις τῶν βαρβάρων [
ἐπέχων ἐσήμαιν᾽, ἐξεβοήθου[ν αὐτίκα
105 ὁπλιζόμενοι [τὸ] παρὸν ἕκαστος πλησίον.
οὕτως ὁ μὲν παρὰ τῷ τροφίμῳ τούτου τότε
ὢν ἐξεβοήθει τήνδ᾽ ἔχων τὴν ἀσπίδα,
εὐθύς τε πίπτει· κειμένης δ᾽ ἐν τοῖς νεκροῖς
τῆς ἀσπίδος τοῦ μειρακίου τ᾽ ᾠδηκότος
110 οὗτος διημάρτηκεν· ὁ δὲ Κλεόστρατος
ἐκεῖθεν ἑτέροις ἐκβοηθήσας ὅπλοις
γέγον᾽ αἰχμάλωτος· ζῇ δὲ καὶ σωθήσεται
ὅσον οὐδέπω. ταυτὶ μὲν οὖν μεμαθήκατε
ἱκανῶς. ὁ γέρων δ᾽ ὁ πάντ᾽ ἀνακρίνων ἀρτίως
115 γένει μὲν αὐτῷ θεῖός ἐστι πρὸς πατρὸς
πονηρίᾳ δὲ πάντας ἀνθρώπους ὅλως
ὑπερπέπαικεν· οὗτος οὔτε συγγενῆ
οὔτε φίλον οἶδεν οὐδὲ τῶν ἐν τῷ βίῳ
αἰσχρῶν πεφρόντικ᾽ οὐδέν, ἀλλὰ βούλεται
120 ἔχειν ἅπαντα· τοῦτο γινώσκει μόνον,   (‘ Comoedia
καὶ ζῇ μονότροπος, γραῦν ἔχων διάκονον.   Florentina’,
οὗ δ᾽ εἰσελήλυθ᾽ ὁ θεράπων ἐν γειτόνων   1 Körte)

---

100 Suppl. several. 102 Suppl. ed. pr. 105 Suppl. Kassel.
117 Corr. Page: ουτως B. 118 ουδε . . . ουτε B. 120–35 are
preserved also in F.

---

[1] I.e. Daos. In Menander's prologue-speeches personal
names are usually avoided. Only one important character is

26

In fact they're lost and in the dark. If you
Listen carefully, you'll learn what [really happened]. 100

(*Lines 100–103, in which the goddess Chance begins her
account of what really happened in that night attack, are
badly mutilated in the papyrus. It seems that Kleo-
stratos had a friend . . .*)

. . . . [There shared Kleostratos' tent (?)]
Another man, a friend (?) [. . . . .] and [. . . . .]
The attack made by the natives [came as a surprise(?)].
The trumpeter kept sounding the alarm. [At once]
The troops streamed out, all armed with what they 105
    found
To hand. That's how the friend of this man's master
Came marching out then with that shield you saw.
He fell immediately. The shield lay there
Among the dead, and when that youngster's corpse
    swelled up,
This man[1] made his great blunder. Kleostratos 110
Marched out of camp with borrowed armour, and
Was captured; but he's still alive, and soon he'll come
Back safely. Well, that's all you need to know
About that. This old man, though, who's just been
Prying into everything—he's his paternal 115
Uncle, the world's most perfect paragon
Of villainy. The names of relative
And friend he doesn't recognize, doesn't care
A fig if any action is dishonest.
He wants to possess everything, that's his 120
One thought. He lives alone, an old slave-woman
Looks after him. Now, where the slave's gone in,

---

named here, and that too only once (Kleostratos, 109), just as
in the *Dyskolos* (Knemon, 6).

MENANDER

ἀδελφὸς οἰκεῖ τοῦδε τοῦ φιλαργύρου
νεώτερος, ταὐτὸν προσήκων κατὰ γένος (5)
125 τῷ μειρακίῳ, χρηστὸς δὲ τῷ τρόπῳ πάνυ
καὶ πλούσιος, γυναῖκ' ἔχων καὶ παρθένου
μιᾶς πατὴρ ὤν, ᾧ κατέλιπεν ἐκπλέων
ὁ μειρακίσκος τὴν ἀδελφήν· σύντροφοι
αὐταί θ' ἑαυταῖς εἰσιν ἐκτεθραμμέναι. (10)
130 ὢν δ', ὅπερ ὑπεῖπα, χρηστὸς οὗτος μακροτέραν
ὁρῶν ἐκείνῳ τὴν ἀποδημίαν τά τε
οἰκεῖα μέτρια παντελῶς, τὴν παρθένον
αὐτὸς συνοικίζειν νεανίσκῳ τινὶ
ἔμελλεν, ὑῷ τῆς γυναικὸς ἧς ἔχει, (15)
135 ἐξ ἀνδρὸς ἑτέρου, προῖκά τ' ἐπεδίδου δύο (16)
τάλαντα· καὶ ποιεῖν ἔμελλε τοὺς γάμους
νυνί. ταραχὴν δὲ τοῦτο πᾶσιν ἐμπεσὸν
τὸ νῦν παρέξει πρᾶγμα· τοὺς ἑξακοσίους
χρυσοῦς ἀκούσας οὑτοσὶ γὰρ ἀρτίως
140 ὁ πονηρός, οἰκέτας τε βαρβάρους ἰδών,
σκευοφόρα, παιδίσκας, ἐπικλήρου τῆς κόρης
οὔσης κρατεῖν βουλήσετ' αὐτός, τῷ χρόνῳ
προὔχων. μάτην δὲ πράγμαθ' αὑτῷ καὶ πόνους
πολλοὺς παρασχὼν γνωριμώτερόν τε τοῖς
145 πᾶ[σ]ιν ποήσας αὑτὸν οἷός ἐστ' ἀνὴρ (17)
ἐ]πάνεισιν ἐπὶ τἀρχαῖα. λοιπὸν τοὔνομα
το]ὐμὸν φράσαι, τίς εἰμι, πάντων κυρία
τούτων βραβεῦσαι καὶ διοικῆσαι· Τύχη. (20)

125 δε B: τε F.   127 εκπλεων B: ετινεαν F.   129 εκτεθραμμ[
F: ειστεθραμμεναι: (sic, with dicolon, and paragraphus at line
beginning) B.   130 Corr. Kassel: υπερυπειπα B, [ως ?] προειπα
F.   133 αυτος B: ουτος F.   137 εμπεσων B.   145, 146 Suppl.
ed. pr. of B.   145–60 are preserved in F (147–48 are torn

Next door, there lives a younger brother of
This money-hungry villain.   He's that young
Man's uncle, too, but *he* has principles   125
As well as riches.   And he's married, with
One daughter.   He became the guardian of
The young man's sister when he sailed away;
The two girls have grown up together.   He's
A man with principles, as I just said;   130
So when he saw how long that young man would
Be away, how very cramped were their resources,
He formed a plan.   The sister should get married
To his young step-son,[1] whom his wife had had
By her previous husband; and for dowry he'd   135
Give two talents.   The wedding was to be
Today, but now this blow has fallen, and
Will raise a storm.   Just now, you understand,
This scoundrel heard of those six hundred coins
Of gold; he's ogled foreign slaves, and mules,   140
And girls.   The young man's sister has become
An heiress, and this rogue, despite his age,
Will want to lay his hands on her.   In vain:
He'll cause himself much toil and trouble, show
His true colours more clearly to the world,   145
And then go back to where he was before.
I've still to tell you who I am, the steward
And judge controlling all this.   I'm called Chance.

(*Exit Chance.   After a short pause Smikrines enters from his house.*)

---

[1] Chaireas.

---

off completely in B, and 146, 149–53 badly mutilated).
147 Suppl. Vitelli.

ΣΜΙΚΡΙΝΗΣ

ἵνα μή τις εἴπῃ μ' ὅτι φιλάργυρος σφόδρα,
150 οὐκ ἐξετάσας πόσον ἐστὶν ὃ φέρει χρυσίον
οὐδ' ὁπόσα τἀργυρώματ', οὐδ' ἀριθμὸν λαβὼν
οὐδενός, ἑτοίμως εἰσενεγκεῖν ἐνθάδε
εἴασα· βασκαίνειν γὰρ εἰώθασί με   (25)
ἐπὶ παντί· τὸ γὰρ ἀκριβὲς εὑρεθήσεται
155 ἕως ἂν οἱ φέροντες ὦσιν οἰκέται.
οἶμαι μὲν οὖν αὐτοὺς ἑκόντας τοῖς νόμοις
καὶ τοῖς δικαίοις ἐμμενεῖν· ἐὰν δὲ μή,
οὐθεὶς ἐπιτρέψει. τοὺς δὲ γινομένους γάμους   (30)
τούτους προειπεῖν βούλομ' αὐτοῖς μὴ ποεῖν.
160 ἴσως μὲν ἄτοπον καὶ λέγειν· οὐκ ἐν γάμοις   (32)
εἰσὶν γὰρ ἥκοντος τοιούτου νῦν λόγου.
ὅμως δὲ τὴν θύραν γε κόψας ἐκκαλῶ
τὸν Δᾶον· οὗτος γὰρ προσέξει μοι μόνος.

ΔΑΟΣ

πολλὴ μὲν ὑμῖν ταῦτα συγγνώμη ποεῖν,
165 ἐκ τῶν δ' ἐνόντων ὡς μάλιστα δεῖ φέρειν
ἀνθρωπίνως τὸ συμβεβηκός.

ΣΜΙΚΡΙΝΗΣ
                            πρός σ' ἐγὼ
πάρειμι, Δᾶε.

---

150 Corr. Körte, Wilamowitz: ὁπόσον ἐσθ' ὁ φέρει F (words
not preserved in B). 156 So F: εκοντασαυτους B. 159 So
F: τουτοισπροσειπεινβουλομαιμηποιειν B. 161 εἰσὶν Henrichs,
Winnington-Ingram: ἐστὶν B.

ASPIS

SMIKRINES

To stop them saying that I'm a slave of Mammon,
I didn't check the amount of gold he's brought,   150
Or even the number of silver cups. I didn't
Count *anything*. I let them take it in
Here willingly. They always like to call
Me names. The exact amount can be discovered
So long as those who carried it are slaves.[1]   155
I think that they'll agree to abide by law
And justice. If they don't, they'll not be allowed
To get away with it. I'm going to tell them to
Call off this wedding that they're fixing now.
Perhaps it's foolish even to mention it.   160
When news like this comes, weddings must be out
For them. Still, I'll knock at the door and call
Daos. He's the one who'll take me seriously.

(*As Smikrines approaches Chairestratos' house, its door
opens and Daos emerges, talking back to the unseen in-
mates within.*)

DAOS

It's very understandable you should behave
Like this, but in the circumstances try your best   165
To bear what's happened reasonably.

SMIKRINES

                      Daos,
I've come for you.

---

[1] In an Athenian court of law, slaves could give evidence
only under torture, and it was commonly believed about this
time that evidence so obtained was more reliable than the
freely given evidence of a free man (cf. A. R. W. Harrison, *The
Law of Athens, II : Procedure*, Oxford 1971, 147).

MENANDER

ΔΑΟΣ
πρὸς ἐμέ;

ΣΜΙΚΡΙΝΗΣ
                ναὶ μὰ τὸν Δία.
ὤφελε μὲν οὖν ἐκεῖνος, ὃν δίκαιον ἦν,
ζῆν καὶ διοικεῖν ταῦτα καὶ τεθνηκότος
170 ἐμοῦ γενέσθαι τῶν ἐμῶν κατὰ τοὺς νόμους
κύριος ἁπάντων.

ΔΑΟΣ
ὤφελεν· τί οὖν;

ΣΜΙΚΡΙΝΗΣ
                    τί γάρ;
πρεσβύτατός εἰμι τοῦ γένους· ἀδικούμενος
ἀεί τε πλεονεκτοῦντα τὸν ἀδελφόν τί μου
ὁρῶν ἀνέχομαι.

ΔΑΟΣ
νοῦν ἔχεις;

ΣΜΙΚΡΙΝΗΣ
                ἀλλ᾽, ὦγαθέ,
175 οὐδὲ μετριάζει· νενόμικεν δὲ παντελῶς
οἰκότριβά μ᾽ ἢ νόθον τιν᾽, ὃς νυνὶ γάμους
ἐπόει διδοὺς οὐκ οἶδ᾽ ὅτῳ τὴν παρθένον,
οὐκ ἐπανενεγκών, οὐκ ἐρωτήσας ἐμέ,
ἐμοὶ προσήκων ταὐτό, θεῖος ὢν ὅπερ
180 κἀγώ.

ASPIS

DAOS
For me?

SMIKRINES
        By Zeus, yes.   Oh,
He *should* have lived.   He was the right man to
Administer this, and take charge of all
My property when I am dead, just as   170
The law prescribes.

DAOS
He should.   What then?

SMIKRINES
             Well, I'm
The oldest in this family.   I submit
To injuries, to seeing my brother take
Advantage of me, always.

DAOS
        Are you serious?

SMIKRINES
             But,
My good friend, he's not even reasonable.   175
He must have thought me totally a slave
Or illegitimate, the way he's marrying
That girl to heaven knows whom.   He didn't consult
Me, didn't enquire.   Yet he's the same relation,
Her uncle, like me.

---

173 αιε B.   τί μου Handley, Reeve: τ' εμου B.   175 μετριαζιμε· B.
176 νοθεν B.   177 τὴν om. B.

MENANDER

ΔΑΟΣ

τί οὖν δή;

ΣΜΙΚΡΙΝΗΣ

        πάντα ταῦτ᾽ ὀργίζομαι
ὁρῶν. ἐπειδὴ δ᾽ ἐστὶν ἀλλοτρίως ἔχων
πρὸς ἐμέ, ποήσω ταῦτ᾽ ἐγώ· τὴν οὐσίαν
οὐχὶ καταλείψω τὴν ἐμὴν διαρπάσαι
τούτοις, ὅπερ δὲ καὶ παραινοῦσίν τινες
185 τῶν γνωρίμων μοι λήψομαι τὴν παρθένον
γυναῖκα ταύτην· καὶ γὰρ ὁ νόμος μοι δοκεῖ
οὕτω λέγειν πως, Δᾶε. ταῦτ᾽ οὖν ὃν τρόπον
πράττοιτ᾽ ἂν ὀρθῶς καὶ σὲ φροντίζειν ἔδει·
οὐκ ἀλλότριος εἶ.

ΔΑΟΣ

        Σμικρίνη, πάνυ μοι δοκεῖ
190 τὸ ῥῆμα τοῦτ᾽ εἶναί τι μεμεριμνημένον,
τὸ " γνῶθι σαυτόν ". ἐμμένειν τούτῳ μ᾽ ἔα,
ὅσα τ᾽ οἰκέτῃ δεῖ μὴ πονηρῷ ταῦτ᾽ ἐμοὶ
ἀνάφερε καὶ τούτων παρ᾽ ἐμοῦ ζήτει λόγον

(Lacuna of one line probably)

σὸν δ᾽ ειμαι†δω[
195 πάντας θερά[ποντ]ας ἐστι.[
σώματα μεγ[. . . λ]αμβανοντ.[(?) οἷα δὲ

188 ορθος B. 189 εἶ om. B, suppl. Sandbach. 190 Corr.
Kassel: ενε B. 195, 196 Suppl. ed. pr., apart from οἷα δὲ
(Arnott, *exempli gratia*).

34

ASPIS

DAOS

So?

SMIKRINES

Seeing all this makes   180
Me angry.   But if he's behaving like
A stranger to me, this is what I'll do.
I'll not leave property of mine for them
To plunder.   No, I'll follow the advice
Given me by some people I know.   I'll marry   185
The girl myself.   In fact, Daos, that's more
Or less, I feel, the meaning of our law.[1]
You too should have been thinking how to have
This done correctly.   You're involved here.

DAOS

Smikrines,
That proverb seems so very wise to me,   190
'Know who you are.'   Let me comply with it.
Pass on to me and question me about
Those matters which concern an honest slave.

(*Here one line seems to have been cut off the papyrus page,
and the following four lines, in which Daos continues his
reply to Smikrines, have suffered more or less serious
damage.*)

Your [. . . . . They are (?)]
All servants.   You may (?) [. . . . .]   195
Their bodies, taking [. . . . . As to (?)]

---

[1] See the note on line 85.   Athenian law gave the option of
marrying an heiress to her male relatives in order of their
seniority.   Smikrines was the oldest member of the girl's
family, and there was no legal embargo on a marriage between
uncle and niece.   His interpretation of Athenian law, therefore,
was correct (cf. Harrison, *The Law of Athens*, I, 9 ff., 132 ff.).

σημεῖ᾽ ἔπεστ[ιν, ὅσα σ]υνήλλαξέν τισιν
ἐκεῖνος ἀποδημῶν ἔχω φράζειν ἐγώ·
ταῦτ᾽, ἂν κελεύῃ τίς με, δείξω καθ᾽ ἕν, ὅπου,
200 πῶς, τοῦ παρόντος. περὶ δὲ κλήρου, Σμικρίνη,
ἢ νὴ Δί᾽ ἐπικλήρου γάμων τε καὶ γένους
καὶ διαφορᾶς οἰκειότητος μηκέτι
Δᾶον ἄγετ᾽ εἰς μέσον· τὰ τῶν ἐλευθέρων
αὐτοὶ δὲ πράττεθ᾽ οἷς τὸ τοιοῦτον ἁρμόσει.

ΣΜΙΚΡΙΝΗΣ

205 δοκῶ δέ σοί τι, πρὸς θεῶν, ἁμαρτάνειν;

ΔΑΟΣ

Φρύξ εἰμι· πολλὰ τῶν παρ᾽ ὑμῖν φαίνεται
καλῶν ἐμοὶ πάνδεινα καὶ τοὐναντίον
τούτων. τί προσέχειν δεῖ σ᾽ ἐμοί; φρονεῖς ἐμοῦ
βέλτιον εἰκότως.

ΣΜΙΚΡΙΝΗΣ

σὺ νυνί μοι δοκεῖς
210 λέγειν ὁμοῦ τι, '' μὴ πάρεχέ μοι πράγματ᾽ '', ἢ
τοιουτότροπόν τι· μανθάνω. τούτων τινὰ
ὀπτέον ἂν εἴη πρὸς ἀγορὰν ἐλθόντι μοι,
εἰ μή τις ἔνδον ἐστίν.

197 Suppl. Sandbach, from ideas by Austin, Barigazzi, and
ed. pr. respectively. 210 πράγματ᾽ '', ἢ Handley: πραγματα B.
211 Corr. Page: τοιουτοντροπον B.

ASPIS

The seals on goods, the contracts he[1] drew up
With people while away—these I can show.
Just ask me, I'll go through them one by one,
Naming the place, occasion, witness. Property   200
Or heiresses, though, bless me!—weddings, blood,
Your different affinities—no, Smikrines,
Don't ever involve *me* in them! Arrange
Your *free* affairs yourselves. You're qualified.

SMIKRINES

In heaven's name, do you believe I'm wrong?   205

DAOS

I come from Phrygia. Much that you approve
Appals me—and the converse.⌋ Why take note
Of *my* opinions? *Yours*, of course, are far
Superior to mine.

SMIKRINES

Now, I presume,
You're saying something like ' Don't bother me ',   210
Or words to that effect. I see. I'd better go
And find one of *them*[2] at the market, if
There's no one in here?

(*After Daos has answered this question, exit Smikrines off
right, in the direction of the market place. Daos is left to
muse alone.*)

---

[1] Kleostratos.
[2] Smikrines means, but does not name, his brother Chaire-
stratos. Thus Menander informs his audience that Chaire-
stratos is to be considered absent from home during the first
act.

MENANDER

ΔΑΟΣ

οὐδείς. — ὦ Τύχη,
οἵῳ μ᾽ ἀφ᾽ οἵου δεσπότου παρεγγυᾶν
215 μέλλεις. τί σ᾽ ἠδίκηκα τηλικοῦτ᾽ ἐγώ;

ΜΑΓΕΙΡΟΣ

ἂν καὶ λάβω ποτ᾽ ἔργον, ἢ τέθνηκέ τις,
εἶτ᾽ ἀποτρέχειν δεῖ μισθὸν οὐκ ἔχοντά με,
ἢ τέτοκε τῶν ἔνδον κυοῦσά τις λάθρα,
εἶτ᾽ οὐκέτι θύουσ᾽ ἐξαπίνης, ἀλλ᾽ οἴχομαι
220 ἀπιὼν ἐγώ. τῆς δυσποτμίας.

ΔΑΟΣ

πρὸς τῶν θεῶν,
μάγειρ᾽, ἄπελθε.

ΜΑΓΕΙΡΟΣ

νῦν δέ σοι τί δοκῶ ποεῖν;
λαβὲ τὰς μαχαίρας, παιδάριον, θᾶττόν ποτε.
δραχμῶν τριῶν ἦλθον δι᾽ ἡμερῶν δέκα
ἔργον λαβών· ᾤμην ἔχειν ταύτας· νεκρὸς
225 ἐλθών τις ἐκ Λυκίας ἀφῄρηται βίᾳ
ταύτας. τοιούτου συμβεβηκότος κακοῦ
τοῖς ἔνδον, ἱερόσυλε, κλαούσας ὁρῶν

215 τηλικουτον B. 218 τετοκετισενδον B. 221 σοι om. B,
suppl. Arnott, Fraenkel. 227 ιεροσυλεσυ B.

---

[1] Kleostratos.

[2] The character here identified as a cook (Greek, μάγειρος)
was a familiar figure in contemporary Athens. He was a man
hired from the market-place to provide a live animal (usually a
sheep), which he then butchered (usually as part of a sacrifice)
and cooked for his hirer. The occasion might range from an

ASPIS

DAOS

No one.—Lady Chance,
Some owner you assign me, after *him*[1]!
What awful crime against you have I done?   215

(*Enter, from Chairestratos' house, a cook*[2] *with his assistant. They do not see Daos at first.*)

COOK

Whenever I get hired, a death occurs
And I'm obliged to leave without my fee.
Or else one of the household has a baby
Whose start was hush-hush—then the party's off
Abruptly. I'm away—no pay—what luck!   220

DAOS

Cook, by the gods, be off!

COOK

What do you think
I'm doing at this moment? Take the knives,
Boy, quickly now. This job I took ten days ago;
My fee, three drachmas. When I came, I thought
The coins were mine. And now a corpse has come   225
From Lycia and snatched them clean away.—You
   crook,[3]
A blow like this falls on the house, when you

informal party of young male friends to a special family
occasion like a wedding, as here (that planned by Chairestratos
for Chaireas and Kleostratos' sister). Cf. H. Dohm, *Mageiros,*
Munich 1964.

[3] Literally ' temple-robber ', a contemporary Attic insult of
general significance (cf. *Dysk.* 640, *Pk.* 176, *Sam.* 678), here
addressed to the cook's assistant.

MENANDER

καὶ κοπτομένας γυναῖκας ἐκφέρεις κενὴν
τὴν λήκυθον; μέμνησο καιρὸν παραλαβὼν
230 τοιοῦτον. οὐ Σπινθήρ᾽, Ἀριστείδην δ᾽ ἔχω,
ὑπηρέτην δίκαιον· ὄψομαί σ᾽ ἐγὼ
ἄδειπνον. ὁ δὲ τραπεζοποιὸς καταμενεῖ
εἰς τὸ περίδειπνον τυχὸν ἴσως.

ΤΡΑΠΕΖΟΠΟΙΟΣ

δραχμὴν ἐγὼ
ἂν μὴ λάβω κοπτόμενος ὑμῶν οὐδὲ ἕν
235 αὐτὸς διοίσω.

ΔΑΟΣ
πρόαγε· τοῦτον οὐ . . [.] . .

(Lacuna of one or two lines)

] . έλλων ἄρ[α
]α πρῶτ[α . .]τα;

ΔΑΟΣ
πάνυ μ[ὲν οὖν.

236 Gaiser suggests that the whole of this line may be pre-
served in anon. comic fr. 287 Kock (*Comicorum Atticorum
Fragmenta*, III, 460), Δᾶος πάρεστι· τί ποτ᾽ ἀπαγγέλλων ἄρα;
237] $\overset{.τα}{\rho α}$ B.   μ[ὲν οὖν suppl. ed. pr.

---

[1] Cooks had a reputation, on the comic stage at least, for
pilfering from their employers (cf. Dohm, *Mageiros* 129 ff.).
[2] The assistant's name is Spinther (= ' Spark '), but he has
been behaving more like Aristides, the Athenian statesman
and general of the early fifth century B.C. whose reputation for
honesty earned him his nickname ' The Just '.

40

See women crying, battering their breasts—
And still you leave with your flask empty[1]!   Do
Remember what a chance you had!   I've got a help   230
Who's honest—Aristides, yes, not Spinther[2]!
I'll see you get no dinner!   But the waiter[3]—
Perhaps *he*'ll stay until the funeral lunch?

(*Exit cook with his assistant, off right.   Enter immedi-
ately, from Chairestratos' house, the waiter himself,
talking back to the unseen women in the house.*)

WAITER

If I don't get my drachma, I'll be just
As cut up as you are!

DAOS

Get on! Him [. . . . . . .]   235

(*The end of 235 is mutilated; then one or two further
lines are missing, cut off the end of the papyrus page.
Two badly mutilated lines follow.   In them the waiter
seems to be questioning Daos about his return from Lycia
with the booty.*)

WAITER

[. . . . .[4]]ing after all
[. . . . .] first?

DAOS

Yes, certainly.

---

[3] Contumelious rivalry between cooks and waiters was a
conventional motif of contemporary comedy.
[4] If Gaiser's suggestion is right (see opposite), this line
would have run ' Daos is here—what news is he bringing after
all? '

MENANDER

ΤΡΑΠΕΖΟΠΟΙΟΣ

κακὸς κακῶ]ς ἀπόλοιο τοίνυν, νὴ Δία,
. . . .] . δ[ε π]εποηκώς, ἀπόπληκτε· χρυσίο[ν
240 ἔχων τοσοῦτο, παῖδας, ἥκεις δεσπότῃ
ταῦτ' ἀποκομίζων, κοὐκ ἀπέδρας; ποταπός π[οτ' εἶ;

ΔΑΟΣ

Φρύξ.

ΤΡΑΠΕΖΟΠΟΙΟΣ

οὐδὲν ἱερόν· ἀνδρόγυνος. ἡμεῖς μόνοι
οἱ Θρᾷκές ἐσμεν ἄνδρες· οἱ μὲν δὴ Γέται,
Ἄπολλον, ἀνδρεῖον τὸ χρῆμα· τοιγαροῦν
245 γέμουσιν οἱ μυλῶνες ἡμῶν.

ΔΑΟΣ

ἐκποδὼν
ἀπαλλάγηθ' ἀπὸ τῆς θύρας· καὶ γάρ τινα
ὄχλον ἄλλον ἀνθρώπων προσιόντα τουτονὶ
ὁρῶ μεθυόντων. νοῦν ἔχετε· τὸ τῆς τύχης
ἄδηλον· εὐφραίνεσθ' ὃν ἔξεστιν χρόνον.

ΧΟ Ρ ΟΥ

239 Suppl. ed. pr.

---

[1] Phrygia, an area of what is now north-west Turkey in
Asia, provided Greece with many slaves. The reputation of
its inhabitants for cowardice and effeminacy was a common-
place.

WAITER

Be damned to you then [damnably], by Zeus,
If [that's what (?)] you've done! Senseless fool!
　When you
Had so much money and slaves, you've brought them 240
　all
Back for your master? You didn't disappear?
　Where do
You come from?

DAOS

　　　　Phrygia.

WAITER

　　　　　　　That means you're no good,
A queer.[1] We Thracians, though, we're men, unique—
The Getic tribe, by Apollo—yes, real men.
That's why we fill the grain-mills.[2]

DAOS

　　　　　　　Off with you! 245
Away from our door! (*Exit waiter.*) There's another
　rabble
Approaching here, I see—some men, quite drunk.
You're sensible. What fortune brings is all
Uncertain. Take your pleasure while you can!

(*Exit Daos, into Chairestratos' home. The 'sensible'
band of drunkards is the chorus, who now enter after the
conventional cue for their first entr'acte performance.*)

[2] The Getai were a Thracian tribe originating from the area
east and south of the Carpathian Mountains. They also pro-
vided Greece with many slaves; indeed Getas is a common
slave name in Menander and elsewhere. Their reputation for
virile vigour is underlined by the reference to grain-mills,
where slaves were often sent to work as a punishment for mis-
behaviour.

ΜΕΡΟΣ Β΄

ΣΜΙΚΡΙΝΗΣ
250 εἰέν· τί δή μοι νῦν λέγεις, Χαιρέστρατε;

ΧΑΙΡΕΣΤΡΑΤΟΣ
πρῶτον μέν, ὦ βέλτιστε, τὰ περὶ τὴν ταφὴν
δεῖ πραγματευθῆναι.

ΣΜΙΚΡΙΝΗΣ
πεπραγματευμένα
ἔσται. τὸ μετὰ ταῦθ᾽, ὁμολόγει τὴν παρθένον
μηθενί· τὸ γὰρ πρᾶγμ᾽ ἐστὶν οὐ σὸν ἀλλ᾽ ἐμόν·
255 πρεσβύτερός εἰμι· σοὶ μέν ἐστ᾽ ἔνδον γυνή,
θυγάτηρ, ἐμοὶ δὲ δεῖ γενέσθαι.

ΧΑΙΡΕΣΤΡΑΤΟΣ
Σμικρίνη,
(KT fr. 692 ?) οὐδὲν μέλει σοι μετριότητος;

ΣΜΙΚΡΙΝΗΣ
διὰ τί, παῖ;

ΧΑΙΡΕΣΤΡΑΤΟΣ
ὢν τηλικοῦτος παῖδα μέλλεις λαμβάνειν;

ΣΜΙΚΡΙΝΗΣ
πηλίκος;

255 συ Β.

44

ASPIS

ACT II

(After the departure of the chorus, enter Smikrines, Chaire-stratos and Chaireas. Smikrines and Chairestratos, who are to be imagined as having met previously in the market place, cf. 211 ff., are in mid-conversation. Chaireas remains in the background until the end of Smikrines' and Chairestratos' discussion.)

SMIKRINES

Well, what's your answer now, Chairestratos?　　250

CHAIRESTRATOS

First, my good fellow, there's the funeral
To organise.

SMIKRINES

It will be organised.
But afterwards, don't you promise the girl
To anyone. This business isn't yours, it's mine
To deal with. I'm the older. You've a wife　　255
And daughter in there. I must have the same!

CHAIRESTRATOS

Does decency mean nothing to you, Smikrines?

SMIKRINES

Bah! Why?

CHAIRESTRATOS

Do you intend to marry a young girl
At *your* age?

SMIKRINES

My age?

MENANDER

ΧΑΙΡΕΣΤΡΑΤΟΣ

ἐμοὶ μὲν παντελῶς δοκεῖς γέρων.

ΣΜΙΚΡΙΝΗΣ

260 μόνος γεγάμηκα πρεσβύτερος;

ΧΑΙΡΕΣΤΡΑΤΟΣ

ἀνθρωπίνως
τὸ πρᾶγμ' ἔνεγκε, Σμικρίνη, πρὸς τῶν θεῶν·
τῇ παιδὶ ταύτῃ γέγονε Χαιρέας ὁδὶ
σύντροφος ὁ μέλλων λαμβάνειν αὐτήν. τί οὖν
λέγω; σὺ μηδὲν ζημιοῦ· τὰ μὲν ὄντα γὰρ
265 ταῦθ' ὅσαπέρ ἐστι λαβὲ σὺ πάντα, κύριος
γενοῦ, δίδομέν σοι· τὴν δὲ παιδίσκην τυχεῖν
καθ' ἡλικίαν ἔασον αὐτὴν νυμφίου.
ἐκ τῶν ἰδίων ἐγὼ γὰρ ἐπιδώσω δύο
τάλαντα προῖκα.

ΣΜΙΚΡΙΝΗΣ

πρὸς θεῶν, Μελιτίδη
270 λαλεῖν ὑπείληφας; τί φής; ἐγὼ λάβω
τὴν οὐσίαν, τούτῳ δὲ τὴν κόρην ἀφῶ
ἵν', ἂν γένηται παιδίον, φεύγω δίκην
ἔχων τὰ τούτου;

ΧΑΙΡΕΣΤΡΑΤΟΣ

τοῦτο δ' οἴει; κατάβαλε.

ΣΜΙΚΡΙΝΗΣ

" οἴει " λέγεις; τὸν Δᾶον ὥς με πέμψατε
275 ἵν' ἀπογραφὴν ὧν κεκόμικεν δή μοι—

268 ἰδών B.

46

ASPIS

CHAIRESTRATOS
I think you're too old.

SMIKRINES
Am I the only older man to marry?   260

CHAIRESTRATOS
Accept the situation decently,
In heaven's name, Smikrines.   This girl's fiancé,
Chaireas here, has been brought up with her.
Here's my suggestion.   I won't let you lose
Anything.   You must take this property,   265
Manage it, all there is.   We give it you.
The girl, though—let her find a bridegroom of
Her own age.   I'll provide two talents dowry
From my own money.

SMIKRINES
                    By the gods, do you think
You're talking to Melitides[1]?   You mean,   270
I take the property, but let him have the girl?
So if they have a son, I'll then stand trial
For taking what's *his*?

CHAIRESTRATOS
                    You think that?   Drop it!

SMIKRINES
You say ' think ', do you?   Send Daos to me;
I'll have an inventory of what he's brought—   275

---

[1] A proverbial blockhead, the Athenian equivalent of Simple
Simon.

MENANDER

ΧΑΙΡΕΣΤΡΑΤΟΣ

$$τί\ χρὴ$$

]εμ' ἢ τί πο[εῖ]ν μ' ἔδει;

ΣΜΙΚΡΙΝΗΣ

. .] . μεν[
. .]εστιν.

ΧΑΙΡΕΣΤΡΑΤΟΣ

    ἐμε .[. .] . .[(?) ᾠόμην
ἀ]εὶ σὲ μὲν λαβ[όν]τα ταύτη[ν τὴν κόρην
280 αὐτὸν δ' ἐκεῖνον τὴν ἐμὴν τῆ[ς οὐσίας
ὑμᾶς καταλείψειν τῆς ἐμαυτοῦ κυρίους.
ἀπαλλαγῆναι τὴν ταχίστην τοῦ βίου
γένοιτό μοι πρὶν ἰδεῖν ἃ μήποτ' ἤλπισα.

ΧΑΙΡΕΑΣ

εἰέν· τὸ μὲν σὸν πρῶτον, ὦ Κλεόστρατε,
285 ἴσως ἐλεῆσαι καὶ δακρῦσαι κατὰ λόγον
πάθος ἐστί, δεύτερον δὲ τοὐμόν· οὐδὲ εἷς
τούτων γὰρ οὕτως ἠτύχηκεν ὡς ἐγώ.
ἔρωτι περιπεσὼν γὰρ οὐκ αὐθαιρέτῳ
τῆ[ς] σῆς ἀδελφῆς, φίλτατ' ἀνθρώπων ἐμοί,
290 οὐθὲν ποήσας προπετὲς οὐδ' ἀνάξιον
οὐδ' ἄδικον ἐδεήθην ἐμαυτῷ κατὰ νόμους
συνοικίσαι τὸν θεῖον ᾧ σὺ κατέλιπες

---

278 ᾠόμην here suppl. Austin.   279 .]εισσε B: corr. and suppl.
Austin. λαβ[όν]τα suppl. ed. pr. τὴν κόρην suppl. Arnott.
280 Suppl. Handley. 289 Suppl. ed. pr.

ASPIS

CHAIRESTRATOS (*interrupting*)

                                    What must
[. . . . .] or what should I have done?   276

(*Lines 276–78 are badly mutilated. Apparently Chaire-
stratos expresses his total helplessness, 275b–76;
Smikrines replies unyieldingly, 277–78a, and then goes
off into his own house.*)

CHAIRESTRATOS

      [. . . . . .] me [. . . . . . I'd] always [thought] 278
That you'd be married to this [girl], and he
Himself to my own daughter.[1] So I'd leave   280
The two of you to inherit my [estate].
Let me depart this life without delay,
Before I see my dreams to nightmares turn.

(*Chairestratos stumbles to his door, and probably dis-
appears inside in a state of collapse. Chaireas, now
alone on the stage, comes forward.*)

CHAIREAS

Ah well! Kleostratos, it's only fair
To mourn and sympathise with your fate first   285
Of all, perhaps; but secondly, with mine,
For none of them has suffered quite like me.
I didn't choose to fall in love with *your*
Sister, O dearest of mankind to me[2]!
I've done nothing that's hasty or vile or   290
Unauthorised. I asked permission for
Her hand in marriage legally from your

---

[1] The 'you' = Chaireas, the 'he' = Kleostratos.
[2] This phrase appears to be paratragic.

49

καὶ τὴν ἐμὴν μητέρα παρ' ᾗ παιδεύεται.
ᾤμην δὲ μακάριός τις εἶναι τῷ βίῳ,
295 ἐλθεῖν δ' ἐπ' αὐτὸ τὸ πέρας οἰηθεὶς σφόδρα
καὶ προσδοκήσας οὐδ' ἰδεῖν δυνήσομαι
τὸ λοιπόν· ἕτερον κύριον δ' αὐτῆς ποεῖ
ὁ νόμος ὁ τοὐμὸν οὐδαμοῦ κρίνων ἔτι.

ΔΑΟΣ

Χαιρέστρατ', οὐκ ὀρθῶς ποεῖς· ἀνίστασο·
300 οὐκ ἔστ' ἀθυμεῖν οὐδὲ κεῖσθαι. Χαιρέα,
ἐλθὼν παραμυθοῦ· μὴ 'πίτρεπε· τὰ πράγματα
ἡμῖν ἅπασίν ἐστιν ἐν τούτῳ σχεδόν.
μᾶλλον δ' ἄνοιγε τὰς θύρας, φανερὸν πόει
σαυτόν· προήσει τοὺς φίλους, Χαιρέστρατε,
305 οὕτως ἀγεννῶς;

ΧΑΙΡΕΣΤΡΑΤΟΣ

Δᾶε παῖ, κακῶς ἔχω.
μελαγχολῶ τοῖς πράγμασιν· μὰ τοὺς θεούς,
οὐκ εἴμ' ἐν ἐμαυτοῦ, μαίνομαι δ' ἀκαρὴς πάνυ·

295 ελθων B.   τερας B: corr. Kassel.   300 ουκετ' B.   305 αγαννως B.

---

[1] I.e., from Chairestratos and his wife. Chairestratos was the girl's guardian during Kleostratos' absence abroad (cf. 127 ff.).

Uncle with whom you left her, from my mother
In whose care she's being groomed.[1]   I thought I was
Lucky in my life, I fully thought and felt   295
I'd reached the very goal.   In future I
Can't even see her.   She belongs to another
By laws which now reject my claim outright.

(*Enter Daos from Chairestratos' house.   He first speaks
back inside to Chairestratos, who is probably to be
imagined at this moment as collapsed on a bed near the
door; then Daos closes the door, and addresses Chaireas.*)

DAOS

Chairestratos, you're doing wrong!   Get up!
You can't lie down and languish.   Chaireas,   300
Come here and reassure him, don't let him
Succumb.   The interests of us all may well
Be anchored in him.

(*As Chaireas moves to join Daos at Chairestratos' door,
however, Daos changes his mind, halts Chaireas, and
turns to address the off-stage Chairestratos behind the
closed door of his house.*)

No—open the door,
Show yourself.   Will you sacrifice your friends,
Chairestratos, so scurvily?

(*Enter Chairestratos.   He is probably helped out by
attendant slaves onto a seat of some kind, which they
place near his door.*)

CHAIRESTRATOS

Daos, my boy,   305
I'm ill.   The affair's produced a black
Depression.   No, by heaven, I can't control myself,

MENANDER

ὁ καλὸς ἀδελφὸς εἰς τοσαύτην ἔκστασιν
ἤδη καθίστησίν με τῇ πονηρίᾳ.
310 μέλλει γαμεῖν γὰρ αὐτός.

ΔΑΟΣ
        εἰπέ μοι, γαμεῖν;
δυνήσεται δέ;

ΧΑΙΡΕΣΤΡΑΤΟΣ
       φησὶν ὁ καλὸς κἀγαθός,
καὶ ταῦτ᾽ ἐμοῦ διδόντος αὐτῷ πάνθ᾽ ὅσα
ἐκεῖνος ἀποπέπομφεν.

ΔΑΟΣ
ὦ μιαρώτατος.

ΧΑΙΡΕΣΤΡΑΤΟΣ
μιαρὸν τὸ χρῆμ᾽· οὐ μὴ βιῶ, μὰ τοὺς θεούς,
315 εἰ τοῦτ᾽ ἐπόψομαι γενόμενον.

ΔΑΟΣ
       πῶς ἂν οὖν
τοῦ σφόδρα πονηροῦ περιγένοιτό τις;

ΧΑΙΡΕΣΤΡΑΤΟΣ
       πάνυ
ἐργῶδες.

ΔΑΟΣ
ἐργῶδες μέν, ἀλλ᾽ ἔνεσθ᾽ ὅμως.

ΧΑΙΡΕΣΤΡΑΤΟΣ
ἔνεστι;

I'm practically deranged.   My noble brother
Is driving me to such distraction by
His villainy!   He's getting married—him!   310

DAOS

Married, you say?   Will he be able?

CHAIRESTRATOS

That's what our
Fine gentleman is saying, even though
I offered him all that the boy's sent home.

DAOS

The perfect fiend!

CHAIRESTRATOS

That creature *is* a fiend.
I'll die, by heaven, if I see it happen!   315

DAOS

So how's this utter villain to be mastered?

CHAIRESTRATOS

That's very hard.

DAOS

Hard, but still possible.

CHAIRESTRATOS

Possible?

---

313 ὦ Austin, Sandbach: ο B.   316 Change of speaker indicated by Lloyd-Jones (τισπανυ B).

MENANDER

ΔΑΟΣ

καὶ μὴν ἄξιον φιλονικίας,
νὴ τὴν Ἀθηνᾶν, τοὔργον.

ΧΑΙΡΕΣΤΡΑΤΟΣ

εἴ τις πρὸς θεῶν

320 ὥρμηκ[.] .. τωνδ᾽ε[.] .[

(Lacuna of one or two lines)

ΔΑΟΣ

] δύο τάλ[αντα
] αὐτῷ τιν᾽ ἐλπίδ[
] . φ[ε]ρόμενον εὐθὺς ἐπ[
προπετῆ, διημαρτηκότ᾽, ἐπτ[οημένον
325 ὄψει μεταχειριεῖ τε τοῦτον εὐπόρω[ς.
(KT fr. 69) ὃ βούλεται γὰρ μόνον ὁρῶν καὶ προσδοκῶν
ἀλόγιστος ἔσται τῆς ἀληθείας κριτής.

ΧΑΙΡΕΣΤΡΑΤΟΣ

τί οὖν λέγεις; ἐγὼ γὰρ ὅ τι βούλει ποεῖν
ἕτοιμός εἰμι.

318 Change of speaker after ἔνεστι suggested by Arnott
(ενεστικαι B). 321, 323, 324, 325 Suppl. ed. pr. 324 προσπετη
B. τιημαρτηκοτ᾽ B: corr. Gaiser.

---

[1] The distribution of parts in lines 316 to 319 is not very
clear. Other possibilities are that 315b–317 are all spoken by
Daos, 318–319a by Chairestratos, and the speech beginning in
319b by Daos again. The distribution suggested in the text
and translation produces lively dialogue and consistent
characterisation, but makes a slave swear by Athena, for
which there appears to be no parallel (cf. Austin, *Menandri
Aspis et Samia*, II, 32).

54

ASPIS

DAOS
And what's more, the job's well worth
The effort, by Athena.

CHAIRESTRATOS
If a man's[1]
Begun (?), by heaven [. . . . .]   320

(After the mutilated line 320, one or two further lines are completely missing, and lines 321–23 badly mutilated. Here Daos begins to outline his ruse to prevent Smikrines from marrying Kleostratos' sister and acquiring her inheritance.)

DAOS
[His[2] present scheme will earn him those (?)] two
   tal[ents].[3]
[Just offer (?)] him a hope [of getting more; (?)]
At once you'll see him bearing down full-tilt
On [this new prospect (?)], all aqu[iver], and
On the wrong track! You'll handle him with ease.   325
A man who only sees and thinks about
His own desires will be a faulty judge
Of actual fact.

CHAIRESTRATOS
Then what's your plan?   I'm ready to
Do anything you like.

[2] Sc. Smikrines'. The supplements in lines 321 to 323 are very tentative (cf. K. Gaiser, *Menander, Der Schild* [Zürich, Stuttgart 1971], 72 f.).
[3] Presumably the 600 gold staters in Kleostratos' booty (see on line 35).

MENANDER

δεῖ τραγῳδῆσαι πάθος
330 ἀλλοῖον ὑμᾶς· ὃ γὰρ ὑπεῖπας ἀρ[τίως
δόξαι σε δεῖ νῦν, εἰς ἀθυμίαν τινὰ
ἐλθόντα τῷ τε τοῦ νεανίσκου πάθει
τῆς τ' ἐκδιδομένης παιδός, ὅτι τε τουτονὶ
ὁρᾷς ἀθυμοῦντ' οὐ μετρίως ὃν νενόμικας
335 υὸν σεαυτοῦ, τῶν ἄφνω τούτων τινὶ
κακῶν γενέσθαι περιπετῆ· τὰ πλεῖστα δὲ
ἅπασιν ἀρρωστήματ' ἐκ λύπης σχεδόν
ἐστιν· φύσει δέ σ' ὄντα πικρὸν εὖ οἶδα καὶ
μελαγχολικόν. ἔπειτα παραληφθήσεται
340 ἐνταῦθ' ἰατρός τις φιλοσοφῶν καὶ λέγων
πλευρῖτιν εἶναι τὸ κακὸν ἢ φρενῖτιν ἢ
τούτων τι τῶν ταχέως ἀναιρούντων.

ΧΑΙΡΕΣΤΡΑΤΟΣ
τί οὖν;

ΔΑΟΣ
τέθνηκας ἐξαίφνης· βοῶμεν " οἴχεται
Χαιρέστρατος " καὶ κοπτόμεθα πρὸ τῶν θυρῶν.
345 σὺ δ' ἐγκέκλεισαι, σχῆμα δ' ἐν μέσῳ νεκροῦ
κεκαλυμμένον προκείσεταί σου.

ΧΑΙΡΕΣΤΡΑΤΟΣ
μανθάνεις
ὃ λέγει;

329 δεῖ Austin: τε B.   330 Corr. Kassel: ουκ'αλλοιον B.
αρ[τίως suppl. ed. pr.   341 φερονιτιν B.   343 βοῶμεν Kassel:
οιμεν B before, βοησομεν B after correction.   344 καὶ om. B.
346 Corr. Kassel: προσκεισεται B.   347 ουλεγει B.   οὐ before

ASPIS

DAOS

You must perform
A sombre tragedy. What you just said   330
Must now come true for you—apparently.
You slump into depression through the ordeal
Of that young man and his intended bride,
And through observing Chaireas sunk in
Deep gloom, the boy you've looked on as your son. 335
So you fall prey to one of these acute
Afflictions. Grief's the likely cause of most
Of this world's ailments. And I know you have
This bitter side to you, this proneness to
Depression. Next, a doctor will be called,   340
An intellectual; ' Pleurisy's the trouble ',
He'll say, or ' phrenic inflammation ', or one of
Those things that's quickly fatal.

CHAIRESTRATOS
So?

DAOS

You're suddenly dead.
We shout ' Chairestratos is gone ', and beat our
   breasts
Outside the door. You're locked indoors. Your 345
   dummy corpse,
All shrouded, will be placed on public view.

CHAIRESTRATOS
Do you grasp what he means?

δῆτ' om. B.   Change of speaker after δῆτ' indicated by Austin
(δητ'ουδ' B).

MENANDER

ΧΑΙΡΕΑΣ
μὰ τὸν Διόνυσον, οὐ δῆτ'.

ΧΑΙΡΕΣΤΡΑΤΟΣ
οὐδ' ἐγώ.

ΔΑΟΣ
ἐπίκληρος ἡ θυγάτηρ ὁμοίως γίνεται
ἡ σὴ πάλιν τῇ νῦν ἐπιδίκῳ παρθένῳ.
350 τάλαντα δ' ἐστὶ σοὶ μὲν ἑξήκοντ' ἴσως,
ταύτῃ δὲ τέτταρ'. ὁ δὲ φιλάργυρος γέρων
ἀμφοῖν προσήκει ταὐτό—

ΧΑΙΡΕΣΤΡΑΤΟΣ
νυνὶ μανθάνω.

ΔΑΟΣ
εἰ μὴ πέτρινος εἶ. τὴν μὲν εὐθὺς ἄσμεν[ος
δώσει παρόντων μαρτύρων τρισχιλ[ίων
355 τῷ πρῶτον αἰτήσαντι, τὴν δὲ λήψεται—

ΧΑΙΡΕΣΤΡΑΤΟΣ
οἰμώξετ' ἆρα.

ΔΑΟΣ
—τῷ δοκεῖν. τήν τ' οἰκίαν
πᾶσαν διοικήσει, περίεισι κλειδία

350 ἐστὶ Austin: ετι B.   352 προσήκοι B.   356 Speech-division
thus indicated by Kassel (αρατωιδοκειν: την B).   357 Corr.
several: διοικησαι B.

58

ASPIS

CHAIREAS

By Dionysus, no!

CHAIRESTRATOS

Nor I.

DAOS

Your daughter thus becomes an heiress, too,
Just like that other female legatee!
But your estate totals some sixty talents;   350
The other girl's, four.[1]   The old miser is
The same relation to them both . . .

CHAIRESTRATOS

Ah, now

I follow!

DAOS

If you're not obtuse.   He'll gladly give
One girl at once to the first applicant
Before three thousand witnesses, and take   355
The other . . .

CHAIRESTRATOS
He'll be hanged first!

DAOS

. . . in his dreams.
He'll supervise the whole house, go round with

---

[1] The whole of Kleostratos' estate, being made up of the 600
gold staters (= two talents, see on line 35), the rest of his
booty, and the ' cramped resources ' (see line 132) he possessed
before going away.

ἔχων, ἐπιβάλλων ταῖς θύραις σημεῖ', ὄναρ
πλουτῶν.

ΧΑΙΡΕΣΤΡΑΤΟΣ
τὸ δ' εἴδωλον τί τοὐμόν;

ΔΑΟΣ
κείσεται,
360 ἡμεῖς τε πάντες ἐν κύκλῳ καθεδούμε[θα
τηροῦν]τες αὐτὸν μὴ προσέλθῃ· πολλ[α

(Lacuna of one or two lines)

```
                              ]··[
                   ]·[··]ν τοὺς φί[λους
                ]·υ πεῖραν ἔσται, τιν[
365           ]πως ἦλθεν ἐπὶ τὴν οἰκίαν
              ]τις γέγον' ὀφείλων· εἴ τινι
           ] διπλάσιον εἰσπράττει πάνυ.
```

ΧΑΙΡΕΣΤΡΑΤΟΣ
εὖ γ' ἐστ]ὶν ὃ λέγεις, Δᾶε, τοῦ τ' ἐμοῦ τρόπου.
τιμωρί]αν δὲ τοῦ πονηροῦ τίν' ἂν ἔχοις
370 λαβεῖν] σφοδροτέραν;

359 Speech-division thus indicated by Kassel (no dicola after
πλουτῶν or τοὐμόν in B, no paragraphus under the line).
361 τηροῦν]τες suppl. Handley, Borgogno. 363 Suppl. ed. pr.
367–8 Change of speaker after πάνυ suggested by Austin (no
dicolon in B). 369 Suppl. Kassel.

---

[1] Chairestratos, on his ' return ' to life, would presumably
prosecute this caller for theft, and if he won his case in an
Athenian court, the thief would be fined twice the value of

The keys and seal the doors—he'll dream that he's
A millionaire.

CHAIRESTRATOS
And what about my dummy?

DAOS
There it will lie, and we'll all sit around   360
On watch, to stop him going too close.   Often (?)   361

*(The end of line 361 is mutilated.   At the top of the
following page of the papyrus two or three lines are
wholly missing, and the next six lines are mutilated badly
enough to prevent convincing restoration.   In them Daos
appears to continue his exposition by listing one or two
incidental consequences that might result from Chaire-
stratos' pretended death.)*

[. . . . .] your friends.   363
You'll have [a chance of (?)] testing [how and why (?)]
[Each caller (?)] had come to the house.   [Suppose 365
   it was (?)]
A man in debt.   If [he stole (?)] something (?) [of
   yours (?)], you
Extort in full the double fine for theft.[1]

CHAIRESTRATOS
Daos, your idea's [fine (?)], just after my
Own heart.   What sharper vengeance could you take
On that rogue?

what he had stolen; this was the law (cf. Fraenkel's note
on Aeschylus, *Agamemnon* 537).   However, the interpretation
of lines 363–67 is highly uncertain, and the supplements sug-
gested in the translation are merely tentative.

MENANDER

ΔΑΟΣ

           λήψομαι, νὴ τὸν Δία,
ὧν] σ' ὠδύνηκε πώποτ' ἀξίαν δίκην·
τὸ γ]ὰρ λεγόμενον ταῖς ἀληθείαις '' λύκος
χ]ανὼν ἄπεισι διὰ κενῆς ''. πράττειν δὲ δεῖ
ἤ]δη. ξενικόν τιν' οἶσθ' ἰατρόν, Χαιρέα,
375 ἀστεῖον, ὑπαλαζόνα;

ΧΑΙΡΕΑΣ

μὰ τὸν Δί', οὐ πάνυ.

ΔΑΟΣ

καὶ μὴν ἔδει.

ΧΑΙΡΕΑΣ

           τί δὲ τοῦτο; τῶν ἐμῶν τινα
ἤξω συνηθῶν παραλαβὼν καὶ προκόμιον
αἰτήσομαι καὶ χλανίδα καὶ βακτηρίαν
αὐτῷ, ξενιεῖ δ' ὅσ' ἂν δύνηται.

(' Comoedia
Florentina',
33 Körte)

ΔΑΟΣ

           ταχὺ μὲν οὖν.

ΧΑΙΡΕΣΤΡΑΤΟΣ

380 ἐγὼ δὲ τί ποῶ;

371, 372, 373, 374 Suppl. ed. pr. 373 Dicolon after κενῆς in B.
δὲ om. B. 376 τοῦτο Kassel: του B. 378–429 are preserved
also in F (378–80, 404–10 in severely mutilated condition).

---

[1] This Greek proverb images the situation of Smikrines, as
he slavers in vain after other men's possessions, more vividly
than the familiar English equivalent, ' Don't count your
chickens before they are hatched '.

DAOS

         I'll impose a fitting punishment,   370
By Zeus, for all the pain he's ever caused
You. Truly, as the proverb says, ' His jaws
Are open, but the wolf will go off empty.'[1]
But now we must act. Chaireas, do you
Know any foreign doctor who's a joker, a   375
Bit bogus[2]?

CHAIREAS

No, by Zeus, I don't!

DAOS

                     Well, you
Should.

CHAIREAS

         Here's a thought. I'll come back with one of
My friends. I'll borrow toupée, cloak, and stick
For him. He'll speak a foreign dialect all he can.

DAOS

Yes, hurry!

(*Exit Chaireas, off right.*)

CHAIRESTRATOS

What do I do?

---

[2] On the Athenian comic stage, apparently, doctors normally affected the Doric dialect. The relationship between dramatic convention and real life is as hard to evaluate here as elsewhere, but in contemporary Greece the leading medical schools (e.g. Cos, Cnidus) were in Doric-speaking areas and to that extent ' foreign ' to Athenians.

ΔΑΟΣ

ταῦτα τὰ βεβουλευμένα· (35)
ἀπόθνησκ᾽ ἀγαθῇ τύχῃ.

ΧΑΙΡΕΣΤΡΑΤΟΣ

ποήσω· μηδένα
ἔξω γ᾽ ἀφίετ᾽, ἀλλὰ τηρεῖτ᾽ ἀνδρικῶς
τὸ πρᾶγμα.

ΔΑΟΣ

τίς δ᾽ ἡμῖν συνείσεται;

ΧΑΙΡΕΣΤΡΑΤΟΣ

μόνῃ
δεῖ τῇ γυναικὶ ταῖς τε παιδίσκαις φράσαι
385 αὐταῖς ἵνα μὴ κλάωσι, τοὺς δ᾽ ἄλλους ἐᾶν (40)
ἔνδον παροινεῖν εἴς με νομίσαντας νεκρόν.

ΔΑΟΣ

ὀρθῶς λέγεις. εἴσω τις ἀγέτω τουτονί.
ἕξει τιν᾽ ἀμέλει διατριβὴν οὐκ ἄρρυθμον
ἀγωνίαν τε τὸ πάθος, ἂν ἐνστῇ μόνον,
390 ὅ τ᾽ ἰατρὸς ἡμῖν πιθανότητα σχῇ τινα. (45)

ΧΟΡΟΥ (46?)

380 ταυτα B: ταδε F. τα om. BF, suppl. Austin. 382 Corr.
Sandbach, Sisti: εξωτ᾽ B, εσωτ᾽ (so Austin) or εγωγ᾽ (so
Vitelli) F. 383 (τίς—συνείσεται;) and 387–90 assigned to Daos
by Gaiser (B names Chaireas as speaker in the right-hand
margin of 383). 389 ενστη F: εστη B. 390 So F (σχηι:τινα: B).

64

DAOS

Follow our   380
Plans.   Die, and good luck to you!

CHAIRESTRATOS

I'll do that.
Let no one go out.   Guard the secret with
Determination.

DAOS
Who'll be in the know with us?

CHAIRESTRATOS
Only my wife and the two girls themselves
Must be informed, to stop them flooding tears;   385
The rest must think me dead, and be allowed
To snipe at me indoors [1] !

DAOS
You're right! Let someone bring
The patient here in.

*The slaves who had helped Chairestratos out at line 305
now help him into his house again.   Daos is alone.*)

Our charade will give, for sure,
Some fine sport and excitement, if it once
Gets moving, and our doctor's plausible!   390

*Exit Daos into Chairestratos' house.   The chorus now
enter to give their second entr'acte performance.*)

[1] An ironic reference to slaves who might abuse when dead a
master they feared and respected when alive.

MENANDER

ΜΕΡΟΣ Γ΄

ΣΜΙΚΡΙΝΗΣ

ταχύ γ᾽ ἦλθ᾽ ὁ Δᾶος πρός με τὴν τῶν χρημάτων (47)
φέρων ἀπογραφήν, πολύ τ᾽ ἐμοῦ πεφρόντικε.
Δᾶος μετὰ τούτων ἐστίν. εὖ γε, νὴ Δία·
καλῶς ἐπόησε. πρόφασιν εἴληφ᾽ ἄσμενος (50)
395 πρὸς αὐτὸν ὥστε μὴ φιλανθρώπως ἔτι
ταῦτ᾽ ἐξετάζειν, ἀλλ᾽ ἐμαυτῷ συμφόρως.
τὰ γὰρ οὐ φανερὰ δήπουθέν ἐστι διπλάσια·
ἐγῷδα τούτου τὰς τέχνας τοῦ δραπέτου.

ΔΑΟΣ

ὦ δαίμονες, φοβερόν γε, νὴ τὸν Ἥλιον, (55)
400 τὸ συμβεβ[ηκός· ο]ὐκ ἂν ᾠήθην ποτὲ
ἄνθρωπο[ν εἰς] τοσοῦτον οὑτωσὶ ταχὺ
πάθος ἐμ[π]εσεῖν. σκηπτός τις εἰς τὴν οἰκίαν
ῥαγδαῖος ἐμπέπτωκε.

ΣΜΙΚΡΙΝΗΣ

     τί ποτε βούλεται; (59)

(Lacuna of two lines)

. . . .]μονον βα[. . .]ν[(62)
405 . . .] . . [.]αρα[
ἄνθρωπος· ὑπ.[

391 So F: προσμ᾽οδαος B.   392 τ[F: γεμου B.   394 ασμενος
B: -ενως F.   396 εξεταζειν F: -ασειν B.   401-4 completely
torn off, and 400, 405-7 severely mutilated, in B.   400, 401,
402 Suppl. Vitelli.   406 Or ἄνθρωπος: ανθρωπος B, -ωπον F.

---

¹ The 'he' is Daos.   Here the Greek plays deliberately (but
untranslatably) on the fact that 'invisible goods' (ἀφανὴς
οὐσία, cf. *Dyskolos* 812) was the technical legal term for all
personal, movable property, as opposed to land.

ASPIS

ACT III

*After the departure of the chorus, enter Smikrines from
his house.)*

SMIKRINES (*sarcastically*)

Daos *has* come quickly with his inventory
of those goods! Great consideration he has shown
Me! Daos is on *their* side. By Zeus, that's fine!
He *has* done well! I'm glad he's given me an
Excuse for looking over items there without   395
further politeness, but with benefit to me.
There surely must be twice the amount that he's
Kept out of sight[1]! I know the tricks of this vile slave!

*At this point Daos enters from Chairestratos' house,
pretending to be very upset, pretending not to see Smikrines
at first. The charade has begun.)*

DAOS

O gods! It's dreadful, the calamity
That has occurred, by Helios! I'd never   400
Have thought a man could sink to such a state
So quickly. A rampaging hurricane
Has struck the house!

SMIKRINES
Whatever does he mean?   403

*The next two lines are entirely missing in both papyri;
then come three badly mutilated lines, from which only the
word* man *in 406 can clearly be made out. Daos here
appears to begin the quotations from tragedy with which he
embroiders his feigned lament; whether Smikrines inter-
poses any aside is uncertain.)*

MENANDER

ΔΑΟΣ

" οὐκ ἔστιν ὅστις π[άντ᾽ ἀνὴρ εὐδαιμονεῖ ᾽᾽·   (6
πάλιν εὖ διαφόρως. ὦ πολ[υτίμητοι θεοί,
ἀπροσδοκήτου πράγμα[τος] κἀ[

ΣΜΙΚΡΙΝΗΣ

410 Δᾶε κακόδαιμον, ποῖ τρέχ[εις;]

ΔΑΟΣ

            καὶ τοῦτό που·
" τύχη τὰ θνητῶν πράγματ᾽, οὐκ εὐβουλία ᾽᾽·
ὑπέρευγε. " θεὸς μὲν αἰτίαν φύει βροτοῖς,   (7
ὅταν κακῶσαι δῶμα παμπήδην θέλῃ ᾽᾽·
Αἰσχύλος ὁ σεμνά—

ΣΜΙΚΡΙΝΗΣ

            γνωμολογεῖς, τρισάθλιε;

ΔΑΟΣ

415 " ἄπιστον, ἄλογον, δεινόν— ᾽᾽

ΣΜΙΚΡΙΝΗΣ

            οὐδὲ παύσεται;

407 Suppl. ed. pr. of B from Euripides fr. 661 Nauck
408 Suppl. several.   409 καια[B (sc. *scriptio plena* for κἀ[c
χἀ[?   The line is not preserved in F).   410 τρέχ[εις] supp
ed. pr. of B.   καὶ τοῦτό που divined by Austin: καιτο[or και
B,]βλαβη/ σπονου F (as read by Lodi, probably incorrectly).   41
σεμνεα B,]οσα F (as read by Vitelli).

---

[1] The opening line of a lost tragedy by Euripides, th
Stheneboia (fragment 661 in A. Nauck, *Tragicorum Graecoru*
Fragmenta, 2nd edition, Leipzig 1889).

ASPIS

DAOS

° There lives no man who prospers over all '[1]:   407
Again, supremely good!   Most [reverend gods],
How unforeseen and [grievous (?)] an affair!

SMIKRINES

Daos, you devil, where's the rush?

DAOS (*as if not hearing Smikrines' question*)

This too, perhaps: 410
' The affairs of men not providence but chance '[2]:
Superb. ' God plants the guilt in mortal men
When he will blight a house completely ': Aeschylus,[3]
Of noble words the—

SMIKRINES (*interrupting*)

Citing mottoes, you
Pathetic worm?

DAOS (*again ignoring the interruption*)

' Creditless, senseless, dread '[4]— '   415

SMIKRINES

Won't he stop, ever?

[2] A line from the lost tragedy *Achilles, Slayer of Thersites* by
the fourth-century dramatist Chaeremon (fr. 2 Nauck[2]; cf.
C. Collard, *Journal of Hellenic Studies* 90 [1970], 22 ff.).
[3] From a lost tragedy, the *Niobe* (fr. 166 Nauck[2] = fr. 277
Lloyd-Jones).
[4] Apparently a fragment from an unknown tragedy.

ΔΑΟΣ
" τί δ' ἔστ' ἄπιστον τῶν ἐν ἀνθρώποις κακῶν; "
ὁ Καρκίνος φήσ'. " ἐν μιᾷ γὰρ ἡμέρᾳ   (75)
τὸν εὐτυχῆ τίθησι δυστυχῆ θεός."
εὖ πάντα ταῦτα, Σμικρίνη.

ΣΜΙΚΡΙΝΗΣ
                    λέγεις δὲ τί;

ΔΑΟΣ
420 ἀδελφός—ὦ Ζεῦ, πῶς φράσω;—σχεδόν τί σου
τέθνηκεν.

ΣΜΙΚΡΙΝΗΣ
          ὁ λαλῶν ἀρτίως ἐνταῦθ' ἐμοί;
τί παθών;

ΔΑΟΣ
          χολή, λύπη τις, ἔκστασις φρενῶν,   (80)
πνιγμός.

ΣΜΙΚΡΙΝΗΣ
          Πόσειδον καὶ θεοί, δεινοῦ πάθους.

ΔΑΟΣ
" οὐκ ἔστιν οὐδὲν δεινὸν ὧδ' εἰπεῖν ἔπος
425 οὐδὲ πάθος— "

416 τί δ' van Leeuwen: τισδ' B,]δ' F.   417 φησ' B: πουφησιν
F.   421–31 Line ends torn off in B.

DAOS (*at last taking note of Smikrines' presence*)
     ' What, of mortal woes,
ls past belief?' So Carcinus says.[1] ' In
One day god brings the victor to defeat '[2]:
All these are jewels, Smikrines!

SMIKRINES
        What do
You mean?

DAOS
    Your brother—O Zeus, how shall I   420
Tell it?—is at death's door!

SMIKRINES
       The man just now
Here, talking to me? What happened to him?

DAOS
Bile, anguish, loss of sanity, a choking spasm.

SMIKRINES
Poseidon and the gods, how terrible!

DAOS
         ' There is
No tale so dread to tell, no blow '—

[1] Carcinus was a productive, not unsuccessful tragedian of the fourth century B.C. (cf. T. B. L. Webster, *Hermes* 82 1954], 300 ff.). The quotation was hitherto not attributed to this dramatist (cf. Nauck [2], p. XII; Austin, II, 39).
[2] Apparently a fragment from an unknown tragedy.

MENANDER

ΣΜΙΚΡΙΝΗΣ

ἀποκναίεις σύ.

ΔΑΟΣ

           " τὰς γὰρ συμφορὰς
ἀπροσδοκήτους δαίμον[ες δι]ώρισαν."
Εὐριπίδου τοῦτ' ἐστί, τὸ δὲ Χαιρήμονος,   (85)
οὐ τῶν τυχόντων.

ΣΜΙΚΡΙΝΗΣ

         εἰσελήλυθ[εν] δέ τις
ἰατρός;

ΔΑΟΣ

      οὐδείς· οἴχεται μὲν Χαιρέας   (87)
430 ἄξων.

ΣΜΙΚΡΙΝΗΣ

τίν' ἄρα;

ΔΑΟΣ

     τουτονί, νὴ τ[ὸν Δία,
ὡς φαίνεται. βέλτιστ', ἐπίσπ[ε]υ[δ'.

426 Suppl. Vitelli: δαιμον[. . . .]ωρισαν F, δαιμονων[B (did B
originally have δαιμόνων τις ὥρισεν? So Austin). 427 τὸ δὲ
Χαιρήμονος Sandbach after Handley: τοδεχα[B, το[...]υρ-
μενον F (as read by Vitelli, probably incorrectly). 428 Suppl.
Vitelli. 429 So ed. pr. of B: ουθεισοιχεταιμεν[B, ουδεισοιχετα-
μενουνοχαιρεας F. 430 Suppl. ed. pr. τ[οὺς θεούς (Austin) is
equally possible. 431 After ἐπίσπ[ε]υ[δ', an answer from either
the doctor (in stage Doric: e.g. ἀλλ' ἐγών Austin) or Chaireas
(e.g. ἀλλὰ χρή Austin).

72

ASPIS

SMIKRINES

You're boring me 425

To death!

DAOS

' The gods ordained that tragedies
Strike unforeseen.' The first's Euripides,[1]
The second is Chaeremon.[2] *They*'re not small fry!

SMIKRINES

Has

A doctor come?

DAOS

No. Chaireas has gone

To fetch one.

SMIKRINES

Who?

*(At this very moment Chaireas enters from the right,
bringing with him the pretended doctor and the pretended
doctor's pretended assistant. They are in a hurry and
make straight for Chairestratos' house.)*

DAOS

This fellow here, by [Zeus (?)], 430
Apparently. *(To the doctor)* Good sir, do hurry!

---

[1] The opening of the *Orestes*.
[2] A previously unknown quotation from a lost tragedy by
him.

MENANDER

ΙΑΤΡΟΣ (?)

$$[- \cup \doteq.$$

ΔΑΟΣ

" δυσάρεστον οἱ νοσοῦντες ἀπορίας ὕπο."

ΣΜΙΚΡΙΝΗΣ

ἐμὲ μὲν ἐὰν ἴδωσιν εὐθὺς ἄσμενον
φήσουσιν ἥκειν, τοῦτ' ἀκριβῶς οἶδ' ἐγώ,
435 αὐτός τ' ἐκεῖνος οὐκ ἂν ἡδέως μ' ἴδοι
436 ..] . . . .[.]ιδ' ἄτοπον οὐδ' ἐπηρόμην

(Lacuna of about sixteen lines)

437   ].ν·

(Lacuna of one line)

ΙΑΤΡΟΣ

439   ] αὐτῶ τὰν χολὰν
440   ]ιμε[..] ἤδη φερομένῳ
             ] διὰ τὰ[ν] παρεῦσαν ἀπορίαν.

439 So B: but αὐτῷ (Austin) may have been intended.   44]
διατη[.] B.

---

[1] The speaker who replies to Daos' command could just as
well be Chaireas, saying something like ' So we must ' in pure
Attic.

[2] From Euripides' *Orestes* (line 232).

[3] Sc. the ' dying ' Chairestratos.

[4] In the Greek the pretended doctor speaks a spurious form
of the Doric dialect which would have been readily compre-
hensible to an Athenian audience for two reasons. By a long
comic tradition stage Doric had become thoroughly familiar,
and the Doricisms introduced by Menander into his text were
all obvious ones (for example, Doric ᾱ for Attic η, ευ for ου, and
a few differences of form in words the Athenians used them-

ASPIS

DOCTOR (?) [1]

> [Sae I do (?).]

(Exeunt Chaireas, doctor and assistant into Chaire-stratos' house. Daos follows them, speaking the next line on exit.)

DAOS

' By their distress the sick are querulous '.[2]

(Daos has departed into Chairestratos' house, leaving Smikrines alone on the stage.)

SMIKRINES

If they see me, I know exactly what they'll say:
I've come at once because I'm overjoyed!
And he himself[3] would not be glad to see me.   435
[. . . . .] odd. I didn't even enquire   436

(After the mutilated line 436 some sixteen lines are entirely missing. In them Smikrines must have completed his soliloquy and the pretended doctor have emerged from Chairestratos' house with his assistant in order to discuss Chairestratos' case with Smikrines. Part of this con-versation is preserved on that page of the papyrus which contains one letter of line 437, and better preserved (though still mutilated) portions of lines 439–68; only 450, 451, and 464–67 are undamaged.)

DOCTOR [4]

[. . . . .] maister's (?) bile.   439
[. . . . .] carrying awa' (?) the noo.   440
[. . . . .] through his present distress.

selves). The English translation adopts an equally spurious form of lowland Scots, which is intended to be equally intelligible.

75

MENANDER

ΣΜΙΚΡΙΝΗΣ

οὔ]πω τοῦτο δήπου μανθάνω.

ΙΑΤΡΟΣ

]σαν.

ΣΜΙΚΡΙΝΗΣ

ταῦτα δήπου μανθάνω.

ΙΑΤΡΟΣ

      α]ὐτὰς τὰς φρένας δή μοι δοκῶ
445   ]. ὀνυμάζεν μὲν ὧν εἰώθαμες
ἁμὲς φ]ρενῖτιν τοῦτο.

ΣΜΙΚΡΙΝΗΣ

             μανθάνω· τί οὖν;
οὐκ ἔστ]ιν ἐλπὶς οὐδεμία σωτηρίας;

ΙΑΤΡΟΣ

καίρια] γάρ, αἰ μὴ δεῖ σε θάλπεν διὰ κενᾶς,
τὰ τοια]ῦτα.

ΣΜΙΚΡΙΝΗΣ

μὴ θάλπ᾽, ἀλλὰ τἀληθῆ λέγε.

ΙΑΤΡΟΣ

450 οὐ πάμπαν οὗτός ἐστί τοι βιώσιμος.
ἀνερεύγεταί τι τᾶς χολᾶς· ἐπισκοτεῖ
    ]εντ .[..] καὶ τοῖς ὄμμασι
      π]υκνὸν ἀναφρίζει τε καὶ
      ] . ας ἐκφορὰν βλέπει.

445 ονυμαζειν B, perhaps correctly.   446 ἁμὲς suppl. Kassel.
]ρνιτιν B. Change of speaker after τοῦτο indicated by Austin
(τοῦτο· B). 447 assigned to Smikrines by Austin (B implies

SMIKRINES

[. . . . .] that I do[n't] quite understand.

DOCTOR

[. . . . .]

SMIKRINES

That I quite understand.

DOCTOR

[. . . . .] the diaphragm itself, I'm thinkin',
[Has intumesced (?).]   We normally ca' this   445
The phrenic oedema.

SMIKRINES

I see.   What happens then?
[Is there] no hope of his recovery?

DOCTOR

[Sic] maladies are [fatal].   I maun nae
Cheer ye wi' vanities.

SMIKRINES

No cheering!   Speak

The truth.

DOCTOR

He willna live at a', I say.   450
He's vomitin' bile.   [The affliction] dims [his sight],
[. . . . .] and for (?) his een
[. . . . .] he aften faims at the mooth, an'
[. . . . .] his look's funereal.

---

that the doctor spoke 447–49a).   447 Suppl. ed. pr.   448
Suppl. Kassel.   450 τοις B.

MENANDER

ΣΜΙΚΡΙΝΗΣ

455 (His words are lost.)

ΙΑΤΡΟΣ
]. προάγωμες, παῖ.

ΣΜΙΚΡΙΝΗΣ

σέ, σὲ

(His remaining words are lost.)

ΙΑΤΡΟΣ
]. μετακαλῇς;

ΣΜΙΚΡΙΝΗΣ

πάνυ μὲν οὖν.
δ]εῦρ' ἀπὸ τῆς θύρας ἔτι.

ΙΑΤΡΟΣ
οὐ]κ ἂν βιῴης τὼς τέως.

ΣΜΙΚΡΙΝΗΣ
] αὐτὸν εὔχου τρόπον ἔχειν
460   ]. πολλὰ γίνεται.

ΙΑΤΡΟΣ

γέλα
] φαμι τᾶς ἐμᾶς τέχνας

457 Suppl. ed. pr.

78

ASPIS

SMIKRINES
[This is grim news! (?)]

DOCTOR
Let's gang awa', lad.

(*The doctor and his assistant move to leave, off right.*)

SMIKRINES
You, 455

[Doctor, hey (?)] you!

DOCTOR
Ye ca' me back?

SMIKRINES
Yes, yes.
[Come over (?)] here, [a little (?)] further from the
  door.

DOCTOR
(*approaching Smikrines, and examining him closely*)

Ye'll nae live [in the future (?)] as ye lived afore!

SMIKRINES
[Nonsense! (?)] *You* ought to pray that you'll
  enjoy good health
Like mine! [But life (?)] sends many [shocks (?).]

DOCTOR
Ye may 460

Mock, [but (?)] I say [nae (?)] skeell [surpasses (?)]
  mine[1]!

---

[1] The interpretation of lines 458–61 is highly uncertain.

MENANDER

σ]ὺ δ᾽ αὐτός μοι δοκῆς
. . . .].[.]κεαλην ἀλλ᾽ ὑπέρχεταί τι τοι
φθιτικὸν νόσαμα. σὺ μὲν ὅλως θανάτους βλέπεις.

ΣΜΙΚΡΙΝΗΣ

465 ἦ που φέρουσιν αἱ γυναῖκες ὡσπερεὶ
ἐκ πολεμίων· ἐπιτάττεται τοῖς γείτοσι
διὰ τῶν ὑδορροῶν.

ΔΑΟΣ

θορυβήσω τουτονί,
ἀλλ᾽ ὅπερ ἔπραττον πρατ[

(Lacuna of between 178 and 214 lines, in which Act
III ended)

462 Suppl. Arnott.   466 ἐπιταττετε B.   467 Above Daos'
words B has ησυχη, referring presumably to their tone of
delivery.

(*And as a new scene, in which Smikrines is teased by
Daos a second time, gets under way, the papyrus breaks
off. Some ten lines are torn off at the foot of this papyrus
page; the next two papyrus pages, which would have con-
tained between 162 and 198 lines, are completely lost;
about six further lines are missing at the top of the badly
mutilated following page. This means a gap of
between approximately 178 and 214 lines, in which the
third act ended and the fourth began. The quality of
Menander's inventiveness makes any attempt to guess what
precisely happened in this gap foolhardy in the extreme.*)

ASPIS

[. . . . .] yet your ain self, I'm thinkin',
[. . . . .] but ye're incubatin' a
Condeetion that's consumptive.   Death sits in your
   een!

(*Exit the doctor, with his assistant, off right.   Smikrines is alone.*)

SMIKRINES

The women will be looting there, just like   465
In conquered houses.   All communication
Will go via the runnels.[1]

(*Enter Daos from Chairestratos' house.   His opening words are an aside.*)

DAOS
                     There he is—
I'll worry him!   As I was (?) doing [. . . . . .]   468

---

[1] Lines 465 to 467a are undamaged and doubtless un-
corrupt, but their interpretation remains a mystery.   The
translation, offered here without confidence, has Smikrines
picturing Chairestratos' womenfolk pillaging his stores and
portable goods as he lies on his deathbed, and communicating
with the world outside by means of the channels which carried
water away from the house.   When death came to an Athenian
house, it brought with it a ritual pollution that necessitated
restrictions on normal modes of access and communication.

---

*The ragging of Smikrines with which it opens could have
been lengthy or brief.   For Daos' ruse to succeed,
Smikrines would have had to transfer his suit from
Kleostratos' sister, thus leaving the way clear again for
Chaireas, to the daughter of Chairestratos.*)

ΜΕΡΟΣ Δ΄

βοῶσιν " οἴχεθ['

470 Χαιρεστρατ[

(ΣΜΙΚΡ.) †δεδρακιχ'.[

τέθνηκε. (?) .[

ἀνὴρ ἀπόλ[ωλε

τὸ μηδὲ ἕ[ν

475 ὑπόλοιπο[ν

ἤδη δικαι[

ἐνθάδ[

μὴ δια[

γραμμ[

480 ον .[

ου .[

υ . . . .[

λαμβαν[

τὸ μὲν ἐγγυᾶν [

485 ἴσως τοιούτου .[

ὑμῖν γενομεν[

πολλῶν σεπ[

ἕτοιμος ἀποφ[

ὃς ἂν κελεύῃ[

490 ἐναντίον σου [

469–90 Assignation of parts and identification of speakers
(apart from 471) are uncertain, but see opposite. 472 τέθνη-
κε: B.   482–97 preserved in P. Cologne 904 (a fragment of
the same codex as P. Bodmer 26, and labelled B like it).
488 e.g. ἀποφ[αίνειν or ἀποφ[έρειν Austin.   489 Or ὅσ' ἂν.

ACT IV

*(Most of Act IV is lost. The badly mutilated lines
469–515 come from the end of the act. Smikrines utters
what remains of line 471; the identity of the man or men
on stage with him, and the general distribution of parts in
lines 469–90, cannot be established for certain, although
the snatches of preserved words and our knowledge of the
plot so far allow a limited amount of plausible guessing.
469 has* they're shouting (*or* men shouting) ' he is
gone ', *472* he is dead, *473* the man has perished;
in 470 Chairestratos *is mentioned by name. It looks
as if this is the moment when the news of Chairestratos'
feigned death finally but expeditiously reaches Smikrines.
Smikrines first hears off-stage cries alleging the death (he
himself is the likeliest speaker of the remaining fragment
of 469), and his interlocutor (who may have just entered)
confirms the sad news. Who can this interlocutor be?
Obviously not Chairestratos himself; and probably not
Daos, who is certainly off-stage between lines 491 and 498.
The choice is between Chaireas and some other possible
character in the play, related to or connected with Chaire-
stratos, whose identity was revealed in the lost portions of
the papyrus (e.g. Chairestratos' wife).
Little can be gleaned from lines 474–82 (474* nothing
(?), *475* remaining, *476* now right, *477* here), *but 483–
90 offer better although still tantalising clues. 483 has
some part of the verb* take, *484* to betroth, *485* maybe *of
such, 486* happen[ing] *to you people, 487* of many, *488*
ready to, *489* whoever (*or* whatever he) orders, *490*
before you; *484–90 apparently belong to one speech.
Is this speech made by Smikrines, formally betrothing
Kleostratos' sister to a new fiancé, namely his interlocutor?
If so, his interlocutor will be Chaireas, the girl's original*

25

MENANDER

*betrothed, and we must presume that Smikrines had just
previously announced his intention of abandoning his
engagement to Kleostratos' sister in order that he might
secure the greater prey of Chairestratos' daughter.*

At 490 this scene ends and its participants go or have

ΚΛΕΟΣΤΡΑΤΟΣ

ὦ φιλτάτη [γῆ
προσεύχομ[αι
πόλλ᾽ ὅν σε .[
πάρειμι τῇ [
495 ὁρῶ δεομεν[
εἰ δ᾽ αὖ διαπ[εσὼν
ὁ Δᾶος, εὐτυ[χέστατον
νομίσαιμ᾽ ἐμαυτό[ν·
παιητέα δ᾽ ἔσθ᾽ ἡ θύρ[α. παῖδες.

ΔΑΟΣ

[τίς εἶ;

ΚΛΕΟΣΤΡΑΤΟΣ

500 ἐγώ.

ΔΑΟΣ

τίνα ζητεῖς; ὁ μ[ὲν γὰρ δεσπότης
τῆς οἰκίας τέθνηκ[ε

ΚΛΕΟΣΤΡΑΤΟΣ

τέθνηκεν; οἴμοι δυ[στυχής.

496 Suppl. Handley.   499 Suppl. Austin (but θύρ[α ed. pr.).

*gone off, leaving the stage momentarily empty. The
missing soldier, Kleostratos, now enters the scene for the
first time, from the right, the conventional direction of
market and harbour.)*

KLEOSTRATOS

O dearest [motherland, how glad I am (?)]	491
[To see you (?)]. Greetings [to you . . . .]	
Whom much [. . . . .]	
I've come to this [house . . . .]	
I see [that I (?)] require [. . . . .]	495
But if Daos [escaped and got home safely, then(?)]	
I'd think myself [of all men in the world (?)]	
The one most fortunate [. . . . .]	
I must knock at the door. [Servants! (?)]	

*(Kleostratos knocks at Chairestratos' door. The door
remains closed, and Daos' remarks, until line 505, are
shouted from inside Chairestratos' house.)*

DAOS

[Who're you ? (?)]

KLEOSTRATOS

It's me!

DAOS

Who's it you want ? The [master] of   500
This house has [only just now (?)] died.   [Please go!]

KLEOSTRATOS

He's died ? Oh no! That's [tragic!]

ΔΑΟΣ

$[\check{a}\pi\epsilon\lambda\theta\epsilon\ \sigma\grave{v}$

καὶ μὴ 'νόχλει πενθ[οῦσι

ΚΛΕΟΣΤΡΑΤΟΣ

οἴμοι τάλας· ὦ θεῖ'· ἀν[

505 ἄνθρωπέ μοι κακόδ[αιμον

ΔΑΟΣ

(His opening words are lost.)

μειράκιον. ὦ Ζεῦ, [

ΚΛΕΟΣΤΡΑΤΟΣ

Δᾶε, τί λέγεις;

ΔΑΟΣ

.[

ἔχω σε.

ΚΛΕΟΣΤΡΑΤΟΣ

κατ[

(Lacuna of about five lines)

	]θανει
510	]τι:
	]. μηδὲ σύ
	ἀ]νοίγετε
	]. ι
	ἐγρ]ηγορὼς
515	]. ομεν.

[<u>ΧΟΡΟΥ</u>]

503 Suppl. ed. pr.   509]θανι B.   512, 514, 518 Suppl. ed.

DAOS

[Go away]
And don't annoy [us (?)] in our mourning, [sir! (?)]

KLEOSTRATOS

Oh no! That's grievous! Uncle! [—Open the door (?)]
For me, you wretched fellow!

(*Daos now obeys, speaking as he comes out.*)

DAOS

[Won't you go away, (?)] 505
Young man? Zeus [and the gods, who's this I see? (?)]

(*Daos has recognised his master. The emotional scene
of reunion that follows is irreparably mutilated.*)

KLEOSTRATOS

What are you saying, Daos?

DAOS

[. . . . .]
I hold you! 508

(*Three letters only are preserved of Kleostratos' response.
After the mutilated line 508, approximately five lines are
lost completely at the top of the next page. Then just a
few letters are preserved from the ends of the last seven
lines in the fourth act. Don't you can be deciphered in
line 511, the plural command open in 512, having
awoken in 514. Presumably the scene of reunion was cut
short by Daos' concise explanation of the strange situation.
Kleostratos' return, however, removes the need for Daos'
ruse. Chairestratos can now rise from the dead. At the
close of the act orders are given probably (512) to open up
Chairestratos' house again and drop the ruse.*)

MENANDER

```
                        ]. ὁμολογῶ
                        ]. ς ἴσος
                    γυ]ναῖκες ἄσμεναι
                        ]ι τἄνδοθεν
520                     ]ν παρείλκυσεν
                    γί]νεται διπλοῦς γάμος
                  τὴν] ἑαυτοῦ θυγατέρα
                        ] τὴν ἀδελφιδῆν πάλιν
                        ] τὴν δὲ πᾶσαν οὐσίαν
525                     ]τα πάνθ' ἕξει πέρας :
                        ]του περιπατεῖ τὸν γείτονα
                        ]ν οὑτοσί, νὴ τὸν Δία
         νὴ τὸν Ἡρακ]λέα, πρόσελθέ μοι
                        ] νὴ τὸν Ἥλιον :
530                     ]ο σῶς Κλεόστρατος :
                        ]νν ᾤμην ἐγώ
                        ]α ποῦ 'στιν; : ἐνθαδὶ
                        ]ραι φίλον λαβὼν
                        ] προσέρχεται
535                     ]ον εὐωχίαν
                    ]εξων δῆλός ἐστιν οὑτοσί·
                    ]αν τε κόπτῃ πολλάκις
                    ]υτῳ κοσμιώτερον πῶ
                 ἀν]ήρ ἐστί μοι τρόπον τινά :
540                 ]ον μοι τοῦτ' ἔχειν τὴν ἐγγύην
                    ]εἰναι μαρτύρων δ' ἐναντίον
```

520–35 preserved in *P. Cologne* 904 (see on 482–97).   521
Suppl. ed. pr.   γάμος Merkelbach: ογαμος B.   522 Suppl.
ed. pr.   523 ἀδελφιδῆν Lloyd-Jones: αδελφην B.   527 Corr.
Arnott: ουτοσιγενη B.   539 Suppl. Turner.   540 So Arnott
τουτ'εχειν̣μοι B.

88

ASPIS

ACT V

(After the conventional choral interlude, Act V begins. The ends of only its first 29 lines are preserved. From their position on the papyrus page it appears that the metre has changed, for the first time in the extant portions of the play, from iambic trimeters to trochaic tetrameters. The identity of the speakers is uncertain; full restitution of the text is impossible. The first ten lines of the act (516– 25) may perhaps be a monologue, spoken by a character who has emerged from Chairestratos' house in order to report on the happy events that have just taken place there. Decipherable are the following words and phrases: I agree 516, equal or fair 517, women glad 518, the provisions from the house (?) 519, delayed (?) 520, the whole estate 524, in the end he'll have [them] all 525; of lines 521–23 a fuller supplementation plausibly provides connected sense as follows:

[. . . . .] a double wedding's being held.   521
[He is giving] his own daughter [to Kleostratos to wed],
While [to Chaireas] on the other hand [he gives] his 523
    niece [away].

Here the ' he ' is obviously Chairestratos. The whole passage seems to announce that the betrothal of Chaireas to Kleostratos' sister and of Kleostratos to Chairestratos' daughter has just taken place off stage, adding some incidental details: the reaction of the womenfolk to the situation (?: 518), the speed at which events had moved (? : a negative may be lost in 520), and the future financial endowment of the betrothed couples (524–25). As all the arrangements are described in the third person, the speaker of these lines, if indeed they are a monologue, is most

89

likely to have been a character who was not a party to, but was still affected by, the planned marriages. The best guess is that he was the slave Daos. Did Daos himself achieve any reward for his past services to Kleostratos (cf. lines 11 f.) and his more recent services in the abortive ruse against Smikrines? If he did receive his freedom and a modest allowance to go with it, such a reward could also have been mentioned hereabouts, but there is no evidence for it in the extant portion of the play.

What follows line 525 is more difficult to elucidate. Another character is now present, and the subject of the ensuing conversation seems to be the events resulting from Kleostratos' happy return. Line 526 yields he walks about; the neighbour, *527* this man here, by Zeus, *528* [by Herac]les, come to me, *529* by Helios. *Apparently the conversation is preceded by asides on the part of one or both speakers. 530 gives* Kleostratos safe, *531* I thought, *532* Where is he? *answered by* Here. *Who is this newcomer, in ignorance (it would seem) posing questions to Daos and learning that Kleostratos has returned safely after all and is now 'here' inside Chairestratos' house? It could just be Smikrines, but is perhaps more likely to have been a new character or someone like Chaireas' medical friend or (perhaps most plausibly) the cook, summoned once again to officiate at the coming weddings.*

533 has taking a friend, *534* he's approaching, *535* festivity, *536* plainly this man here will [. . .], *537* if [one (?)] beats [him (?)] frequently, *538* I make [him] more docile, *539* I must somehow [chastise the man (?)]. *The interpretation of these scraps is doubtful in the extreme; one possibility is that Daos proposes to the cook a scheme for punishing Smikrines (cf. Getas' scheme propounded to the cook at the end of the* Dyskolos, *885 ff.).*

*At the end of line 539 there is a change of speaker, and
apparently a change of subject with it. 540 has that for
me the betrothal involves this, 541 and before wit-
nesses, 542 and for Chaireas, what he wishes, 543 for I
[. . .] this estate, 544 a textually corrupt reference to
causing me annoyance. If lines 516–25 were correctly
interpreted above as a monologue describing the off-stage
betrothal of Chaireas and Kleostratos to the two girls, it
follows that their betrothal ceremonies were already
formally completed, and lines 540–44 cannot be their stage
enactment. Could it be that Smikrines enters the stage
just before line 539, unaware that other characters are
already on it? In that case his approach would be
signalled at 534 (cf. 536 (?)) by one of those characters,
and Smikrines would speak all or most of lines 540–44 as a
soliloquy, still musing on his plan to marry Chairestratos'
daughter (540–41) and ready to give Chaireas anything he
wanted within reason (542). Smikrines would still be
unaware of Kleostratos' arrival home and Chairestratos'
resurrection from the dead, and a scene in which his
illusions were cruelly and jeeringly dispelled by—say—
Daos and the cook would provide a fitting and typically
Menandrean close to the play (cf. the ending of the
Dyskolos).*

*How many lines are lost after 544? The missing final
sheet of the papyrus could theoretically have contained
anything from one to about 96 lines (no page of this
papyrus has more than fifty lines on it, and a minimum of
four lines' space would be needed for the colophon). How-
ever, a final act with fewer than a hundred verses is
improbable for Menander; his shortest last act extant (in
the Samia) contains 122 verses. It would be safe to
assume, therefore, that between 71 and 96 lines have been
lost, giving a last act of between 100 and 125 lines. The*

] Χαιρέᾳ δ' ἃ βούλεται
] γὰρ τήνδ' ἐγὼ τὴν οὐσίαν
544   ]μοι παρενοχλοῦντος†:

(Lacuna of between 71 and 96 lines, up to the end of the play)

Other fragments of Ἀσπίς, *which cannot be placed in their precise context*

1 (68 Körte-Thierfelder, 74 Kock)

Quoted by Stobaeus, *Eclogae* 4. 8. 7 (ψόγος τυραννίδος). Μενάνδρου Ἀσπίδος·

ὦ τρισάθλιοι,
† τί πλέον ἔχουσι τῶν ἄλλων; βίον
ὡς οἰκτρὸν ἐξαντλοῦσιν οἱ τὰ φρούρια
τηροῦντες, οἱ τὰς ἀκροπόλεις κεκτημένοι.
5 εἰ πάντας ὑπονοοῦσιν οὕτω ῥᾳδίως
ἐγχειρίδιον ἔχοντας αὐτοῖς προσιέναι,
οἵαν δίκην διδόασιν.

Fragment 1, line 2 e.g. ἔχειν ζητοῦσι Cobet. 6 αὑτοῖς Körte: αὐτοῖς mss. SA of Stobaeus, αὐτοὺς M.

---

[1] This puzzling fragment was perhaps spoken by Chairestratos or one of his supporters distressed by Smikrines' selfish greed. Its context cannot be even approximately defined. But what is the point of the reference to fort-guarding and citadel-holding commanders who risk assassination by the dagger? It is unlikely to have been motivated by any situation or talk in the drama itself, and no recent historical event known to us can be singled out as its direct inspiration. Every Athenian knew the story of Harmodios and Aristogeiton, who concealed their swords under a sprig of myrtle before assassinating Hipparchos, younger brother of the tyrant of Athens, in 514 B.C. And when in 379 B.C. one Melon and six associates

*hypothesised scene of Smikrines' victimisation would
easily take up all that remained of the play (the correspond-
ing scene in the Dyskolos goes on for 70 lines), apart from
the conventional last ten lines or so of all, in which
general revelling would be announced, requests made for
torch and garlands, and a prayer for Victory enunciated.)*

---

*Other fragments of Aspis, which cannot be placed in their
precise context*

1

*Quoted by Stobaeus, Eclogae 4. 8. 7 (the section headed
' Censure of Tyranny ').*

                      Triply unhappy men!
Why do they want a bigger share than all
The others?   What a wretched life they go through,
   those
Who guard the forts, who hold the citadels!
If they suspect that it's so easy for the world   5
To come and see them with a dagger, what
Amends they make![1]

struck down with daggers the polemarchs of Thebes (Xeno-
phon, *Hellenica* 5. 4. 1), the exploit made a considerable stir in
Athens. If such events seem impossibly remote from Menan-
der's period, it is easy enough to substitute a long list of suc-
cessful assassinations in the Greek world between 322 and 291
B.C.; the pages of one historian, Diodorus, alone provide six
examples between 322 and 314 (Harpalos 322, Perdikkas 321,
Demades and his son 320–19, Alketas 319, Nikanor 317, Alex-
ander son of Polyperchon 314). A recent assassination may
well have inspired Menander's words here; but so long as the
Aspis cannot be safely dated from other evidence, it will be
impossible to identify which assassination it was. And this
fragment on its own will continue to be useless as a guide for
dating the *Aspis*.

MENANDER

2 (73 KT, 79 K)

Stephanus of Byzantium, p. 324 Meineke. καὶ ἀπὸ τῆς "Ιβηρος γενικῆς 'Ιβηρὶς τὸ θηλυκόν·

'Ελληνίς, οὐκ 'Ιβηρίς·

Μένανδρος 'Ασπίδι.

3 (75 KT, 81 K)

Erotian, p. 36 Nachmanson. ἔμυξεν· ἐστέναξεν. μέμνηται τῆς λέξεως καὶ Μένανδρος ἐν 'Ασπίδι.

4 (76 KT, 82 K)

Pollux, 10. 137. ὡμοίωται δὲ τῷ κιβωτίῳ παραπλήσιόν τι σκεῦος κανδύτανες, οὗ μέμνηται καὶ Μένανδρος ἐν 'Ασπίδι.

5a, 5b

Fragments 5a, 5b are the two sides of a tiny scrap of B, perhaps deriving from the gap or broken lines between 403 and 407 (= 5a), and between 436 and 439 (= 5b), respectively.

a   ]ερφην[
     ].νταπ[
     ]ενην[

b   ].[..].[
     ]νυμφιον[
     ]δη μαλ[

ASPIS

2

Stephanus of Byzantium, p. 324 Meineke.

A Greek girl, not Iberian.[1]

3

Erotian, p. 36 Nachmanson, says that in this play Menander used the word ἔμυξεν *in the sense of* ' sighed '.

4

Pollux, 10. 137 says that in this play Menander used the word κανδύτανες, *meaning* ' boxes '.

5a, 5b

A tiny scrap of papyrus. 5a is one side, containing some letters of three successive lines without any coherent word, perhaps deriving from the gap or broken lines between 403 and 407. 5b is the other side, perhaps from the gap or broken lines between 436 and 439; bridegroom *or* best man *can be read in the second of its three lines, and* very *in the third.*

---

[1] ' Iberian ' from the Caucasian area of Iberia (= the modern Georgia), presumably. Menander's reference may have been to one of the slave women in Kleostratos' booty.

GEORGOS

(THE FARMER)

GEORGOS (The Farmer)

Manuscripts[1]

B = *P. British Museum* 2823a, three tiny scraps from
papyrus codex written in the fourth century A.D. It
contains six largely unintelligible fragments of line
middles in each case; the first of these coincides with
part of verses 3–5 of fragment 1, and the other five are
printed here as frs. 9a–9e. First edition: H. J. M.
Milne, *JEA* 16 (1930), 192 f.; no photograph has been
published.

Berl. = *P. Berlin* 21106, a scrap of a papyrus roll per-
haps from the Fayum written in the first century B.C.
It contains broken fragments of lines 25–31. First
edition: H. Maehler, *Mus. Helv.* 24 (1967), 77 f.; no
photograph has been published.

[1] M. P. Zappone, *Quad. Triest. sul Teatro Antico* 3 (1973),
59 ff., believes that *P. Oxyrhynchus* 2826 (*The Oxyrhynchus
Papyri* 38 [1971], 16 f.) may derive from the *Georgos*. This
new scrap comes from a scene where a young man appears to
be complaining about a situation in which he considered a
certain young woman to be his wife. The unnamed ' young
man ' in the *Georgos* could have uttered a similar complaint on
learning that Kleainetos planned to marry Myrrhine's
daughter, but the kind of situation reflected in this scrap is so
basic to so many New-Comedy plots that its one point of con-
tact, unsupported by any others, hardly justifies the attribu-
tion to the *Georgos*. Accordingly, *P. Oxyrhynchus* 2826 is not
printed here.

INTRODUCTION

' = *PSI* 100, a narrow strip of papyrus now in 'lorence and dating from the fourth century A.D. It ontains the ends of lines 79–98, the beginnings of '9–128. First edition: T. Lodi and G. Vitelli, *PSI* 1 1912), 168 f. and XIII f.; no photograph has been ublished.

; = *P. Geneva* 155, one leaf (paginated 6 and 7) of a odex written between 350 and 600 A.D. It contains ines 1–87 of the play. First edition: J. Nicole, *Le aboureur de Ménandre*, Basle and Geneva 1897–98. 'hotographs of both sides of the leaf appear in E. M. 'hompson and others, *Fascimiles of Ancient Manu- cripts, New Palaeographical Society*, 1 part 4 (1906), lates 74 and 75; of lines 1–44, in W. G. Waddell, *Selections from Menander*, Oxford 1927, plate I.

'ragments 1–7 are quotations, and fr. 8 a description, rom a variety of sources. See Introduction, pp. xxiv f.

* * *

The Geneva page of the *Georgos* contains 87 con- inuous lines of text from the closing two scenes of an ct. The scrap of Florence papyrus, which overlaps he final nine lines of the Geneva fragment, shows that he end of the act came only eight lines after the Geneva fragments breaks off. But which act of the Georgos was this?

The possibilities are limited to two, because the two ides of the Geneva fragments were numbered by the original scribe as pages 6 (F) and 7 (ζ) of the codex. These two pages held 44 and 43 lines of text

respectively. If the text of the *Georgos* began at the
top of page 1, and if each of the missing page
similarly contained 43 or 44 lines, around 215 to 220
lines must have been lost before the Geneva frag
ment opens, and the act-break in the Florence
papyrus must have come somewhere between line
311 and 316. This appears to be too early for the end
of a Menandrean play's second act (this break come
at line 426 in *Dyskolos*, c. 395 in *Aspis*, c. 361 in *Samia*)
yet much too late for the end of a first act (c. 251 in
Aspis, 232 in *Dyskolos*, c. 198 in *Samia*).

One of the two protases stated above must accord
ingly be rejected: either the play text did not begin
at the top of p. 1 of the Geneva codex, or the missing
pages did not average 43 to 44 lines. The general
view today is that the whole of the first page and
perhaps even some of the second were taken up not
with the text of the play itself but with preliminary
matter—a verse hypothesis, didascalic information
and a cast-list, for example (cf. *Dyskolos*, *Heros*)
perhaps even a potted biography of the author. In
that event the act-break could be assumed to have
closed a first act of normal length, between 224 and
268 lines. Alternatively, however, it is possible that
the text of the play did begin at the top of p. 1 of the
Geneva codex, but that the missing pages each con-
tained more than the 43 or 44 lines of pp. 6 and 7
perhaps even as many as 50 or 51 lines. In the
Bodmer codex, for example, the pages of the *Aspis*
vary in length between 42 and 50 lines. If the lost
Geneva pages averaged 51 lines each, the act-break
could be calculated to have closed the second act of
the *Georgos* at about line 350.

Which is the likelier hypothesis? It is hard to

know. A further piece of evidence here is infuriatingly Janus-faced.[1] The Florentine scrap of papyrus preserves a few letters from the end of each of the lines immediately preceding the act-break. The lines at the end of the first acts of Menandrean comedies regularly introduce the initial appearance of the chorus of revellers with a series of verbal formulas repeated with some variation from play to play (cf. *Asp.* 246 ff., *Dysk.* 230 ff., *Epit.* 169 ff., *Pk.* 261 ff.). There are, however, no parallel formulas in use to herald the chorus' entry at the end of the second act. The line-endings in the Florentine scrap just before the act-break could perhaps be supplemented in either of two places (lines 90, 92) with one of the first-act verbal formulas ($\pi\rho\sigma\acute{\epsilon}\rho\chi\epsilon\tau\alpha\iota$), but the remains of the final line of the act ( ]σ' $\acute{\epsilon}\gamma\acute{\omega}$) do not square with the regular (but admittedly not invariable: cf. *Asp.* 248) last line of Menandrean first acts where the speaker departs from the stage with the remark ' This is not the time for getting in the way (sc. of the chorus), I think ', the last Greek word here normally being $\delta\sigma\kappa\epsilon\hat{\iota}$. The argument from verbal formulas, accordingly, is inconclusive. Too little of the Florentine scrap is preserved, and too few of Menander's comedies survive.

The line-numbering in this edition agrees basically with that of Sandbach's Oxford Text (*Menandri Reliquiae Selectae*, Oxford 1972) and Körte's third Teubner edition (*Menandri quae supersunt*, I, Leipzig 1945); the unplaced scraps of the British Museum papyrus, however, are here given the status of separately numbered fragments.

[1] For a fuller discussion of this point, see my note in *ZPE* 31 (1978), 16 ff.

INTRODUCTION

No hypothesis, didascalic notice, or cast-list survives for this play. Its production date is unknown and unguessable.

*   *   *

Dramatis personae, so far as is known:

A young man

Myrrhine, an old woman whose present marital status is uncertain

Philinna, an old woman, perhaps Myrrhine's former nurse

Daos, slave in the young man's family

Gorgias, son of Myrrhine

Kleainetos, an old farmer

In the missing sections of the play several other characters probably had speaking parts. These are likely to have included a god or goddess as prologue, and two persons connected with the young man—his wealthy father (who was Myrrhine's next-door neighbour), and a friend of unknown name. In addition, Myrrhine's daughter (whose off-stage cries are heard at line 112 and perhaps also at 113), the young man's step-sister, and a second slave in the young man's household named Syros played minor roles, but it is uncertain whether any of them, apart from Myrrhine's daughter, had speaking parts or not. There was certainly a chorus, perhaps of tipsy revellers, to perform the entr'actes.

ΓΕΩΡΓΟΣ

(*SCENE: Probably a street in Athens, with two houses visible to the audience.   One belongs to Myrrhine and her two children, the other to the young man's father.*)

(*The Geneva fragment preserves 87 lines from near the end of one of the play's first two acts.   What came before the young man's monologue partially preserved in lines 1–21 cannot now be safely reconstructed, but some at least of the plot antecedents are clearly detailed or implied in the extant portions of text.   The young man, whose name is not known, had got a free girl pregnant (15 f., 30) some nine months ago (87).   For a reason no longer clearly preserved, but most probably timidity in the face of parental opposition, he has failed to marry the girl, and now on return from a business trip to Corinth (6) he suddenly learns that his father has arranged for him to marry his own step-sister, the daughter of his father's second marriage (7 ff.).   Such unions were certainly sanctioned by Attic law (cf. C. W. Keyes, TAPA 71 [1941], 217 ff.; A. R. W. Harrison, The Law of Athens, I, Oxford 1968, 21 ff.).   The pregnant girl, whose baby is now due, was one of two children of the young man's next-door neighbour, a woman of uncertain marital status named Myrrhine.   The other child was a grown-up son called Gorgias, who was employed as a hired labourer, apparently because of his family's poverty, by one*)

cf
SAMIA

GEORGOS

(The Farmer)

Kleainetos, the farmer from whom the play takes its title, ostensibly an old bachelor or widower (73) of considerable means.

The loss of the play's opening scenes inevitably means that some important details of the past history of leading characters are shrouded in mystery. How did the young man come to meet Myrrhine's daughter? Did he get drunk, rape her under cover of darkness, and then seek amends by a promise of marriage, as Aeschinus did in Terence's Adelphoe (470 ff.), or was his experience more akin to that of Moschion in the Samia (38 ff.)? Why did the young man allow nine months to pass without marrying the girl he had wronged? What was his father's purpose in sending his son off to Corinth on business and in selecting for him a different bride? Who was the father of Myrrhine's children? Had she herself been raped before marriage to another man by an unknown assailant, then given birth to twins and brought them up as if they were the legitimate offspring of a marriage now ended by the death of her husband? Or had she conceived her children in wedlock, but afterwards been separated from her husband through one of the vicissitudes of life so beloved by contemporary dramatists? In either case a reunion between Myrrhine and the father of her children would be a likely development in the later stages of the plot.

MENANDER

And finally, was Kleainetos' function in the play merely
that of benefactor to Myrrhine and her family, or did he
turn out to be the long-lost father of Myrrhine's children?
Most of the answers to these questions could have been
and no doubt were provided in expository scenes whose
participants were the human characters involved in the
events. If Kleainetos was the father of Myrrhine's
children, however, the full story of their past relation-

(The Geneva fragment begins with the young man in
mid-speech.)

ΝΕΑΝΙΣΚΟΣ

$$] \ \pi\rho οσι\grave{ω}ν \ \pi\rho\acute{α}ττων \ (\cup \backsimeq)$$
$$] \ \acute{υ}ποφοβο\acute{υ}μενος \ (\cup \backsimeq \ ?)$$

(Kock fr. 99) ἦν δ' οὐ πονηρὸς οὐδ' ἐδόκουν (≃ — ∪ ≃).
ἡνίκα δ'] ὁ μειρακίσκος ἐν ἀγρῷ διετέλει,
5 ἔτυχε τὸ] συμβεβηκὸς ὅ μ' ἀπολώλεκε
ἀπόδη]μον εἰς Κόρινθον ἐπὶ πρᾶξίν τινα·
κατιὼν ὑ]πὸ νύκτα γινομένους ἑτέρους γάμους
καταλαμ]βάνω μοι, τοὺς θεοὺς στεφανουμένους,
τὸν πατέ]ρα θύοντ' ἔνδον· ἐκδίδωσι δὲ

In the apparatus to this play, those corrections and supple-
ments whose author is not named were made by the ed. pr. of
the Geneva papyrus, J. Nicole, *Le Laboureur de Ménandre*,
Basle and Geneva 1897–98.   1–3 The original line-endings are
omitted (certainly in 1, 3; probably in 2) by G.   3 ἦν δ'—
ἐδόκουν mss. of Choeroboscus, *Scholia in Theodosii Canones*,
2. 340 Hilgard (δὲ οὐ CO: δὲ ὁ V. οὐδ' ἐδόκουν CV: οὐδὲ δήπου
O):]ηρ[...]νδ[..]δοκουν G.   4 Suppl. tentatively Arnott.
5 Suppl. Grenfell, Hunt. ωμ'απολοληκε G.   7 κατιὼν suppl.
Körte, Wilamowitz. γινομενητουσγαμους G: corr. Dziatzko.
8 Suppl. and corr. Grenfell, Hunt: θεουσεστεφανους G.

106

GEORGOS

*ship and present separation would not have been known
to any individual human character. It is accordingly
probable that some divine figure as prologue revealed
enough information about the couple's past history
for the audience to appreciate their subsequent experiences
with an appropriate sense of irony.*)

(*When the Geneva fragment begins, the young man is alone
on the stage, in the middle of a monologue which describes
his recent tribulations. The first few lines of the papyrus
are doubly defective, having carried originally an im-
perfect text and now being badly mutilated, but the speaker
at this point appears to be finding excuses for his dilatori-
ness in marrying Myrrhine's daughter.*)

YOUNG MAN

[I then (?)] approached [her mother (?)], acted [like (?)]
[A gentleman, with no (?)] misgivings. I
Was *not* a villain, nor did [people (?)] think
Me one. [But when] that boy[1] was staying on
The farm, [there fell the] blow that's knocked me flat! 5
[Away] on business at the time I was,
In Corinth. [I got back] at dusk, and found
[Another] wedding fixed for me, wreaths on
The gods, [my] father sacrificing in

---

[1] Sc. Gorgias. Despite the speaker's description of him as
a ' boy ', he was legally the head of Myrrhine's family, and his
approval (as well as that of the speaker's father) was necessary
before the wedding desired by the speaker could take place.
Gorgias at this stage knew nothing of his sister's pregnancy.

10 αὐτὸς ὁ] πατήρ· ὁμοπατρία γάρ ἐστί μοι
ἐξ ἧς ἔχει] νυνὶ γυναικὸς τρεφομένη
ἡβῶσ' ἀ]δελφή. [τ]ίνα δὲ δυσφεύκτῳ κακῷ
τρόπον μάχωμ' οὐκ οἶδ]α· πλὴν οὕτως ἔχω·
ἐλήλυθ' ἐκ τῆς οἰ]κίας οὐδὲν φράσας
15 ἔνδον], λ[ι]πὼν δὲ τὸν γάμον· τὴν φιλτάτην
οὐδ'] ἄν ποτ' ἀδικήσαιμ' ἄν· οὐ γὰρ εὐσεβές.
κό]πτειν δὲ μέλλων τὴν θύραν ὀκνῶ πάλαι·
οὐ]κ οἶδα γὰρ τὸν ἀδελφὸν εἰ νῦν ἐξ ἀγροῦ
ἐ]νθάδ' ἐπιδημεῖ· πάντα προνοεῖσθαί με δεῖ.
20 ἀλλ' ἐκποδὼν ἄπειμι καὶ βουλεύσομαι
τοῦτ' αὔθ', ὅπως δεῖ διαφυγεῖν με τὸν γάμον.

ΜΥΡΡΙΝΗ

ἀ]λλ' ὡς πρὸς εὔνουν, ὦ Φίλιννα, τοὺς λόγους
π]οουμένη σε πάντα τἀμαυτῆς λέγω.
ἐν τ]οῖσδ' ἐγὼ νῦν εἰμι.

10 Suppl. Bury.   11–16 Plausible supplementation of these lines is well-nigh impossible, and the text printed here is merely *exempli gratia*.   11 Suppl. Arnott (μεθ' ἧς ἔχει already Sandbach). τρεφομενης G.   12 ἡβῶσ' suppl. van Leeuwen.   13 τρόπον μάχωμ' suppl. Sudhaus, οὐκ οἶδ]α Blass.   14 ἐλήλυθ' suppl. Sandbach, ἐκ τῆς οἰ]κίας Grenfell, Hunt.   15 ἔνδον suppl. Arnott.   16 Suppl. Arnott. ποτ' om. G, suppl. Richards.   17–23 Suppl. ed. pr.   19 Corr. several: μ'εδει G.   21–22 Here and often elsewhere G omits all indication of a change of speaker. Parallel omissions may be assumed elsewhere in this play where the presence of a paragraphus or dicolon is not recorded in this apparatus. The identity of the speakers and the part-divisions were worked out simultaneously by several scholars (notably Dziatzko, Grenfell and Hunt, van Leeuwen, Wilamowitz) directly after the first edition

GEORGOS

There[1]—he's [the man who] gives away the bride,　　10
His daughter by his present wife, my [big (?)]
Step-sister!　How [to find] an exit from
This maze, [I've no idea].　This is my
Position, though—[I've left our] house.　I told
[Them] nothing, but I've skipped their wedding.　I　15
Could [never] wrong my darling, that would be
Immoral.　I've been scared of knocking at the door
For ages, though I meant to.　I don't know
If now her brother's come here from the farm.
I must take all precautions.　Well, I'll go away　　20
And plan my tactics—how to dodge that wedding!

(*The young man now goes off, either into his own house or
off stage to the left. Myrrhine and Philinna, who is
probably Myrrhine's old nurse, now enter from the right,
deep in conversation. They are making for Myrrhine's
house.*)

MYRRHINE

Philinna, it's because you're sympathetic
I'm talking to you, telling all my problems.
I'm [in] this trouble now.

---

[1] Before the bridegroom came to the bride's house on the
evening of the wedding day, the bride's father made a sacrifice
to the gods who supervised marriage, especially Zeus and
Hera.　Statues of the gods would be garlanded.　On the
events of an ancient Greek wedding day see particularly W.
Erdmann, *Die Ehe im alten Griechenland*, Munich 1934, 250 ff.,
and H. Licht, *Sexual Life in Ancient Greece* (translated by
J. H. Freese, London 1932), 42 ff.

(which is erratic in this respect).　22, 28 φιλινα G (28 φιλιννα
Berl.).　24–25 Suppl. Blass.

MENANDER

ΦΙΛΙΝΝΑ

καί, νὴ τὼ θεώ,

25 ἔγ]ωγ᾽ ἀκούουσ᾽, ὦ τέκνον, μικροῦ δέω
πρ]ὸς τὴν θύραν ἐλθοῦσα καὶ καλέσασα τὸν
ἀ]λαζόν᾽ ἔξω τοῦτον εἰπεῖν ὅσα φρονῶ.

ΜΥΡΡΙΝΗ

μ]ὴ σύ γε, Φίλιννα· χαιρέτω.

ΦΙΛΙΝΝΑ

τί " χαιρέτω ";

οἰ]μωζέτω μὲν οὖν τοι[ο]ῦτος ὤν. γαμεῖ
30 ὁ μι]αρὸς οὗτος ἠδικηκὼς τὴν κόρην;

ΜΥΡΡΙΝΗ

τί γὰρ] τοσούτους κατατ[εμὼ]ν προσέρχεται
ὄζους] ὁ θεράπων ἐξ ἀγροῦ Δᾶος; βραχύ,
φ[ί]λη, μεταστῶμεν.

25–31 Some letters from near the beginnings of these lines are preserved also in Berl. 26–27 Suppl. ed. pr. 27]λαζονεξω[Berl.,]ζων᾽εξω G. 28 Suppl. Blass. G's colon after the first χαιρέτω may be intended to indicate a change of speaker. 29–30 Line openings suppl. ed. pr. 29 τοι[.]ντως G, where the gap is of one broad or two narrower letters: corr. Grenfell, Hunt. γαμειν G: corr. van Leeuwen, Wilamowitz. 31–34 Supplementation and part-division here are highly speculative, and the text printed is purely *exempli gratia*. 31–32 τί γὰρ suppl. Austin, κατατ[εμὼ]ν . . . ὄζους van Leeuwen (κατατ[εμὼ]ν also Dziatzko, in a different sense). 33 Suppl. Sudhaus.

---

[1] The two goddesses Demeter and Persephone.

GEORGOS

PHILINNA

(treating Myrrhine as if she were still a young girl)
                          And by the Ladies,[1] as
I listen, my poor child, I almost feel   25
Like walking to that door, and asking this
Impostor out, and saying what I think!

(Myrrhine stops Philinna as she moves to the young man's door.)

MYRRHINE
Philinna, don't!   Leave him alone!

PHILINNA *(in high dudgeon)*
                          Alone?   What can
You mean?   No—*damn* him and his conduct!   Can
This monster make a marriage when he's wronged   30
This girl?

(At this point Daos, a slave in the young man's family, can be seen approaching through the side-entrance on the left which is imagined to lead in from the country.   He is accompanied by a fellow-slave, Syros.   They are both carrying large bundles of freshly cut leafy branches.)

MYRRHINE *(catching sight of Daos)*
    [Why else (?)] is Daos coming here—
The servant, from the farm—with all the [branches (?)] he's
Been [chopp]ing (?) up [2]?   Let's move a bit, dear.

---

[2] Part-division and supplementation of a defective text are here both uncertain, and the reference to the greenery is purely conjectural.   Such greenery, however, was normally used to decorate houses on festive occasions such as weddings.   Cf. the note on line 10.

MENANDER

ΦΙΛΙΝΝΑ

τί δ᾽ ἡμῖν, εἰπέ μοι,

34 τούτου μέλει;

ΜΥΡΡΙΝΗ

καλόν γ᾽ ἂν εἴη, νὴ Δία.

ΔΑΟΣ

\text{(Cf.)}
Kock fr. 96) ἀγρὸν εὐσεβέστερον γεωργεῖν οὐδένα
    οἶμαι· φέρει γὰρ μυρρ[ίνην, κιττὸν] καλόν,
Kock fr. 899) ἄνθη τοσαῦτα· τἄλλα δ᾽ ἄν τις καταβάλῃ,
    ἀπέδωκεν ὀρθῶς καὶ δικαίως, οὐ [πλέον,
    ἀλλ᾽ αὐτὸ τὸ μέτρον. ὁ Σύρος, εἰσένεγχ᾽ ὅμως
40 ὅσ᾽ ἂν φέρωμεν· ταῦτα πάντ᾽ εἰς τοὺς γάμους.
    ὦ χαῖρε πολλά, Μυρρίνη.

ΜΥΡΡΙΝΗ

νὴ καὶ σύ γε.

34 τούτου om. G (leaving a blank space of 6 letters): suppl.
ed. pr. μελει· G (see on line 28). 35 εὐσεβέστερον γεωργεῖν
οὐδένα mss. of Stobaeus, *Ecl.* 4. 15b. 25, citing a different
version of lines 35–38 which mss. MA of this anthology either
falsely attribute to the *Georgos*, or conflate from two comic
sources (one of which will have been this passage of the
Georgos): γεωργεινευσε[11 letters]ενα G. 36 Suppl. ed. pr.
from Stob. (ἄνθη καλά, / κιττόν, δάφνην). 37 τἄλλα—κατα-
βάλῃ is quoted from Menander by the scholiast on Aristides,
3. 541 Dindorf: ταλλαδα[11 letters]η G. 38 Suppl. ed. pr.
40 ὅσ᾽ ἂν φέρωμεν tentatively Arnott: πανταοσαφερομεν G. 41
μυρρινη:νη (with the νη apparently altered to νυ) G.

GEORGOS

PHILINNA

(*opposing Myrrhina's attempt to move back out of the way of the approaching slaves*)

       Tell me, what
Concern is he of ours?

MYRRHINE (*emphatically*)
   It would be *best*, by Zeus.

(*The two women do move into the background. Daos and Syros reach the middle of the stage and put down their burdens. At first they do not notice the women.*)

DAOS

I don't think anybody farms on land   35
More *holy*. It produces myrtle trees,
Fine [ivy],—and the flowers![1] Sow other crops,
Though, and it yields a just and fair return,
No [surplus], just the standard quantity.
Still, Syros, you must take our loads in. They're 40
All for the wedding.

(*Syros picks up the bundles and departs with them into the young man's house. As Daos turns to shepherd him in, he sees Myrrhine.*)
     Myrrhine, hello.

MYRRHINE (*coming forward, with Philinna*)
Hello to you, too.

---

[1] Myrtles were closely associated with Aphrodite, ivy with Dionysus, Apollo and the Muses.

ΔΑΟΣ

οὔ σε καθεώρων, γεννικὴ καὶ κοσμία
γύναι. τί πράττεις; βούλομαί σ᾽ ἀγαθῶν λόγων,
μᾶλλον δὲ πράξεων ἐσομένων, ἂν οἱ θεοὶ
45 θ]έλωσι, γ[εῦσ]αι καὶ φθάσαι πρῶτο[ς φράσας.
ὁ Κλεαίνετος γάρ, οὗ τὸ μειράκιον [τὸ σὸν
ἐ]ργάζεται, πρώην ποτ᾽ ἐν ταῖς ἀμ[πέλοις
σκ[ά]πτων διέκοψε τὸ σκέλος χρησ[τῶς] πάνυ.

ΜΥΡΡΙΝΗ

τάλαιν᾽ ἐγώ.

ΔΑΟΣ

θάρρει· τὸ πέρας δ᾽ ἄκουέ μου.
50 ἀπὸ τοῦ γὰρ ἕλκους, ὡς τριταῖον ἐγένετο,
(Kock fr. 98) βουβὼν ἐπήρθη τῷ γέροντι, θέρμα τε
ἐπέλαβεν αὐτόν, καὶ κακῶς ἔσχεν πάνυ.

ΦΙΛΙΝΝΑ

(Kock fr. 903) ἀλλ᾽ ἐκκορηθείης σύ γ᾽· οἷα τἀγαθὰ
ἥκεις ἀπαγγέλλων.

ΜΥΡΡΙΝΗ

σιώπα, γρᾴδιον.

ΔΑΟΣ

55 ἐνταῦθα χρείας γενομένης αὐτῷ τινος

42, 44 Corr. Grenfell, Hunt: καθεωρουνγενικη and εαν G.
45–46 γ[εῦσ]αι and τὸ σὸν suppl. Blass, the rest Grenfell, Hunt.
κλαιενετος G: corr. ed. pr. 47 ἐ]ργάζεται deciphered and
suppl. Blass. 48 χρησ[τῶς] suppl. several from Aelian, *Epist.*

GEORGOS

DAOS

(with formal, but apparently sincere, politeness throughout)

Good and noble lady,
I didn't see you. How d'you do? I'd like
To [treat (?)] you to good news—or rather,
God willing, to your future prospects, and to be   45
The first [to tell (?)]. Kleainetos, you see—
That's where [your] youngster works—the other day
Was in his vineyard digging, when he well
And truly gashed his leg.

MYRRHINE
Oh dear!

DAOS
Cheer up,
And hear me out. The third day saw the old   50
Man's wound puffed out and swollen, he was gripped
By fever, and became extremely ill.

PHILINNA
Drat you! Is *this* the splendid news you've come
To tell us?

MYRRHINE
Quiet, mother.

DAOS
He required
Someone to nurse him at this juncture, but   55

2, which plagiarises this passage. 49 ταλαιν'εγω: G. 52
επελαβεν (but with no dicolon after πανυ) G. 54 ηκεισαπαγ-
γελλων: G.

κηδεμ[ό]νος, οἱ μὲν οἰκέται καὶ βάρβ[αρ]οι,
ἐφ᾽ οἷς ἐκεῖνός ἐστιν, οἰμώζειν μ[ακ]ρὰν
ἔλ[ε]γον ἅπαντες, ὁ δὲ σὸς ὑός, οἱον[εὶ
νομίσας ἑαυτοῦ πατέρα, ποιήσας [ἃ δεῖ,
60 ἤλειφεν, ἐξέτριβεν, ἀπένιζεν, φαγεῖν
προσέφερ[ε], παρεμυθεῖτο, πάνυ φαύλως ἔχειν
δ[ό]ξ[α]ντ᾽ ἀνέστησ᾽ αὐτὸν ἐπιμελούμενος.

ΦΙΛΙΝΝΑ

φ]ίλον τέκν[ο]ν.

ΔΑΟΣ

νὴ τὸν Δί᾽, εὖ δῆθ᾽ οὑτοσί.
ἀναλ]αμβάνων γὰρ αὐτὸν ἔνδον καὶ σχολὴν
65 ἄγ]ων, ἀπαλλαγεὶς δικέλλης καὶ κακῶν—
οὕτω] τίς ἐστι σκληρὸς ὁ γέρων τῷ βίῳ—
τοῦ μειρακίου τὰ πράγματ᾽ ἀνέκρινεν, τίνα
ἔστ᾽], οὐχὶ παντάπασιν ἀγνοῶν ἴσως.
κοινου]μένου δὲ τοῦ νεανίσκο[υ] τ[ά] τε
70 περὶ τ]ῆς ἀδελφῆς ἐμβαλόντος σοῦ τε καὶ
τῆς ἀπορί]ας, ἔπαθέ τι κοινὸν καὶ χάριν

56 κηδεμ[ό]νος deciphered and suppl. Grenfell and Hunt, Weill.
βάρβ[αρ]οι ed. pr. 57 μ[ακ]ρὰν suppl. Grenfell, Hunt. 58
ἔλ[ε]γον deciphered and suppl. Grenfell, Hunt (? ελ[.]γαν
G). οἱον[εὶ Blass. 59 Suppl. Sudhaus. 61 Corr. Richards:
παρεμυθειτ᾽οπανυφαυλοσεχει G. 62 δ.ξ.ντ᾽ G: suppl. Richards,
Wilamowitz. επιμελουμενον G: corr. ed. pr. 63 φ]ίλον
τεκν[ο]ν: G, suppl. Kaibel, assigned to Philinna by Sandbach.
δηταγ᾽ουτωσει G: corr. Grenfell, Hunt. 64 Suppl. and corr.
Sandbach: (4 letters)]αβων G. 65 Suppl. and corr. Kaibel (did
G have αγαγ]ων ?). 66 Suppl. Blass. 67 Suppl. Blass, Ellis.
68 Suppl. Préchac, Wilamowitz. 69 κοινου]μένου suppl.
Sandbach. νεανίσκο[υ] Grenfell, Hunt. τ[ά] τε Blass: τ[.]δε

GEORGOS

The servants in whose hands he found himself
Weren't Greeks,[1] and so they all consigned him to
Perdition, but your son behaved as if
He thought the man was his own father,[2] he
Did what was needed—embrocations, towelling,   60
He'd wash him, serve his meals, and cheer him up.
He'd looked so poorly, but your son's support
Has set him on his feet.

PHILINNA
Dear boy!

DAOS
                         Yes, Gorgias,
Well done, by Zeus!—Indoors, as he got better, he
[Had] time to think, freed from the bother of   65
His mattock—[that's how] hard the old man's life
Is—he inquired about [the] lad's affairs,
Although not wholly unaware perhaps
Of his position.   Well, the boy [responded].
He talked [about] his sister, you, and [all]   70
[Your problems (?)].[3]   The old man's reaction was

---

[1] Cf. Sir Kenneth J. Dover, *Greek Popular Morality*, Oxford
1974, 114: ' Since slaves were often of foreign birth, captives
in war or the children of captives, their ' natural ' relation to
their individual owners and to the Athenian citizen body
generally was assumed to be enmity and resentment.'

[2] It would be a neat irony if Kleainetos finally turned out to
be Gorgias' real father, after all: see the introduction to this
play, pp. 106 f.

[3] The problems caused by Myrrhine's poverty, presumably.
At this point Daos is unaware of the additional one caused by
the pregnancy of Myrrhine's daughter.

G.   70 Suppl. Blass.   εμβαλλοντος σου και (*sic*) G: corr. and
suppl. Blass.   71 Suppl. Arnott.

τῆ]ς ἐπιμελείας ᾤετ' ἐκ παντὸς λόγου
δεῖ]ν αὐτὸν ἀποδοῦναι, μόνος τ' ὢν καὶ γέρων
ν]οῦ[ν] ἔσχε· τὴν γὰρ παῖδ' ὑπέσχ[ητ]αι γαμεῖν.
(Kock fr. 922 ?) κ]εφάλαιόν ἐστι τοῦτο τοῦ παντὸς λόγου.
76 ἥ]ξ[ου]σιν ἤδη δεῦρ', ἄπεισιν εἰς ἀγρὸν
(Kock anon. fr. 183) αὐτὴ]ν λαβών. παύσεσθ[ε] πενίᾳ μαχόμενοι,
δυσνουθετήτῳ θηρίῳ καὶ δυσκόλῳ,
(Kock fr. 928) κ]αὶ ταῦτ' [ἐν] ἄστει. δεῖ γὰρ ἢ πλουτεῖν ἴσως
80 ἢ ζῆν ὅπως μὴ μάρτυρας τ[ο]ῦ δυστυχεῖν
πολλούς τις ἕξει τοὺς ὁρῶντας. ἔστι δὲ
ἀγρὸ]ς εἰς τὸ τοιοῦτ' εὐκτὸν ἥ τ' ἐρημία.
εὐ]αγγελίσασθαι πρ[ὸ]ς σε ταῦτ' ἐβουλόμην.
ἔρρ]ωσο πολλά.

MΥΡΡΙΝΗ

καὶ σύ.

ΦΙΛΙΝΝΑ

τί πέπονθας, τέκνον;
85 τί πε]ριπατεῖς τρίβουσα τὰς χεῖρας;

ΜΥΡΡΙΝΗ

τί γάρ;
Φί]λινν', ἀπορούμαι νῦν τί ποιῆσαί με δεῖ.

72 Suppl. ed. pr. ωνετ' G: corr. Richards. 73 Suppl. Jackson, Richards. μονως G: corr. Grenfell, Hunt. 74 ν]οῦ[ν] suppl. Grenfell, Hunt. ὑπέσχ[ητ]αι ed. pr. 75 Suppl. ed. pr. (but Quintilian, 3. 11. 27 cites κεφάλαιόν ἐστιν as a Menandrean locution). 76 Suppl. Grenfell, Hunt. 77–78 αὐτὴ]ν suppl. Sudhaus, the rest Blass from Theophylactus Simocatta, Epist. 29 (πεπαύμεθα πενίᾳ—δυσκόλῳ): παυσεσθ[(8–9 letters)]χομενοι, θηρι[G. 79–81 Suppl. Weil

GEORGOS

The normal one.   He felt on all accounts
He [must] repay his debt for your son's care.
He's lonely, old—and showed his sense.   He's planned
To wed your daughter!   That's the crucial point   75
Of my whole story.   They'll be here directly, he'll
Take [her] off to his farm.   Your battle with
That obstinate, perverse brute poverty—
And [in] the city, too—will cease.   One should
Be rich, perhaps—or live without a crowd   80
Of witnesses to notice one's bad luck.
In such conditions [country] solitude's
The answer.—Well, I wished to bring you this
[Great] news.   Good-bye!

MYRRHINE
Good-bye then.

(*Daos goes off into the young man's house.   Myrrhine
begins to pace about the stage in a highly agitated state.*)

PHILINNA
                     What's the matter,
My child?   [Why] are you walking up and down,   85
Wringing your hands?

MYRRHINE
          You ask?   I can't think what to do
Just now, Philinna.

---

with the help of the scholiast on Hesiod, *Op.* 637: ασπειδ[(12
letters)]νισως, οπ[..]μημ[(7 letters)]τ[.]νδυστυχειν / π[.]λλους G.
79–87 The final letters of these lines are preserved also in F.
82 Suppl. Weil.   83–86 πρ[ό]s suppl. Grenfell, Hunt, the rest
ed. pr.   84]ωσω G.   συγετι G: corr. Kaibel.   86 δει: F.

MENANDER

ΦΙΛΙΝΝΑ

περὶ τίνος;

ΜΥΡΡΙΝΗ

(Kock fr. 851 =
Körte fr. 760?)

ἡ παῖς ἐστι τοῦ τόκου, φίλη,

88 [ὁμοῦ]

(After line 87 the Geneva papyrus breaks off. The
last few letters of some of the following eleven lines
are preserved in F, as follows:]τόδε (or]τὸ δὲ) 88,
]ει 89,]ται 90,]εται 92,]ει 94,]σ᾽ ἐγώ 96. Between
lines 96 and 97 there appears to have been an indi-
cation of an act-break, [XOPO]Υ. Then]τι 98.
There follows a lacuna of probably between 16 and 29
lines [1] before the other side of F preserves the open-
ing letters of a sequence of 30 lines, as follows:)

ΓΟΡΓΙΑΣ (in mid-speech)

99 τοιοῦ[τ
100 στροβει[
    τοῦτ᾽ ἐ[
    ἐγώ· τί ποιη[σ
    αὐτῶν ἰδω[

ΦΙΛΙΝΝΑ

πρὸ τῶν θυρῶ[ν

87 Suppl. De Stefani. φιλη F, [..]λινν G. 88 [ὁμοῦ] suppl.
Sudhaus from Harpocration, 137. 36, and the scholiast on
Apollonius of Rhodes, *Argon.* 2. 121. 96–97 [XOPO]Υ suppl.
De Stefani, Körte. 99–128 F identifies the speakers at 104
and 105, and marks part-divisions by paragraphi under lines
103, 104, 109, 110, 112 and 115. The other part-divisions and
identifications of speaker given here, apart from that at 113,
follow the suggestions of De Stefani.

GEORGOS

PHILINNA
What [about]?

MYRRHINE
Her baby's [due],
My dear . . .   88

(*At this point the Geneva papyrus breaks off, but the last
few letters of some of the following eleven lines are pre-
served on a papyrus scrap now in Florence. Although its
remains are too scanty for any profitable attempt to recon-
struct the dialogue (the only translatable expressions are 88
this or and the, 96 I), this scrap shows by its indication of
an act-break after line 96 that the scene between the anxious
Myrrhine and her companion Philinna had only nine more
lines to run. Doubtless Myrrhine told Philinna a little
more about her daughter's impending confinement before
they went off into Myrrhine's house, and the chorus
entered for its first or second entr'acte. The difficulties
which interfere with our identifying which act-break this
was are fully discussed in the introduction to this play,
pp. 99 ff.*

*What happened after this act-break? The same side of
the Florence scrap (F) preserves a meaningless syllable
at the end of the second line of the new scene, and then
there is a lacuna whose probable extent may be calculated
at between 16 and 29 lines.[1] Thereafter the other side of
F presents us with the opening portions of 30 lines of text.
The first five of these lines seem to be the end of a soliloquy
by Gorgias, and it would be reasonable to suppose that
he entered from the country at the beginning of the new*

---

[1] The figure of ' no more than 25 ' lines, which is generally
given by editors as an estimate of this lacuna, thus needs to be
revised: see Arnott, *ZPE* 31 (1978), 25.

MENANDER

ΓΟΡΓΙΑΣ

105 οὐδεὶς γάρ εἰμ' ἕ[τερος

ΦΙΛΙΝΝΑ

τί ἐστιν;

ΓΟΡΓΙΑΣ

οὐδέν. α[
τὴν μητέρ' επη[
Φίλιννα, κάλεσον [

ΦΙΛΙΝΝΑ

μὰ τὼ θεώ, τέκνο[ν

ΓΟΡΓΙΑΣ (?)

110 σὺ γὰρ παρ' ἡμῶν α[
ἐν γειτόνων ὄντ[

ΜΥΡΡΙΝΗΣ ΘΥΓΑΤΗΡ (from off-stage)

τὴν Ἄρτεμιν [

ΓΟΡΓΙΑΣ or ΦΙΛΙΝΝΑ
(His or her words are lost.)

ΜΥΡΡΙΝΗΣ ΘΥΓΑΤΗΡ (again from off-stage)

ἐγὼ καλῶ τ[

105 Suppl. Sudhaus.   109 Suppl. Lodi.   113 Assigned to
Myrrhine's daughter by Arnott.

*act and that the lacuna was entirely filled by his entrance
monologue. From its close survive a few meaningful
expressions:* such (99), whirl *or* distress (100), this
(101), I. What [am I to (?)] do? (102), of them . . .
see (103). *Gorgias evidently is in a state of uncertainty,
possibly about what he should do now that Kleainetos has
announced his intention to marry Gorgias' sister. At line
104 Philinna enters from Myrrhine's house, saying some-
thing about* before the doors. *Gorgias then resumes,
perhaps without having noticed Philinna as yet, with* I'm
no [different (?)] (105). *The two then engage in a con-
versation which may have continued at least to the end of
F's 30 lines, but although a few words or phrases can be
made out and assigned to their speakers, at all but a few
points the drift of the dialogue remains uncertain.*
What's the matter? *says Philinna, presumably with
reference to the other's agitation, and Gorgias directly
replies* Nothing (106). *Gorgias continues with a
reference to* my mother (107), *adding* Philinna, call . . .
(108). *Is Gorgias asking Philinna to call his mother
out? We cannot be certain. Philinna replies firmly to
Gorgias' request:* No, by the Ladies,[1] no, my boy (109).
*Next Gorgias (if he is rightly identified as the speaker)
makes a mysterious comment,* From us, you see, you . . .
among neighbours . . . (110–11). *At this point an off-
stage cry is heard from Myrrhine's daughter, now in the
agony of labour, calling on* Artemis, *the goddess of
childbirth* (112), *and she may have followed this up in the
next line with* I call [on her for aid (?)], *perhaps after an
intervention by one of the characters on stage. At 114 one
of the pair on stage asks* And now what['s to be] done?,
continuing with a further, less intelligible question, or how

---

[1] The goddesses Demeter and Persephone.

MENANDER

ΓΟΡΓΙΑΣ or ΦΙΛΙΝΝΑ

καὶ νῦν τί ποι[

115 ἢ πῶς μαλακ[

ΦΙΛΙΝΝΑ or ΓΟΡΓΙΑΣ

116 τὸ παιδίον κα[

(After line 116 attribution of these *disiecta membra* to
named speakers is impossible. The beginnings of
lines 117–28 are preserved in F as follows: τί ταῦτά
τις λε[117, ἡμῖν ὑπόλοιπον [118, παρρησίαν τ' ην[
119, ὁρῶντα ταυτ[120, ἡμᾶς τε τοὺς [121, οὐδεὶς
ἔπειτ[α 122, οὐδ' ἄξιόν γ' ἐστ[ὶν 123, ὑμῖν ἐγὼ [
124, ἅπασι καὶ τ[125, ἔχειν α[126, κομματ[127,
οἰκειότη[128.)

122, 126 οὐδεὶς and ἔχειν tentatively deciphered by Arnott.

. . weak . . . ? (*114–15*). *The other replies with a
reference to* the child *or* the young slave (*116*). *There
can be little doubt that Philinna and Gorgias, provoked
partly by the off-stage cries of Myrrhine's daughter and
partly no doubt by Kleainetos' plans, are discussing what
they must do about the girl, of whose pregnancy Gorgias,
her brother, had been unaware. The details of their
conversation, however, become progressively more diffi-
cult to focus after line 116, when it becomes totally
impossible to know who is saying what. The broken
phrases that emerge from F's torn scrap are now all
generalities:* what is one to . . . this ? (*117*), left for us
(*118*), and candour (*119*), seeing this (*120*), and us the
(*121*), nobody (?) then (*122*), and it's not worth (*123*),
to you I (*124*), to all and (*125*), to have (?) (*126*),
stamp (*127*), relationship (*128*). *Here F breaks off,
leaving each modern reader to work out for himself how
Menander might have developed his plot. We know that
at some point later in the play there was a conversation
between Kleainetos and Gorgias on the injuries sustained
by poor people (see frs. 1, 5, 9, possibly also 2 and 3),
and somebody upbraided the young man who had wronged
Myrrhine's daughter (fr. 4). And the dramatic con-
ventions required that this young man and the girl he had
violated would be successfully married in the end. The
rest, however, is pure speculation.*)

MENANDER

Other fragments of Γεωργός, *which cannot be placed in their precise context*

1 (Lines 129–33 Körte-Thierfelder, fragment 93 Kock)

The complete fragment is cited by Stobaeus, *Ecloga* 4. 32b. 24 (πενίας ψόγος) with the heading Μενάνδρου Γεωργῷ. The middle portions of lines 3–5 only are preserved on a tiny fragment of papyrus in the British Museum (fr. 1 verso of B: see below, *Georgos* fr. 9).

ΚΛΕΑΙΝΕΤΟΣ (?)
εὐκαταφρόνητόν ἐστι, Γοργία, πένης,
κἂν πάνυ λέγῃ δίκαια· τούτου γὰρ λέγειν (KT line 130)
ἕνεκα μόνου νομίζεθ' οὗτος, τοῦ λαβεῖν.
καὶ συκοφάντης εὐθὺς ὁ τὸ τριβώνιον
5 ἔχων καλεῖται, κἂν ἀδικούμενος τύχῃ.

2 (1 KT, 94 K)

The whole fragment is cited by Stobaeus, *Ecloga* 4. 41. 28 (ὅτι ἀβέβαιος ἡ τῶν ἀνθρώπων εὐπραξία) with the heading Μενάνδρου Γεωργῷ. Line 5 alone is cited without the play-title but with the author's name by the *Etymologicum Magnum* 685. 38, by a grammarian in J. A. Cramer, *Anecdota Graeca e codd. Oxon.* i. 333. 31, and by a late scholiast on a Venice ms. (B) of Homer, *Iliad* 4. 396 (iv. 383. 30 Dindorf) and with neither title nor author's name by the scholiasts on Sophocles, *Oedipus Tyrannus* 1191 and Euripides, *Orestes* 343, and the sixth-century philosophic commentator Elias writing both on Porphyrius' *Isagoge* and on Aristotle's *Categoriae*, *C.A.G.* XVIII part 1, pp. 45 and 252 respectively.

GEORGOS

*Other fragments of Georgos, which cannot be placed in
their precise context*

1

*A passage quoted by Stobaeus, Eclogae 4. 32b. 24 (the
section headed ' Censure of Poverty '). The middle
portions of lines 3–5 are also preserved on a tiny scrap
of P. British Museum (see below, Georgos fr. 9).*

KLEAINETOS (?)

It's easy, Gorgias, to scorn a poor
Man, even when he's wholly in the right;
The target of his words is thought to be
Pure grabbing. Wear a shabby cloak—you're
  promptly called
A swindler, even though the injured party!   5

*These words were probably addressed to Gorgias by
Kleainetos in a scene where the former had been com-
plaining of the difficulties his poverty had put in the way
of any action against the doubtless wealthy young man
who had caused his sister's pregnancy. Cf. frs. 2 and 3.*

2

*The whole passage is cited by Stobaeus, Eclogae 4. 41. 28
(the section headed ' That human prosperity is unstable ').
The final line seems to have become proverbial, being
quoted by a number of later writers (who fail to identify
its precise source), as listed on the facing page.*

Fragment 1   Identity of speaker suggested by Körte.   Line 3
μόνου mss. of Stobaeus: μονον B.

MENANDER

ΚΛΕΑΙΝΕΤΟΣ (?)

ὁ δ’ ἠδικηκώς, ὅστις ἔσθ’ οὗτός ποτε,
τὴν ὑμετέραν πενίαν κακοδαίμων ἔσθ’, ὅτι
τοῦτ’ ἠδίκηκεν οὗ τυχὸν μεταλήψεται.
εἰ καὶ σφόδρ’ εὐπορεῖ γάρ, ἀβεβαίως τρυφᾷ·
5 τὸ τῆς τύχης γὰρ ῥεῦμα μεταπίπτει ταχύ.

3 (2 KT, 95 K)

The whole fragment is cited by the lexicographer
Orion, *Antholognomici* 7. 9 (F. W. Schneidewin,
Conjectanea Critica, Göttingen 1839, 51), with its
heading given as τοῦ αὐτοῦ (sc. the same source as for
Orion's previous extract, 7. 8, which is falsely de-
rived ἐκ τοῦ Γεωργίου (*sic*!) but is in reality Menan-
der, *Epitrepontes* fr. 9, q.v.). Lines 1 and 2 are cited
also by Stobaeus, *Eclogae* 3. 1. 62 (περὶ ἀρετῆς) with
the heading Μενάνδρου Γεωργῷ (so ms. M: γεωργῶι
A), and lines 3 and 4 by Stobaeus, *Eclogae* 3. 20. 22
(περὶ ὀργῆς) with the heading τοῦ αὐτοῦ (= Μενάν-
δρου).

ΚΛΕΑΙΝΕΤΟΣ (?)

οὗτος κράτιστός ἐστ’ ἀνήρ, ὦ Γοργία,
ὅστις ἀδικεῖσθαι πλεῖστ’ ἐπίστατ’ ἐγκρατῶς·
τὸ δ’ ὀξύθυμον τοῦτο καὶ λίαν πικρὸν
δεῖγμ’ ἐστὶν εὐθὺς πᾶσι μικροψυχίας.

Fragment 2 Identity of speaker suggested by Körte. Line 4
τρυφᾷ mss. SA of Stobaeus, τρυφᾶν M. 5 γάρ omitted by gram-
marian in Cramer, *Anecd. Oxon.* and by ms. V of Elias on
Porph., and misplaced (τὸ γὰρ τῆς) by scholiast on Eur. *Or.*
343.

GEORGOS

KLEAINETOS (?)

'he man who's fouled your poverty has an
Jnlucky star, whoever he may be,
}ecause he's fouled a thing which could be his.
Ie may be very rich, but luxury's
Jnstable. Fortune's tide can swiftly ebb.   5

*'urther remarks in all probability addressed by Klein-
os to Gorgias in the scene discussed above (fr. 1).

3

*f fragment cited in its entirety by the lexicographer
)rion, Antholognomici, 7. 9, and in its separate halves
*y Stobaeus, Eclogae 3. 1. 62 (the section headed ' On
*'xcellence': lines 1–2) and 3. 20. 22 (' On Anger':
ines 3–4).

KLEAINETOS (?)

[he best man, Gorgias, is he who can
}ear most offences with self-discipline.
[his venom and excessive rancour is
A sign of weakness simply in men's eyes.

*'f these remarks also were addressed by Kleainetos to
*iorgias in the scene discussed above (on fr. 1), Menander
*nust have presented Kleainetos, the title figure of the play,
is something closely akin to a sententious old bore.

'ragment 3   Identity of speaker suggested by Körte.
.ine 2 ἐπίστατ' ἐγκρατῶς Orion: ἐπίσταται βροτῶν Stobaeus.

MENANDER

4 (4 KT, 100 K)

The late Byzantine scholar Maximus Planudes com‐
menting on Hermogenes, Περὶ ἰδεῶν (*Rhet. Gr.* 5.52
Walz), citing παρὰ τῷ Μενάνδρῳ ἐν Γεωργῷ·

ΤΟΥ ΝΕΑΝΙΣΚΟΥ ΕΤΑΙΡΟΣ (?)

ἐμβεβρόντησαι; γέλοιον· ὃς κόρης ἐλευθέρας
εἰς ἔρωθ’ ἥκων σιωπᾷς καὶ μάτην ποιουμένους
περιορᾷς γάμους σεαυτῷ.

5 (3 KT, 97 K)

Orion, *Antholognomici* 1. 19 (p. 43 Schneidewin), with
the heading ἐκ τοῦ Γεωργοῦ·

ΚΛΕΑΙΝΕΤΟΣ

εἰμὶ μὲν ἄγροικος, καὐτὸς οὐκ ἄλλως ἐρῶ,
καὶ τῶν κατ’ ἄστυ πραγμάτων οὐ παντελῶς
ἔμπειρος, ὁ δὲ χρόνος τί μ’ εἰδέναι ποεῖ
πλέον.

6 (5 KT)

An anonymous glossary on a sixth-century papyrus
(*P. Oxyrhynchus* 1803, fol. 2 recto, lines 36–37)
[Μένανδρος ἐν Γε]ωργῷ·

ὡς σχολῇ πορεύεθ’ οὑτοσί.

Fragment 4 Identity of speaker suggested by Körte.

Fragment 5 Identity of speaker suggested by Schneidewin.
Line 1 Corr. Schneidewin: ἄλλος ms.

Fragment 6 [Μένανδρος ἐν] suppl. Körte (but there are several
other ways in which this gloss could have been introduced).
Γε]ωργῷ Grenfell, Hunt.   The fragment could alternatively be
printed with πορεύεται as the end of one trochaic tetrameter
line and οὑτοσί the beginning of another.

4

Quoted by Maximus Planudes in his commentary on Hermogenes, On Types (Rhet. Gr. 5. 525 Walz).

A COMPANION OF THE YOUNG MAN (?)

Are you crazy? It's preposterous! Here you've lost
  your heart to a
Free-born girl, and then say nothing! When a
  wedding's fixed for you,
You ignore it without reason!

*This outburst in trochaic tetrameters was clearly vented
upon the young man who had got Myrrhine's daughter
pregnant. It is tempting to suppose that these words were
spoken by a friend of the young man, in whose company
he had returned on stage for the first time after his exit at
line 21.*

5

Cited by Orion, Anthولognomici 1. 19.

KLEAINETOS

I'm from the country—no, I shan't deny
It, and in city business I've no great
Experience. My years have taught me, though,
A little extra.

These words must have been spoken by Kleainetos.

6

*Cited by an anonymous glossary on a sixth-century
papyrus (P. Oxyrhynchus 1803).*

    How slow that fellow's walking!

Context and speaker are uncertain.

MENANDER

7 (6 KT, 101 K)

A scholiast on Aristophanes, *Plutus* 652 writes
ἀκριβῶς δὲ δεδήλωκεν ὅτι ἐπὶ κακῷ ἔλεγον οἱ
'Αθηναῖοι τὰ πράγματα, καὶ Μένανδρος δὲ ἐν
Γεωργῷ·

> ἐν πράγμασιν, ἐν μάχαις.

The *Suda*, s.v. πράγματα, writes and cites similarly,
but without naming the play-title. The fragment
may form the end of one trochaic tetrameter and the
beginning of the next, or it may mutilate an iambic
trimeter.

8

Quintilian, *Institutio Oratoria* 11. 3. 91. etiam si
iuuenem agant, cum tamen in expositione aut senis
sermo, ut in Hydriae prologo, aut mulieris, ut in
Georgo, incidit, tremula uel effeminata uoce pro-
nuntiant.

7

A scholiast on Aristophanes, Plutus 652, and the tenth-century lexicon entitled the Suda, s.v. πράγματα, argue that in Attic Greek the noun πράγματα (normally = 'affairs') could be used pejoratively in the sense of 'troubles'. They cite in support this fragment:

In troubles, in battles . . .

Context and speaker are unknown.

8

Quintilian, Institutio Oratoria 11. 3. 91, writes: ' Even if they act the part of a young man, when his narrative happens to quote an old man's words, as in the prologue of the *Hydria*, or a woman's, as in the *Georgos*, the actors speak in a quavering or effeminate sort of voice.' *The implication of Quintilian's remark is that a young man (the one who had violated Myrrhine's daughter?) had a narrative speech in the Georgos in which he reported some remarks made by a woman (Myrrhine herself?). It is possible but by no means certain (Quintilian's words here are imprecise) that this speech came in the first act of the play and had the expository function of a prologue. If this was so, then the young man's 'prologue' is likely to have been a secondary or supplementary prologue, since the main prologue of this play was probably delivered by some divinity who had access to information denied to the human characters in the play (see the preliminary discussion, p. 106 f).*

MENANDER

9a–9e (Lines 134–63 Körte-Thierfelder)

Fragments 9a to 9e inclusive are five tiny scraps of
P. British Museum 2823a (= B) which do not overlap
any otherwise known part of the play.   A sixth scrap,
which has been identified as part of *Georgos* fr. 1 (see
above), secures the attribution of the other five to
this play.

a (fr. 1 recto Milne)

]ο. . . . .[

]ορατ. . . .   (KT line 135)

]τερ. . .

b (fr. 2 verso M.)

] . . .κο.ω[

] . εινοσ. [

] .ατην γυναῖκα μ[

]ραιδιον . τωνδ' ο[(KT 140)

5   ⏑—⏑—]νυνί γε κακὸν ὁ Ζεὺς [⏑⏟

⏑—⏑—⏟]φροντίδ' ἐξεργά[ζεται

⏑—⏑—⏟]την, ἐὰν μὴ συν[τριβ

⏑—⏑—⏟]ἐὰν μὴ συντριβ[

⏑—⏑—⏟]ὡς τάχιστά μοι, γέρ[ον,

10   ]. π. . . . ιεισπ. .σο[(KT 146)

Fragment 9b, line 4   Remains of a gloss (].α.) above the line.
6 φιλοσοφιαν inserted as a gloss above φροντιδ'.   6, 9 Suppl.
Milne.   7 Suppl. Körte.   7, 8 Obviously dialogue: probably
between Gorgias and Kleainetos, if this scrap comes from the
same page as fr. 1.

GEORGOS

9a–9e

*P. British Museum 2023a consists of six small frag-
ments of line-middles from the play on three scraps of
papyrus with text written on both sides. One of these six
forms part of fragment 1 (see above). It is a reasonable
hypothesis that the three scraps originally belonged to one
page of papyrus, and that consequently the other five
fragments (here numbered frs. 9a–9e consecutively)
derive from the same area of the play as fr. 1, in which
Gorgias is being addressed apparently by the old farmer
Kleainetos. It is impossible to say, however, which side
of the papyrus page came first, or what was the original
disposition of the fragments on the page. None of the
scraps yields a single passage of connected sense, and only
an occasional word or phrase in frs. 9b–9e is capable of
translation. The verso side of the page contained frs. 1,
9b and 9d. 9b is clearly part of a dialogue, presumably
the one between Gorgias and Kleainetos; we can read
woman (line 3), now Zeus . . . evil/unfortunate (5),
achieves his (?) heart's desire (6), if . . . not
smashed] (7), a phrase which the other speaker seems to
repeat in the line following, and as quickly as you can to
me, old man (9). 9d is less informative, with only
thought (?) to do (2) and seem/think (5). Could
Gorgias and Kleainetos be discussing the blow caused by
the pregnancy to Kleainetos' plan to marry Myrrhine's
daughter? Was it the young man who was described as
achieving his heart's desire, or someone else (Kleainetos,
Gorgias, Myrrhine?) who was described as not doing so?*

*We cannot be certain whether the other side of the papy-
rus page preceded or followed the verso. To judge from
the few tantalising words and phrases that can be de-
ciphered, it may have contained the description of a rape.*

c (fr. 2 recto M.)

]εια[.] ἀργύριον υ[
]ν ἐσκοπεῖτο πον[
] .. τοῦθ' ὁ ἀδικῶν π[
] . εν .. οντες ...... [(KT 150)
5   ]ονυ..... εττακο[
]ὄπισθε κατεβαλ.[
] . κἀκεῖνος ὅτι π .[
] ... κον. νε.. σ[
] ... ν ὕπτιο .[

d (fr. 3 verso M.)   e (fr. 3 recto M.)

]κ[(KT 155)   ]σκοπει.. [
]α δρᾶν ἐφρο .[   ]νον ενχε[
]κλεες χρημ[   ]. .κε[
] . .ρυτα[   ]ιτικων[(KT 160)
5]του δοκε[   ]ε.τοσ.. [
]τοδεοιν[(KT 160)   ] ..οιγ[
]τασ[

Fragment 9c, line 3 ` Körte reads τουθ: 5 Remains of a gloss
(ον]ειδος?) above τακο[.

Fragment 9d, line 2   ἐφρόν[τισε Körte.

Fragment 9e, line 4   πολ]ιτικῶν Körte.

136

GEORGOS

*The fragments from this side of the page are 9a, 9c and
9e. Of these 9a preserves nothing susceptible to trans-
lation, and 9e merely one word (line 1, consider). 9c,
however, has* money *(line 1),* considered *(2),* this
thing . . . the malefactor *(3),* threw down behind
(6), and he, because/what (7) and on his/its back *(9).
A reference to ' the malefactor ' who ' threw down behind '
fits remarkably well into the description of a rape. The
narrator perhaps could most plausibly be identified as
Myrrhine. But was she describing an incident in her own
past, or her daughter's violation nine months ago?*

DIS EXAPATON

(Twice a Swindler)

DIS EXAPATON (Twice a Swindler)

Manuscript

O = an Oxyrhynchus papyrus as yet unnumbered and only provisionally and incompletely published. It consists of thirteen broken fragments from three consecutive columns of a roll written in the second half of the third century A.D. or just later. First edition of the portions published: lines 11–30, 91–112, E. W. Handley, *Menander and Plautus: A Study in Comparison* (Inaugural Lecture: University College London, 1968); lines 47–63, 89–90, F. H. Sandbach, *Menandri Reliquiae Selectae*, Oxford 1972, 39 f. (by courtesy of E. W. Handley). No photograph has yet been published.

Fragments 1–5 are scraps or quotations of the play from various sources. See Introduction, pp. xxiv f.

Fragments 6a–6d are mutilated texts on two tiny scraps of papyrus (*P. Antinoopolis* 122) dating from the third century A.D. and tentatively attributed to the *Dis Exapaton*. First edition: J. W. B. Barns, *The Antinoopolis Papyri*, iii, London 1967, 122 ff.; no photograph has been published.

*   *   *

The Oxyrhynchus fragments have no title or author's name affixed, and no part of their splintered

INTRODUCTION

text coincides with any previously known quotation from Menander's *Dis Exapaton*. The single clue to the identification of the new papyrus is the unprecedented circumstance that its fragments appear to contain the Greek original for lines 494 to 562 of Plautus' comedy, the *Bacchides*. Well over a century ago Friedrich Ritschl (*Parerga zu Plautus und Terenz*, Berlin 1845: reprinted Amsterdam 1965, 404 ff.) clearly demonstrated that this Plautine play was adapted from Menander's *Dis Exapaton*, when he observed that fr. 111 Körte-Thierfelder, cited by Stobaeus from the *Dis Exapaton*, was exactly translated by *Bacch.* 816 f., that fr. 112 KT fitted well into the context of the slave's lying story about the priest of Diana at Ephesus in *Bacch.* 306–13, and that the text of the Roman play is sprinkled with references to the double deception of the Greek play's title (*Bacch.* 975, 1090, 1128).

Synoptic comparison of the Menander papyrus with the Plautine adaptation is informative in many ways,[1] and not only to the student of Roman comedy concerned with Plautus' methods of composition and his relation to the Greek models he adapted for the Roman stage. Judicious scrutiny of the Plautine text is advantageous for Menandrean scholars as well. For instance, *Bacch.* 107 clearly echoes the typical Menandrean formula for introducing the chorus of tipsy revellers at the end of his first acts (*Asp.* 246 ff., *Dysk.* 230 ff., *Epit.* 169 ff., *Pk.* 261 ff.); accordingly,

---

[1] Cf. the works cited in my survey *Menander, Plautus, Terence* (*Greece & Rome, New Surveys in the Classics* 9, Oxford 1975), 38 ff., to which C. Questa's valuable introduction to his second edition of the *Bacchides* (Florence 1975) now needs to be added.

the opening act of the *Dis Exapaton* must have ended at the point corresponding to *Bacch.* 108. The new Oxyrhynchus papyrus contains the end of Menander's second act (line 63 of the Greek text), where the chorus enter for their interlude directly after Sostratos and his father have gone off stage into their house. The corresponding point in the *Bacchides* is Mnesilochus' exit into his father's house at 525. Plautus' adaptation of Menander's second act thus extended to 417 lines. In the left-hand margin by line 63 in the *Dis Exapaton* papyrus, directly before the act-break, the scribe has written the number ΤΞΔ (=364). Although there are no parallels in parchment or papyrus manuscripts for scribes totalling in this way the number of lines or verses in a section of the work they are copying, it can hardly be doubted by anyone who compares the figure of 417 lines in the Plautine adaptation that the marginal number in the papyrus represents the number of lines in an exceptionally long second act of Menander's play.

The line-numbering in this edition corresponds with that in Handley's preliminary edition and in Sandbach's Oxford Text (*Menandri Reliquiae Selectae*, Oxford 1972).

No hypothesis or didascalic notice is preserved for this play. Its production date is therefore unknown. Many attempts,[1] however, have been made to work out a plausible date for the play from two supposed references to the Athenian environment which Plautus may have retained in the *Bacchides*. At *Bacch.* 911 f. the trickster slave Chrysalus refers to some insults heard by ' Clinia from Demetrius '. It

---

[1] Most recently by K. Gaiser, *Philologus* 114 (1970), 81 ff., and C. Questa, *op. cit.* 9 f.

has been suggested that the Demetrius there mentioned was the philosopher and rhetorician who ruled Athens between 317 and 307 B.C., in which case the allusion would have been as mysterious to Plautus' Roman audience as it is today to us. No Clinia or Clinias is known to have tangled at any time politically or rhetorically with this Demetrius, and so the alleged historical reference is altogether unverifiable. In fact, if this allusion does go back to Menander's *Dis Exapaton*, a more plausible explanation of it can be advanced from the world of the contemporary theatre than from that of political history. An ephemerally celebrated scene involving characters named Kleinias and Demetrios, in a recently produced but now unidentifiable comedy, would in this case have been the source of the allusion —an allusion which thus becomes totally useless for dating the *Dis Exapaton*.

The second reference is *Bacch.* 900 f., which at first sight looks far more promising. Here the same Chrysalus announces that one of the Bacchis sisters has climbed the Acropolis in order to visit the Parthenon, which ' is now open '. Another Demetrius, the Macedonian adventurer nicknamed Poliorcetes, used the Parthenon as his private harem and orgy centre in the winter of 304/3 B.C. (so Teles fr. 8.4 Hense², Plut. *Demetr.* 23–28). Doubtless the Parthenon reverted to its normal uses after Demetrius' departure from Athens in 302, and was reopened to visitors. Could *Bacch.* 900 f. refer to this reopening and so date the Greek original to 301 or thereabouts? Possibly: but Chrysalus' remark is far too general and imprecise for other interpretations to be ruled out. We know too little about the day-to-day running of the temples on the Acropolis during Menander's lifetime to exclude other, less exotic reasons[1] for temporary closure of the Parthenon than the whim of a self-important general.

If neither *Bacch.* 900 f. nor 911 f. provides secure evidence for the dating of Menander's *Dis Exapaton*, equally unstable are the subjective arguments based on the subtle interplay of thematic motif and plot incident in the Roman adaptation. Clearly the intrigue of the *Bacchides* is more complex than that of the *Dyskolos*; clearly too some interesting (but hardly unconventional) ideas on loyalty, friendship and the education of young men are competently woven into the fabric of the plot. Yet to argue from this that the *Dis Exapaton* must have been a work of Menander's ripe maturity begs too many questions about the relationship of dramatic maturity to age in years, about the originality of the devices and themes in the play, and about the fidelity of the Plautine adaptation to Menander's intentions.

*   *   *

Although the Oxyrhynchus papyrus preserves no cast-list for the *Dis Exapaton*, the plot structure and characters of the *Bacchides* are unlikely to have been significantly different in sequence of events and appearances. Plautus, however, certainly altered

---

[1] Such as the annual audit of the temple treasures, cleaning, or repair. The *opisthodomos*, for example, was damaged by fire earlier in the fourth century, and only one casual reference to this event is preserved today (Demosthenes, 24. 136). How often might other such disasters have occurred without any mention in surviving records?

he names of three of Menander's characters, and
nay well have tampered with more, substituting
nore grandiloquently sounding Greek names for
Menander's own everyday and typical ones. In the
ollowing list of *dramatis personae*, the Plautine names
ire bracketed and characters who do not appear in
he Oxyrhynchus fragments are asterisked.

Dramatis personae, in order of speaking, so far as is
cnown:

i) In the Oxyrhynchus fragments:

The father of Moschos (his name is unknown: =
    Philoxenus in Plautus)
Lydos, Moschos' tutor (= Lydus)
Sostratos, a young man (= Mnesilochus)
The father of Sostratos (his name is unknown[1]: =
    Nicobulus)
Moschos, a young friend of Sostratos (= Pistoclerus)
Syros, Sostratos' slave (= Chrysalus)

ii) Characters in the *Bacchides* whose counterparts
    must have appeared in the *Dis Exapaton*:

* A *hetaira* living in Athens (Bacchis of Athens)
* Her sister, also a *hetaira*, newly arrived from Samos[2]
    (Bacchis of Samos)
* A parasite, attendant on the soldier (Cleomachus'
    parasite)
* A soldier, Sostratos' rival for the affections of the
    hetaira from Samos (Cleomachus)

---

[1] The assumption that he was called Demeas in Menander's
play is probably false (see on fr. 2, below).
[2] Handley's suggestion that Menander may have named her
Chrysis is attractive but uncertain.

Mute characters in the Plautine adaptation include Pistoclerus' attendants carrying provisions, Mnesilochus' attendants carrying luggage, Cleomachus' page (who may have had a small speaking role in a lost early scene of the *Bacchides*), and one or more of Nicobulus' slaves armed with leather straps. All or some of their equivalents may have appeared in the lost scenes of Menander's play, which also included a chorus, perhaps of tipsy revellers, to perform the entr'actes.

ΔΙΣ ΕΞΑΠΑΤΩΝ

(*SCENE: A street in Athens, with two houses visible to the audience. One belongs to a hetaira living in Athens (Bacchis of Athens, in the Plautine adaptation), the other to Sostratos' father.*)

(*The broken text of the Oxyrhynchus papyrus straddles the end of the second, and the beginning of the third, act of the Dis Exapaton. Many of the play's earlier events, however, in the lost scenes of the first and second acts, can be conjectured with some security from three different pieces of evidence. The most important of these is the Plautine adaptation of Menander's play, although its own opening three-and-a-half scenes are now lost in the lacuna that affects the Palatine manuscripts of Plautus at this point. Nevertheless the grammarians of Rome quoted enough fragments from the opening scenes of the Latin adaptation for a plausible reconstruction of its lost beginning to be feasible. There is no indication that here the Roman poet made any startling alteration to his Greek model in dramatic structure or plot outline. The other two pieces of evidence are of relatively minor weight, except insofar as they complement or reinforce information provided by the Bacchides. The text of the Oxyrhynchus papyrus itself contains a few references to preceding events, especially in the conversation between Sostratos and his father when they discuss the lies that*)

DIS EXAPATON
(Twice a Swindler)

the slave Syros had told Sostratos' father about Sostratos' experiences in Ephesus (*Dis Ex. 53–58*). *And just after the discovery and provisional publication of the Oxyrhynchus papyrus, a further tiny scrap of papyrus has turned up containing the opening four words of Menander's play (fr. 1, below).*

This new scrap appears to confirm the conclusions based on the Plautine fragments, that the opening scene of the Dis Exapaton was a lively conversation between Moschos and the hetaira domiciled in Athens. The function of this scene and of a prologue speech by Moschos that probably followed would have been primarily expository. The audience would have learnt that Moschos had a young friend called Sostratos, who had been sent with the slave Syros by Sostratos' father from Athens to Ephesus in order to effect the repayment of a debt, and that while away Sostratos had fallen in love with a hetaira living in Samos. This hetaira, however, had engaged her services for a year to a soldier, who took her to Athens. Sostratos had written to Moschos asking him to find out where in Athens the hetaira from Samos was now staying. In the play's opening scene Moschos would have learnt that the hetaira to whom he was talking was the sister of the girl for whom he was searching on his friend's behalf, and that Sostratos' inamorata was coming *very soon to visit her sister. This visit occurred probably directly after Moschos had delivered his prologue speech, by which time Moschos himself was already half in love with the hetaira of Athens. The two sisters accordingly found it easy to use Moschos as their minion, securing his help with the organisation of a ' Welcome Home ' party for the sister from Samos, and winning his support for a proposed attempt to release the sister from her contract with the soldier.*

Menander's second act probably began with Moschos returning from market to the hetaira's house with provisions for the coming party, and being intercepted by his old tutor Lydos, who first scolded him for getting involved with a hetaira and then accompanied him into the hetaira's house in order to keep his eye on Moschos. At this point Syros and Sostratos arrived back in Athens with their business in Ephesus successfully completed. Syros was seen on stage first, and Moschos was able to explain to him that Sostratos' girlfriend had been traced, but that she urgently needed money to secure her release from her military contract. Syros promised help out of the money that Sostratos had recovered in Ephesus, which amounted to 240 minas in the Plautine version of the story. Syros

---

A fragment of Δὶς Ἐξαπατῶν, containing the play's opening words

1

A papyrus of the *Institut Français d'Archéologie Orientale du Caire*, inv. 337, first published (with a photograph: plate IIa) by B. Boyaval, *ZPE* 6 (1970),

*hen met Sostratos' father. Realising that a plausible
reason would now be needed for any failure to hand over
the money in full to the father, Syros pretended that it had
been deposited at Ephesus with one Theotimos, the priest
of Artemis there, because Sostratos and he had been
threatened there by pirates directly after recovering the
debt.*

*When Sostratos himself arrived on stage, he overheard
Lydos complaining to Moschos' father about Moschos'
indecent conduct at the party in the hetaira's house.
Lydos then explained to Sostratos that Moschos had there
been misbehaving with a hetaira, and the circumstantial
evidence produced by Lydos led Sostratos reasonably but
wrongly to assume that the girl in Moschos' arms was the
girl whom Sostratos loved. Sostratos' indignation at this
perfidy was misinterpreted by Lydos and Moschos' father,
who between them thought that Sostratos was upset
merely because his friend Moschos had fallen into the
clutches of a hetaira. This is where the text of the
Oxyrhynchus papyrus begins, in mid-scene with three
characters on stage in conversation with each other:
Moschos' father, Lydos, and Sostratos.)*

---

*A fragment of Dis Exapaton, containing the play's
opening words*

1

*P. IFAO inv. 337, part of a work that seems originally to
have contained plot-summaries of Menandrean plays, has
the following entry:*

5 ff. This scrap, written in the second century A.D.
was almost certainly part of a work containing plot
summaries of some plays by Menander (cf. *P. Oxy*
1235).

$$\Delta i s \ \text{'E} \xi \alpha \pi \alpha \tau \hat{\omega} \nu, \ o[\hat{v} \ \dot{\alpha} \rho \chi \acute{\eta} \cdot$$

$$\pi \rho \grave{o} s \ \tau \hat{\omega} \nu \ \theta \epsilon \hat{\omega} \nu, \ \mu \epsilon \iota \rho \acute{\alpha} \kappa \iota o[\nu$$

(The text of the Oxyrhynchus papyrus. Very little
remains of its first ten lines, which have not yet been
published. At line 11 Moschos' father is in mid-
speech.)

ΜΟΣΧΟΥ ΠΑΤΗΡ

11   σ]ὺ δ' ἐκεῖνον ἐκκάλε[ι
       ]ν, νουθέτει δ' ἐναν[τίον
αὐτόν τε σῶσον οἰκίαν θ' ὅλην φίλων.
Λυδέ, προάγωμεν.

ΛΥΔΟΣ
εἰ δὲ κἀμὲ καταλίποις—

ΜΟΣΧΟΥ ΠΑΤΗΡ

15 προάγωμεν. ἱκανὸς ο[ὖ]τος.

Fragment 1 Supplements by Boyaval.

The Oxyrhynchus papyrus In the apparatus to the text here
printed, those corrections and supplements whose author is not
named were made by E. W. Handley, *Menander and Plautus
A Study in Comparison*, London 1968. 13 θ' ὅλην deciphered
Rea.

DIS EXAPATON

Dis Exapaton, which [begins thus:]

THE HETAIRA OF ATHENS (?)

In heaven's name, young man . . .

It seems reasonably certain (cf. the immediately preceding introductory note) that Menander gave his play a lively beginning, with Moschos and the hetaira of Athens entering together in heated conversation. The woman, to whom the opening words clearly belong, uses her oath as a preface either to a command to Moschos (presumably a command to stop pestering her) or to a question (presumably asking why he had accosted her). Doubtless Moschos then went on to explain about his commission from Sostratos to search for a hetaira newly arrived in Athens from Samos . . .

(The translation of the Oxyrhynchus papyrus. At line 11 Moschos' father is addressing Sostratos, asking him to help with the moral rehabilitation of Moschos.)

MOSCHOS' FATHER

. . . .] you must fetch him out,   11
. . . .] and face him, tick him off,
And rescue him and all his family
Who love him. Lydos, let's be off.

LYDOS

(wishing to stay behind with Sostratos for Moschos' wigging)

                  But if
You left me here too . . .

MOSCHOS' FATHER *(turning to go)*

                Let's be off. He'll be   15
Enough!

MENANDER

ΛΥΔΟΣ

αὐτῷ, Σώστρα[τε,

χρῆσαι πικρῶς· ἔλαυν' ἐκεῖνον τὸ[ν] ἀκρα[τῆ·
ἅπαντας αἰσχύνει γὰρ ἡμᾶς τοὺ[ς] φίλους.

ΣΩΣΤΡΑΤΟΣ

ἤδη 'στὶν οὗτος φροῦδος. ἐμπλή[κτως ἔχει·
τούτου καθέξει. Σώστρα[τ]ον προήρπασας.
20 ἀρνήσεται μέν, οὐκ [ἄ]δηλόν ἐστί μοι—
ἰτάμη γάρ—εἰς μέσον τε π[ά]ντες οἱ θεοὶ
ἥξουσι. μὴ τοίνυν [.]ον[......] νὴ Δία.
κακὴ κακῶς τοίνυν—ἐ[π]άν[αγε, Σ]ώστρατε·
ἴσως σε πείσει· δοῦλο[ς ....]ρα[.....
25 ἐγὼ μάλισθ'· ἡ δ' ὡ[ς κενὸν συ]μπεισάτω
ἔχοντα μηδ[έν. πᾶν ἀποδώσω τ]ῷ πατρὶ
τὸ χ]ρυσίον· π[ι]θαν[ευομέν]η γὰρ παύσεται
ὅταν] ποτ' αἴσθητα[ι, τὸ τῆς πα]ροιμίας,
νεκρῷ] λέγουσα [μῦθον· ἀλλ'] ἤδη [με] δεῖ
30 ἐλθεῖν ἐπ'] ἐκεῖνον. [ἀλλ' ὁρῶ γὰ]ρ τ[ουτο]νὶ

---

17 παντας O (but with απ...[in the right-hand margin).
18 Suppl. tentatively Arnott. 22 νὴ Δία deciphered by
Webster. 30 ἐλθεῖν suppl. Austin, the rest ed. pr.

---

[1] Moschos.
[2] A proverb applied to situations, as the ancient paroemiographers note, where the listener takes no notice of what is said to him.

DIS EXAPATON

LYDOS (*as he reluctantly leaves with Moschos' father*)
    Savage him, Sostratos, assail
That libertine! He shames us all, his friends!

(*Moschos' father and Lydos now leave the stage, prob-
ably to the spectators' right and in the direction of the city
centre, where they may be imagined to live. Sostratos is
left alone, and the agitation of his thoughts is indicated
partly by the incoherent terseness of what he says, partly
by the sudden switches between first and second and
between second and third persons in his references to him-
self and to the girl he loves.*)

SOSTRATOS

Too late, he's[1] come to grief. [She's fickle (?),] she'll
Enslave him! Sostratos was your first catch—
Oh, she'll deny it, that's quite clear to me—   20
She fights back, every single god'll be
Named in her oaths. So don't [. . .] yes, by Zeus!
So damn the bitch!

(*Sostratos moves in the direction of the hetaira's house,
intending to confront her, but as he reaches the door, he
changes his mind.*)

     No, Sostratos—come back,
She may persuade you! I'm her slave (?), [. . .],
Lock, stock and barrel. Let her win me over   25
When I am [broke] and penniless. [I'll give (?)]
My father [all the] money. She will stop
Her blarney [once] she sees she's lecturing
[A corpse, as] people say.[2] [Well], now [I]'ve got
[To find] my father. [Why, he's] here, [I see,]   30
[Approaching] . . .

(Of the next 16 lines, in which a conversation between Sostratos and his father begins, hardly anything survives. The text appears to resume with Sostratos' father in mid-speech.)

ΣΩΣΤΡΑΤΟΥ ΠΑΤΗΡ

47   ]έδωκεν δέ σοι
          ] τὸν τόκον

ΣΩΣΤΡΑΤΟΣ

        ] . ειδον· μηδὲ ἐν
50   ἐγκ]άλει χρηστῷ ξένῳ.
   ἥ]κω κομίζων δεῦρό σοι.

ΣΩΣΤΡΑΤΟΥ ΠΑΤΗΡ

]σα· τ[ὸ χρυ]σίον [δό]θ' ὑμεῖς, παῖ, ταχύ.

ΣΩΣΤΡΑΤΟΣ

λήψει π]αρ' [ἡ]μῶν· μὴ πρόσεχε κενῷ λόγῳ.
οὐ γὰρ] παρώρμη[σ' ο]ὐδ' ἐπεβούλευσ' οὐδὲ εἷς.

ΣΩΣΤΡΑΤΟΥ ΠΑΤΗΡ

55 οὐ πρὸς Θ]εό[τ]ιμον [κ]ατετέ[θ]η τὸ χρυσίον;

54 οὐ γὰρ suppl. Arnott, the rest ed. pr.

---

[1] Sostratos' father refers to Theotimos (cf. lines 55–56), the priest of Artemis at Ephesus with whom, in Syros' story (cf. Plautus, *Bacch.* 306 ff.), the recovered debt was finally deposited for safety.

[2] In Syros' story (here cf. *Bacch.* 279 ff.), the original debtor had plotted with the crew of a pirate ship in Ephesus harbour to attack the vessel on which Sostratos was embarking and steal the money back.

DIS EXAPATON

(Virtually nothing survives of lines 31–46, but part at least of their probable content may be guessed from the surrounding context and an occasional decipherable phrase in the papyrus. Sostratos' father entered, and after greeting and being greeted by his son (this was their first meeting since Sostratos' return from Ephesus), the father doubtless lamented the failure of his son and Syros to bring the recovered money to Athens. Sostratos then revealed that Syros had been lying: some badly mutilated lines contain the remark ' If Syros was standing by me now and said the sun up there was shining, I should think it was dark, that night had come.' The papyrus text as published resumes at line 47, with Sostratos' father speaking.)

SOSTRATOS' FATHER

[. . . . .] and he[1] gave it you   47
[. . . . . adding all (?)] the interest?

SOSTRATOS

[Yes. . . . .] I saw him do it (?).   Don't
[. . . . .] malign a first-class friend.   50
[. . . . .] I've brought it here for you.

SOSTRATOS' FATHER

[. . . . .] give me the money quickly, son.

SOSTRATOS

We['ll let] you [have it].   Just ignore that fatuous
Tale.   No-one anchored near or hatched a plot.[2]

SOSTRATOS' FATHER

The money was[n't] then deposited   55
[With] Theotimos?

ΣΩΣΤΡΑΤΟΣ

τί '' πρὸς Θεό[τ]ιμον ''; α[ὐ]τὸς ἐφύλαττεν λαβών,
τ[ό τε πρὸ]ς βί[ο]ν διφο[ρ]εῖ, πάτερ.

ΣΩΣΤΡΑΤΟΥ ΠΑΤΗΡ

χρηστὸς σφόδρα·
ἐφ[ρόντι]σέ τι.   τί οὖν ὁ Σύρος ἐβούλετο;

ΣΩΣΤΡΑΤΟΣ

ἐ[ατέο]ν.   μετ' ἐμοῦ δ' ἀκολούθει καὶ λαβὲ
60 τὸ [χρ]υσίον.

ΣΩΣΤΡΑΤΟΥ ΠΑΤΗΡ

παίζεις;

ΣΩΣΤΡΑΤΟΣ

ἀκολούθει καὶ λαβέ.

ΣΩΣΤΡΑΤΟΥ ΠΑΤΗΡ

οὐ[κοῦ]ν ἀκολουθῶ.   δὸς μόνον, καλῶς τέ μοι
ὡς [δεῖ] κέχρησαι.   πρὶν λαβεῖν μάχομαι [τ]ί σοι;
63 ἐμ[οὶ] δὲ πάντων τοῦτο προὐργιαίτερον.

XO P OY

56 τί suppl. Sandbach, the rest ed. pr.   62 τί rather than τι?
63 In the left-hand margin of O the number ΤΞΔ (= 364)
appears: see the introduction to this play, p. 142.

158

DIS EXAPATON

SOSTRATOS

[What? With] him? Looked after it
Himself, you mean, dad—he makes money grow!

SOSTRATOS' FATHER

He's really first-class. Used his brains (?). So what
Was Syros up to?

SOSTRATOS

[Never mind.] Just come with me
And get the money.

SOSTRATOS' FATHER
You're not teasing?

SOSTRATOS

Come   60

And get it.

SOSTRATOS' FATHER
Then I'll come. Just give it me, and you'll
Have done your [duty] well. No point in squabbling
Before I get it! This caps everything!   63

(*Sostratos now leads his father off stage, in order to hand
the money over to him. The papyrus remains do not
reveal whether Sostratos and Syros had hidden this money
somewhere in Sostratos' house, or whether it had been left
in a safe and secret place in another part of the city.
After the departure of Sostratos and his father, the chorus
enter to give what would have been their second entr'acte
performance.*)

ΜΕΡΟΣ Γ΄

(The first 25 lines of the third act are badly mutilated and have not yet been published. They contain a conversation between Sostratos and his father, which continues down to line 90.)

ΣΩΣΤΡΑΤΟΣ (in mid-speech here ?)

89   ] . μοι.

ΣΩΣΤΡΑΤΟΥ ΠΑΤΗΡ

ταῦτ᾽ ἄπειμι πρὸς ἀγορὰν
90 πρ]άττ[ων. ὅ] τι πράττῃς ἄλλο δέδοται τοῦτό σοι.

ΣΩΣΤΡΑΤΟΣ

κα]ὶ μ[ὴν δο]κῶ μ[ο]ι τὴν καλήν τε κἀγαθὴν
ἰδεῖν ἐρωμένην ἂν ἡδ[έ]ως κενὸς
πιθανευομένην καὶ προσδοκῶσαν αὐτ[ί]κα—
φησὶν δ᾽ ἐν αὐτῇ—πᾶν ὃ κομίζω χρυσίον·
95 " πάνυ γὰρ κομίζει τοῦ[το] καί, νὴ τοὺς θεούς,
ἐ[λ]ευθερίως—τί[ς] μᾶλλον;—ἀξί[ω]ς τ᾽ ἐμοῦ."
α[ὕ]τη δ᾽ ἱ[κα]ν[ῶς], καλῶς ποοῦ[σ]ά [γ᾽], εὑρέθη
ο[ἵ]αν ποτ᾽ ᾤ[μ]ην οὖσα, τὸν δ᾽ ἀβέλτερον
Μόσχον ἐλεῶ. καὶ τὰ μὲν ἔγωγ᾽ ὀργίζομαι,
100 τὰ δ᾽ οὐκ ἐκεῖνον τοῦ γεγονότος αἴτιον

92 ἡδ[έ]ως suppl. and deciphered Lloyd-Jones, Sandbach.
98 Corr. ed. pr.: οια O. 99 ἐλεῶ deciphered Rea.

DIS EXAPATON

ACT III

The choral interlude allows, by the stage convention, enough time for the off-stage transfer of the money. After the departure of the chorus, Sostratos and his father return to the stage with their transaction completed, but the first 25 lines of the new act, which contain all but the final remarks of their conversation, are extremely mutilated and have not been published. As their conversation closes, Sostratos' father refers to two tasks ahead of them: some unexplained business (it was probably spelled out in the preceding context) which he himself had to attend to in the city centre, and his son's obligation to scold Moschos.)

SOSTRATOS (*only the end of his remark is preserved*)

. . . .] to me (?).

SOSTRATOS' FATHER

I'll go to town and fix   89
this business.   You've that other job [to] do.   90

Sostratos' father goes off to the right in the direction of the city centre, leaving Sostratos alone.)

SOSTRATOS

And now I'm broke, I do believe I'd like
To see my fine and dandy lady-friend
Come with her blarney and her instant hopes
Of all the cash I'm bringing.   To herself
She'll say, ' Oh yes, he brings it like a gentleman,   95
I swear—yes, he's the best—and just as I
Deserve.'   She's [pretty well], though, proved to be
What I once thought her!   Serve her right, too!   But
I pity that fool Moschos.   In a way I'm mad
At him, yet I don't feel that *he*'s to blame   100

ἀδικήματος νενόμικα, τὴν δ᾽ ἰταμωτάτην
πασῶν ἐκείνην.

ΜΟΣΧΟΣ

εἶτ᾽ ἀκούσας ἐνθάδε
εἶναί με, ποῦ γῆς ἐστι; χαῖρε, Σώστρατε.

ΣΩΣΤΡΑΤΟΣ

καὶ σύ.

ΜΟΣΧΟΣ

τί κατηφὴς καὶ σκυθρωπός, εἰπέ μοι;
105 καὶ βλέμμα τοῦθ᾽ ὑπόδακρυ; μὴ νεώτερον
κακὸν κατείληφάς τι τῶν [γ᾽] ἐνταῦθα;

ΣΩΣΤΡΑΤΟΣ

ναί.

ΜΟΣΧΟΣ

εἶτ᾽ οὐ [λέ]γεις;

ΣΩΣΤΡΑΤΟΣ

ἔνδον γὰρ ἀμέλει, Μόσχε.

ΜΟΣΧΟΣ

πῶς;

107 Suppl. Sandbach.

---

[1] Sostratos.

DIS EXAPATON

'or this atrocious episode—it's her,
That brazen queen of tarts!

*As Sostratos comes close to breaking down in his distress,
Moschos emerges from the hetaira's house.   His opening
remark is addressed back into the house he is leaving,
before he catches sight of Sostratos.)*

MOSCHOS
He's heard I'm here,
But where on earth is *he*[1]?—Oh, Sostratos,
Hello!

SOSTRATOS (*bleakly*)
Hello.

MOSCHOS
Crestfallen?   Scowling?   Tell
Me, why?   That blear-eyed look, too!   Have you met 105
With some new trouble *here*?

SOSTRATOS
Yes.

MOSCHOS (*after waiting for Sostratos to continue*)
Won't you [tell],
Then?

SOSTRATOS (*pointing to the hetaira's house*)
Moschos, it's in *there*, of course.

MOSCHOS
How do
You mean?

MENANDER

ΣΩΣΤΡΑΤΟΣ

τ[   ] φιλοῦντα τὸν πρὸ τοῦ χρόνον

          ]α· τοῦτο πρῶτον ὧν ἐμὲ

110   ] ἠδίκηκας.

ΜΟΣΧΟΣ

                 ἠδίκηκα δὲ

ἐγὼ σέ; μὴ γένοιτο τοῦτο, Σώστρατε.

ΣΩΣΤΡΑΤΟΣ

112 οὐκ ἠξίουν γοῦν οὐδ' ἐγώ.

ΜΟΣΧΟΣ

                 λέγεις δὲ τί;

(After line 112 the Oxyrhynchus papyrus has trace
of a further line, and then breaks off.)

(*Doubtless the misunderstanding between Sostratos and
Moschos was quickly cleared up, with few or none of the
comic delaying tactics that enliven the opening of the
corresponding scene in Plautus' Bacchides (534 ff.), and
after that the double swindle of Menander's title would
have been organised by the slave Syros. Without more of
the Greek text, however, it is impossible to gauge how
closely Plautus followed Menander's plot in the scenes*

DIS EXAPATON

SOSTRATOS

[You (?)] previously [claimed to be (?)]
[My (?)] friend, [and you've betrayed me (?)]. That's
  the first
[Vile (?)] wrong you've done me.[1]

MOSCHOS (*mystified*)

Wrong I've done you? That   110
Must never happen, Sostratos.

SOSTRATOS

It's not
What I expected, either.

MOSCHOS

What's your point?   112

---

[1] The openings of lines 108–10 in the papyrus text are badly
mutilated, and the supplements here suggested (in the square
brackets) are merely an attempt to achieve logically consistent
sense.

*that followed. Careful comparison between the extant
Menandrean scenes and the corresponding parts of the
Plautine adaptation reveals that the Roman dramatist
neither alters the outline of the original plot nor adds new
incidents of any importance, but that at times he takes a
totally independent line with the details of scenic structure
and the composition of individual speeches or dialogue.
In both plays, for example, the young traveller (Sostratos/
Mnesilochus) hands over to his father the money he has
brought back from Ephesus. Here Menander writes two*

short scenes of dialogue between father and son, with an act-break dividing them during which the transfer is imagined to occur off stage. The Roman theatre, however, dispensed with act-breaks, and Plautus achieved continuity by cutting the two Menandrean scenes of dialogue, removing the father altogether from the stage at this point, and writing a long monologue for the son,

---

Four fragments quoted from Δὶς Ἐξαπατῶν by ancient authors

2 (109 Körte-Thierfelder, 123 Kock)

The late Roman allegorist Fulgentius, writing about Bellerophon, *Mitologiae* 3. 1. Bellerofonta posuerunt quasi βουληφοροῦντα . . . nam et Menander similiter in *Disexapaton* comoedia ita ait:

> βουληφόρως
> τὴν ἡμετέραν δή, Δημέα, προκατέλαβες
> ὅρασιν.

id est: consiliarie nostram, Demea, praeoccupauisti uisionem.

Fragment 2, line 2 τὴν and δή om. Fulgentius, suppl. Bentley and Sandbach respectively.

Fragment 2 has no counterpart in Plautus' Bacchides, and Fulgentius sometimes makes mistakes over the attribution of individual citations. Accordingly some scholars (Webster, Studies in Menander[2], Manchester 1960, 86; Gaiser, Wien. Stud. 79 [1966], 194 f.) have suggested that this passage derives not from Menander's Dis Exapaton but from the same dramatist's second Adelphoi. This suggestion is attractive, but the absence

who left the stage briefly (525–29) at its close in order to effect the transfer, and then returned to find his young friend (Moschos/Pistoclerus) newly arrived on stage. It seems reasonable to assume that Plautus maintained in the later scenes of the Bacchides a similar fidelity to the outlines of Menander's story, and a similar independence over the details of scenic structure and dialogue.)

Four fragments quoted from Dis Exapaton by ancient authors

2

Cited by Fulgentius, Mitologiae, 3. 1, who writes as follows: ' They have interpreted Bellerophon to mean βουληφορῶν (= Counselling)—for Menander also in his comedy Dis Exapaton speaks similarly, thus:

Counsel-wise,
You have anticipated, Demeas,
Our own impression.

of any echo in Plautus' Bacchides is not a compelling argument in its favour, in view of the Roman poet's independent attitude to details in his Greek models. If this fragment is after all correctly attributed by Fulgentius, it is most likely to have been spoken by a slave (Syros?), perhaps to one of the old men he was swindling; its language is affected (βουληφόρως, here translated ' counsel-wise', has a Homeric ring; ὅρασιν, translated 'impression', smacks more of the philosophy school than of everyday speech) in a way that best suits the grandiloquent mumbo-jumbo of an impudent trickster.

MENANDER

3 (110 KT, 124 K)

An anonymous lexicographer in his Συναγωγὴ λέξεων
χρησίμων (Bekker, *Anecdota Graeca* 1. 436. 17), and
the *Suda* lexicon: ἀπόστα· οὐ μόνον ἀπόστηθι
λέγουσιν. καὶ παράστα. Μένανδρος Παιδίῳ (fr. 317
KT)· . . . Δὶς Ἐξαπατῶντι·

ἐμοὶ παράστα· τὴν θύραν κόψας ἐγὼ
καλῶ τιν᾽ αὐτῶν.

4 (111 KT, 125 K)

The line is cited by Stobaeus, *Eclogae* 4. 52b. 27 (περὶ
ζωῆς), with the full heading Μενάνδρου Δὶς Ἐξαπα-
τῶντος. Without the play-title but with the author's
name it is cited by [Plutarch], *Consol. ad Apoll.* 119e;
Clement of Alexandria, *Stromata* 6. 2 (p. 436. 10
Stählin); a scholiast on Homer, *Odyssey* 15. 246; and
Eustathius, commenting on the same line of Homer,
1781. 2. It appears also in the collection of mono-
stichs ascribed to Menander, 583 Jäkel.

ΣΥΡΟΣ

ὃν οἱ θεοὶ φιλοῦσιν, ἀποθνῄσκει νέος.

Cf. Plautus, *Bacchides* 816–17 (Chrysalus) quem di
diligunt / adulescens moritur, dum ualet, sentit, sapit.

Fragment 4   ὃν γὰρ θεὸς φιλεῖ mss. of Men. *monost.* 583.

DIS EXAPATON

3

An anonymous lexicographer in his Collection of Useful Terms (Bekker, Anecdota Graeca 1. 436. 17) and the Suda Lexicon quote this and another fragment (317 Körte-Thierfelder) to illustrate Menander's use of παράστα (' stand by ') and ἀπόστα (' stand off ') as alternative forms to παράστηθι and ἀπόστηθι, which are the regular 2nd person singular, strong aorist active imperative forms of παρίστημι and ἀφίστημι.

Stand by my side.   I'll hammer on the door
And summon one of them.

Context and speaker are uncertain. In Plautus' Bacchides, the soldier's young slave, accompanied by his parasite, knocks on a door at 810, and Nicobulus, accompanied by Philoxenus, at 1117.

4

Quoted by Stobaeus, Eclogae 4. 52b. 27 (the section headed ' On Life '), and by several other authors (who fail to indicate its precise source), as listed on the facing page.

SYROS

He whom the gods love dies while still a youngster.

This line, celebrated in antiquity (to judge from the number of its quoters) and given its modern currency by the mistranslation in Byron's Don Juan, IV. xii (the moribund subject in Menander is singular, not plural), was faithfully translated by Plautus at Bacch. 816–17.   Far from being a sentimental sigh about the Schuberts of this world, it was part of a caustic comment by the slave Syros

MENANDER

5 (112 KT, 126 K)

Three Byzantine lexica—Photius, the *Suda*, and the
Etymologicum Genuinum (R. Reitzenstein, *Geschicht*
der griechischen Etymologika, Leipzig 1897, p. 194)—
cite the fragment under the entry ζάκορος· νεωκόρος
Μένανδρος Δὶς Ἐξαπατῶντι·

$$οὐ \ Μεγάβυζος \ ἦν$$
ὅστις γένοιτο ζάκορος.

Two papyrus scraps which are hesitantly assigned to Δὶς
Ἐξαπατῶν

6a–6d (frs. 121 a i, ii; b i, ii Austin, *C.G.F.*)

Two tiny scraps of papyrus (*P. Antinoopolis* 122) yield
four brief and uninformative passages which have
tentatively been attributed to this play because in
one of them (fr. 6a, line 1) a character named Lydos
is addressed.   In later Greek comedy this name up to
now is known only from the *Dis Exapaton*, but note
the title *Lydos* by Antiphanes (ii. 70 Kock); fr. anon.
720 Kock; Plautus, *Cornicula* fr. vi; Atilius fr. i
Ribbeck; and Cicero, *Pro Flacco* 65: *quis umquam*
Graecus comoediam scripsit in qua seruus primarium
partium non Lydus esset?   Even if it is ridiculously
exaggerated, Cicero's question should warn us against
too easy an acceptance of these papyrus scraps as part
of the *Dis Exapaton*.   In any case they are too brief
and too mutilated to be tested by any comparison
with the text of Plautus' *Bacchides*.   Fragment 6a =
the first scrap, h(orizontal)-f(ibres) side; 6b = the

DIS EXAPATON

*(Chrysalus) to Nicobulus (the father of Sostratos/
Mnesilochus) about the old man's stupidity on the occasion
of the first swindle.*

5

*Three Byzantine lexica—Photius, the Suda, and the
Etymologicum Genuinum—cite this fragment in order to
illustrate the use of the word* ζάκορος *(a temple warden):*

> Whoever got the warden's job,
> It wasn't Megabyzos.

*Megabyzos was the family or cult name of the warden of
the temple of Artemis at Ephesus.   Although Plautus does
not translate the words of this fragment literally in his
Bacchides (the reference would clearly have made little
sense to his Roman audience), their original context was
almost certainly the scene in which the slave Syros
(Chrysalus) was telling his elaborate lie to Sostratos'
father (Nicobulus) about the deposit of the money with
Theotimos, the priest of Artemis at Ephesus (cf. Bacch.
306–13).   If Syros had been embroidering his story too
cleverly with circumstantial details like the names of the
priest and the warden of the temple—Theotimos and
Megabyzos respectively—the old man could well have cut
in with a remark such as this fragment, thus challenging
Syros' story.*

*Two papyrus scraps which are hesitantly assigned to Dis
Exapaton*

6a–6d

*P. Antinoopolis 122 consists of two tiny shreds of papyrus
with text on both sides, providing four broken snatches of*

MENANDER

second scrap, h.-f. side; 6c = the first scrap, v(ertical)-f. side; 6d = the second scrap, v.-f. side. The fibre pattern suggests that line 6 followed 5, and 16 followed 15, with no lines lost between.

a

```
      ]ην Λυδέ .[
      ]ειδεστησ[
      ]ν· οἶμαι δε[
      ]ειν· τρ. [
5     ].. ω .[
```

b

```
      ]ῆλθες :—ου[
      ]ζουσ' ὅτ' ο.[
      ]υκειασεν[
      ]σ' ἐντεῦθε[ν
10    ]. ας :—ανε[
```

c

```
      ]. ωνεσ. [
      ]. ευρος δοκ[
      ]μυσον· ε[
      ].[.].δεκα[
15 μὰ τὴν] Δήμητ[ρα
```

d

```
      ε]λθων θ[
      ]. ιν λαμβα[ν
      ]αφείη τη[
      ]τοῖς θεοῖς[
20    ]. ονες δ' ι.[
      ]. ντον.[
```

Fragments 6a–6d Suppl. ed. pr. (J. W. B. Barns, *The Antino-opolis Papyri* iii, London 1967, 122 ff.). 13 Μυσόν ? (ed. pr.).

DIS EXAPATON

dramatic text. All four come from the middle of lines. One (fr. 6b) has two dicola (lines 6, 10), and another has a name in the vocative (fr. 6a, 1); if the two shreds of papyrus come from the same page, as appears likely, they evidently provide the remains of a dialogue. Only a few words and phrases can now be translated: fr. 6a, line 1 an address to Lydos, *3* I think; *6b, 6* . . . you came. —Not . . . (?), *7* when (?), *9* from here/there; *6c, 13* Mysian (?: the Mysians lived in the north-west corner of Asia Minor, and were proverbially considered beneath contempt), *14* ten, *15* [No, by] Demet[er]; *6d, 16* having come, *17* take, *19* the gods. The sole reason for assigning these scraps to Dis Exapaton is the address to ' Lydos ' in fr. 6a, 1. Lydos may well have been a common slave name in later Greek comedy (Cicero, Pro Flacco 65, asks ' What Greek ever wrote a comedy without a Lydos being the main slave part? '), but up to now the name in later Greek comedy is known only from the Oxyrhynchus fragments of Dis Exapaton. Nothing in the scraps, however, either supports or hinders the attribution, and the remains are all too tattered for any attempt to match them with the text of Plautus' Bacchides.*

DYSKOLOS

(The Peevish Fellow)

DYSKOLOS (The Peevish Fellow)

Manuscripts

B = *P. Bodmer* 4, the second play (between *Samia* and *Aspis*) in a papyrus codex of the third century A.D. It is a virtually complete text of the play. First edition: V. Martin, *Papyrus Bodmer IV. Ménandre: Le Dyscolos*, Cologny-Geneva 1958, with photographs.[1] Subsequently two tiny scraps that had been detached from one page of this codex, containing bits of lines 756–63, 806–10, and 773–77, were identified and published by R. Kasser and C. Austin in *Papyrus Bodmer XXVI. Ménandre: Le Bouclier*, Cologny-Geneva 1969, 48 f., with a photograph.

Berl. = *P. Berlin* 21199, a scrap of papyrus from Hermupolis dating from the sixth or seventh century A.D., and containing the beginnings of lines 452–57 and the ends of 484–89. First edition: H. Maehler, *ZPE* 4 (1969), 113, with a photograph.

H = a fragment of vellum codex, also from Hermupolis, written in the fourth century A.D. and now in Oxford (Bodleian Library, Gr. Class, g. 50 [P]). It contains the beginnings of lines 140–50 and the ends of 169–74. First edition: B. Grenfell and A. Hunt,

---

[1] W. E. Blake's edition (New York 1966) also contains photographs.

Mélanges Nicole, Geneva 1905, 220 ff.; no photograph has been published.

O = *P. Oxyrhynchus* 2467, two tiny scraps of papyrus from the second century A.D., containing the ends of lines 263–72 and 283–90. First edition: E. G. Turner, *The Oxyrhynchus Papyri* 27 (1962), 137, with a photograph.

Oslo = *P. Oslo* 168, a tiny scrap of papyrus roll from an unknown source. Dating to the third or second century B.C., it is by far the earliest fragment of the *Dyskolos* yet known. It contains portions of lines 766–73. First edition: S. Eitrem and L. Amundsen, *Papyri Osloenses* 3 (1936), 259, publishing it as an unidentified literary fragment. Identification, as well as its correct dating, was achieved by J. Lenaerts, *Papyrus Littéraires Grecs (Papyrologica Bruxellensia 13* [1977]), 23 ff., where the scrap is republished with a photograph.

*   *   *

Of the *Dyskolos'* original 969 lines, only nine (650–53, 703–7) are totally lost, and another twenty or so are damaged beyond even ramshackle repair. No other play by Menander is preserved in a state so near completeness. Furthermore, the Bodmer papyrus prefixes to its text a short verse hypothesis or plot-summary, a didascalic notice, and a cast-list. The hypothesis is attributed on the papyrus to Aristophanes of Byzantium, the famous editor and scholar who worked at Alexandria in the second half of the third and the beginning of the second centuries B.C. This attribution is clearly spurious (cf. Handley's edition of the play, pp. 121 ff.; and R. Pfeiffer, *History of Classical Scholarship*, Oxford 1968, 190 ff.), for the scansion and language of the hypothesis excite suspicion, and the précis of the plot is inaccurate. It names only Sostratos, for example, as Knemon's rescuer from the well, and then makes Knemon play a part in arranging the marriage between Gorgias and Sostratos' sister. The cast-list seems to be more reliable, whatever its origins may have been. It purports to list the speaking characters of the play in their order of appearance, with brief identifications attached to most of them. If Sostratos' mother had a small speaking part in the *Dyskolos*, as I now believe likely (see the critical apparatus on line 430), her omission from the list between Getas and Simiche is its one real inaccuracy.

It is the didascalic notice, however, which provides information of true value. The material from which it derives was assembled in Alexandria not long after Menander's death from the public records of Athens. Although the text as we have it on the papyrus contains an irritating corruption, its fairly certain emendation enables us to date the play's first production to a winter's day early in 316 B.C., when in the dramatic competition that formed an important part of the festival of the Lenaea the *Dyskolos* won first prize. Menander was then in his middle twenties, a playwright with between four and eight years' practical experience. Did he deserve this early—and apparently not often repeated—success?

ΑΡΙΣΤΟΦΑΝ(ΟΥΣ) ΓΡΑΜΜΑΤΙ[Κ](ΟΥ)
Η ΥΠΟΘΕΣΙΣ

ἔχων θυγατέρα δύσκολος μητρὸς μέν, ἣν
ἔγημ' ἔχουσαν υἱόν, ἀπελείφθη τάχος
διὰ τοὺς τρόπους, μόνος δ' ἐπ' ἀγρῶν διετέλει.
τῆς παρθένου δὲ Σώστρατος σφοδρῶς ἐρῶν
5 προσῆλθεν αἰτῶν· ἀντέπιφθ' ὁ δύσκολος.
τὸν ἀδελφὸν αὐτῆς ἔπιθεν· οὐκ εἶχ' ὅ τι λέγοι
ἐκεῖνος. ἐμπεσὼν δὲ Κνήμων εἰς φρέαρ
τὸν Σώστρατον βοηθὸν εἶχε διὰ τάχους.
κατηλλάγη μὲν τῇ γυναικί, τὴν κόρην
10 τούτῳ δ' ἐδίδου γυναῖκα κατὰ νόμους ἔχειν.
τούτου δ' ἀδελφὴν λαμβάνει τῷ Γοργίᾳ
τῷ τῆς γυναικὸς παιδί, πρᾶος γενόμενος.

ἐδίδαξεν εἰς Λήναια ἐπὶ Δημογένους ἄρχοντ(ος) καὶ
ἐνίκα. ὑπεκρίνατο Ἀριστόδημος Σκαρφεύς. ἀντεπι-
γράφετ(αι) Μισάνθρωπος.

Hypothesis and didascalic notice taken from the Bodmer
papyrus.

Hypothesis   1 μέν, ἣν Bingen, Pfeiffer: μονην B.   2 Corr. van
Groningen: ετημεν B.   5 Corr. Mayer, Pfeiffer: αντετιφθ' B.
6 ἔπιθεν Diano, London seminar: επειθεν B.   οτιποει B, with
λεγοι added in margin.   10 τηγυναικα B.   ἔχειν Lloyd-Jones:
ερων B.   11 τουτω B.

Didascalic notice   Δημογένους ed. pr.: διδυμογενης B.   Σκαρ-
φεύς ed. pr.: σκαφευς B.   αντεπιγραφετ' B.

HYPOTHESIS
BY ARISTOPHANES THE SCHOLAR[1]

A peevish man, who had a daughter, soon
Was left through his behaviour by his wife,
Already mother of a son.   He lived
A hermit in the country.   Sostratos
Fell madly for the girl.   He came and asked.   5
The peevish man resisted.   He won over
Her brother, who was at a loss for words.
Knemon fell in a well, was quickly helped
By Sostratos.   He made up with his wife
And gave away the girl as legal wife   10
To him, whose sister then on Gorgias,
His wife's son, he bestowed, now mollified.

(DIDASCALIC NOTICE)

(Menander) produced (this play) at the Lenaea festival when Demogenes was archon[2] and won first prize.   Aristodemus of Scarphe[3] was his principal actor.   It has an alternative title ' *The Misanthrope* '.

[1] This attribution to Aristophanes of Byzantium is spurious: see above, p. 177 f.

[2] Demogenes was eponymous archon of Athens from summer 317 to summer 316, and the Lenaea festival was celebrated each year in January.   The date of the play's first production was thus January 316 B.C.

[3] This actor is otherwise unknown.   Scarphe, otherwise known as Scarpheia, was an important town in Locris near Thermopylae.   It was the birthplace of another comic actor who won fame in Athens, Lycon, active in the 320s.

ΤΑ ΤΟΥ ΔΡΑΜΑΤ(ΟΣ) ΠΡΟΣΩΠΑ

Πάν, ὁ θεός
Χαιρέας, ὁ παράσιτος
Σώστρατος, ὁ ἐρασθείς
Πυρρίας, ὁ δοῦλος

Κνήμων, ὁ πατήρ
παρθένος θυγατὴρ Κνήμων(ος)
Δᾶος
Γοργίας, ὁ ἐκ μ[η]τρὸς ἀδελφ[ός
Σίκων μάγειρος
Γέτας, ὁ δοῦλο[ς
Σιμίχη γραῦς
Καλλιππίδης π[α]τὴρ τοῦ Σωστράτ[ου

Cast-list, as it appears in the Bodmer papyrus.

After Γέτας, ὁ δοῦλος the entry μήτηρ Σωστράτου seems to have
been omitted (see on line 430). B here and elsewhere has
σιμικη (see on 636).

DRAMATIS PERSONAE, in order of speaking:

The god Pan, speaker of the prologue
Chaireas, a friend of Sostratos[1]
Sostratos, a young man in love
Pyrrhias, a slave in Sostratos' family
Knemon, the peevish old fellow
Knemon's daughter, still unmarried
Daos, the slave of Gorgias
Gorgias, a young farmer, half-sister to Knemon's daughter
Sikon, a cook
Getas, a slave in Sostratos' family
Sostratos' mother[2]
Simiche, an old woman, Knemon's slave
Kallippides, Sostratos' father

Mute characters: a group of people accompanying Sostratos's mother to the sacrifice at the shrine of Pan (these include Plangon, Sostratos' sister; Parthenis, a hired girl-piper; and two male slaves, Donax and Syros); Myrrhine, Knemon's wife and Gorgias' mother by a former marriage; the piper who accompanies the scene from 880 to 958; and—if it can be called a mute—the sheep brought by Sikon on his first appearance. There is a conventional chorus of tipsy revellers, characterised here as Pan-worshippers, to perform the entr'actes.

[1] The cast-list in the papyrus identifies Chaireas as a ' parasite ' (see the note after line 49). If this identification has any authority—and of that we cannot be certain—its implication will be only that Chaireas' friendship for Sostratos was bought rather than freely given.
[2] Omitted by the cast-list in the papyrus.

ΔΥΣΚΟΛΟΣ

(*SCENE: Phyle, a village about thirteen miles north-west of Athens on the slopes of Mount Parnes. A country lane, backed by three buildings. In the centre is a shrine dedicated to Pan and the Nymphs. On one side of it (spectators' left, probably) is Knemon's farmhouse; on*

ΠΑΝ

(KT fr. 115) τῆς Ἀττικῆς νομίζετ' εἶναι τὸν τόπον,
Φυλήν, τὸ νυμφαῖον δ' ὅθεν προέρχομαι
Φυλασίων καὶ τῶν δυναμένων τὰς πέτρας
ἐνθάδε γεωργεῖν, ἱερὸν ἐπιφανὲς πάνυ.
5 τὸν ἀγρὸν δὲ τὸν [ἐ]πὶ δεξί' οἰκεῖ τουτονὶ
Κνήμων, ἀπάνθρωπός τις ἄνθρωπος σφόδρα
καὶ δύσκολος πρὸς ἅπαντας, οὐ χαίρων τ' ὄχλῳ—
" ὄχλῳ " λέγω; ζ[ῶ]ν οὗτος ἐπιεικῶς χρόνον
πολὺν λελάληκεν ἡδέως ἐν τῷ βίῳ
10 οὐδενί, προσηγόρευκε πρότερος δ' οὐδένα
πλὴν ἐξ ἀνάγκης γειτνιῶν παριών τ' ἐμέ,

In the apparatus to this play, those corrections and supplements whose author is not named were made by the ed. pr., V. Martin, *Papyrus Bodmer IV. Ménandre: Le Dyscolos*, Cologny-Geneva 1958. 10 οὐδενί Diano, Lloyd-Jones: ουδεν B.

184

DYSKOLOS
(The Peevish Fellow)

*he other, Gorgias' farmhouse.   The time is early morn-
ng.)*

*The god Pan enters from his shrine, to deliver the pro-
ogue.)*

PAN

magine that the scene's in Attica—
.t's Phyle—and the shrine from which I come
3elongs to the villagers and people who
Can farm the rocks here; it's a holy place
Of great renown.[1]   This farm here on the right's[2]   5
Where Knemon lives, a hermit of a man,
Peevish to everybody, loathing crowds—
Crowds' do I say?   He's lived a good long time
And never spoken willingly to anyone
n his life, never been the first to greet a man,   10
With one exception: me, his neighbour, Pan.

[1] The shrine of Pan and the Nymphs at Phyle was indeed
celebrated, but for the purposes of his play Menander is forced
to alter its site from the steep cliff face on the side of a gorge,
where it was in real life (cf. Handley's edition of the *Dyskolos*,
pp. 24 f.; a photograph of it forms the frontispiece to Bingen's
second edition of the play), to a country lane bounded by
arms.
[2] Pan's right, presumably, and the audience's left; but the
wording is ambiguous.

τὸν Πᾶνα. καὶ τοῦτ' εὐθὺς αὐτῷ μεταμέλει,
εὖ οἶδ'. ὅμως οὖν, τῷ τρόπῳ τοιοῦτος ὤν,
χήραν γυναῖκ' ἔγημε, τετελευτηκότος
15 αὐτῇ νεωστὶ τοῦ λαβόντος τὸ πρότερον
υἱοῦ τε καταλελειμμένου μικροῦ τότε.
ταύτῃ ζυγομαχῶν οὐ μόνον τὰς ἡμέρας
ἐπιλαμβάνων δὲ καὶ τὸ πολὺ νυκτὸς μέρος
ἔζη κακῶς. θυγάτριον αὐτῷ γίνεται·
20 ἔτι μᾶλλον. ὡς δ' ἦν τὸ κακὸν οἷον οὐθὲν ἂν
ἕτερον γένοιθ', ὁ βίος τ' ἐπίπονος καὶ πικρός,
ἀπῆλθε πρὸς τὸν υἱὸν ἡ γυνὴ πάλιν
τὸν πρότερον αὐτῇ γενόμενον. χωρίδιον
τούτῳ δ' ὑπάρχον ἦν τι μικρὸν ἐνθαδὶ
25 ἐν γειτόνων, οὗ διατρέφει νυνὶ κακῶς
τὴν μητέρ', αὑτόν, πιστὸν οἰκέτην θ' ἕνα
πατρῷον. ἤδη δ'. ἐστὶ μειρακύλλιον
ὁ παῖς ὑπὲρ τὴν ἡλικίαν τὸν νοῦν ἔχων·
προάγει γὰρ ἡ τῶν πραγμάτων ἐμπειρία.
30 ὁ γέρων δ' ἔχων τὴν θυγατέρ' αὐτὸς ζῇ μόνος
καὶ γραῦν θεράπαιναν, ξυλοφορῶν σκάπτων τ', ἀε[
πονῶν, ἀπὸ τούτων ἀρξάμενος τῶν γειτόνων
καὶ τῆς γυναικὸς μέχρι Χολαργέων κάτω
μισῶν ἐφεξῆς πάντας. ἡ δὲ παρθένος
35 γέγονεν ὁμοία τῇ τροφῇ τις, οὐδὲ ἓν
εἰδυῖα φλαῦρον. τὰς δὲ συντρόφους ἐμοὶ

---

12 Corr. several: τουστ' B. 14 τελευτηκοτος B. 15 λαμβα
νοντος B. 16 Corr. several: ποτε B. 18 Corr. Diano: πολ
τησνυκτος B. 26 θ' ἕνα several: θεναμα B. 31 σκαπτον
αιε[B. 36 φλαρουν B.

---

[1] Ancient Greeks did not dare walk past a shrine of Pan (se
the note below, on line 433) without greeting its tenant god

He's forced to greet me when he passes,[1] and
That makes him rueful right away, I know for sure!
And yet, despite his character, he married a
Widow, whose former husband had just died   15
And left her just then with a baby son.
He squabbled with her not just every day
But took up too a good part of each night
In living miserably.   A baby girl
Came—still worse.   When these troubles reached a 20
   point
Beyond all hope of change, and life was hard
And bitter, his wife left him and went back
To the son she'd had earlier.   He owned
A tiny plot of land here in the neighbourhood,[2]
And there with difficulty he now supports   25
His mother, himself, and one loyal family slave.
The boy's already quite grown up, with an
Old head upon his shoulders that belies
His age.   Experience matures a man.
The old husband lives his own life, with his daughter 30
And an old servant woman, carrying wood
And digging, always working.   He detests
The whole world, from his wife and neighbours here
Right to Cholargos[3] down there, every single man.
His daughter, though, is innocent like her   35
Upbringing, pure in thought.   She cherishes

who would be represented by a statue placed outside the
entrance to the shrine.

[2] Gorgias' house is separated from Knemon's by the shrine
of Pan, but the land of the two farms is imagined to be con-
tiguous.

[3] A village ten miles or so down the road to Athens, virtually
at sea level.

Νύμφας κολακεύουσ' ἐπιμελῶς τιμῶσά τε
πέπεικεν αὐτῆς ἐπιμέλειαν σχεῖν τινα
ἡμᾶς· νεανίσκον δὲ καὶ μαλ' εὐπόρου
40 πατ[ρ]ὸς γεωργοῦντος ταλάντων κτήματα
ἐντα]ῦθα πολλῶν, ἀστικὸν τῇ διατριβῇ,
ἥκο]ντ' ἐπὶ θήραν μετὰ κυνηγέτου τινὸς
φίλο]υ, κατὰ τύχην παραβαλόντ' εἰς τὸν τόπον
ἔρωτ'] ἔχειν πως ἐνθεαστικῶς ποῶ.
45 ταῦτ'] ἐστὶ τὰ κεφάλαια, τὰ καθ' ἕκαστα δὲ
ὄψεσθ'] ἐὰν βούλησθε· βουλήθητε δέ.
καὶ γὰ]ρ προσιόνθ' ὁρᾶν δοκῶ μοι τουτονὶ
τὸν ἐρῶντα τόν τε συγκ[υνηγέτη]ν ἅμα,
αὐτοῖς ὑπὲρ τούτων τι σ[υγκοινουμ]ένους.

ΧΑΙΡΕΑΣ

(ΚΤ fr. 120) τί φής; ἰδὼν ἐνθένδε παῖδ' ἐλευθέραν
51 τὰς πλησίον Νύμφας στεφ[ανο]ῦσαν, Σώστρατε,
ἐρῶν ἀπῆλθες εὐθύς;

ΣΩΣΤΡΑΤΟΣ

εὐθ[ύς].

39 τεκαι B. 43 παραλαβοντ' B. 44 Suppl. Bingen. 46 βου-
λεσθε B. 48 Suppl. several. 49 τισσ[B. 50 Suppl. ed. pr.:
εντανθαπα [......]θεραν B, ἐνθένδε or ἐνθέν γε πᾶς δ' ἐλευθε-
ρῶν mss. of Ammonius, Diff. 202, p. 53 Nickau. 52 Suppl.
several.

---

[1] The parasite, a conventional figure on the contemporary
comic stage, was usually a poor young man who obtained free
board from a richer friend in return for services of various
kinds. One of his specialities was acting as jester at his friend's
parties (cf. Handley's edition of the Dyskolos, on 57 ff.).

ith loving care the Nymphs who share my shrine;
he worships us, and so she's made us take
ome little care of her.   There is a boy
hose father's very rich and farms land here   40
orth many talents.   This boy lives in town,
ut he's [come] with a sportsman [friend (?)] to hunt
nd accidentally reached this very spot.
ve put him under a spell, and made him fall
n love.   That]'s the synopsis.   Now [you'll see]   45
he details, if you like: you'd better like!
n fact], I think I see that lovesick youth
pproaching with . his [hunting (?)] friend; they're both
bsorbed in their [discussion] of the affair.

Exit Pan into his shrine. Sostratos and his friend
haireas, identified in the cast list as a ' parasite ',[1] *now*
ater deep in conversation on their way from the estate of
ostratos' father, which must be imagined as situated off
age to the right.)

CHAIREAS

hat's that you say ?   You saw a girl from here,   50
free girl, Sostratos, crowning the Nymphs next door[2]
nd you emerged *in love*, at first sight ?

SOSTRATOS

At first sight.

---

[2] Sc. putting garlands on the heads of their statues.

MENANDER

ΧΑΙΡΕΑΣ

                                    ὡς ταχύ·
ἢ τοῦτ' ἐβεβούλευσ' ἐξιών, ἐρᾶ[ν] τινος;

ΣΩΣΤΡΑΤΟΣ

σκώπτεις· ἐγὼ δέ, Χαιρέα, κακῶς ἔχω.

ΧΑΙΡΕΑΣ

55 ἀλλ' οὐκ ἀπιστῶ.

ΣΩΣΤΡΑΤΟΣ

                        διόπερ ἥκω παραλαβὼν
σὲ πρὸς τὸ πρᾶγμα, καὶ φίλον καὶ πρακτικὸν
κρίνας μάλιστα.

ΧΑΙΡΕΑΣ

                        πρὸς τὰ τοιαῦτα, Σώστρατε,
οὕτως ἔχω· παραλαμβάνει τις τῶν φίλων
ἐρῶν ἑταίρας· εὐθὺς ἁρπάσας φέρω·
60 μεθύω, κατακάω, λόγον ὅλως οὐκ ἀνέχομαι·
πρὶν ἐξετάσαι γὰρ ἥτις ἐστί, δεῖ τυχεῖν.
τὸ μὲν βραδύνειν γὰρ τὸν ἔρωτ' αὔξει πολύ,
ἐν τῷ ταχέως δ' ἔνεστι παύσασθαι ταχύ.
γάμον λέγει τις καὶ κόρην ἐλευθέραν·
65 ἕτερός τίς εἰμ' ἐνταῦθα· πυνθάνομαι γένος,
βίον, τρόπους. εἰς πάντα τὸν λοιπὸν χρόνον
μνείαν γὰρ ἤδη τῷ φίλῳ καταλείπομαι
ὅσ' ἂν διοικήσω περὶ ταῦτα.

53 Corr. several: εβουλευσ' B. 56 απρακτικον B. 62 αυξάνει
B. 68 ὅσ' ἂν Handley: ὡσαν B.

DYSKOLOS

CHAIREAS

Quick work! Or had you planned, on leaving, to
Fall for a girl?

SOSTRATOS

You're laughing at me, Chaireas,
But I feel awful.

CHAIREAS

I believe you.

SOSTRATOS

That is why   55
I've brought you in on it. I thought you were a friend
And practical especially.

CHAIREAS

That, Sostratos,
Is what I am in such things. Say a friend's in love
With a *hetaira*.[1] I'm called in, snatch and bring
Her right away—get drunk, burn doors down—I'm   60
Deaf to all reason. You must strike before
You check on her identity. Delays
Increase a passion dangerously; brisk starts
Mean brisk conclusions. Say a man suggests
Marriage, a free girl. I'm a different man   65
Then—dossier on family, money, character.
I leave my friend in that case with a permanent
Record of my efficiency, you see!

---

[1] In the ancient Greek world, *hetairai* ranged from common
prostitutes to highly educated courtesans who might be good
dancers, musicians and conversationalists too. Their houses
seem to have been at the mercy of drunken bands of young
louts who would retaliate against locked doors by firing them
with torches (cf. Headlam's note in the Headlam–Knox edition
of Herodas, on 2. 34–7).

MENANDER

ΣΩΣΤΡΑΤΟΣ

                            καὶ μάλ᾽ εὖ,
οὐ πάνυ δ᾽ ἀρεσκόντως ἐμοί.

ΧΑΙΡΕΑΣ

                           καὶ νῦν γε δεῖ
70 ταῦτα διακοῦσαι πρῶτον ἡμᾶς.

ΣΩΣΤΡΑΤΟΣ

                              ὄρθριον
τὸν Πυρρίαν τὸν συγκυνηγὸν οἴκοθεν
ἐγὼ πέπομφα—

ΧΑΙΡΕΑΣ

πρὸς τίν᾽;

ΣΩΣΤΡΑΤΟΣ

                         αὐτῷ τῷ πατρὶ
ἐντευξόμενον τῆς παιδὸς ἢ τῷ κυρίῳ
τῆς οἰκίας ὅστις ποτ᾽ ἐστίν.

ΧΑΙΡΕΑΣ

                          Ἡράκλεις,
75 οἷον λέγεις.

ΣΩΣΤΡΑΤΟΣ

                ἥμαρτον· οὐ γὰρ οἰκέτῃ
ἥρμοττ᾽ ἴσως τὸ τοιοῦτον. ἀλλ᾽ οὐ ῥᾴδιον

---

76 Corr. Kamerbeek: ἥρμοστ᾽ B. τοιουτ᾽ B.

DYSKOLOS

SOSTRATOS

'hat's very good, (*aside*) but doesn't suit me at all!

CHAIREAS

And first now we must hear about this problem.　　　70

SOSTRATOS

At first light I sent Pyrrhias out—he's my
Hunting companion[1]—on an errand.

CHAIREAS

　　　　　　　　　　　Where?

SOSTRATOS

To meet the girl's father in person, or
Whoever's the head of the household.

CHAIREAS

　　　　　　　　　　　　　Heracles,

What *are* you saying?

SOSTRATOS

　　　　　　　　Yes, I did wrong.　Such jobs　75
Are not for slaves, perhaps.　When you're in love,

---

[1] There is a difficulty here, caused partly by tears in the
papyrus at crucial points of lines 42 and 48, partly by some un-
characteristically loose writing by Menander.　Here, at line 71,
Sostratos identifies his slave Pyrrhias as his 'hunting com-
panion'; in the prologue, however, Pan says that Sostratos
had been hunting with a 'sportsman [friend (?)]' (42 f.), and
goes on apparently to identify that '[hunting (?)] friend' as
Chaireas (48), if τὸν . . . συγκ[υνηγέτη]ν is correctly supple-
mented there.　In fact no other supplement approaches that in
plausibility, given the length of the papyrus gap and the general
configuration of Pan's speech as he introduces Chaireas to the
audience.

ἐρῶντα συνιδεῖν ἐστι τί ποτε συμφέρει.
καὶ τὴν διατριβὴν ἥτις ἔστ' αὐτοῦ πάλαι
τεθαύμακ'· εἰρήκειν γὰρ εὐθὺς οἴκαδε
80 αὐτῷ παρεῖναι πυθομένῳ τἀνταῦθά μοι.

ΠΥΡΡΙΑΣ

πάρες, φυλάττου, πᾶς ἄπελθ' ἐκ τοῦ μέσου·
μαίνεθ' ὁ διώκων, μαίνεται.

ΣΩΣΤΡΑΤΟΣ
                    τί τοῦτο, παῖ;

ΠΥΡΡΙΑΣ

φεύγετε.

ΣΩΣΤΡΑΤΟΣ
        τί ἐστι;

ΠΥΡΡΙΑΣ
                βάλλομαι βώλοις, λίθοις·
ἀπόλωλα.

ΣΩΣΤΡΑΤΟΣ
βάλλει; ποῖ, κακόδαιμον;

ΠΥΡΡΙΑΣ
                                οὐκέτι
85 ἴσως διώκει;

Though, it's not easy to make out what's best.
And why's Pyrrhias so long?   For ages I've
Been wondering.   I told him to come straight home
When he'd discovered there the facts for me.   80

*At this point Pyrrhias enters from the left, running
blindly and breathlessly.)*

PYRRHIAS

Let me pass, look out, everybody get
Out of my way.   He's mad, the man who's chasing me,
Mad.

SOSTRATOS
What's this, boy?

PYRRHIAS
Run!

SOSTRATOS
What's the matter?

PYRRHIAS
Earth and stones
Being thrown at me.   I'm all in.

SOSTRATOS
Thrown?   You wretch, where are
You off to?

*Pyrrhias has been attempting to reach the opposite exit.
Now he stands still, and for the first time gingerly looks
round, over his shoulder.)*

PYRRHIAS
He's not chasing me perhaps now?

MENANDER

ΣΩΣΤΡΑΤΟΣ

μὰ Δί'.

ΠΥΡΡΙΑΣ

ἐγὼ δ' ᾤμην.

ΣΩΣΤΡΑΤΟΣ

τί δὲ

λέγεις;

ΠΥΡΡΙΑΣ

ἀπαλλαγῶμεν, ἱκετεύω σε.

ΣΩΣΤΡΑΤΟΣ

ποῖ;

ΠΥΡΡΙΑΣ

ἀπὸ τῆς θύρας ἐντεῦθεν ὡς πορρωτάτω.
'Οδύνης γὰρ ὑὸς ἢ κακοδαιμονῶν τις ἢ
μελαγχολῶν ἄνθρωπος οἰκῶ[ν . . . . .]ει
90 τὴν οἰκίαν πρὸς ὅν μ' ἔπεμπ[ες —◡‿
μεγάλου κακοῦ· τοὺς δακτύλους [κατέαξα γὰρ
σχεδόν τι προσπταίων ἅπα[ντας.

ΣΩΣΤΡΑΤΟΣ

['Ηράκλεις,

ἐλθὼν τί πεπαρῴνηκε δεῦρο;

85 τιδ'αιᵉ B.   88 κακοδαίμων B.   90–95 Supplementation,
speech-division and assignation of parts are highly uncertain;
the text printed is *exempli gratia*.   90 Suppl. Page.   91 Suppl.
several.   92 ἅπα[ντας suppl. ed. pr., 'Ηράκλεις Handley.

SOSTRATOS

No, 85

By Zeus.

PYRRHIAS

I thought he was.

SOSTRATOS

What do you mean?

PYRRHIAS

Let's go

From here, please.

SOSTRATOS

Where?

PYRRHIAS

As far as we can from

That door there![1]   He's a son of grief, berserk,
A lunatic, the man you sent me to,
Who lives [there (?)], in that house!   [O gods above (?)], 90
What hideous trouble!   [I have] stubbed and [broken]
Just every single toe!

SOSTRATOS

[O Heracles (?)],

What's he been up to, coming here?

[1] Sc. Knemon's.

ΧΑΙΡΕΑΣ

[παραφρονῶν
εὔδηλός ἐστι.

ΠΥΡΡΙΑΣ

νὴ Δί᾽, ἐξώλ[ης ἄρα,
95 Σώ]στρατ᾽, ἀπολο[ίμην· ἔχε] δέ πως φυλακτικῶς
ἀλλ᾽ οὐ δύναμαι λ[έγειν· προ]σέστηκεν δέ μοι
τὸ πνεῦμα. κόψας [τὴν θύ]ραν τῆς οἰκίας
τὸν κύριον ζητεῖν [ἔφ]ην· προῆλθέ μοι
γραῦς τις κακοδαίμων, α[ὐτ]όθεν δ᾽ οὗ νῦν λέγων
100 ἕστηκ᾽, ἔδειξεν αὐτὸν ἐπὶ τοῦ λοφιδίου
ἐκεῖ περιφθειρόμενον ἀχράδας ἢ πολὺν
κύφων᾽ ἑαυτῷ συλλέγονθ᾽.

ΧΑΙΡΕΑΣ
ὡς ὀργίλως.

ΠΥΡΡΙΑΣ

τί, ὦ μακάρι᾽; ἐγὼ μὲν εἰς τὸ χωρίον
ἐμβὰς ἐπορευόμην πρὸς αὐτὸν καὶ πάνυ
105 πόρρωθεν, εἶναί τις φιλάνθρωπος σφόδρα
ἐπιδέξιός τε βουλόμενος, προσεῖπα καὶ
" ἥκω τι," φημί, " πρός σε, πάτερ, ἰδεῖν τί σε
σπεύδων ὑπὲρ σοῦ πρᾶγμ᾽." ὁ δ᾽ εὐθύς, " ἀνόσι‹
ἄνθρωπε," φησίν, " εἰς τὸ χωρίον δέ μου

93 Suppl. several.   94 Suppl. Handley (ἐξώλ[ης several).   95‹
98 Suppl. several.   98 προῆλθε Sandbach: προσῆλθε B.   10‹
In the left-hand margin B appears to identify the speaker o‹
the words ὡς ὀργίλως as χα]ιρ (σωσ]τρ and π]υρ are possibl‹
interpretations of the traces, however).   105 εἶναιφιλάνθρω‹
πόστις B.   108 ὁ δ᾽ om. B, suppl. several.

DYSKOLOS

CHAIREAS

He's [mad (?)],

Quite clearly!

PYRRHIAS

By Zeus, Sostratos, I'd [sooner be (?)]
Completely pulverised!   Keep on the alert,   95
Though.   Oh, I can't [speak properly], I'm short
Of breath.   I knocked at [the] door of the house
And [said] I'd like to see the owner.   Out came a
Pathetic hag, and from here, where I'm standing now[1]
Talking to you, she pointed him out on the hill,   100
Going round his bloody pears and picking up
A load of troubles for himself!

*(Pyrrhias has worked himself into a fury.   Chaireas'
next remark, aside to Sostratos, refers to the tone and
vocabulary of Pyrrhias' last words.)*

CHAIREAS
What fury!

PYRRHIAS

What, *dear* sir ?—Then I stepped onto his land
And walked towards him.   I was still a good
Way from him, but I wanted to be a   105
Friendly and tactful sort of fellow, so
I greeted him. ' I've come,' I said, ' on business,
To see you, sir, on business, it's to your
Advantage.'   Right away, ' Damned heathen,' he

---

[1] Lines 89 to 99 inclusive are irritatingly damaged in the
papyrus; supplements, part-division, and general interpreta-
tion are highly uncertain in several places, especially between
lines 90 and 95.

110 ἥκεις σύ; τί μαθών; ” βῶλον αἴρεταί τινα·
τὴν αὐτὴν ἀφίησ᾽ εἰς τὸ πρόσωπον αὐτό μου.

ΧΑΙΡΕΑΣ

ἐς κόρακας.

ΠΥΡΡΙΑΣ

ἐν ὅσῳ δ᾽ “ ἀλλά σ᾽ ὁ Ποσειδῶν— ” λέγων
κατέμυσα, χάρακα λαμβάνει πάλιν τινά·
ἐκάθαιρέ μ᾽ αὐτῇ, “ σοὶ δὲ κἀμοὶ πρᾶγμα τί
115 ἔστιν; ” λέγων, “ τὴν δημοσίαν οὐκ οἶσθ᾽ ὁδόν; ”
ὀξύτατον ἀναβοῶν τι.

ΧΑΙΡΕΑΣ

μαινόμενον λέγεις
τελέως γεωργόν.

ΠΥΡΡΙΑΣ

τὸ δὲ πέρας· φεύγοντα γὰρ
δεδίωχ᾽ ἴσως με στάδια πέντε καὶ δέκα,
περὶ τὸν λόφον πρώτιστον, εἶθ᾽ οὕτω κάτω
120 εἰς τὸ δασὺ τοῦτο, σφενδονῶν βώλοις, λίθοις,
ταῖς ἀχράσιν ὡς οὐκ εἶχεν οὐδὲν ἀλλ᾽ ἔτι.
ἀνήμερόν τι πρᾶγμα, τελέως ἀνόσιος
γέρων. ἱκετεύω σ᾽, ἄπιτε.

ΣΩΣΤΡΑΤΟΣ

δειλίαν λέγεις.

110 σύ om. B, suppl. Kassel and (without its mark of interrogation) Page.   111 ἀφίησιν B.   112 ησκορακας B.   113 In the right-hand margin B has μαστιγγ[α, a misinterpretation presumably of χάρακα.   114 μ᾽ αὐτῇ Arnott (after Handley's ταύτη μ᾽ἐκάθαιρε): ταύτην B.   118 Corr. several: δεδιωκ᾽ B.

Said, ' trespassing on my land?   What's your game?'   110
He picked a lump of earth up, which he threw
Smack in my face!

CHAIREAS
Hell!

PYRRHIAS
While I shut my eyes
And said 'Poseidon blast you,' he'd now grabbed a
  stake
Again and flogged me with it, said ' What dealings
Do we have?   Don't you know the public road?'   115
He bawled fortissimo.

CHAIREAS
This farmer sounds
A perfect madman.

PYRRHIAS
Here's the ending.   I
Took to my heels, and he's chased after me
Some fifteen stades,[1] first round the hill, then right
Down into this copse, slinging sods and stones,   120
Those pears, too, when he'd nothing else left.   What
A savage brute, an absolutely vile
Old man!   Get out of here, *please*!

SOSTRATOS
That is cowardice!

---

[1] Nearly two miles.   A stade measured 202 yards.

MENANDER

ΠΥΡΡΙΑΣ

οὐκ ἴστε τὸ κακὸν οἷόν ἐστι· κατέδεται
125 ἡμᾶς.

ΧΑΙΡΕΑΣ

    τυχὸν ἴσως ὅδ' ὀδυνώμενός τι νῦν
τετύχηκε· διόπερ ἀναβαλέσθαι μοι δοκεῖ
αὐτῷ προσελθεῖν, Σώστρατ'. εὖ τοῦτ' ἴσθ' ὅτι
πρὸς πάντα πράγματ' ἐστὶ πρακτικώτερον
εὐκαιρία.

ΠΥΡΡΙΑΣ

    νοῦν ἔχεθ'.

ΧΑΙΡΕΑΣ

    ὑπέρπικρον δέ τί
130 ἐστιν πένης γεωργός, οὐχ οὗτος μόνος,
σχεδὸν δ' ἅπαντες. ἀλλ' ἕωθεν αὔριον
ἐγὼ πρόσειμ' αὐτῷ μόνος, τὴν οἰκίαν
ἐπείπερ οἶδα. νῦν δ' ἀπελθὼν οἴκαδε
καὶ σὺ διάτριβε. τοῦτο δ' ἕξει κατὰ τρόπον.

ΠΥΡΡΙΑΣ

135 πράττωμεν οὕτως.

ΣΩΣΤΡΑΤΟΣ

    πρόφασιν οὗτος ἄσμενος
εἴληφεν· εὐθὺς φανερὸς ἦν οὐχ ἡδέως
μετ' ἐμοῦ βαδίζων, οὐδὲ δοκιμάζων πάνυ
τὴν ἐπιβολ]ὴν τὴν τοῦ γάμου. κακὸν δέ σε

125 τυχῶν B. ὅδ' ὀδυνώμενος Kraus, Zuntz: ουδυνωμένος B.
128 πρακτικώτατον B before correction. 135 πράττομεν B.
136 Corr. several: εἴληφενευθὺς B.

DYSKOLOS

PYRRHIAS

You don't realise the mess we're in!   He will
Eat us alive!

CHAIREAS

          He may perhaps have been   125
A bit upset just now.   So, Sostratos, I think
We ought to put off seeing him.   You can
Be pretty sure, in all you do, that tact's
A more effective course.

PYRRHIAS

          You make good sense.

CHAIREAS

Poor farmers are hot-tempered—not just him,   130
But nearly all of them.   Tomorrow, at first light,
I'll go and see him by myself; I know
The house.   And you had better go back home
As well, and wait there.   This'll be all right.

PYRRHIAS

Let's do that.

(*As Pyrrhias speaks, exit Chaireas off right.*)

SOSTRATOS

          He's delighted to have found   135
An excuse!   It was clear right from the start
He didn't want to come with me or think
Much of my [plan] to marry.   As for you—

MENANDER

κακῶς ἄπ]αντες ἀπολέσειαν οἱ θεοί,
140 μαστιγία.]

ΠΥΡΡΙΑΣ
τί] δ' ἠδίκηκα, Σώστρατε;

ΣΩΣΤΡΑΤΟΣ
κακὸν ἐπό]εις τὸ χωρίον τι δηλάδη
κλέπτων.]

ΠΥΡΡΙΑΣ
ἔκλεπτον;

ΣΩΣΤΡΑΤΟΣ
ἀλλ' ἐμαστίγου σέ τις
οὐδὲν ἀδικοῦντα;

ΠΥΡΡΙΑΣ
καὶ πάρεστί γ' οὑτοσὶ
αὐτός· ὑπάγω, βέλτιστε· σὺ δὲ τούτῳ λάλει.

ΣΩΣΤΡΑΤΟΣ
145 οὐκ ἂ[ν] δυναίμην· ἀπίθανός τίς εἰμ' ἀεὶ

140–50 Portions of these lines (the opening 1½ metra,
generally) are preserved in H. 140 Suppl. several:]εηδι
κηκα B,]δ' or]σ'ηδικη[H.   141 Suppl. Ritchie:]εις B,
]...εις H.   142 Suppl. Arnott:]επον: B,].[.].[.]εκλεπτ
ον H.   The point at which Pyrrhias begins to speak is un-
certain.   143]οῦντα: B.   143–44 Speech assignment thus
given by several (B has dicola after ουτοσι and]βελτιστε; in
H, where the end of 144 is missing, there is no dicolon after
βελτιστε, probably none after υπαγω, while some scholars think
that they can see]ρρι (= Πυ]ρρί(ας)) written in the left-hand
margin of 143).   145 Suppl. Grenfell, Hunt:]αιμην B.

DYSKOLOS

May all the gods blast you [to kingdom come],
[You rogue! (?)]

PYRRHIAS
[What] have I done wrong, Sostratos? 140

SOSTRATOS
It's quite plain.   You [damaged (?)] his land, [you
   stole (?)]
Something.

PYRRHIAS
I stole?

SOSTRATOS
You mean, a man lashed out
At you when you weren't guilty?

PYRRHIAS
Yes—and look!
He's here himself now!   (*To Knemon*) Sir, I'm off!
   (*To Sostratos*) *You* talk to him!

(*With these words Pyrrhias departs off right.   Knemon
now becomes visible, entering from the left at a resolutely
brisk pace.   The length of the ancient Greek stage makes
it possible for Sostratos to complete his speech and take
refuge at the back of the stage, as far as possible from the
door of Knemon's house, before Knemon reaches the
centre of the stage.*)

SOSTRATOS
I couldn't!   When I talk, my arguments 145

ἐν τῷ λαλεῖν. ποῖον λέγει[ν δεῖ τουτο]νί;
οὐ πάνυ φιλάνθρωπον βλ[έπειν μ]οι φαίνεται,
μὰ τὸν Δί'· ὡς δ' ἐσπούδακ'. ἐπ[ανά]ξω βραχὺ
ἀπὸ τῆς θύρας· βέλτιον. ἀλλὰ κ[αὶ β]οᾷ
150 μόνος βαδίζων· οὐχ ὑγιαίνειν μ[οι] δοκεῖ.
δέδοικα μέντοι, μὰ τὸν Ἀπόλλω καὶ θεούς,
αὐτόν· τί γὰρ ἄν τις μὴ οὐχὶ τἀληθῆ λέγοι;

KNHMΩN

εἶτ' οὐ μακάριος ἦν ὁ Περσεὺς κατὰ δύο
τρόπους ἐκεῖνος, ὅτι πετηνὸς ἐγένετο
155 κοὐδενὶ συνήντα τῶν βαδιζόντων χαμαί,
εἶθ' ὅτι τοιοῦτο κτῆμ' ἐκέκτηθ' ᾧ λίθους
ἅπαντας ἐπόει τοὺς ἐνοχλοῦντας; ὅπερ ἐμοὶ
νυνὶ γένοιτ'· οὐδὲν γὰρ ἀφθονώτερον
λιθίνων γένοιτ' ἂν ἀνδριάντων πανταχοῦ.
160 νῦν δ' οὐ βιωτόν ἐστι, μὰ τὸν Ἀσκληπιόν.
λαλοῦσ' ἐπεμβαίνοντες εἰς τὸ χωρίον
ἤδη. παρ' αὐτὴν τὴν ὁδὸν γάρ, νὴ Δία,
εἴωθα διατρίβειν· ὃς οὐδ' ἐργάζομαι
τοῦτο τὸ μέρος τοῦ χωρίου, πέφευγα δὲ
165 διὰ τοὺς παριόντας. ἀλλ' ἐπὶ τοὺς λόφους ἄνω
ἤδη διώκουσ'. ὦ πολυπληθείας ὄχλου.
οἴμοι· πάλιν τις οὑτοσὶ πρὸς ταῖς θύραις
ἕστηκεν ἡμῶν.

146 Lloyd-Jones opposes any change of speaker (B has paragraphus and]νι: while H may have paragraphus). 147, 148, 149 Suppl. several. 148 ωσδ' B: ουδ' altered to ως H. 151 καιτουσθεους B. 156 ωιλιθινους B. 159 ἂν om. B. 164 τοῦτο τὸ μέρος τοῦ χωρίου Barrett, Thierfelder: τοιουτοτομεροσχωριου B. 167 προταις B.

DYSKOLOS

Are always unconvincing!—How [could one (?)]
    describe
[A man like *him*[1] (?)]? His look doesn't seem to me
At all benevolent, by Zeus no! What
Determination! I'll move from the door
A bit. That's better. Why, he's walking by himself, 150
Yelling. He doesn't look sane. Apollo and the gods,
I'm scared of him—why not admit the truth?

(*Knemon, who now occupies the centre of the stage, has not
noticed Sostratos yet. He addresses the audience.*)

KNEMON

Well, wasn't that Perseus such a lucky fellow,[2]
On two accounts? He had some wings, and so
Didn't meet any pedestrians on the ground.   155
And then he owned a sort of instrument
With which he petrified all who annoyed him!
I wish *I* had one now! Then nothing would
Be commoner all over than stone statues!
But now life's not worth living, by Asclepius.   160
Today men trespass on my land and—talk!
You think I usually waste my time along
The roadside? I don't cultivate at all
That part of my land, I've abandoned it because
Of all the travellers. Now they chase me up   165
Onto the hill-tops. Oh, the teeming, swarming crowds!
Oh no! Here's one more of them, standing by
Our door!

---

[1] Sc. Knemon.
[2] Perseus' winged sandals were given to him by the god
Hermes, to help him on his crusade against the Gorgon
Medusa. When he killed her, he cut off her head, which had
the power even in death to turn all who looked on it to stone.

MENANDER

ΣΩΣΤΡΑΤΟΣ

ἆρα τυπτήσει γέ με;

ΚΝΗΜΩΝ

ἐρημίας οὐκ ἔστιν οὐδαμοῦ τυχεῖν,
170 οὐδ᾽ ἂν ἀπάγξασθαί τις ἐπιθυμῶν τύχῃ.

ΣΩΣΤΡΑΤΟΣ

ἐμοὶ χαλεπαίνει;—περιμένω, πάτερ, τινὰ
ἐνταῦθα· συνεθέμην γάρ.

ΚΝΗΜΩΝ

           οὐκ ἐγὼ 'λέγον;
τουτὶ στοὰν νενομίκατ᾽ ἢ τὸ τοῦ Λεώ;
πρὸς τὰς ἐμὰς θύρας, ἐὰν ἰδεῖν τινα
175 βούλησθε, συντάττεσθ᾽ ἀπαντᾶν· παντελῶς,
καὶ θῶκον οἰκοδομήσατ᾽, ἂν ἔχητε νοῦν,
μᾶλλον δὲ καὶ συνέδριον. ὦ τάλας ἐγώ·
ἐπηρεασμὸς τὸ κακὸν εἶναί μοι δοκεῖ.

---

168 τυπησεις B. 169–74 Scraps of the ends of these lines are
preserved in H. 173 τουτοτι B. Λεώ (as proper name)
Koumanoudis, Wycherley: λεω B. 175 Corr. Lloyd-Jones:
συνταττεσθεπαντα B. 176 Corr. several: εαν B. 177 συνε
δριον:ω B (without, however, any paragraphus under the
beginning of the line).

---

¹ In the Athenian agora there were several stoas, long open
colonnades, where people could shelter from rain, sun or wind,
walk, watch processions, meet friends, talk, and transact many
kinds of official or private business.
² Leos was one of the Athenian heroes after whom a political
tribe was named. According to the legend he sacrificed his

DYSKOLOS

SOSTRATOS (*aside*)

I wonder if he means to hit me?

KNEMON (*still addressing the audience*)

A man can't find privacy anywhere,
Not even if he wants to hang himself!　　　　　　　170

(*Sostratos comes tentatively forward.　His first remark is
made aside, then he plucks up courage to address Knemon.*)

SOSTRATOS

Is he annoyed with me?—Sir, here I'm waiting
For someone, by arrangement.

KNEMON

　　　　　　　　　Didn't I say so?　Do
You people think this is a stoa,[1] or
The shrine of Leos[2]?　If you want to see
A man, arrange to meet him at my door.　　　　　　175
Yes—build a bench, if you've a mind to it,
Or better still, a council chamber!　Oh, it breaks
My heart!　It's interference that's the trouble,
In my judgment!

(*Knemon storms off into his house, leaving Sostratos alone
on stage.*)

daughters for the good of the city.　His shrine (which may
have been identical with that of his daughters, the so-called
Leokoreion) seems to have been a popular rendezvous in the
Athenian agora (cf. H. A. Thompson and R. E. Wycherley,
The Agora of Athens [*The Athenian Agora, volume XIV*:
Princeton 1972], 121 ff.).

ΣΩΣΤΡΑΤΟΣ

οὐ τοῦ τυχόντος, ὡς ἐμοὶ δοκεῖ, πόνου
180 τουτὶ τὸ πρᾶγμά γ᾽, ἀλλὰ συντονωτέρου·
πρόδηλόν ἐστιν. ἆρ᾽ ἐγὼ πορεύσομαι
ἐπὶ τὸν Γέταν τὸν τοῦ πατρός; νὴ τοὺς θεούς,
ἔγωγ᾽. ἔχει τι διάπυρον καὶ πραγμάτων
ἔμπειρός ἐστι παντοδαπῶν· τὸ δύσκολον
185 τὸ τοῦδ᾽ ἐκεῖνος πᾶν ἀπώσετ᾽, οἶδ᾽ ἐγώ.
τὸ μὲν χρόνον γὰρ ἐμποεῖν τῷ πράγματι
ἀποδοκιμάζω· πόλλ᾽ ἐν ἡμέρᾳ μιᾷ
γένοιτ᾽ ἄν. ἀλλὰ τὴν θύραν πέπληχέ τις.

ΚΟΡΗ

οἴμοι τάλαινα τῶν ἐμῶν ἐγὼ κακῶν·
190 τί νῦν ποήσω; τὸν κάδον γὰρ ἡ τροφὸς
ἱμῶσ᾽ ἀφῆκεν εἰς τὸ φρέαρ.

ΣΩΣΤΡΑΤΟΣ

                ὦ Ζεῦ πάτερ
καὶ Φοῖβε Παιάν, ὦ Διοσκόρω φίλ[ω,
κάλλους ἀμάχου.

ΚΟΡΗ

              θερμὸν δ᾽ ὕδωρ πρ[οσέταξέ μοι
ποιεῖν ὁ πάππας εἰσιών.

180 γ᾽ om. B, suppl. several.   183 τι om. B, suppl. several
185 τὸ τοῦδ᾽ several: τοτουτουδ᾽ B.   πᾶν om. B, suppl. Dian
(other supplements are possible).   απωσαιτ᾽ B.   187 πολλ
δ᾽ανημεραῖ B.   192 Corr. Sandbach: διοσκουρω B.   193 καλου
B.   δ᾽ om. B, suppl. several.   πρ[οσέταξε suppl. ed. pr., μο

DYSKOLOS

SOSTRATOS

This operation needs,
think, no ordinary effort, it demands   180
initiative! That's evident. Shall I
etch Getas, father's slave? Yes, by the gods,
l do that. He's a ball of fire, experienced in
ll kinds of things. I'm certain he'll shake all
at dragon's peevish temper out of him.   185
don't approve of temporising in
is matter. A great deal could happen in
single day—but somebody's unlatched *his* door!

(*nter, from Knemon's house, his daughter, carrying a
rge jar. She doesn't see Sostratos at first.*)

GIRL

m so unhappy, oh, it's all gone wrong!
hat am I going to do now? Nurse was hauling up 190
he bucket, and she dropped it in the well!

SOSTRATOS (*enraptured*)

ather Zeus, Healer Phoebus, dear Dioscuri,[1]
hat irresistible beauty!

GIRL (*still unaware of Sostratos' presence*)
                    Daddy [told me],
hen he came in, to heat some water.

[1] Castor and Polydeuces, the twin sons of Zeus and Leda.

---

veral. 194–201 Supplementation is uncertain; the text
pplied is *exempli gratia.* 194 εἰσιών Zuntz: εξιων B.

MENANDER

ΣΩΣΤΡΑΤΟΣ

ἄνδρε[ς, τρέμω.

KOPH

195 ἐὰν δὲ τοῦτ' αἴσθητ', ἀπολεῖ κακ[ῶς πάνυ
παίων ἐκείνην. οὐ σχολὴ μάτ[ην λαλεῖν·
ὦ φίλταται Νύμφαι, παρ' ὑμῶν λη[πτέον.
αἰσχύνομαι μέν, εἴ τινες θύουσ' ἆ[ρα
ἔνδον, ἐνοχλεῖν—

ΣΩΣΤΡΑΤΟΣ

ἀλλ' ἂν ἐμοὶ δῷ[ς, αὐτίκα
200 βάψας ἐγώ σοι τ[ὴν ὑδρίαν ἥ]ξω φέρων.

KOPH

ναὶ πρὸς θεῶν, ἀ[νύσας γ'.]

ΣΩΣΤΡΑΤΟΣ

ἐλευθερίως γέ πως
ἄγροικός ἐστιν. ὦ [πολυτί]μητοι θεοί,
τίς ἄν με σῶσαι δ[αιμό]νων;

KOPH

τάλαιν' ἐγώ,
τίς ἐψόφηκεν; ἆρ' ὁ [πά]ππας ἔρχεται;

---

194 τρέμω suppl. Peek. 195 τουτουτο B. Suppl. Kass.
196 B has either εκεινην·ου or εκεινην:ου (without paragraphu
however). Suppl. Gallavotti, Georgoulis. 197 Suppl. Barret
198 θυος B.

DYSKOLOS

SOSTRATOS

Audience,

'm trembling! (?)]

GIRL

If he hears about this, he'll   195
Curse and (?)] beat her to death. No time for [idle
talk! (?)]
• dearest Nymphs, *you* must [supply] our water.
[there's a sacrifice, though, going on in there
Perhaps], I'd hesitate to interfere . . .

SOSTRATOS (*advancing to the girl*)

Well, if
You give] it me, I'll fill [the jar] for you, and have   200
t here [in no time].

GIRL (*handing Sostratos the jar*)

By the gods, yes, [hurry! (?)]

SOSTRATOS
(*aside, as he goes off into the shrine with the jar*)

country girl, yet there's a kind of poise . . .
• [honoured] gods, what power could save me now?

*The girl is now alone on stage. Immediately the noise of
door being unbolted is heard.*)

GIRL

Oh no! Who's at the door? Is daddy coming?

---

uppl. several. 199 δῶ[ς suppl. several, αὐτίκα Shipp.   200
Spíav suppl. several. 201 Suppl. Webster. 203 με Lloyd-
ones: εμε B. δ[αιμό]νων suppl. Barrett.

205 ἔπειτα πληγὰς λ[ή]ψομ᾽, ἄν με καταλάβῃ
    ἔξω.

ΔΑΟΣ

    διατρίβω σοι διακονῶν πάλαι
ἐνταῦθ᾽, ὁ δὲ σκάπτει μόνος. πορευτέον
πρὸς ἐκεῖνόν ἐστιν. ὦ κάκιστ᾽ ἀπολουμένη
Πενία, τί σ᾽ ἡ[μ]εῖς τηλικοῦτ᾽ ἐφεύρομεν;
210 τί τοσοῦτον ἡμῖν ἐνδελεχῶς οὕτω χρόνον
ἔνδον κάθησαι καὶ συνοικεῖς;

ΣΩΣΤΡΑΤΟΣ

                              λάμβανε
τηνδί.

ΚΟΡΗ

    φέρε δεῦρο.

ΔΑΟΣ

            τί ποτε βούλεθ᾽ οὑτοσὶ
ἄνθρωπος;

205 Corr. several: εαν B.   207 σκεπτει B.   211 καθοσαι B
212 ποτε βούλεθ᾽ Szemerényi: ποτ᾽εβουλετο B.   213-2[
Speech assignments first divined by Grassi (B has dicola aft[
πατρος 213 and κακοδαιμων 214, a paragraphus under 214, an[
πυρριας (!) in the right-hand margin).

'll get a hiding if he finds me outside!

*(The girl moves back towards her door, but the door which
opens is that of Gorgias' house. Daos, Gorgias' slave,
emerges. His opening remark is addressed to Gorgias'
mother inside the house. At first he does not notice the
girl, who is now probably standing half-hidden by her
slightly open door.)*

DAOS

've spent a long time doing housework here
For you, while master's working on the farm
Without help. I must join him.—Poverty!
Damn and blast you! Why did we plumb your
  depths?
Why settle here, coming to stay with us   210
So long, without a break?

*(Sostratos now re-enters from the shrine with the jar full
of water. He offers it to the girl without being aware of
Daos' presence.)*

SOSTRATOS
Here, take it.

GIRL (*from her doorway*)
                              Bring
It over here.

DAOS (*aside*)
This fellow here—whatever does
He want?

                                                            215

ΣΩΣΤΡΑΤΟΣ

ἔρρωσ’, ἐπιμελοῦ τε τοῦ πατρός.
οἴμοι κακοδαίμων.—παῦε θρηνῶν, Σώστρατε·
215 ἔσται κατὰ τρόπον.

ΔΑΟΣ

κατὰ τρόπον τί;

ΣΩΣΤΡΑΤΟΣ

μὴ φοβοῦ,
ἀλλ’ ὅπερ ἔμελλες ἄρτι, τὸν Γέταν λαβὼν
ἐπάνηκ’, ἐκείνῳ πᾶν τὸ πρᾶγμ’ εἰπὼν σαφῶς.

ΔΑΟΣ

τουτὶ τὸ κακὸν τί ποτ’ ἐστίν; ὡς οὔ μοι πάνυ
τὸ πρᾶγμ’ ἀρέσκει. μειράκιον διακονεῖ
220 κόρῃ· πονηρόν. ἀλλά σ’, ὦ Κνήμων, κακὸν
κακῶς ἅπαντες ἀπολέσειαν οἱ θεοί.
ἄκακον κόρην μόνην ἀφεὶς ἐν ἐρημίᾳ
ἐᾷς, φυλακὴν οὐδεμίαν, ὡς προσῆκον ἦν,
ποιούμενος. τουτὶ καταμανθάνων ἴσως
225 οὗτος προσερρύη, νομίζων ὡσπερεὶ
ἕρμαιον. οὐ μὴν ἀλλὰ τἀδελφῷ γε δεῖ
αὐτῆς φράσαι με τὴν ταχίστην ταῦθ’, ἵνα
ἐν ἐπιμελείᾳ τῆς κόρης γενώμεθα.
ἤδη δὲ τοῦτ’ ἐλθὼν ποήσειν μοι δοκῶ.

218 τουτοτιτο B.   223 προσῆκον several: προκεν B.   224 κατα
μαθανων B.   226 αδελφωι (without the article) B.

DYSKOLOS

SOSTRATOS

Good-bye, and look after your father!

(*As Sostratos says this to the girl, she goes off into her house with the jar.*)

It's agonising . . .—Oh, stop moaning, Sostratos!
It'll be all right!

DAOS (*overhearing, and aside*)
What'll be all right?

SOSTRATOS (*still unaware of Daos' presence*)
Don't panic, do 215
As you intended just now—fetch Getas,
Explain the whole affair clearly to him!

(*With these words, exit Sostratos off right. Daos is now alone on stage.*)

DAOS

What's this chicanery? I don't at all like
What's going on! A young man doing things for
A girl—that's wrong! Knemon, I hope that all 220
The gods will damn and blast you for your sins!
You leave an innocent girl all alone,
In isolation, and without her due
Protection! Probably this youth found out
And stole here in a flash, believing he'd 225
Struck lucky! However, I'd better tell
Her brother about it without delay,
So we can keep the girl out of harm's reach.
I think I'd better go and do this now,

230 καὶ γὰρ προσιόντας τούσδε, Πανιστάς τινας,
  εἰς τὸν τόπον δεῦρ' ὑποβεβρεγμένους ὁρῶ,
  οἷς μὴ 'νοχλεῖν εὔκαιρον εἶναί μοι δοκεῖ.

ΧΟΡΟΥ

ΜΕΡΟΣ Β΄

ΓΟΡΓΙΑΣ

οὕτω παρέργως δ', εἰπέ μοι, τῷ πράγματι
φαύλως τ' ἐχρήσω;

ΔΑΟΣ

πῶς;

ΓΟΡΓΙΑΣ

ἔδει σε, νὴ Δία,
235 τὸν τῇ κόρῃ προσιόντα, Δᾶ', ὅστις ποτ' ἦν,
  ἰδεῖν τότ' εὐθύς, τοῦτο τοῦ λοιποῦ χρόνου
  εἰπεῖν θ' ὅπως μηδείς ποτ' αὐτὸν ὄψεται
  ποιοῦντα· νυνὶ δ' ὥσπερ ἀλλοτρίου τινὸς
(ΚΤ fr. 122) πράγματος ἀπέστης. οὐκ ἔνεστ' ἴσως φυγεῖν
240 οἰκειότητα, Δᾶ', ἀδελφῆς· ἔτι μέλει
  ἡμῖ[ν]. ὁ πατὴρ ἀλλότριος εἶναι βούλεται

230 Corr. Lloyd-Jones, van Groningen: παιανιστας B. 235
Δᾶ' om. B, suppl. Eitrem (other supplements are possible).
236 ιδειντουτ' B. 239 απετης B. ενεστ'ισως B and mss. AN
of scholia to Euripides, *Andr.* 975: ἔνεστί σοι ms. M of the
scholia. 240 Corr. Handley, Robertson: επιμελει B. 241
ἡμῖ[ν] several: ειμη[.] B, where the missing letter is prob-
ably ς.

For I can see these people coming here,   230
Right here, some rather drunk Pan-worshippers.   I think
It would be tactful not to clash with them.

(*Exit Daos, off left. The approaching band of drunken
Pan-worshippers is the chorus, who now enter from the
right after the conventional cue for their first entr'acte
performance.*)

ACT II

(*After the departure of the chorus, enter Gorgias and
Daos from the left. They are in mid-conversation.*)

GORGIAS

But tell me, did you treat the matter as
So slight and unimportant?

DAOS

How do you mean?

GORGIAS

[Daos, (?)]
You should, by Zeus, have seen the man accosting   235
The girl, whoever he was, right away, and told
Him that he'd better not be seen doing *that* again,
In future! As it is, you stood aside, as if
None of your business! Daos, you can't escape
From blood ties with a sister, I don't think.   240
We're still responsible. Her father may

219

αὐ[τ]ῆς πρὸς ἡμᾶς· μὴ τὸ τούτου δύσκολον
μ[ι]μώμεθ' ἡμεῖς. ἂν γὰρ αἰσχύνῃ τινὶ
αὕτη] περιπέσῃ, τοῦτο κἀμοὶ γίνεται
245 ὄνειδο]ς· ὁ γὰρ ἔξωθεν οὐ τὸν αἴτιον
ὅστις] ποτ' ἐστὶν οἶδεν, ἀλλὰ τὸ γεγονός.
κόψωμε]ν.

ΔΑΟΣ

ὦ τᾶν, τὸν γέροντα, Γοργία,
δέδοικ'· ἐ]ὰν γὰρ τῇ θύρᾳ προσιόντα με
λάβῃ, κρ]εμᾷ παραχρῆμα.

ΓΟΡΓΙΑΣ

δυσχρήστως γέ πως
250 ἔχει ζυ]γομαχῶν· τοῦτον οὔθ' ὅτῳ τρόπῳ
ἀναγκάσει τις εἰς τὸ βέλτι[ον ......]ν
οὔτ' ἂν μεταπεῖσαι νουθετῶν ο[.......]ς·
ἀλλ' ἐμποδὼν τῷ μὲν βιάσασθαι [τὸν ν]όμον
ἔχει μεθ' αὑτοῦ, τῷ δὲ πεῖσαι τὸν τρ[όπο]ν.

ΔΑΟΣ

255 ἔπισχε μικρόν· οὐ μάτην γὰρ ἥκ[ομ]εν,
ἀλλ' ὥσπερ εἶπον ἔρχετ' ἀνακάμψας πάλιν.

ΓΟΡΓΙΑΣ

ὁ τὴν χλανίδ' ἔχων; οὗτός ἐστιν ὃν λέγεις;

242 Corr. several: μηδετο B. 244 Suppl. Lloyd-Jones, London
seminar. 247 Suppl. Kassel. 249 λάβῃ suppl. Roberts,
κρ]εμᾷ several. 250 τουτω B. 251 ἀναγκάσει Arnott, Sand-
bach: αναγκασειε B. 255 Corr. several: επισχεσμικρον B.
256 ωσπερανειπον B. 257 ουτην B.

220

DYSKOLOS

Not want to fraternise with us; let's not
Copy his peevishness. If [she]'s the victim of
A scandal, that will bring [disgrace] on me
As well. Outsiders never know [which] man's   245
Responsible—they only see the event.
[Let's knock. (?)]

DAOS

        Gorgias, sir, [I'm afraid of] the
Old man. The minute [he finds] me going near
His door, he'll [string] me [up]!

GORGIAS

        Yes, [he's] a nuisance
In some ways, with his quarrelling. How can   250
One *force* him to reform, or change his mind
By good advice? Those are [dark mysteries (?)]!
Against the use of force, he's got [the] law
On his side; and against persuasion, his
[Character]!

DAOS

        Stop a moment! Why, our journey   255
Hasn't been in vain—he's coming back again,
Just as I said![1]

GORGIAS

        The man in that smart cloak[2]—
Is that the one you mean?

---

[1] Presumably in that part of the conversation which is presumed to have taken place off stage before the beginning of this scene.

[2] The garment referred to was an elegant cloak of fine wool, suitable wear for a rich and fashionable townsman, but capable of causing offence to suspicious, poorer countrymen like Gorgias.

MENANDER

ΔΑΟΣ
οὗτος.

ΓΟΡΓΙΑΣ
κακοῦργος εὐθὺς ἀπὸ τοῦ βλέμματος.

ΣΩΣΤΡΑΤΟΣ
τὸν μὲν Γέταν οὐκ ἔνδον ὄντα κατέλ[α]βον,
260 μέλλουσα δ' ἡ μήτηρ θεῷ θύειν τινί,
οὐκ οἶδ' ὅτῳ—ποεῖ δὲ τοῦθ' ὁσημέραι,
περιέρχεται θύουσα τὸν δῆμον κύκλῳ
ἅπαντ'—ἀπέσταλκ' αὐτὸν αὐτόθεν τινὰ
μισθωσόμενον μάγειρον. ἐρρῶσθαι δὲ τῇ
265 θυσίᾳ φράσας ἥκω πάλιν πρὸς τἀνθάδε.
καί μοι δοκῶ τοὺς περιπάτους τούτους ἀφεὶς
αὐτὸς διαλέξεσθ' ὑπὲρ ἐμαυτοῦ. τὴν θύραν
κόψω δ', ἵν' ᾖ μοι μηδὲ βουλεύσασθ' ἔτι.

ΓΟΡΓΙΑΣ
μειράκιον, ἐθελήσαις ἂν ὑπομεῖναι λόγον
270 σπουδαιότερόν μου;

ΣΩΣΤΡΑΤΟΣ
καὶ μαλ' ἡδέως· λέγε.

263–72 Scraps of the very ends of these lines are preserved in
O. 266 Corr. Winnington-Ingram: καμοι B. 267 Corr.
several: διαλεξασθαι B. 270 ηδως B.

222

DYSKOLOS

DAOS
Yes.

GORGIAS
Clearly a rogue,
From his expression!

(*The richly cloaked Sostratos, whose approach has already been signalled in the preceding four lines, now enters from the right. He is unaware of Daos' and Gorgias' presence.*)

SOSTRATOS
Getas wasn't in, I found.
My mother's going to make an offering to   260
Some god, I don't know who—she does this every day,
Goes with her offerings all around the whole
District—well, she's sent Getas out to hire
A cook[1] nearby.   I've said good-bye to *that*
Venture, and here I am, back on the job!   265
I think I'll cut out these excursions, and
Do my own speaking for myself.   I'll knock
At his door; that will guillotine for me
Further reflection!

(*Sostratos is just about to knock on Knemon's door when Gorgias accosts him.*)

GORGIAS
Young man, would you mind
Listening to some quite serious advice from me?   270

SOSTRATOS (*surprised but polite*)
Yes, with great pleasure.   Go ahead!

---

[1] See the note on the translation of *Aspis* 215–16.

MENANDER

ΓΟΡΓΙΑΣ

εἶναι νομίζω πᾶσιν ἀνθρώποις ἐγὼ
τοῖς τ᾽ εὐτυχοῦσιν τοῖς τε πράττουσιν κακῶς
πέρας τι τούτου καὶ μεταλλαγήν τινα·
καὶ τῷ μὲν εὐτυχοῦντι μεχρὶ τούτου μένειν
275 τὰ πράγματ᾽ εὐθενοῦντ᾽ ἀεὶ τὰ τοῦ βίου,
ὅσον ἂν χρόνον φέρειν δύνηται τὴν τύχην
μηδὲν ποήσας ἄδικον· εἰς δὲ τοῦθ᾽ ὅταν
ἔλθῃ προαχθεὶς τοῖς ἀγαθοῖς, ἐνταῦθά που
τὴν μεταβολὴν τὴν εἰς τὸ χεῖρον λαμβάνειν·
280 τοῖς δ᾽ ἐνδεῶς πράττουσιν, ἂν μηδὲν κακὸν
ποιῶσιν ἀποροῦντες, φέρωσι δ᾽ εὐγενῶς
τὸν δαίμον᾽, εἰς πίστιν ποτ᾽ ἐλθόντας χρόνῳ,
βελτίον᾽ εἶναι μερίδα προσδοκᾶν τινα.

(KT fr. 250, 8–11)

τί οὖν λέγω; μήτ᾽ αὐτός, εἰ σφόδρ᾽ εὐπορεῖς,
285 πίστευε τούτῳ, μήτε τῶν πτωχῶν πάλιν
ἡμῶν καταφρόνει· τοῦ διευτυχεῖν δ᾽ ἀεὶ
πάρεχε σεαυτὸν τοῖς ὁρῶσιν ἄξιον.

ΣΩΣΤΡΑΤΟΣ

ἄτοπον δέ σοί τι φαίνομαι νυνὶ ποεῖν;

ΓΟΡΓΙΑΣ

ἔργον δοκεῖς μοι φαῦλον ἐζηλωκέναι,
290 πείσειν νομίζων ἐξαμαρτεῖν παρθένον
ἐλευθέραν ἢ καιρὸν ἐπιτηρῶν τινα

273 Corr. several: τουτο B. 279 λαμβανει B. 283–90 Scraps of the very ends of these lines are found in O. 284 μητ᾽ B: μηδ᾽ ms. S of Stobaeus, *Ecl.* 3. 22. 19. O has the variant (or gloss) ευτυχεις written above ευπορεις. 286 τουδιευτυχειν B:

DYSKOLOS

GORGIAS

For all
Mankind, I think—successes, failures too—
There is a boundary, a turning point
In their positions.   The successful man's
Worldly prosperity continues just so long   275
As he can buttress his good fortune by
Avoiding any crimes.   However, if
He's lured to evil by his affluence,
His fortune switches then, I think, into decline.
If, on the other hand, the less successful,   280
Despite their poverty, keep clear of evil,
Shouldering their destiny with honour, and
Achieving in the end a credit balance, they'll
Expect their stock to improve.   My message, then,
  is this:
You may be very rich, but don't you bank on it,   285
Don't trample, either, on us down-and-outs!   Always
Show onlookers that you deserve a durable
Prosperity!

SOSTRATOS (*after the lecture, even more mystified*)

You feel I'm doing something now
That's out of place?

GORGIAS

You've set your heart, I think,
On a foul deed.   You're hoping to seduce   290
An innocent free girl, or looking for a chance

τοῦδ' εὐτυχεῖν S of Stob.   287 Corr. Gesner: σαυτὸν B, S of
Stob.   288 Corr. several: τισοι B.   289 εξηλωκεναι B.

κατεργάσασθαι πρᾶγμα θανάτων ἄξιον
πολλῶν.

ΣΩΣΤΡΑΤΟΣ

Ἄπολλον.

ΓΟΡΓΙΑΣ

οὐ δίκαιόν ἐστι γοῦν
τὴν σὴν σχολὴν τοῖς ἀσχολουμένοις κακὸν
295 ἡμῖν γενέσθαι. τῶν δ᾽ ἁπάντων ἴσθ᾽ ὅτι
πτωχὸς ἀδικηθείς ἐστι δυσκολώτατον.
πρῶτον μέν ἐστ᾽ ἐλεινός, εἶτα λαμβά[νει
οὐκ εἰς ἀδικίαν ὅσα πέπονθ᾽, ἀλλ᾽ εἰς [ὕβριν.

ΣΩΣΤΡΑΤΟΣ

μειράκιον, οὕτως εὐτυχοίης, βραχ[ύ τί μου
300 ἄκουσον.

ΔΑΟΣ

εὖ γε, δέσποθ᾽, οὕτω πολλά [σοι
ἀγαθὰ γένοιτο.

ΣΩΣΤΡΑΤΟΣ

καὶ σύ γ᾽ ὁ λαλῶν, πρ[όσεχε δή.
κόρην τιν᾽ εἶδο[ν ἐνθαδί· τ]αύτης ἐρῶ.
εἰ τοῦτ᾽ ἀδίκημ᾽ ε[ἴρηκ]ας, ἠδίκηκ᾽ ἴσως.
τί γὰρ ἄν τις εἴποι; π[λὴν π]ορεύομ᾽ ἐνθάδε
305 οὐχὶ πρὸς ἐκείνη[ν, βο]ύλομαι δ᾽ αὐτῆς ἰδεῖν
τὸν πατέρ᾽. ἐγὼ γά[ρ], ὢν ἐλεύθερος, βίον
ἱκανὸν ἔχων, ἕτοιμός εἰμι λαμβάνειν

292 Corr. Kraus, Oguse: κατεργασεσθαι B.   296 αδικησθεις B.
297 Corr. Blake: ελεεινος B.   298, 299 Suppl. several.   302
ἐνθαδί suppl. several.   303, 304 Suppl. several.

ɔ do an action for which you deserve
he sentence of a thousand deaths!

SOSTRATOS (*horror-struck at the accusation*)

Apollo!

GORGIAS

t any rate, it isn't right that your
eisure should injure us, who have none. When a poor 295
▌an's injured, he's the bitterest foe of all, for sure.
t first, he's just pathetic; later, he takes all
▌is tribulations as a [personal]
nsult], not just as mischief!

SOSTRATOS

Young man, *please*
et [me] say *some*thing!

DAOS (*ignoring Sostratos' intervention*)

Bravo master, [you] 300
▌eserve a shower of blessings!

SOSTRATOS

And you listen too,
⌐ou interrupter!—[Here] I saw a girl,
love her. If [you call] that ' crime ', then I must be
▖ criminal. What else can one say ? [Only that]
'm coming here not for *her*, it's her father 305
'd like to see. I'm free-born, I've enough
▌oney, and I'm prepared to marry her

αὐτὴν ἄπροικον, πίστιν ἐπιθεὶς διατελεῖν
στέργων. ἐπὶ κακῷ δ' εἰ προσελήλυθ' ἐνθάδε,
310 ἢ βουλόμενος ὑμῶν τι κακοτεχνεῖν λάθρα,
οὗτός μ' ὁ Πάν, μειράκιον, αἱ Νύμφαι θ' ἅμα
ἀπόπληκτον αὐτοῦ πλησίον τῆς οἰκίας
ἤδη ποήσειαν. τετάραγμ', εὖ ἴσθ' ὅτι,
οὐδὲ μετρίως, εἴ σοι τοιοῦτος φαίνομαι.

ΓΟΡΓΙΑΣ

315 ἀλλ' εἴ τι κἀγὼ τοῦ δέοντος σφοδρότερον
εἴρηκα, μηδὲν τοῦτο λυπείτω σ' ἔτι.
ἅμα γὰρ μεταπείθεις ταῦτα καὶ φίλον μ' ἔχεις.
οὐκ ἀλλότριος δ' ὤν, ἀλλ' ἀδελφὸς τῆς κόρης
ὁμομήτριος, βέλτιστε, ταῦτά σοι λέγω.

ΣΩΣΤΡΑΤΟΣ

320 καὶ χρήσιμός γ' εἶ, νὴ Δί', εἰς τὰ λοιπά μοι.

ΓΟΡΓΙΑΣ

τί χρήσιμος;

ΣΩΣΤΡΑΤΟΣ

γεννικὸν ὁρῶ σε τῷ τρόπῳ—

ΓΟΡΓΙΑΣ

οὐ πρόφασιν εἰπὼν βούλομ' ἀποπέμψαι κενήν,
τὰ δ' ὄντα πράγματ' ἐμφανίσαι. ταύτῃ πατήρ

---

310 τι om. B, suppl. several.   313 εὖ om. B, suppl. severa[l]
315 ἀλλετι B.   317 αιμαγαρ B.

DYSKOLOS

Without a dowry, and I'll swear an oath
always to cherish her! Young man, if I've
come here with evil intent, planning an   310
intrigue behind your backs, may this Pan[1] and
the Nymphs together strike me senseless on
the spot, here by the house.[2] Let me tell you,
I'm most upset if *that*'s the kind of man
you think me!

GORGIAS

        Well, if I've spoken a bit   315
too strongly, don't let that aggrieve you any more!
You've put things in a new light, won me to
your side, too! My dear sir, I'm no outsider, I'm
the girl's half-brother, that's why I can say
this!

SOSTRATOS

   And, by Zeus, you'll be able to help   320
me now!

GORGIAS

     Help? How do you mean?

SOSTRATOS

              I see you've got
a kind heart . . .

GORGIAS (*interrupting*)

         I don't want to send you off
with frivolous excuses, I prefer

[1] Sostratos points to the statue of Pan placed at the entrance
to the shrine (see the note on line 12).
[2] Whose house? The Greek is ambiguous, but the reference
is most probably to the shrine of Pan.

ἐσθ᾿ οἷος οὐδεὶς γέγονεν οὔτε τῶν πάλαι
325 ἄνθρωπος οὔτε τῶν καθ᾿ ἡμᾶς.

ΣΩΣΤΡΑΤΟΣ

ὁ χαλεπός;
σχεδὸν οἶδ᾿.

ΓΟΡΓΙΑΣ

ὑπερβολή τίς ἐστι τοῦ κακοῦ.
τούτῳ ταλάντων ἔστ᾿ ἴσως τουτὶ δυεῖν
τὸ κτῆμα. τοῦτ᾿ αὐτὸς γεωργῶν διατελεῖ
μόνος, συνεργὸν δ᾿ οὐδέν᾿ ἀνθρώπων ἔχων,
330 οὐκ οἰκέτην οἰκεῖον, οὐκ ἐκ τοῦ τόπου
μισθωτόν, οὐχὶ γείτον᾿, ἀλλ᾿ αὐτὸς μόνος.
ἥδιστόν ἐστ᾿ αὐτῷ γὰρ ἀνθρώπων ὁρᾶν
οὐδένα. μεθ᾿ αὑτοῦ τὴν κόρην ἐργάζεται
ἔχων τὰ πολλά· προσλαλεῖ ταύτῃ μόνῃ,
335 ἑτέρῳ δὲ τοῦτ᾿ οὐκ ἂν ποήσαι ῥᾳδίως.
τότε φησὶν ἐκδώσειν ἐκείνην, ἡνίκ᾿ ἂν
ὁμότροπον αὑτῷ νυμφίον λάβῃ.

ΣΩΣΤΡΑΤΟΣ

λέγεις
οὐδέποτε.

ΓΟΡΓΙΑΣ

μὴ δὴ πράγματ᾿, ὦ βέλτιστ᾿, ἔχε·
μάτην γὰρ ἕξεις. τοὺς δ᾿ ἀναγκαίους ἔα
340 ἡμᾶς φέρειν ταῦθ᾿, οἷς δίδωσιν ἡ τύχη.

329 ανθρωπον B. 337 νυμφ᾿ον B. 338 ουδεποτ᾿ει B.

o spell out the plain truth. Her father is
nique. There's never been a man like him,   325
a earlier times or nowadays.

SOSTRATOS

                    This terror?
think I know him!

GORGIAS

                    A catastrophe—
, beats them all. This property of his is worth
bout two talents,[1] and he farms it still
ll by himself, without a man to help—   330
o family slave, no hired hand from the area,
o neighbour—it's all done by him, and him alone.
is greatest pleasure's seeing nobody.
e usually works with just his daughter by his side.
o her alone he'll talk, he wouldn't easily   335
o *that* to someone else! He says he won't
arry her till he finds a bridegroom who
hares his own outlook.

SOSTRATOS
That means never!

GORGIAS

                    So, my friend,
on't you give yourself trouble, it'll be
seless. Leave us to bear the burden, we're   340
is relatives, by gift of fortune!

---

[1] It would accordingly be an estate of considerable value
ee the note on *Aspis* 35) and presumably also of considerable
ze—well beyond the capacity of any real-life farmer. In fact
nemon does not contrive to farm *all* his land (cf. 163 ff.).

MENANDER

ΣΩΣΤΡΑΤΟΣ

πρὸς τῶν θεῶν οὐπώποτ᾽ ἠράσθης τινός,
μειράκιον;

ΓΟΡΓΙΑΣ

οὐδ᾽ ἔξεστί μοι, βέλτιστε.

ΣΩΣΤΡΑΤΟΣ

πῶς;

τίς ἐσθ᾽ ὁ κωλύων;

ΓΟΡΓΙΑΣ

ὁ τῶν ὄντων κακῶν
λογισμός, ἀνάπαυσιν διδοὺς οὐδ᾽ ἡντινοῦν.✓

ΣΩΣΤΡΑΤΟΣ

345 οὔ μοι δοκεῖς· ἀπειρότερον γοῦν διαλέγει
πε[ρὶ τ]αῦτ᾽. ἀποστῆναι κελεύεις μ᾽. οὐκέτι
τοῦτ᾽ ἐσ]τὶν ἐπ᾽ ἐμοί, τῷ θεῷ δέ.

ΓΟΡΓΙΑΣ

τοιγαροῦν
οὐδὲ]ν ἀδικεῖς ἡμᾶς, μάτην δὲ κακοπαθεῖς.

ΣΩΣΤΡΑΤΟΣ

οὔκ, εἰ λά]βοιμι τὴν κόρην.

343 τισεθ᾽ου B.   345 Corr. Browning (cf. the plagiarism of this
passage in Aristaenetus, *Epist.* 2. 17): διατελει B.   346 τ]αῦτ
suppl. several.   348 Suppl. several.   349 Suppl. Sandbach.

DYSKOLOS

SOSTRATOS

By the gods,
Young fellow, have you never been in love?

GORGIAS

My friend,
I can't!

SOSTRATOS

Why? What's to stop you?

GORGIAS

Adding up
Our present hardships—that allows no time at all
For hobbies!

SOSTRATOS

No, I see you never were in love.   345
That's why you talk about it too naively! ' Stop ',
You say, yet [that]'s no longer in *my* power,
But in the god's[1]!

GORGIAS

So you're [not] hurting us—
Just suffering pointlessly!

SOSTRATOS

[Not if] I win the girl!

---

[1] Sostratos means Eros, the god of love; the audience,
however, knows that it was Pan who made Sostratos fall in
love (39 ff.). Menander's lack of precision is deliberate.

ΓΟΡΓΙΑΣ

οὐκ ἂν λάβοις.

350 ......]υνα† συνακολουθήσας ἐμοὶ
αὑτὸν] παραιτῇ· πλησίον γὰρ τὴν νάπην
ἐργάζε]θ᾽ ἡμῶν.

ΣΩΣΤΡΑΤΟΣ

πῶς;

ΓΟΡΓΙΑΣ

λόγον τιν᾽ ἐμβαλῶ

.... περὶ] γάμου τῆς κόρης· τὸ τοιοῦτο γὰρ
ἴδοιμι κἂ]ν αὐτὸς γενόμενον ἄσμενος.
355 εὐθὺς μαχεῖται πᾶσι, λοιδ[ορούμενο]ς
εἰς τοὺς βίους οὓς ζῶσι· σὲ δ᾽ [ἄγοντ᾽ ἂν] ἤδη
σχολὴν τρυφῶντά τ᾽, οὐδ᾽ ὁρ[ῶν ἂν]έξεται.

ΣΩΣΤΡΑΤΟΣ

νῦν ἐστ᾽ ἐκεῖ;

ΓΟΡΓΙΑΣ

μὰ Δί᾽, ἀλλὰ μ[ικρ]ὸν ὕστερον

ἔξεισιν ἣν εἴωθεν.

ΣΩΣΤΡΑΤΟΣ

ὦ τᾶν, τὴν κόρην

360 ἄγων μεθ᾽ αὑτοῦ, φής;

350–54 Supplementation of B's already corrupt text is *highly*
uncertain; the text printed here is *exempli gratia*. 350
συνκολουθησας B. 351 αὑτὸν] παραιτῇ Fraenkel:]παρατης B.
352 Suppl. several. εμβαλωι B. 354 Suppl. Blake, Post. 356

234

DYSKOLOS

GORGIAS

You won't, [as you'll discover if you (?)] come   350
With me and [ask him. He farms in (?)] the valley
Near us.

SOSTRATOS

Discover? How?

GORGIAS

I'll introduce
The subject [of] his daughter's marriage. That's
A thing that I myself would like to see
Take place. But he'll wade into everybody,   355
Fire insults at the lives they lead. [If] he sees you
In all your pampered ease, he won't agree
Even to look at you.

SOSTRATOS
Is he there now?

GORGIAS

He isn't,
By Zeus, but he'll emerge soon on his usual road . . .

SOSTRATOS (*interrupting*)

My dear friend, do you mean he'll have the girl   360
With him?

Corr. and suppl. Kraus, Lloyd-Jones: B may have had
γεδ['αναγον]τ'ιδηι. 357 ὁρ[ῶν suppl. several. 358 Suppl.
several. 359 Speech-division thus indicated by ed. pr. (no
dicolon, no paragraphus in B). οταν B.

ΓΟΡΓΙΑΣ

    ὅπως ἂν τοῦτό γε

τύχῃ.

ΣΩΣΤΡΑΤΟΣ

βάδιζ'· ἕτοιμός εἰμ'.

ΓΟΡΓΙΑΣ

    οἷον λέγεις.

ΣΩΣΤΡΑΤΟΣ

ἀλλ', ἀντιβολῶ, συναγώνισαί μοι.

ΓΟΡΓΙΑΣ

      τίνα τρόπον;

ΣΩΣΤΡΑΤΟΣ

ὅντινα τρόπον; προάγωμεν οἷ λέγεις.

ΔΑΟΣ

      τί οὖν;
ἐργαζομένοις ἡμῖν παρεστήξεις ἔχων
365 χλανίδα;

ΣΩΣΤΡΑΤΟΣ

  τί δὴ γὰρ οὐχί;

ΔΑΟΣ

    ταῖς βώλοις βαλεῖ
εὐθύς σ', ἀποκαλεῖ τ' ὄλεθρον ἀργόν. ἀλλὰ δεῖ

361 Corr. Blake: βαδιζεινετοιμος: οιλεγεις: B. **365** Corr. Handley: γαρδη B. βαλλει B.

GORGIAS

Perhaps, perhaps not.

SOSTRATOS

Come on, I'm ready!

GORGIAS

What an idea!

SOSTRATOS

Please, do help me!

GORGIAS

How?

SOSTRATOS

How?   Let's walk on to where you mentioned.

DAOS

What?

Do you plan to stand by us while we work,
Wearing a cloak[1]?

SOSTRATOS

Why ever not?

DAOS

Straight off, he'll throw 365
His sods at you, call you a lazy devil.   No,

[1] See the note on line 257.

MENANDER

σκάπτειν μεθ' ἡμῶν σ'. εἰ τύχοι γάρ, τοῦτ' ἰδὼν
ἴσως ἂν ὑπομείνειε καὶ παρὰ σοῦ τινα
λόγον, νομίσας αὐτουργὸν εἶναι τῷ βίῳ
370 πένητ'.

ΣΩΣΤΡΑΤΟΣ

ἕτοιμος πάντα πειθαρχεῖν· ἄγε.

ΓΟΡΓΙΑΣ

τί κακοπαθεῖν σαυτὸν βιάζῃ;

ΔΑΟΣ

βούλομαι
ὡς πλεῖστον ἡμᾶς ἐργάσασθαι τήμερον,
τοῦτόν τε τὴν ὀσφῦν ἀπορρήξανθ' ἅμα
παύσασθ' ἐνοχλοῦνθ' ἡμῖν προσιόντα τ' ἐνθάδε.

ΣΩΣΤΡΑΤΟΣ

375 ἔκφερε δίκελλαν.

372 ημερας (for ἡμᾶς) B.

---

¹ When Sostratos returns from his work in the fields at line
522, he is clearly not wearing his incriminating cloak, and it
seems most likely that he does not resume wearing it until his
entry at the beginning of the last act.   One possibility is that
he goes off here at line 371 carrying the cloak, returns similarly
carrying it at 522, and then deposits it in the shrine of Pan
when he goes in there at 619 (cf. Handley's edition of the
Dyskolos, on 370).

You'd better do some digging with us. If he saw
That, he just might—perhaps—agree to listen to,
Yes, even you, because he thought your life
Was that of a poor farmer.

SOSTRATOS

I'm prepared to do 370
All I am told.   Lead on.

*(Either at this point, or directly before his exit at line 392,
Sostratos must take off his smart cloak,[1] revealing under-
neath a short tunic more suitable for energetic work out-
doors under a hot sun.)*

GORGIAS
Why force yourself
To suffer?

DAOS *(aside)*

I'd like *us* to get as much work done
Today as possible, and *him* to slip a disc
At the same time.   Then he'll stop bothering us
And coming here.

SOSTRATOS
Bring out a mattock.[2]

---

[2] The δίκελλα, here translated ' mattock ', was an agri-
ultural tool used for digging, breaking up the surface of the
ground, and for shifting dung (cf. lines 584 ff.).   It probably
combined the broad, horizontal blade of a mattock with a pair
of hoe-like prongs (cf. W. K. Pritchett, *Hesperia* 25 [1956],
290 f.; K. D. White, *Agricultural Implements of the Roman
World*, Cambridge 1967, 47 f., 66 ff.).

MENANDER

ΔΑΟΣ

τὴν παρ' ἐμοῦ λαβὼν ἴθι.
τὴν αἱμασιὰν ἐποικοδομήσω γὰρ τέως
ἐγώ· ποιητέον δὲ καὶ τοῦτ' ἐστί.

ΣΩΣΤΡΑΤΟΣ

δός.

ἀπέσωσας.

ΔΑΟΣ

ὑπάγω, τρόφιμ'· ἐκεῖ διώκετε.

ΣΩΣΤΡΑΤΟΣ

οὕτως ἔχω· παραποθανεῖν ἤδη με δεῖ
380 ἢ ζῆν ἔχοντα τὴν κόρην.

ΓΟΡΓΙΑΣ

εἴπερ λέγεις
ἃ φρονεῖς, ἐπιτύχοις.

ΣΩΣΤΡΑΤΟΣ

ὦ πολυτίμητοι θεοί,
οἷς ἀποτρέπεις νυνὶ γὰρ ὡς οἴει με σύ,
τούτοις παρώξυμμ' εἰς τὸ πρᾶγμα διπλασίως.
εἰ μὴ γὰρ ἐν γυναιξίν ἐστιν ἡ κόρη
385 τεθραμμένη μηδ' οἶδε τῶν ἐν τῷ βίῳ
τούτῳ κακῶν μηδὲν ὑπὸ τηθίδος τινὸς
δεδισαμένη μαίας τ', ἐλευθερίως δέ πως
μετὰ πατρὸς ἀγρίου μισοπονήρου τῷ τρόπῳ,
πῶς οὐκ ἐπιτυχεῖν ἐστι ταύτης μακάριον;

DYSKOLOS

DAOS

Here, 375

Take mine, and go.   And while you're occupied,
I'll build the wall up.   That needs doing, too.

SOSTRATOS

Pass it.   You've saved my life!

DAOS

I'm off then, master.

Follow on there.

(*Exit Daos, off left*)

SOSTRATOS

So that's my fortune—I must now
Die in the attempt, or win the girl and *live*! 380

GORGIAS

If you mean what you say, good luck to you!

SOSTRATOS

O honoured gods!   The arguments you've used
To put me off now, so you think, have made me twice
As eager for the venture.   If the girl
Hasn't grown up in a horde of women, if 385
She's ignorant of the vices in this life, and all
The fears trumped up by aunts or nurses, if her life's
Been, well, sincere, with a fierce father who's
A natural foe to vice—why then, it *must*

---

376 Corr. several: ετιγαροικοδομησω B.   377–78 Speech-divi-
sion thus indicated by ed. pr. (δος:απεσωσασυ·παγω B).   386
τουτων B.   387 δειδισαμένη Gallavotti: δεδεισαμενη B.   388
μεταυτουπατροσαγριου B.

241

390 ἀλλ' ἡ δίκελλ' ἄγει τάλαντα τέτταρα
αὕτη· προαπολεῖ μ'. οὐ μαλακιστέον δ' ὅμως,
ἐπείπερ ἦργμαι καταπονεῖν τὸ πρᾶγμ' ἅπαξ.

ΣΙΚΩΝ

τουτὶ τὸ πρόβατόν ἐστιν οὐ τὸ τυχὸν καλόν.
ἄπαγ' εἰς τὸ βάραθρον. ἂν μὲν αἰρόμενος φέρω
395 μετέωρον, ἔχεται τῷ στόματι θαλλοῦ, κράδης
κατεσθίει τὰ θρῖ', ἀποσπᾷ δ' εἰς βίαν.
ἐὰν δ' ἀφῇ χαμαί τις, οὐ προέρχεται.
τοὐναντίον δὴ γέγονε· κατακέκομμ' ἐ[γὼ
ὁ μάγειρος ὑπὸ τούτου νεωλκῶν τὴν ὁδ[όν.
400 ἀλλ' ἐστὶν εὐτυχῶς τὸ νυμφαῖον τοδ[ὶ
οὗ θύσομεν. τὸν Πᾶνα χαίρειν. παῖ Γέ[τα,
τοσοῦτ' ἀπολείπῃ;

ΓΕΤΑΣ

      τεττάρων γὰρ φορ[τίον
ὄνων συνέδησαν αἱ κάκιστ' ἀπολού[μεναι
φέρειν γυναῖκές μοι.

391 Corr. Kraus, Maas: προσαπολει B. 394 βαραθμον B.
396 εἰς van Groningen: ες B. 397 τισχαμαι B. 398 δὴ γέγονε
Barber: δ'ηγαγον B. 400 Suppl. several. 403 ακακισταπολυ[
B.

---

[1] In modern terms, about 110 kilogrammes or 242 pounds
(cf. the note on *Aspis* 84), an obvious exaggeration.

Be bliss to win her! But this mattock weighs   390
Four talents,[1] it'll kill me first. No slacking, though,
Once I've begun to sweat at this affair!

*Exeunt Gorgias and Sostratos, off left. The stage is now
empty and silent for a few seconds. Then confused noises
are heard off to the right. These become gradually louder,
finally resolving into the bleating of a lamb, the rattling of
pots and pans, and human cursing. At length the cook
Sikon enters, dragging behind him a very reluctant sheep.)*

SIKON

This sheep here is no ordinary beauty—damn
And blast it to perdition! If I lift it up
And carry it in the air, its teeth lock on a shoot,   395
It wolfs the fig-leaves, pulling hard away
From my grip. If you lower it to the ground,
Though, it won't budge. So here's a paradox: this
   sheep's
Got me, the cook, all in a stew, through hauling it
Along the road! But here's the shrine, thank heavens, 400
Where we're to sacrifice. Hail, Pan! Getas,
My boy, so far behind?

*After Sikon has made the conventional salutation to the
god Pan (see above, on line 12), he looks back off-stage in
the direction of Getas, who now enters, also from the right,
staggering under an enormous load of pots, pans, rugs,
cushions and mattresses.)*

GETAS

            Yes, damn the women!
They fastened up four donkey-loads for me
To carry!

MENANDER

ΣΙΚΩΝ

πολύς τις ἔρ[χεται
405 ὄχλος, ὡς ἔοι[κε. στρ]ώματ᾽ ἀδιήγηθ᾽ ὅσα
φέρεις.

ΓΕΤΑΣ

τί δ᾽ ἐγὼ [νῦν;]

ΣΙΚΩΝ

ταῦτ᾽ ἔρεισον δεῦρ᾽.

ΓΕΤΑΣ

ἰδού.

ἐὰν ἴδῃ γὰρ ἐνύ[πνιο]ν τὸν Πᾶνα τὸν
Παιανιοῖ, τού[τ]ῳ βαδιούμεθ᾽, οἶδ᾽ ὅτι,
θύσοντες εὐθύς.

ΣΙΚΩΝ

[τ]ίς δ᾽ ἑόρακεν ἐνύπνιον;

ΓΕΤΑΣ

410 ἄνθρωπε, μή με κόφθ᾽.

ΣΙΚΩΝ

ὅμως εἶπον, Γέτα,
τίς εἶδεν;

406 νῦν suppl. Sandbach. ερεισονταυτα B. Speech-division after
δεῦρο indicated by ed. pr. (δευροιδου: B). 407 αν B. 407–8
πανατε/τονπαιανιοι B. 408 βαζιουμεθ᾽ B. 409 ενθυσ[..]ιδ᾽εωρα
κεν B (did the papyrus originally have ενθυς:τιδ᾽?). 410
μημοι B.

---

[1] The village of Paiania was situated on the eastern side of
Mount Hymettos, a good twenty miles by road or track south-
east of Phyle. Getas mentions it here less for any association

SIKON

There's a great crowd coming, clear
Enough. The cushions you've got on your back— 405
What a tremendous number!

GETAS (*at last puffing up to the front door of the shrine*)
What do I do [now (?)]?

SIKON

Rest that against here.

(*Getas obeys Sikon, unloading himself of his pack and
placing it against the wall of the shrine*).

GETAS

There. You see, if she
Dreams of Pan of Paiania,[1] we'll trot
Straight off to sacrifice to him there, that's for sure!

SIKON

Who's had a dream?

GETAS

Don't grate me, sir!

SIKON

Do tell 410
Me, Getas, all the same, who had this dream?

it may have had with the worship of Pan (although Mount
Hymettos itself had some celebrity in this connection: see
Handley's edition of the *Dyskolos*, *ad loc.*), than because he is
gloomily thinking of the effort that would be required to carry
his enormous load over the rugged country between Phyle and
Paiania.

MENANDER

ΓΕΤΑΣ

ἡ κεκτημένη.

ΣΙΚΩΝ

τί πρὸς θεῶν;

ΓΕΤΑΣ

ἀπολεῖς. ἐδόκει τὸν Πᾶνα—

ΣΙΚΩΝ

τουτονὶ λέγεις;

ΓΕΤΑΣ

τοῦτον.

ΣΙΚΩΝ

τί ποιεῖν;

ΓΕΤΑΣ

τῷ τροφίμῳ τῷ Σωστράτῳ—

ΣΙΚΩΝ

κομψῷ νεανίσκῳ γε—

ΓΕΤΑΣ

—περικρούειν πέδας—

ΣΙΚΩΝ

415 Ἄπολλον.

414 Corr. several: γενεανισκωι B. παιδας B.

GETAS

My mistress.

SIKON

By the gods, what was it?

GETAS

You'll kill me!

She saw Pan . . .

SIKON (*interrupting*)

This one here, you mean?

(*Sikon points to the statue of Pan by the front door of the shrine.*)

GETAS

Yes.

SIKON

What was he

Doing?

GETAS

He had Sostratos, our master's son . . .

SIKON

A fine

Boy!

GETAS

Pan was putting chains on him . . .

SIKON

Apollo!

247

ΓΕΤΑΣ

—εἶτα δόντα διφθέραν τε καὶ
δίκελλαν ἐν τοῦ πλησίον τῷ χωρίῳ
σκάπτειν κελεύειν.

ΣΙΚΩΝ

ἄτοπον.

ΓΕΤΑΣ

ἀλλὰ θύομεν
διὰ τοῦθ᾽, ἵν᾽ εἰς βέλτιον ἀποβῇ τὸ φοβερόν.

ΣΙΚΩΝ

μεμάθηκα. πάλιν αἴρου δὲ ταυτὶ καὶ φέρε
420 εἴσω. ποῶμεν στιβάδας ἔνδον εὐτρεπεῖς
καὶ τἄλλ᾽ ἕτοιμα· μηδὲν ἐπικωλυέτω
θύειν γ᾽ ἐπὰν ἔλθωσιν· ἀλλ᾽ ἀγαθῇ τύχῃ.
καὶ τὰς ὀφρῦς ἄνες ποτ᾽, ὦ τρισάθλιε·
ἐγώ σε χορτάσω κατὰ τρόπον τήμερον.

ΓΕΤΑΣ

425 ἐπαινέτης οὖν εἰμι σοῦ καὶ τῆς τέχνης
ἔγωγ᾽ ἀεί ποτ᾽, οὐχὶ πιστεύω δ᾽ ὅμως.

ΧΟΡΟΥ

415 δ᾽ονταδιαφθεραν B. 416 ἐν om. B, suppl. ed. pr. τοῦ
πλησίον London seminar: τωπλησιον B. 418 αποβαιη B.
420 ποιησωμεν B. 422 θύειν Fraenkel, London seminar:
θυσειν B. 423 Corr. several: ανεσπογ᾽ B.

DYSKOLOS

GETAS

Next 415

Pan handed him a jerkin and a mattock, then
Told him to dig the neighbour's land!

SIKON

Extraordinary!

GETAS

That's why we're sacrificing here, to get
A better sequel to this frightful dream.

SIKON

I see.
Well, pick *them* up again, and carry them inside.   420
Let's have some couches ready in there, and the rest
All shipshape. When they come, the sacrifice must go
Without snags. Here's to that! And do please stop
That scowling, you wet blanket! I'll give you today
A proper feed.

GETAS

That's why I've always praised   425
You and your skill—I'll never *trust* you, though!

(*In Sikon's speech, lines 419–20, ' them ' obviously refers
to the load which Getas put down at 407.   Getas presum-
ably resumes his burden with a scowl of displeasure while
the cook speaks 421–22.   Sikon probably goes off (with
his sheep) into the shrine during the complimentary part
of Getas' remarks at 425–26, thus leaving Getas all alone
to deliver his critical clausula before he too disappears
into the shrine.   When the stage is empty, the chorus
enter to give their second entr'acte performance.*)

MENANDER

ΜΕΡΟΣ Γ΄

ΚΝΗΜΩΝ

γραῦ, τὴν θύραν κλείσασ᾽ ἄνοιγε μηδενί,
ἕως ἂν ἔλθω δεῦρ᾽ ἐγὼ πάλιν· σκότους
ἔσται δὲ τοῦτο παντελῶς, ὡς οἴομαι.

ΜΗΤΗΡ ΣΩΣΤΡΑΤΟΥ

430 Πλαγγών, πορεύου θᾶττον· ἤδη τεθυκέναι
ἡμᾶς ἔδει.

ΚΝΗΜΩΝ

τουτὶ τὸ κακὸν τί βούλεται;
ὄχλος τις· ἄπαγ᾽ ἐς κόρακας.

ΜΗΤΗΡ ΣΩΣΤΡΑΤΟΥ

αὔλει, Παρθένι,
(KT fr. 121) Πανός· σιωπῇ, φασί, τούτῳ τῷ θεῷ
οὐ δεῖ προσιέναι.

430–31, 432–4, 436–7 Ritchie assigns these speeches to
Sostratos' mother with dramatic plausibility (B nowhere
mentions this character as a speaking part, and assigns 430–31
specifically to Getas).   434 δεῖ B: δεῖν mss. of (i) scholia of
Aristophanes, *Lys.* 2 and (ii) *Suda*, s.v. Πανικῷ δείματι.

---

[1] This character's intervention in the dialogue during this
scene is an attractively bold conjecture of modern scholarship
for which, however, there is no written evidence in the cast list
and marginal or interlinear part-assignations of the Bodmer
papyrus.   See apparatus criticus on line 430.

[2] To play 'Pan's hymn' was presumably the musical
equivalent of the spoken greetings normal on more ordinary
occasions (cf. lines 12, 401, 572 f.).   Pan was a dangerous god,
capable of inducing such things as ' panic ' terror if crossed or
neglected.

DYSKOLOS

ACT III

*(After the chorus' departure, Knemon enters from his house
all equipped for a day's farming. His opening remarks
are addressed to his servant Simiche inside the house.)*

KNEMON

Old woman, bar the door, don't open it
To anybody till I come back home
Again. It'll be quite dark then, I expect.

*(At this point, Knemon turns away from the door in the
direction of his fields, which are to be imagined off right.
But before he can move, he is engulfed by a crowd of
people coming to sacrifice at the shrine of Pan. These
include Sostratos' mother, her daughter Plangon, and a
hired girl named Parthenis who is playing the ancient
Greek double pipes.)*

SOSTRATOS' MOTHER [1]

Hurry, Plangon! By now the sacrifice   430
Should have been over! ·

KNEMON (*aside*)

What's the meaning of
This devilry? A horde! To hell with them!

SOSTRATOS' MOTHER

Play Pan's hymn, Parthenis. They say one shouldn't
Approach this god in silence. [2]

*(The hullabaloo of the sacrificial party's arrival finally
brings Getas out of the shrine to greet them with grumbles.)*

251

MENANDER

ΓΕΤΑΣ

νὴ Δί᾽, ἀπεσώθητέ γε.
435 ὦ ῾Ηράκλεις, ἀηδίας· καθήμεθα
χρόνον τοσοῦτον περιμένοντες.

ΜΗΤΗΡ ΣΩΣΤΡΑΤΟΥ

εὐτρεπῆ

ἅπαντα δ᾽ ἡμῖν ἐστι;

ΓΕΤΑΣ

ναὶ μὰ τὸν Δία·
τὸ γοῦν πρόβατον· μικροῦ τέθνηκε γάρ.

ΜΗΤΗΡ ΣΩΣΤΡΑΤΟΥ

τάλαν·

οὐ περιμένει τὴν σὴν σχολήν. ἀλλ᾽ εἴσιτε·
440 κανᾶ πρόχειρα, χέρνιβας, θυλήματα
ποιεῖτε. ποῖ κέχηνας, ἐμβρόντητε σύ;

ΚΝΗΜΩΝ

κακοὶ κακῶς ἀπόλοισθε. ποιοῦσίν γέ με
ἀργόν· καταλιπεῖν γὰρ μόνην τὴν οἰκίαν

436 New speaker before εὐτρεπῆ suggested by several, identified
(see above, on 430–31) by Ritchie (περιμενοντεσευτρ:επη B).
438–41 Speech-divisions and identification of speakers un-
certain: here the former follow B, the latter Blake. 438
ταλαιν᾽ B. 440 προχρεια B. 441 κεχονας B.

---

[1] All these were needed for a sacrifice: spring water for
lustration; a basket for the barley grains whose sprinkling on
the victim was part of the preliminary ritual; and cakes (either

DYSKOLOS

GETAS

By Zeus, you've
Arrived here safely!   Heracles, how tedious!   435
We've been kept waiting such a long time!

SOSTRATOS' MOTHER

Is
Everything ready for us?

GETAS

By Zeus, yes—at least
The *sheep* is.   The suspense has all but killed
It!

SOSTRATOS' MOTHER
Poor thing, it can't wait for your convenience!

(*Here she turns to address her attendants*)

In you all go!   Prepare the baskets, water, cakes.[1] 440
What are *you* staring at, you imbecile?

*While these lines are being spoken, Getas and the party
move off into the shrine, and line 441 is most probably
addressed to the last loitering attendant to leave the stage,
although it could just possibly refer to the bemused
Knemon, left all alone now on the stage after Sostratos'
mother has followed Getas and the party inside.*)

KNEMON

You filthy scum, to hell with you!—They stop
Me doing any work.   I couldn't leave

dible ones, of meal sprinkled with honey and wine, or cakes of
incense: ancient accounts differ) for another part of the
ceremony.

MENANDER

οὐκ ἂν δυναίμην. αἱ δὲ Νύμφαι μοι κακὸν

445 a[ὖ]ται· παροικοῦσ', ὥστε μοι δοκῶ πάλιν
με]τοικοδομήσειν, καταβαλὼν τὴν οἰκίαν,

(KT fr. 117) ἐντ]εῦθεν. ὡς θύουσι δ' οἱ τοιχωρύχοι·
κοίτας φέρονται, σταμνί', οὐχὶ τῶν θεῶν
ἕνεκ', ἀλλ' ἑαυτῶν. ὁ λιβανωτὸς εὐσεβὲς √

450 καὶ τὸ πόπανον· τοῦτ' ἔλαβεν ὁ θεὸς ἐπὶ τὸ πῦρ
ἅπαν ἐπιτεθέν· οἱ δὲ τὴν ὀσφῦν ἄκραν
καὶ τὴν χολήν, ὅτι ἔστ' ἄβρωτα, τοῖς θεοῖς
ἐπιθέντες αὐτοὶ τἆλλα καταπίνουσι. γραῦ,
ἄνοιγε θᾶττον τὴν θύραν. [ποιητέ]ον

455 ἐστὶν γὰρ ἡμῖν τἄνδον, ὡ[ς ἐμοὶ] δοκεῖ.

ΓΕΤΑΣ

τὸ λεβήτιον, φῄς, ἐπιλέλη[σθ]ε; παντελῶς
ἀποκραιπαλᾶτε. καὶ τί νῦν ποιή[σ]ομεν;

445 a[ὖ]ται Stoessl : a[.]. αρ B, where the third letter could be
γ, π, or τ. 448 Corr. ed. pr.:]αιφερονται B, κοίτας φέροντες
ms. A of Athenaeus, 4. 146e. 449–52 The opening three (five
apparently in 450, but B may have had an error there) letters of
these lines, which are torn off in B, are supplied from some of
the ancient citations (Ath.; Porphyry, *De Abst.* 2. 17) or from
Berl. 449 ἑαυτῶν A of Ath.: εαυτον B. εὐσεβὲς A of Ath., B:
εὐσεβὴς mss. of Porph. 451 ἐπιτεθέν A of Ath., B: τεθέν mss
of Porph. 452–57 The opening 6 to 8 letters of these lines are
preserved in Berl. 452]την B, .]αιτην Berl. ὅτι ἔστ' A of
Ath., B: ὀστέα τὰ (in error for ὀστᾶ τ' ?) ms. L of Clement of
Alex., *Strom.* 7. 6. 31. 453 ἐπιθέντες A of Ath., B: ἐπιτιθέντες
L of Clem. καταπίνουσι A of Ath., B: ἀναλίσκουσι L of Clem.
454 Suppl. Blake. 456 Corr. and suppl. Zuntz: επιλελη[..]α
B.

DYSKOLOS

The house all unattended.   These Nymphs are
Nothing but trouble to me, being next door.   445
I think I'll pull my house down, build another
Away from here!—Look how the devils sacrifice.
They bring hampers and wine-jars, not to please
The gods, but their own guts.   Their piety
Extends to incense and the cake[1]—that's all put on   450
The fire, the god can take *that*.   And they serve
The gods with tail-bone and gall-bladder, just because
Men can't eat them.[2]   The rest they guzzle down
Themselves.—Old woman, quick, open the door!
We'd better [do] the inside jobs, [I] think.   455

*Knemon's final remarks are made while he knocks
vigorously on his door.   When it is opened, he disappears
inside.   After a few seconds, Getas enters from the shrine.
His opening remarks are addressed back into the shrine,
to unseen servant-women in the sacrificial party.*)

GETAS

The stew-pot?   You've forgotten it, you say?
You're all asleep—with hangovers!   Well, what

---

[1] Specifically, a small round cake usually made of barley.
[2] Though Knemon's anger and character lead him to
exaggerate here, there is enough truth in what he says to have
made an audience think hard about their religious observances.
Although Knemon's views were in no way novel (they belong
to a tradition going back a century at least), they were parti-
cularly relevant at the time of Menander's play, when philo-
sophers such as Theophrastus (allegedly a teacher of Menander)
were seriously interested in the problem, and when legislation
was being considered against useless extravagance (see Hand-
ley's edition of the *Dyskolos*, ad loc.).

ἐνοχλητέον τοῖς γειτνιῶσι τῷ θεῷ
ἐσθ᾽, ὡς ἔοικε. παιδίον. μὰ τοὺς θεούς,
460 θεραπαινίδια γὰρ ἀθλιώτερ᾽ οὐδαμοῦ
οἶμαι τρέφεσθαι. παῖδες. οὐδὲν ἄλλο πλὴν
κινητιᾶν ἐπίσταται—παῖδες καλοί—
καὶ διαβαλεῖν ἐὰν ἴδῃ τις. παιδίον.
τουτὶ τὸ κακὸν τί ἐστι; παῖδες. οὐδὲ εἷς
465 ἐστ᾽ ἔνδον. ἤήν. προστρέχειν τις φαίνεται.

ΚΝΗΜΩΝ
τί τῆς θύρας ἅπτει, τρισάθλι᾽, εἰπέ μοι,
ἄνθρωπε;

ΓΕΤΑΣ
μὴ δάκῃς.

ΚΝΗΜΩΝ
ἐγώ σε, νὴ Δία,
καὶ κατέδομαί γε ζῶντα.

ΓΕΤΑΣ
μή, πρὸς τῶν θεῶν.

ΚΝΗΜΩΝ
ἐμοὶ γάρ ἐστι συμβόλαιον, ἀνόσιε,
470 καὶ σοί τι;

458 τοιγιτνιωσι B.   462 επιστανται B.   464 τί om. B, suppl
ed. pr.   465 ην B.   466 Corr. several: απει B.   466–67 Change
of speaker after ἄνθρωπε indicated by several (ανθρωπεμη B
with no paragraphus under 466).   468 τῶν om. B, suppl
ed. pr.

Shall we do now? Apparently, disturb
Pan's next-door neighbours!

(*Getas goes to Knemon's door, and bangs on it loudly
every time he calls for a servant to open it for him.*)

         Servant!—By the gods,
I don't think there's a poorer set of girls   460
Anywhere living! Servants!—They don't know
A thing, apart from sex—Good servants, hoy!
—And telling tales if they are caught. Hoy, servant!
What's gone wrong here? Servants!—There's no-
  one in.
Aha! There's someone dashing to the door,   465
Apparently.

(*The door is flung open, to reveal an enraged Knemon.*)

        KNEMON
    Tell me, you wretched cur, why are
You clinging to my door?

        GETAS
        Don't bite my head
Off!

        KNEMON
  That I will, by Zeus, and eat you up
Alive, too!

        GETAS
  By the gods, no!

        KNEMON
        Villain, have
I ever signed a contract with you?

MENANDER

ΓΕΤΑΣ
συμβόλαιον οὐδέν· τοιγαροῦν
προσελήλυθ᾽ οὐ χρέος σ᾽ ἀπαιτῶν οὐδ᾽ ἔχων
κλητῆρας, ἀλλ᾽ αἰτησόμενος λεβήτιον.

ΚΝΗΜΩΝ
λεβήτιον;

ΓΕΤΑΣ
λεβήτιον.

ΚΝΗΜΩΝ
μαστιγία,
θύειν με βοῦς οἴει ποεῖν τε ταῦθ᾽ ἅπερ
475 ὑμεῖς ποεῖτ᾽;

ΓΕΤΑΣ
οὐδὲ κοχλίαν ἔγωγέ σε.
ἀλλ᾽ εὐτύχει, βέλτιστε. κόψαι τὴν θύραν
ἐκέλευσαν αἱ γυναῖκες αἰτῆσαί τέ με.
ἐπόησα τοῦτ᾽· οὐκ ἔστι· πάλιν ἀπαγγελῶ
ἐλθὼν ἐκείναις. ὦ πολυτίμητοι θεοί,
480 ἔχις πολιὸς ἄνθρωπός ἐστιν οὑτοσί.

ΚΝΗΜΩΝ
ἀνδροφόνα θηρί᾽· εὐθὺς ὥσπερ πρὸς φίλον
κόπτουσιν. ἂν ἡμῶν προσιόντα τῇ θύρᾳ

---

473 λεβοιτιον twice in B. Change of speaker after the second
λεβήτιον indicated by ed. pr. (λεβοιτιονμαστιγια B). 474
ποιεινδε B. 475 κωχλειαν B. 476 κομψαι B. 478 απαγγελλω
B.

DYSKOLOS

GETAS

Contract, no—   470

That's why I haven't come collecting debts from you
Or serving summonses—but just to borrow
A stew-pot.

KNEMON

A stew-pot?

GETAS

A stew-pot.

KNEMON

You
Scoundrel, do you think I offer cattle when
I sacrifice, and act just like you?

GETAS (*his first remark aside*)

Cattle? I   475

Don't think you'd even give a snail!—Good-bye,
Then, my dear sir! The women told me to
Knock at your door and ask. I've done that. You
   don't have
One. I'll go back and let them know. O honoured
   gods,
This fellow here's a silver-haired old viper!   480

(*Exit Getas, back into the shrine. Knemon is alone.*)

KNEMON

They're all man-eating tigers, think it's like
A friend's house, come right up and knock. Just let

λάβω τιν᾿, ἂν μὴ πᾶσι τοῖς ἐν τῷ τόπῳ
παράδειγμα ποιήσω, νομίζεθ᾿ ἕνα τινὰ
485 ὁρᾶν με τῶν πολλῶν. ὁ νῦν δ᾿ οὐκ οἶδ᾿ ὅπως
διευτύχηκεν οὗτος, ὅστις ἦν ποτε.

ΣΙΚΩΝ

κάκιστ᾿ ἀπόλοι᾿. ἐλοιδορεῖτό σοι; τυχὸν
ᾔτεις σκατοφάγως· οὐκ ἐπίστανταί τινες
(KT fr. 125) ποιεῖν τὸ τοιοῦθ᾿· εὕρηκ᾿ ἐγὼ τούτου τέχνην.
490 διακονῶ γὰρ μυρίοις ἐν τῇ πόλει
τούτων τ᾿ ἐνοχλῶ τοῖς γείτοσιν καὶ λαμβάνω
σκεύη παρ᾿ ἁπάντων. δεῖ γὰρ εἶναι κολακικὸν
τὸν δεόμενόν του. πρεσβύτερός τις τ[ῇ θύρᾳ
ὑπακήκο᾿· εὐθὺς πατέρα καὶ πάππα[ν καλῶ.
495 γραῦς· μητέρ᾿. ἂν τῶν διὰ μέσου τ[ις ᾖ γυνή,
ἐκάλεσ᾿ ἱερέαν. ἂν θεράπων [νεώτερος,
βέλτιστον. ὑμεῖς δ᾿ ἐκκρεμανν[ύοισθε δή·

483 λαβων B. 484–89 Scraps of the ends of these lines are
preserved in Berl. 485 ουραν B.]νδ᾿ουκ Berl: νννουκ B.
487 ελυδωρειτο B. 488 καταφαγ᾿ως B. 491 τ᾿ several: τι B.
494–500 Supplementation here is highly speculative, and the
text offered is *exempli gratia*. 494 πατέρα several: πατερ B.
πάππα[ν καλῶ suppl. several. 495 γρας B. τ[ις ᾖ γυνή suppl.
several (τ[ις and γυνή ed. pr. already). 496 ἱερέαν Handley:
ιερειαν B. νεώτερος suppl. Sandbach, tentatively. 497–98
Corr. and suppl. Arnott, *exempli gratia*: δεκρεμανν[(or -ανν[
or -ανη[) B.

¹ Literally in the Greek, 'priestess'. In Menander's
Athens, however, the title and function of priestess seem to
have been as much a mark of social status as of any particular
religious vocation.

DYSKOLOS

Me catch a man approaching *our* door! If
I don't make an example of you to the whole
Community, consider me—a cipher!   485
This fellow though, whoever he was, somehow got
Away just now!

(*Exit Knemon, into his house. Just as he slams the door,
Sikon emerges from the shrine. His opening remarks are
contemptuously addressed to Getas, who must either be
imagined by the audience as an unseen auditor inside the
shrine, or have come on stage with Sikon to be a silent
spectator, standing in the background, of what ensues.
Getas' visible presence would certainly add piquancy to
the following scene.*)

SIKON
Be damned to you! He told
You off? Perhaps you asked with the finesse
Of a pig! Some folk don't know how to do a thing
Like that. There's a technique to it that I've   490
Discovered. I help millions in the town,
Pestering their neighbours, borrowing pans from all
Of them. A borrower must use soft soap.
Suppose an older man answers the door. [I call]
[Him] ' Father ' straight away, or ' Dad '. If it's   495
A hag, then ' Mother '. If [a] middle-aged
[Woman], I call her ' Madam '.[1] If a [youngish (?)]
slave,
' Good chap '.

(*Here Sikon either turns to address Getas directly, if
Getas is on stage with him, or indicates by a wave in the
direction of the cave that he has Getas in mind, if Getas is
imagined to be still in the shrine.*)

You people, though—[be (?)] hanged! O what

MENANDER

ὢ τῆς ἀμαθίας· " παιδίον, παῖ "· [φλήναφος.
ἐγώ, " πρόελθε, πατρίδιον, σὲ β[ούλομαι."

ΚΝΗΜΩΝ
500 πάλιν αὖ σύ;

ΣΙΚΩΝ
π[αῖ, τί το]ῦτ';

ΚΝΗΜΩΝ
                       ἐρεθίζεις μ' ὡσπερεὶ
ἐπίτηδες. οὐκ [εἴρη]κά σοι πρὸς τὴν θύραν
μὴ προσιέναι; [τὸ]ν ἱμάντα δός, γραῦ.

ΣΙΚΩΝ
                              μηδαμῶς,
ἀλλ' ἄφες.

ΚΝΗΜΩΝ
ἄφε[ς;]

ΣΙΚΩΝ
               βέλτιστε, ναὶ πρὸς τῶν θεῶν.

ΚΝΗΜΩΝ
ἧκε πάλιν.

---

499 Suppl. Barrett.   500 Suppl. Handley.   503 τῶν om. B,
suppl. ed. pr.

DYSKOLOS

Stupidity! [Claptrap like (?)] ' Boy! Slave! ' *My*
   approach
Is ' Come on, dad, [I want (?)] you! '

(*As he speaks the last sentence, Sikon suits his action to the
words and knocks on Knemon's door. Knemon comes out
angrily.*)

KNEMON

You again? 500

SIKON (*taken aback by Knemon's fierceness*)
[Oh, what's (?)] this?

KNEMON

Looks as if you're nettling me
On purpose! Didn't I [tell] you not to come
To my door? Woman, pass [the] strap!

(*As Knemon speaks this command, addressed to Simiche
inside his house, he seizes Sikon; then he takes the strap
and belabours the cook with it.*)

SIKON

No! Let me go!

KNEMON

Let go?

SIKON

Yes, by the gods! Good chap!

(*Sikon breaks free of Knemon's grasp.*)

KNEMON

Come back!

MENANDER

ΣΙΚΩΝ

ὁ Ποσειδῶν σε—

ΚΝΗΜΩΝ

καὶ λαλεῖς ἔτι;

ΣΙΚΩΝ

505 χυτρόγαυλο[ν] αἰτησόμενος ἦλθον.

ΚΝΗΜΩΝ

(KT fr. 671?)   οὐκ ἔχω
οὔτε χυτρό[γ]αυλον οὔτε πέλεκυν οὔθ' ἅλας
οὔτ' ὄξος οὔτ' ἄλλ' οὐδέν, ἀλλ' εἴρηχ' ἁπλῶς
μὴ προσι[έ]ναι μοι πᾶσι τοῖς ἐν τῷ τόπῳ.

ΣΙΚΩΝ

ἐμοὶ μὲν οὐκ εἴρηκας.

ΚΝΗΜΩΝ

ἀλλὰ νῦν λέγω.

ΣΙΚΩΝ

510 νή, σὺν κακῷ γ'. οὐδ' ὁπόθεν ἄν τις, εἰπέ μοι,
ἐλθὼν λάβοι φράσαις ἄν;

---

505 αιτουμενος B. 507 So B: Choeroboscus in Theodosius,
Can. 1. 259. 16 Hilgard, however, appears to cite this line with
οὔτ' ὄξος οὔτ' ὀρίγανον, but he may be confusing this passage
with one in another play of Menander, or even be referring
to a similar passage in a different play. 510 Corr. several:
ουθ' B apparently altered to ουκ.

DYSKOLOS

SIKON

Poseidon send you . . .

KNEMON (*interrupting Sikon's imprecation*)
Babbling still?

SIKON
I came to ask 505
You for a skillet.[1]

KNEMON
I don't have a skillet, or
Cleaver, or salt, or vinegar, or anything
Else. I've told all the neighbourhood to keep
Away from me—just that!

SIKON
You've not told me!

KNEMON
Well, I'm
Telling you now!

SIKON (*feeling his sore shoulders*)
Yes, worse luck! Tell me, couldn't you just 510
Say where a man could go and get one from?

---

[1] The cook carefully avoids repeating Getas' unfortunate word 'stew-pot' (λεβήτιον). The substituted word χυτρό-γαυλος, a deep earthenware pot of bucket shape, may have been intended to sound a little over-technical. The translation 'skillet' attempts to convey something of this; it must of course be taken in its more traditional sense of ' cooking-pot '.

ΚΝΗΜΩΝ

οὐκ ἐγὼ ᾽λεγον;

ἔτι μοι λαλήσεις;

ΣΙΚΩΝ

χαῖρε πόλλ᾽.

ΚΝΗΜΩΝ

οὐ βούλομαι

χαίρειν παρ᾽ ὑμῶν οὐδενός.

ΣΙΚΩΝ

μὴ χαῖρε δή.

ΚΝΗΜΩΝ

ὦ τῶν ἀνηκέστων κακῶν.

ΣΙΚΩΝ

καλῶς γέ με

515 βεβωλοκόπηκεν. οἷόν ἐστ᾽ ἐπιδεξίως
αἰτεῖν· διαφέρει, νὴ Δί᾽. ἐφ᾽ ἑτέραν θύραν
ἔλθῃ τις; ἀλλ᾽ εἰ σφαιρομαχοῦσ᾽ ἐν τῷ τόπῳ
οὕτως ἑτοίμως, χαλεπόν. ἆρά γ᾽ ἐστί μοι
κράτιστον ὀπτᾶν τὰ κρέα πάντα; φαίνεται.
520 ἔστιν δέ μοι λοπάς τις. ἐρρῶσθαι λέγω
Φυλασίοις. τοῖς οὖσι τούτοις χρήσομαι.

514–15 καλῶς με βεβωλοκόπηκεν is cited by Aelius Dionysius (in
Aldus Manutius, *Horti Adonidis* p. 234a) without any source
being named. 516 Corr. several: εφαιτεραν $\overset{το}{B}$. 517 εντοπωι
B. 520 μοικαιλοπας B. 521 φυλασιτοισουσι B.

---

[1] The λοπάς, a shallow earthenware casserole, is illustrated in
B. A. Sparkes and L. Talcott, *Pots and Pans of Classical Athens*,
Princeton, 1958, fig. 44.

DYSKOLOS

KNEMON (*threatening Sikon again*)
Did I not tell you? Will you go on babbling
Away at me?

SIKON (*backing away*)
Good-bye!

KNEMON
I won't be 'good-bye'd' by
Any of you!

SIKON
Bad-bye, then!

KNEMON
Oh, what desperate
Afflictions!

(*Exit Knemon into his house, leaving Sikon alone on stage.*)

SIKON
Yes, he's ploughed me nicely! The   515
Importance of the shrewd appeal—by Zeus, how that
Does matter!

(*Sikon now changes from his rueful, self-mocking mood
to one of positive thinking.*)

—Must one try another door? Though if
They're *so* quick with their boxing lessons here,
I foresee snags!—Will it be best to roast
All this meat? That's the answer! I've a casserole.[1] 520
Farewell to Phyle! I'll use what I've got.

(*Exit Sikon, into the shrine. As he disappears, Sostratos
limps stiffly onto the stage from the left.*)

MENANDER

ΣΩΣΤΡΑΤΟΣ

ὅστις ἀπορεῖ κακῶν, ἐπὶ Φυλὴν ἐλθέτω
κυνηγετῶν. ὢ τρισκακοδαίμων, ὡς ἔχω
ὀσφῦν, μετάφρενον, τὸν τράχηλον, ἑνὶ λόγῳ
525 ὅλον τὸ σῶμ'. εὐθὺς γὰρ ἐμπεσὼν πολὺς
νεανίας ἐγώ τις, ἐξαίρων ἄνω
σφόδρα τὴν δίκελλαν, ὡς ἂν ἐργάτης, βαθὺ
ἔπαιον. ἐπεκείμην φιλοπόνως, οὐ πολὺν
χρόνον. εἶτα καὶ μετεστρεφόμην τι, πηνίκα
530 ὁ γέρων πρόσεισι τὴν κόρην ἄγων ἅμα
σκοπούμενος. καὶ νὴ Δί', ἐλαβόμην τότε
τῆς ὀσφύος, λάθρα τὸ πρῶτον· ὡς μακρὸν
ἦν παντελῶς δὲ τοῦτο, λορδοῦν ἠρχόμην,
ἀπεξυλούμην ἀτρέμα δ'. οὐδεὶς ἤρχετο.
535 ὁ δ' ἥλιος κατέκα', ἑώρα τ' ἐμβλέπων
ὁ Γοργίας ὥσπερ τὰ κηλώνειά με
μόλις ἀνακύπτοντ', εἶθ' ὅλῳ τῷ σώματι
πάλιν κατακύπτοντ'. "οὐ δοκεῖ μοι νῦν," ἔφη,
"ἥξειν ἐκεῖνος, μειράκιον." "τί οὖν," ἐγὼ
540 εὐθύς, "ποῶμεν; αὔριον τηρήσομεν
α[ὐ]τόν, τὸ δὲ νῦν ἐῶμεν;" ὅ τε Δᾶος παρῆν
ἐπ[ὶ] τὴν σκαπάνην διάδοχος. ἡ πρώτη μὲν οὖν
ἔφο]δος τοιαύτη γέγονεν· ἥκω δ' ἐνθάδε,
διὰ] τί μὲν οὐκ ἔχω λέγειν, μὰ τοὺς θεούς,
545 ἕλκ]ει δέ μ' αὐτόματον τὸ πρᾶγμ' εἰς τὸν τόπον.

523 κυνηγετῶν Quincey: κυνηγετησων B. τρισκακοδαίμων,
ὡς several: τρισκακοδαιμονως B. 528 ἔπαιον Sandbach: εγαι
πλειον B. 531 Corr. Handley: ποτε B. 536 κηλωναειμε B.
541 εασομεν B. 542 Suppl. Lloyd-Jones. 543 Suppl. several.
545 Suppl. Barrett, London seminar.

DYSKOLOS

SOSTRATOS

f anybody's short of troubles, let
Him come to Phyle for the hunting.   Oh,
The pain!   It crucifies my loins, back, neck—
In short, my whole body!   You see, I tore   525
Hard into it straight off, the young fanatic!
Swinging the mattock heftily up, like
A labourer, I'd smash in deep.   I kept
On strenuously—not too long.   Then I'd turn round
A bit, and look to see when the old man   530
Would turn up with the girl.   That's when, by Zeus,
I felt my back.   First, furtively.   But as
It went on, hours and hours, I started to
Go bow-backed.   I was quietly stiffening up.
But no-one came.   The sun was frizzling me.   535
And Gorgias would look and see me going up
Just like a see-saw,[1] slightly up, then down
Again with all my strength.   ' Young man,' he said,
I don't think he'll come now.'   ' What shall we do
Then?' I replied at once; ' look out for him   540
Tomorrow, and call it a day now?'   Daos
Arrived to take the digging over.   So that's how
The first assault has ended.   And I'm here.   Why? I
Can't tell you, by the gods, but of its own
Accord the venture draws me to this spot.   545

*(The door of the shrine bursts open, emitting a cloud of
smoke.   Through it Getas enters, shouting back at Sikon,
who remains inside unseen.)*

---

[1] Literally in the Greek, the counterpoised beams which
were sometimes used as the mechanism for drawing water up
from the shallower wells.

ΓΕΤΑΣ

τί τὸ κ]ακόν; οἴει χεῖρας ἑξήκοντά με,
ἄνθρ]ωπ᾽, ἔχειν; τοὺς ἄνθρακάς σοι ζωπυρῶ·
δέχο]μαι, φέρω, πλύνω, κατατέμνω σπλάγχν᾽ ἅμα
μάττω· περιφέρω τὰ κ[εράμια, νὴ το]υτονί,
550 ὑπὸ τοῦ καπνοῦ τυφλὸς [γεγονώ]ς. τούτοις ὄνος
ἄγειν δοκῶ μοι τὴν ἑορτή[ν.]

ΣΩΣΤΡΑΤΟΣ

[π]αῖ Γέτα.

ΓΕΤΑΣ

ἐμὲ τίς;

ΣΩΣΤΡΑΤΟΣ

ἐγώ.

ΓΕΤΑΣ

σὺ δ᾽ εἶ τίς;

ΣΩΣΤΡΑΤΟΣ

οὐχ [ὁρᾷ]ς;

ΓΕΤΑΣ

ὁρῶ·

τρόφιμος.

546, 547 Suppl. several. ανθρακασοι B.   548–550 Supplementa
tion and correction are highly uncertain, and the text printed
is *exempli gratia*.   548 δέχο]μαι suppl. Kraus.   φέρω, πλύνω
Barber, Kraus: πολυνωφερω B.   549 Suppl. Arnott (νὴ also
Kraus).   550 ὄνος several: ολος B.   552 συδετις B.

DYSKOLOS

GETAS

'What] *now*, damn you?   [Man], do you think that I've
Got sixty hands?   I've made the charcoal glow for you.
I [take (?)], fetch, wash, cut offal up, all in
One breath.   I make cakes, shift the [pots, by Pan (?)]
Here,[1] and [get] blinded by the smoke.   I'm just   550
The donkey at the feast,[2] as far as *they*'re
Concerned!

SOSTRATOS
Getas, boy!

GETAS (*his eyes still smarting from the smoke*)
Who wants me?

SOSTRATOS
I do.

GETAS (*still not recognising Sostratos*)
Who're you?

SOSTRATOS
Can't you [see]?

GETAS
Yes, it's master.

[1] If this supplement is right (and it is highly speculative),
Getas' oath would be accompanied by a gesture in the direction
of the statue of Pan, which stood at the entrance to his shrine
(see the note on line 12).

[2] Apparently an adaptation of the proverb ὄνος ἄγω μυστήρια,
' I'm the donkey celebrating the Mysteries ' (cf. Aristophanes,
Frogs 159).   The donkey's role in the celebration of such
festivals consisted in carrying the sacred utensils, while the
human participants enjoyed themselves.

MENANDER

ΣΩΣΤΡΑΤΟΣ

τί ποιεῖτ᾽ ἐνθάδ᾽, [εἰ]πέ μοι;

ΓΕΤΑΣ

τί γάρ;

τεθύκαμεν ἄρτι καὶ παρασκευάζομεν
555 ἄριστον ὑμῖν.

ΣΩΣΤΡΑΤΟΣ

ἐνθάδ᾽ ἡ μήτηρ;

ΓΕΤΑΣ

πάλαι.

ΣΩΣΤΡΑΤΟΣ

ὁ πατὴρ δέ;

ΓΕΤΑΣ

προσδοκῶμεν. ἀ[λ]λὰ πάραγε σύ.

ΣΩΣΤΡΑΤΟΣ

μικρὸν διαδραμών γ᾽. ἐνθαδὶ τρ[ό]πον τινὰ
γέγον᾽ οὐκ ἄκαιρος ἡ θυσία· παραλήψομαι
τὸ μειράκιον τουτὶ γάρ, ἐλθὼν ὡς ἔχω,
560 καὶ τὸν θεράποντ᾽ αὐτοῦ· κεκοινωνηκότες
ἱερῶν γὰρ εἰς τὰ λοιπὰ χρησιμώτεροι
ἡμῖν ἔσονται σύμμαχοι πρὸς τὸν γάμον.

ΓΕΤΑΣ

τί φῄς; ἐπ᾽ ἄριστόν τινας παραλαμβάνειν
μέλλεις πορευθείς; ἕνεκ᾽ ἐμοῦ τρισχίλιοι

557 γ᾽ om. B, suppl. several. 558 ηθυσιαν B. 559 Corr.
Sandbach: παρελθων B. 561 χρησιμωτεραι B.

272

DYSKOLOS

SOSTRATOS

Tell me, what
Are *you* doing here?

GETAS

Why, we've just finished with
The sacrifice, we're getting lunch prepared.   555

SOSTRATOS

Is mother here?

GETAS

A long while.

SOSTRATOS
Father?

GETAS

We're
Expecting him.   But come on in.

SOSTRATOS

Yes, after I've
Run a small errand.   In one way, the sacrifice
Here's been quite timely.   I'll go just as I
Am and invite this young man here and his   560
Servant.   If they share in the offerings, they'll
Be better champions of our wedding plan
In future!

GETAS

What do you say?   You intend
To go and invite guests to lunch?   Well, *I*

565 γένοισθ'. ἐγὼ μὲν γὰρ πάλαι τοῦτ' οἶδ', ὅτι
οὐ γεύσομ' οὐδενός· πόθεν γάρ; συνάγετε
πάντας. καλὸν γὰρ τεθύκαθ' ἱερεῖον, πάνυ
ἄξιον ἰδεῖν. ἀλλὰ τὰ γύναια ταῦτά μοι—
ἔχει γὰρ ἀστείως—μεταδοίη γ' ἄν τινος;
570 οὐδ' ἄν, μὰ τὴν Δήμητρ', ἁλὸς πικροῦ.

ΣΩΣΤΡΑΤΟΣ

καλῶς

ἔσται, Γέτα, τὸ τήμερον· μαντεύσομαι
τοῦτ' αὐτός, ὦ Πάν—ἀλλὰ μὴν προσεύχομαι
ἀεὶ παριών σοι—καὶ φιλανθρωπεύσομαι.

ΣΙΜΙΧΗ

ὦ δυστυχής· ὦ δυστυχής· ὦ δυστυχής.

ΓΕΤΑΣ

575 ἄπαγ' εἰς τὸ βάραθρον· τοῦ γέροντός τις γυνὴ
προελήλυθεν.

ΣΙΜΙΧΗ

τί πείσομαι; τὸν γὰρ κάδον
ἐκ τοῦ φρέατος βουλομένη τοῦ δεσπότου,
εἴ πως δυναίμην, ἐξελεῖν αὐτὴ λάθρᾳ,
ἀνῆψα τὴν δίκελλαν ἀσθενεῖ τινι

568 ἰδεῖν. ἀλλὰ τὰ γύναια several: ιδειντιν'αλλαγυναια B. 577
Corr. several: βουλομενου B. 579 ενηψα B. (with *a* above)

---

[1] See note on line 12.

DYSKOLOS

Don't care if there's three thousand of you!   There's 565
One thing I've known a long time—*I* shan't taste
A thing; how could I?   Round up all the guests!
You've had a *fine* sheep killed, a *real* joy to the eyes!
These females, though—they're charming, but would
   they
Give *me* a taste of something?   By Demeter, not 570
Even a grain of kitchen salt!

SOSTRATOS

          Getas, today
It'll be all right, I'll forecast that myself, O Pan!
—I always pray to you as I go past[1]—and I'll
Be generous!

(*With these consoling remarks to the grumbling Getas,
Sostratos goes off left, in search of Gorgias and Daos.
Suddenly Knemon's door opens, and out comes Simiche,
Knemon's old female slave, in a state of tragic misery.*)

SIMICHE (*not noticing Getas' presence*)
        O tragedy!   O tragedy!
O tragedy!

GETAS (*aside*)
        To hell with her!   Look who's 575
Come out—the old man's woman.

SIMICHE
                What will happen
To me?   I hoped to fish the bucket up
Out of the well myself, if possible,
Without my master knowing, so I tied

MENANDER

580 καλῳδίῳ σαπρῷ, διερράγη τέ μοι
τοῦτ᾽ εὐθύς—

ΓΕΤΑΣ

ὀρθῶς.

ΣΙΜΙΧΗ

—ἐνσέσεικά θ᾽ ἀθλία
καὶ τὴν δίκελλαν εἰς τὸ φρέαρ μετὰ τοῦ κάδου.

ΓΕΤΑΣ

ῥῖψαι τὸ λοιπόν σοι σεαυτὴν ἔστ᾽ ἔτι.

ΣΙΜΙΧΗ

ὁ δ᾽ ἀπὸ τύχης κόπρον τιν᾽ ἔνδον κειμένην
585 μέλλων μεταφέρειν, περιτρέχων ταύτην πάλαι
ζητεῖ βοᾷ τε—καὶ ψοφεῖ γε τὴν θύραν.

ΓΕΤΑΣ

φεῦγ᾽, ὦ πονηρά, φεῦγ᾽· ἀποκτενεῖ σε, γραῦ·
μᾶλλον δ᾽ ἀμύνου.

ΚΝΗΜΩΝ

ποῦ ᾽στιν ἡ τοιχωρύχος;

ΣΙΜΙΧΗ

ἄκουσα, δέσποτ᾽, ἐνέβαλον.

---

581 Getas' interruption indicated by ed. pr. (B has no para-
graphus under line 581, certainly no dicolon after ὀρθῶς,
probably no dicolon before it). 581 θ᾽ ἀθλία Jacques: τ᾽ἀθλια
B. 584 ὁ δ᾽ several: οιδ᾽ B. 585 μελλοντων B.

The mattock to a flimsy, rotten bit   580
Of rope, and it snapped on me right away . . .

GETAS

Good!

SIMICHE (*deaf to all interruptions*)

. . . and,
Oh dear, I've dropped the mattock in the well
Now, with the bucket! . . .

GETAS

Still one thing to do—
Jump in yourself!

SIMICHE

. . . and master wants to shift some dung
That's lying in the yard, as luck would have it, and 585
For ages he's been searching for it, bawling and
Rushing around, and . . . he's rattling the latch!

(*Simiche cowers in terror as the door of Knemon's house
opens, and Knemon rushes out in a rage.*)

GETAS

Poor thing,
Run, run! He'll murder you, old woman! No,
   stand up
To him!

KNEMON

Where is the culprit?

SIMICHE

Master, I
Didn't mean to drop it in!

277

MENANDER

ΚΝΗΜΩΝ

βάδιζε δὴ

590 εἴσω.

ΣΙΜΙΧΗ

τί ποιεῖν δ', εἰπέ μοι, μέλλεις;

ΚΝΗΜΩΝ

ἐγώ;

δήσας καθιμήσω σε.

ΣΙΜΙΧΗ

μὴ δῆτ', ὦ τάλαν.

ΓΕΤΑΣ

ταὐτῷ γε τούτῳ σχοινίῳ, νὴ τοὺς θεούς·
κράτιστον, εἴπερ ἐστὶ παντελῶς σαπρόν.

ΣΙΜΙΧΗ

τὸν Δᾶον ἐκ τῶν γειτόνων ἐγὼ [καλ]ῶ.

ΚΝΗΜΩΝ

595 Δᾶον καλεῖς, ἀνόσι', ἀνῃρηκυῖα [με;
οὔ σοι λέγω; θᾶττον βάδιζ' εἴσω. [τάλας

592–93 These lines are given to Getas by Webster (in B there is
no paragraphus under 592, no dicolon visible after ταλαν in
591), but other assignments are possible. 595 ανηρεικυια B.
με suppl. several.

---

¹ The text hereabouts (lines 595 to 599) is both defective and
corrupt, and certain restoration is impossible. Nevertheless, a
change of tone is clearly discernible in the remainder of
Knemon's speech and in the words of Getas that immediately
follow Knemon's exit here. Knemon appears suddenly to
realise (in vivid contrast to what he has said earlier: cf. 169 f.)

278

DYSKOLOS

KNEMON (*with a gesture to the door*)
        Get in!

    SIMICHE

                      Tell me, what are 590
You going to do?

    KNEMON
    Me? I'll let *you* down on the rope!

    SIMICHE
No, no! Oh dear!

    GETAS
        Yes—best use, by the gods,
That same rope, if it's *really* rotten through
And through!

    SIMICHE (*making for Gorgias' door*)
        I'll [shout for] Daos, from next door.

    KNEMON (*going after her*)
You'll shout for Daos, will you? You've ruined me, 595
You heathcn! Can't I tell you? Get inside,
Quickly!

(*Exit Simiche into Knemon's house. There is a slight
pause before Knemon continues his specch.*[1])

the difficulties of isolation, and with this realisation his
character reveals for the first time a sympathetic facet.
Getas' speech (603 ff.) underpins this sympathy. Menander is
laying the foundations for Knemon's appearance in the fourth
act.

ἐγώ, τάλας τῆς νῦν ἐρημίας, [τάλας
ὡς οὐδὲ εἷς. καταβήσομ' εἰ[ς τὸ φρέαρ· τί γὰρ
ἔτ' ἐστὶν ἄλλ';

ΓΕΤΑΣ

ἡμεῖς ποριοῦ[μεν ἁρπάγην

600 καὶ σχοινίον.

ΚΝΗΜΩΝ

κακὸν κάκ[ιστά σ' οἱ θεοὶ
ἅπαντες ἀπολέσειαν εἴ τι μ[οι λαλεῖς.

ΓΕΤΑΣ

καὶ μάλα δικ[αίως. εἰσ]πεπήδηκεν πάλιν.
ὦ τρισκακοδα[ίμων οὗ]τος· οἷον ζῇ βίον.
τοῦτ' ἐστὶν εἰλικρ[ινὴς] γεωργὸς Ἀττικός·
605 πέτραις μαχόμ[εν]ος θύμα φερούσαις καὶ σφάκον
ὀδύνας ἐπισπᾶ[τ', ο]ὐδὲν ἀγαθὸν λαμβάνων.
ἀλλ' ὁ τρόφιμος [γ]ὰρ οὑτοσὶ προσέρχεται
ἄγων μεθ' α[ὑ]τοῦ τοὺς ἐπικλήτους. ἐργάται
ἐκ τοῦ τόπου τ[ιν]ές εἰσιν· ὦ τῆς ἀτοπίας.

596–99 Supplementation of B's gaps is uncertain; the text
printed is *exempli gratia*.   596–97 Suppl. Winnington-
Ingram.   597 τῆς νῦν ἐρημίας Shipp: τησερημιαστησνυν[B
598 Suppl. Handley.   599 ἔτ' Handley: ειτ' B. ποριοῦ[με
ἁρπάγην suppl. several.   600 Suppl. Gallavotti, Page.   60
Suppl. Fraenkel.   602 δικ[αίως suppl. ed. pr., εἰσ]πεπήδηκε
several.   604 Suppl. J. Martin (εἰλικρ[ινῶς] ed. pr.).   60
σκαφο ⁻ (where ⁻ is a sign for ν) B.   606 ἐπισπᾶ[τ' severa
επιστα[B.

This isolation makes me [ache],
Yes! ache—[ache (?)] more than anybody.   I'll go
  down
The well.   What (?)] else can one do?

GETAS (*addressing Knemon directly*)
                    We'll provide
A grapple (?)] and a rope.

KNEMON
                    May all [the gods]   600
Damn, smash and blast [you] to perdition, if [you say]
A [word to me]!

*As Getas begins his next speech, Knemon goes off into his
house, slamming the door and leaving Getas alone on the
stage.*)

GETAS
                    And I'll deserve it!   He's
Off [in] again.   O poor, poor devil, what
A life he leads!   There goes a perfect specimen
Of Attic farmer.   Wages war on rocks that grow   605
Savory and sage,[1] reaps aches and pains, and gets
No profit.   But here comes my master, with
His guests in tow.   They're just farm-labourers from
The neighbourhood!   How extraordinary!

[1] Typical wild plants in the barren, stony soil of the Attic
hills.

610 οὗτος τί τούτους δεῦρ᾽ ἄγει νῦν; ἢ πόθεν
γεγονὼς συνήθης;

ΣΩΣΤΡΑΤΟΣ
οὐκ ἂν ἐπιτρέψαιμί σοι
ἄλλως ποῆσαι.

ΓΟΡΓΙΑΣ
πάντ᾽ ἔχομεν.

ΣΩΣΤΡΑΤΟΣ
ὦ Ἡράκλεις,
τουτὶ δ᾽ ἀπαρνεῖται τίς ἀνθρώπων ὅλως,
ἐλθεῖν ἐπ᾽ ἄριστον συνήθους τεθυκότος;
615 εἰμὶ γάρ, ἀκριβῶς ἴσθι, σοὶ πάλαι φίλος,
πρὶν ἰδεῖν. λαβὼν ταῦτ᾽ εἰσένεγκε, Δᾶε, σύ,
εἶθ᾽ ἧκε.

610 αγεινννν B. 611 γονως B. 612 παντ᾽ ἔχομεν assigned to
Gorgias by Webster (in B there is no paragraphus under 612
no dicola before or after the phrase). 616 Corr. Gallavott
(who prefers, however, τάδ᾽ to ταῦτ᾽): ταυταδ᾽εισενεγκεδεσυ B

---

[1] Behind the ebullient exaggeration lies a grain of truth
To the contemporary Athenian, a marriage tie could involve
friendly relations with any member of the bride's family, and

DYSKOLOS

Why's he now bringing *them* here? How's he got   610
To know *them*?

(*As Getas concludes his speech, Sostratos enters with
Gorgias and Daos from the left. Sostratos and Gorgias
are in mid-conversation. Getas now either steps into the
doorway of the shrine in order to eavesdrop on the following
conversation, or perhaps more plausibly makes his exit
into the shrine.*)

SOSTRATOS
I'd not dream of letting you

Refuse!

GORGIAS
Thank you, but we can't.

SOSTRATOS
              Heracles!
Who in the world declines an invitation
Point blank, to come to lunch after his friend
Has had a sacrifice? I've been your friend—   615
That's definite—a long time, since before I met
You.[1] Here, take these in, Daos, then come yourself.

(*Sostratos takes Gorgias' farming implements from him
and hands them over to Daos, who makes for Gorgias'
house with them. Gorgias stops Daos, and addresses
him.*)

Sostratos had at least fallen in love with Gorgias' half-sister
some time before meeting him!

ΓΟΡΓΙΑΣ

μηδαμῶς μόνην τὴν μητέρα
οἴκοι καταλείπων· ἀλλ' ἐκείνης ἐπιμελοῦ
ὧν ἂν δέηται· ταχὺ δὲ κἀγὼ παρέσομαι.

ΧΟΡΟΥ

ΜΕΡΟΣ Δ'

ΣΙΜΙΧΗ

620 τίς ἂν βοηθήσειεν; ὦ τάλαιν' ἐγώ.
τίς ἂν βοηθήσειεν;

ΣΙΚΩΝ

'Ηράκλεις ἄναξ.
ἐάσαθ' ἡμᾶς, πρὸς θεῶν καὶ δαιμόνων,
σπονδὰς ποῆσαι. λοιδορεῖσθε, τύπτετε·
οἰμώζετ'. ὦ τῆς οἰκίας τῆς ἐκτόπου.

ΣΙΜΙΧΗ

625 ὁ δεσπότης ἐν τῷ φρέατι.

ΣΙΚΩΝ

πῶς;

---

[1] Menander marks carefully the successive stages of the
ceremony at the shrine. The sacrifice is now long past, and
the lunch itself just completed. At this point libations are

DYSKOLOS

GORGIAS

Leave mother by herself at home? Never! See to
Whatever she needs. I'll be back soon, too.

*(Daos now goes off into Gorgias' house with the imple-
ments, while Sostratos leads Gorgias into the shrine.
When the stage is empty, the chorus enter to give their
entr'acte performance.)*

ACT IV

*(After the chorus' departure, Simiche dashes out from
Knemon's house in a tragic state of distress.)*

SIMICHE

Who'll come and bring assistance? Oh dear me!   620
Who'll come and bring assistance?

(Sikon comes angrily out of the shrine.)

SIKON

             O Lord Heracles!
By all the gods and spirits, do let us get on
With our libations[1]! You insult and clout us, you—
May go to hell! What an incredible
House!

SIMICHE

Master's in the well!

SIKON

             How did that happen? 625

offered to the gods as a prelude to the drinking which concludes
the party.

MENANDER

ΣΙΜΙΧΗ

ὅπως;
ἵνα τὴν δίκελλαν ἐξέλοι καὶ τὸν κάδον
κατέβαινε, κᾆτ' ὤλισθ' ἄνωθεν, ὥστε καὶ
πέπτωκεν.

ΣΙΚΩΝ

οὐ γὰρ ὁ χαλεπὸς γέρων σφόδρα;

ΣΙΜΙΧΗ

οὗτος.

ΣΙΚΩΝ

καλά γ' ἐπόησε, νὴ τὸν Οὐρανόν.
630 ὦ φιλτάτη γραῦ, νῦν σὸν ἔργον ἐστί.

ΣΙΜΙΧΗ

πῶς;

ΣΙΚΩΝ

ὅλμον τιν' ἢ λίθον τιν' ἢ τοιοῦτό τι
ἄνωθεν ἔνσεισον λαβοῦσα.

ΣΙΜΙΧΗ

φίλτατε,

κατάβα.

627 κατωλισθ' B.   628 σφοδραῖ B.   629–33 οὗτος in line 629 is
assigned to Simiche by Kassel, Thierfelder (in B no para-
graphus under the line, no dicola before or after the word); and
the change of speaker after κατάβα in line 633 is indicated by
ed. pr. (in B no paragraphus under the line, no dicola after the
word); the intrusive ι at the end of σφοδραῖ, καταβαῖ, however,

286

DYSKOLOS

SIMICHE

How? He was going down to fish the mattock
out and the bucket, then he slipped while at
the top, and so he's fallen in.

SIKON

Not that

crabby old terror?

SIMICHE

Yes.

SIKON

By Heaven, he's done
himself justice! And now it's up to you,   630
My dear old girl!

SIMICHE

How?

SIKON

Take a mortar or a rock,
Or something of the sort, and drop it on
Him from above!

SIMICHE

Dear fellow, do go down!

---

may possibly mistranscribe a blotched : in the model copied.
33 καταβαῖ B.

MENANDER

ΣΙΚΩΝ

Πόσειδον, ἵνα τὸ τοῦ λόγου πάθω,
ἐν τῷ φρέατι κυνὶ μάχωμαι; μηδαμῶς.

ΣΙΜΙΧΗ

635 ὦ Γοργία, ποῦ γῆς ποτ᾽ εἶ;

ΓΟΡΓΙΑΣ

               ποῦ γῆς ἐγώ;
τί ἐστι, Σιμίχη;

ΣΙΜΙΧΗ

          τί γάρ; πάλιν λέγω·
ὁ δεσπότης ἐν τῷ φρέατι.

ΓΟΡΓΙΑΣ

              Σώστρατε,
ἔξελθε δεῦρ᾽.

ΣΙΜΙΧΗ

ἡγοῦ, βάδιζ᾽ εἴσω ταχύ.

635 πουτισποτει: πουποτ᾽ειμιγησεγω Β.   636 Here and else-
where (926, 931, cast list, character indications in B's margins)
B spells the name σιμικη: corr. Marzullo, Schmid.

---

[1] Sikon's proverb is taken from the old fable (a version of
which is preserved in the Aesopic collection, no. 122 Hausrath)
about the gardener and the dog. When the gardener went
down a well to rescue his dog, the dog bit him because he
thought his master had come to drown him.

DYSKOLOS

SIKON

Poseidon! Like the victim in the fable, fight
The dog inside the well[1]? Never!

*(Simiche now turns to bang loudly on Gorgias' door,
shouting for him at the same time.)*

SIMICHE

Where *are*   635
You, Gorgias?

*(Gorgias, hearing the clamour, dashes out from the
shrine.)*

GORGIAS

Where *am* I? What's this, Simiche?

SIMICHE

You ask? Again I tell you, master's in the well!

GORGIAS *(shouting into the entrance of the shrine)*
Come out here, Sostratos!

SIMICHE *(to Gorgias, as Sostratos comes out of the
shrine)*

You lead—go in,
Hurry!

*(Simiche and Sostratos follow Gorgias into Knemon's
house, leaving Sikon alone on the stage. He has been an
amused spectator of all this bustling.)*

ΣΙΚΩΝ

εἰσὶν θεοί, μὰ τὸν Διόνυσον. οὐ δίδως
640 λεβήτιον θύουσιν, ἱερόσυλε σύ,
ἀλλὰ φθονεῖς; ἔκπιθι τὸ φρέαρ ἐμπεσών,
ἵ]να μηδ' ὕδατος ἔχῃς μεταδοῦναι μηδενί.
νυ]νὶ μὲν αἱ Νύμφαι τετιμωρημέναι
(KT fr. 118) εἴσ'] αὐτὸν ὑπὲρ ἐμοῦ δικαίως. οὐδὲ εἷς
645 μάγειρον ἀδικήσας ἀθῶος διέφυγεν·
ἱεροπρεπής πώς ἐστιν ἡμῶν ἡ τέχνη·
ἀλλ' εἰ]ς τραπεζοποιὸν ὅ τι βούλει πόει.
τί δ'; ἆ]ρα μὴ τέθνηκεν; πάππαν φίλτατον
649 καλο]ῦσ' ἀποιμώζει τις· οὐδὲν τοῦτό γε

(Lacuna of perhaps four lines)

654 δηλονότι καθ[
655 οὕτως ἀνιμησ[
    τὴν ὄψιν αὐτοῦ ι ιν[
    οἴεσθ' ἔσεσθαι, πρὸς θεῶν; βεβ[αμ]μένου,
    τρέμοντος; ἀστείαν. ἐγὼ μὲν ἡδέως
    ἴδοιμ' ἄν, ἄνδρες, νὴ τὸν Ἀπόλλω τουτονί.

---

639 διονυσιου B. 641 εκπεσων B. 645-46]γ_ρον and
]πρεπης B: full text in Athenaeus, 9. 383 f. 645 ἀθῷος msc. o
Ath.: αθωιως B. 647 Suppl. Webster. 648 τί δ'; suppl.
Bingen, ἆ]ρα ed. pr. 649 Suppl. several. 654 δηλονοθι B.
656 τιν[or τη[B. 657 εσεσθε B. βεβ[αμ]μένου suppl. M_ _.

---

[1] See the note on *Aspis* 227.
[2] See the note on *Aspis* 232.
[3] Outside the street door of Greek houses, an altar or
emblem (usually in the form of a pointed pillar) was erected to
Apollo Agyieus (that is, Apollo viewed in his capacity as god of

DYSKOLOS

SIKON

By Dionysus, the gods *do*
Exist! So you won't lend a stewing-pot, 640
You crook,[1] to sacrificers? No—you're greedy!
Fall in and drink the well dry—you won't have
A dribble then of water left to share
With anyone! Today the Nymphs [have] given me
Revenge on him—and rightly! No-one hurts a *cook*, 645
And gets away scot-free. Our art's a sacred art,
I think. [With] *waiters*,[2] [though], do what you like!
[Oh, (?)] surely he's not died? A girl is crying,
She's [call]ing ' Dearest daddy .' That's nothing 649
[To do with me, however (?) . . . .]

(*Lines 650 to 653 inclusive, according to the first editor's
calculations, have been torn off the top of a folio of the
papyrus and so lost, and lines 654 to 656 are badly
mutilated. In the gap Sikon continues his monologue.
Presumably he hears some off-stage cries which indicate
that Knemon has not died but been rescued. He pictures
to himself the scene.*)

Clearly [. . . . .] 654
That's how [they'll (?)] haul [him] up [. . . . .] 655
And his appearance, [once he's been fished out (?)]—
Can you imagine, by the gods, what it'll
Be like? A drowned rat, shivering! Lovely! By
Apollo here,[3] I'd love to see that, gentlemen!

(*Sikon's ' gentlemen ' was addressed to the audience. He
now turns to the entrance of the shrine, shouting inside to
the women members of the sacrificial party who are
imagined to be inside.*)

streets and highways). Here Sikon points to a stage equiv-
alent set up outside Knemon's door.

660 ὑμεῖς δ' ὑπὲρ τούτων, γυναῖκες, σπένδετε·
εὔχεσθε τὸν γέροντα σωθῆναι—κακῶς,
ἀνάπηρον ὄντα, χωλόν· οὕτω γίνεται
ἀλυπότατος γὰρ τῷδε γείτων τ[ῷ] θεῷ
καὶ τοῖς ἀεὶ θύουσιν. ἐπιμελὲς δέ μοι
665 τοῦτ' ἐστίν, ἄν τις ἆρα μισθώσητ' ἐμέ.

ΣΩΣΤΡΑΤΟΣ

ἄνδρες, μὰ τὴν Δήμητρα, μὰ τὸν Ἀσκληπιόν,
μὰ τοὺς θεούς, οὐπώποτ' ἐν τὠμῷ βίῳ
εὐκαιρότερον ἄνθρωπον ἀποπεπνιγμένον
ἑόρακα—μικροῦ· τῆς γλυκείας διατριβῆς.
670 ὁ Γοργίας γάρ, ὡς τάχιστ' εἰσήλθομεν,
εὐθὺς κατεπήδησ' εἰς τὸ φρέαρ, ἐγὼ δὲ καὶ
ἡ παῖς ἄνωθεν οὐδὲν ἐποοῦμεν· τί γὰρ
ἐμέλλομεν; πλὴν ἡ μὲν αὑτῆς τὰς τρίχας
ἔτιλλ', ἔκλα', ἔτυπτε τὸ στῆθος σφόδρα·
675 ἐγὼ δ' ὁ χρυσοῦς, ὡσπερεί, νὴ τοὺς θεούς,
τροφὸς παρεστώς, ἐδεόμην γε μὴ ποεῖν
(KT fr. 126?) ταῦθ', ἱκέτευον, ἐμβλέπων ἀγάλματι
οὐ τῷ τυχόντι. τοῦ πεπληγμένου κάτω
ἔμελε δ' ἔλαττον ἤ τινός μοι, πλὴν ἀεὶ
680 ἕλκειν ἐκεῖνον—τοῦτ' ἐνώχλει μοι σφόδρα.
μικροῦ γε, νὴ Δί', αὐτὸν εἰσαπολώλεκα·
τὸ σχοινίον γάρ, ἐμβλέπων τῇ παρθένῳ,
ἀφῆκ' ἴσως τρίς. ἀλλ' ὁ Γοργίας Ἄτλας

661 ευχεσθαι B. 663 Corr. several: αλλ'υποτατος B. τ[ῷ] θεῷ deciphered and suppl. by several. 664 καιτους B. 668 απο πενιγμενον B. 678–79 του π.κ./ εμελε δ' Kraus (εμελεν already ed. pr.): τοδε π.κ./ εμελλον B. 680 ενοχλι B. 683 ισωτρις B.

DYSKOLOS

And ladies, you must pour libations, to   660
Help them.   Pray that the old man's rescue may
Be bungled, leaving him disabled and
A cripple.   Then he'll be the quietest of
Neighbours to Pan here and all sacrificers.   It's
Crucial for *me*, too, if I'm ever hired!   665

(*Exit Sikon, into the shrine. Directly afterwards,
Sostratos comes on stage from Knemon's house, his face
beaming.*)

SOSTRATOS

Gentlemen, by Demeter, by Asclepius,
By all the gods, I've never in my life
Seen anybody choose a better time
For *nearly* getting drowned!   What paradise
It's been!   You see, we'd hardly got inside   670
When Gorgias jumped down the well, and up
Above the girl and I *did nothing*.   Well,
What could we do?   True, she was tearing her
Hair, crying, passionately beating her
Breast.   I stood near her, by the gods, just like   675
A nanny—precious fool I was!   I tried to tell
Her not to act like that, I asked and asked—
And gazed on that rare masterpiece.   I couldn't have
Cared less about the injured man down there!
The constant hauling, though—I found that a   680
Great nuisance.   I've almost manslaughtered[1] him,
By Zeus!   You see, through gazing into the
Girl's eyes, I dropped the rope—about three times!

[1] The Greek verb εἰσαπολώλεκα, which ' I've . . . man-
slaughtered ' here translates, may also have been specially
coined for the occasion.

ἦν οὐχ ὁ τυχών· ἀντεῖχε καὶ μόλις ποτὲ
685 ἀνενήνοχ' αὐτόν. ὡς δ' ἐκεῖνος ἐξέβη,
δεῦρ' ἐξελήλυθ'· οὐ γὰρ ἐδυνάμην ἔ[τ]ι
κατέχειν ἐμαυτόν, ἀλλὰ μικροῦ [τὴν κόρην
ἐφίλουν προσιών· οὕτω σφόδρ' ἐ[μμανῶς ἐγὼ
ἐρῶ. παρασκευάζομαι δὴ—τὴν θ[ύραν
690 ψοφοῦσιν. ὦ Ζεῦ Σῶτερ, ἐκτόπου θ[έας.

ΓΟΡΓΙΑΣ

(KT fr. 677) βούλει τι, Κνήμων; εἰπέ μοι.

ΚΝΗΜΩΝ

τί [δεῖ λέγειν;
φαύλως ἔχω.

ΓΟΡΓΙΑΣ

θάρρει.

ΚΝΗΜΩΝ

τεθάρ[ρηκ'· οὐκέτι
ὑμῖν ἐνοχλήσει τὸν ἐπίλοιπον γὰ[ρ χρόνον
694 Κνήμων.

---

684 αντειχηκαμολις B.   685 δ' om. B, suppl. Page.   688
προσιον B. ἐ[μμανῶς ἐγὼ suppl. Fraenkel.   691 Suppl. Arnott
(here and in 688 other supplements are possible).   692 τε-
θάρ[ρηκ' suppl. Barrett, οὐκέτι ed. pr.   693 γὰ[ρ suppl. several,
χρόνον ed. pr.

---

[1] In Greek mythology Atlas, son of Iapetus, was the Titan
who held the sky up and prevented it from falling onto the
earth.   He came to be identified with one or more peaks of the
Atlas Mountains in North-West Africa.
[2] If the Greek text here is correctly interpreted and supple-
mented, Sostratos breaks off in mid-sentence on hearing
Knemon's door open.

But Gorgias was no ordinary Atlas,[1] he
Held on, and in the end's managed to bring him up. 685
As *he* emerged, I came out here.   I couldn't
Control my feelings any more, I nearly went
Up to [the girl] and kissed her—that's how [madly
  (?)] I'm
In love.   I'm getting ready now to . . .[2] Oh, the
  [latch]
Is rattling.   Saviour Zeus, what a strange [sight]!   690

(*During the last two lines of Sostratos' speech, the door of
Knemon's house opens, and through it, by means of the
 'ekkyklema' or rolling platform used in the ancient
theatre to reveal interiors to the audience (cf. Sandbach's
note, Commentary ad loc.; P. D. Arnott, Greek Scenic
Conventions, 78 ff.), there appears on stage a couch on
which the injured Knemon is reclining.   Knemon's
daughter and Gorgias accompany him.   Sostratos mean-
while retires to the rear of the stage.*)

GORGIAS

Want anything, Knemon?   Tell me.

KNEMON

What [need I say (?)]?
I'm poorly.

GORGIAS
Do cheer up!

KNEMON
[I] *have* cheered up!
[No more] will Knemon trouble you, in [time]
To come.

MENANDER

ΓΟΡΓΙΑΣ

τοιοῦτόν ἐστ᾽ ἐρημία κ[ακόν.
(KT fr. 686a) ὁρᾷς; ἀκαρὴς νῦν παραπόλωλας ἀρτίως.
τηρούμενον δὴ τηλικοῦτον τῷ βίῳ
ἤδη καταζῆν δεῖ.

ΚΝΗΜΩΝ

χαλεπῶς μὲν οἶδ᾽ ὅτι
ἔχω· κάλεσον δέ, Γοργία, τὴν μητέρα.

ΓΟΡΓΙΑΣ

ὡς ἔνι μάλιστα. τὰ κακὰ παιδεύειν μόνα
700 ἐπίσταθ᾽ ἡμᾶς, ὡς ἔοικε.

ΚΝΗΜΩΝ

θυγάτριον,
βούλει μ᾽ ἀναστῆσαι λαβοῦσα;

ΣΩΣΤΡΑΤΟΣ

μακάριε
702 ἄνθρωπε.

ΚΝΗΜΩΝ

τί παρέστηκας ἐνταῦθ᾽, ἄθλι[ε;

(Lacuna of perhaps five lines, in which one or both of
the following citations may originally have occurred.)

695 νυνπαραπολωλασα[B: παραπόλωλας ἀρτίως (with νῦν omitted)
mss. of *Etymologica* (*Genuinum, Gudianum, Magnum*) s.v.
ἀκαρής. 699–700 ὡς ἔνι—ἔοικε assigned to Gorgias by several
(in B there is a paragraphus under line 698, but none under 700
and no dicola after μητέρα in 698 or after ἔοικε in 700).

DYSKOLOS

GORGIAS
This is the [tragedy], you see,
Of isolation. Just now you've escaped   695
Death by a whisker! At your age you ought
To end your days now under someone's care.

KNEMON
I'm not so well, I know, but, Gorgias, call
Your mother.

GORGIAS
With all speed. Only disasters,
It seems, can educate us!

*(Gorgias goes off briefly into his own house in order to
bring his mother, Knemon's former wife, onto the stage.
Knemon meanwhile turns to his daughter.)*

KNEMON
Daughter dear,   700
Please hold me and help me to stand up.

*(As the girl's arm goes round the old man's waist, Sostratos
betrays his presence by an envious comment.)*

SOSTRATOS
Lucky
Fellow!

KNEMON *(now on his feet, and addressing Sostratos)*
Why are *you* standing there, you worm?   702

*(Lines 703 to 707 inclusive, according to the first editor's
calculations, have been torn off the top of the other side of
the papyrus folio from lines 650 to 653, and so been lost*

*along with them; and lines 708 to 711 are badly mutilated.
In the gap Sostratos clearly retired once again into the
background, and Gorgias escorted his mother onto the
stage; but whether these movements were accompanied by
further interventions by Gorgias and Sostratos into the
dialogue, or whether Knemon was the sole speaker in the
gap, it is no longer possible to say. By 708, however,
Knemon has already launched into the great harangue*

Two fragments of Δύσκολος, *quoted by ancient authors*

1 (II p. 51 Körte-Thierfelder, III p. 37 Kock)

Quoted by Julian, *Misopogon* 342a. οὕτω μὲν οὖν ἐγὼ
καὶ ἐν Κελτοῖς, κατὰ τὸν τοῦ Μενάνδρου Δύσκολον,
αὐτὸς ἐμαυτῷ πόνους προσετίθην. The last four
words here may be a paraphrase or an imperfect cita-
tion of Menander's own words.

2 (647 KT, 930 K)

Stobaeus, *Eclogae* 4. 53. 5 (σύγκρισις ζωῆς καὶ θανά-
του).

ἡδύ τ' ἀποθνήσκειν ὅτῳ ζῆν μὴ πάρεσθ' ὡς
βούλεται.

708

]εσοις ἐβουλόμην
Μυρ]ρίνη καὶ Γοργία

Fragment 1 ἐγὼ καὶ M, καὶ om. SBW.
Fragment 2 was attributed to the *Dyskolos* by Handley and
Luria. πάρεσθ' Grotius: παρέσται SA.

*which continues until line 747; its solemnity is partly
indicated by a change of metre from iambic trimeters to
trochaic tetrameters, and these tetrameters continue to be
used right up to the end of the fourth act. It is just
possible that one or two of the remarks made by Knemon
in the missing lines have been preserved in fragments 1 and
2 below.)*

Two fragments, quoted by ancient authors

1

*Quoted (or paraphrased) by Julian in his satire The
Beard-Hater, 342a, where he writes:* ' So that is how I,
even among the Celts, according to Menander's
Peevish Fellow, used to impose labours upon myself.'
Here the words ' I used to impose labours upon myself '
*may be a paraphrase or loose reminiscence (the Greek
words are not metrical as they stand) of words in the
play.*

2

*Quoted by Stobaeus, Eclogae 4. 53. 5 (the section headed
' Comparison of Life and Death ').*

He who can't live as he wishes welcomes the approach
   of death.

*In our mss. of Stobaeus, this line has lost its original tag
identifying the source of the quotation, but its attribution
to the Dyskolos is a plausible conjecture.*

---

*(In line 709 Knemon addresses [Myr]rhine and Gorgias,
from which it may be inferred that Myrrhine was the
name of Gorgias' mother and Knemon's wife. In lines*

710 ε . [   ]ον προειλόμην·

ουχισω . [. . . .] . κ . [.]ν οὐδ’ ἂν εἷς δύναιτό με

τοῦτο με[τα]πεῖσαί τις ὑμῶν, ἀλλὰ συγχωρήσετε.

ἕν δ’ ἴσω[ς] ἥμαρτον, ὅστις τῶν ἁπάντων ᾠόμην

αὐτὸς αὐ[τ]άρκης τις εἶναι καὶ δεήσεσθ’ οὐδενός.

715 νῦν δ’ [ἰ]δὼν ὀξεῖαν οὖσαν ἄσκοπόν τε τοῦ βίου

τὴν τε[λ]ευτήν, εὗρον οὐκ εὖ τοῦτο γινώσκων τότε.

δεῖ γὰρ [εἶ]ναι καὶ παρεῖναι τὸν ἐπικουρήσοντ’ ἀεί.

ἀλλὰ μὰ τὸν Ἥφαιστον—οὕτω σφόδρα διεφθάρμην
   ἐγὼ

τοὺς βίους ὁρῶν ἑκάστους τοὺς λογισμούς θ’ ὃν
   τρόπον

720 πρὸς τὸ κερδαίνειν ἔχουσιν—οὐδέν’ εὔνουν ᾠόμην

ἕτερον ἑτέρῳ τῶν ἁπάντων ἂν γενέσθαι· τοῦτο δὴ

ἐμποδὼν ἦν μοι. μόλις δὲ πεῖραν εἷς δέδωκε νῦν

Γοργίας, ἔργον ποήσας ἀνδρὸς εὐγενεστάτου.

τὸν γὰρ οὐκ ἐῶνθ’ ἑαυτὸν προσιέναι πρὸς τὴν θύραν,

---

711 Either οὐχὶ σω.[or οὐκ ἴσως[?   713 ὅστις Winnington-
Ingram: οτι B.   ωμην B.   714 δεησεθ’ B.   715 [ἰ]δὼν suppl.
several.   ασκαπτον B.   716 ευτογινωσκων B.   717 Suppl. and
corr. several: [..]ναικαπαρειναι B.   718 σφοδραεφθαρμην B.
719 λογισμουσ’ον B.   724 ἐῶνθ’ ἑαυτὸν Fraenkel: εωντ’αυτον
B.   πρὸς τὴν θύραν Arnott: τηθυραῖ B.

DYSKOLOS

708 and 710 respectively the words I wished *and* I chose
deliberately *are decipherable. It seems clear that
Knemon began his tetrameter speech by explaining to
Myrrhine and Gorgias why he had originally decided
upon his misanthropic life of isolation.*)

[. . . . .] nor could any one of you 711
Change my views about this—you'll just reconcile
   yourselves to that.
One mistake, perhaps, I *did* make—I believed that I
   was the
One man in the world who could be self-contained,
   and wouldn't require
Help from any man. However, I've seen now that 715
   death can strike
Suddenly and with no warning, and I've realised that
   my
Past belief was wrong. You always need someone
   who'll lend a hand,
Someone on the doorstep. By Hephaestus, I thought
   nobody
On this earth could show real friendship to another—
   that's how far
Off the rails I'd gone through studying all the 720
   different ways of life,
How men in their calculations angle for gain. That
   was my
Obstacle, but one man has succeeded now in proving
   me
Quite wrong—Gorgias, by acting with a truly noble
   heart.
I'm the man who never let him turn his steps towards
   my door,

725 οὐ βοηθήσανθ' ἑαυτῷ πώποτ' εἰς οὐδὲν μέρος,
οὐ προσειπόντ', οὐ λαλήσανθ' ἡδέως, σέσωχ' ὅμως.
εἶπ' ἂν ἄλλος, καὶ δικαίως, '' οὐκ ἐᾷς με προσιέναι·
οὐ προσέρχομ'. οὐδὲν ἡμῖν γέγονας αὐτὸς χρήσιμος·
οὐδ' ἐγώ σοι νῦν.'' τί δ' ἐστί, μειράκιον; ἐάν τ' ἐγὼ
730 ἀποθάνω νῦν—οἴομαι δέ, καὶ κακῶς ἴσως ἔχω—
ἄν τε περισωθῶ, ποοῦμαί σ' υἱόν, ἅ τ' ἔχων τυγχάνω
πάντα σαυτοῦ νόμισον εἶναι. τήνδε σοι παρεγγυῶ·
ἄνδρα δ' αὐτῇ πόρισον. εἰ γὰρ καὶ σφόδρ' ὑγιαί-
νοιμ' ἐγώ,
αὐτὸς οὐ δυνήσομ' εὑρεῖν· οὐ γὰρ ἀρέσει μοί ποτε
735 οὐδὲ εἷς. ἀλλ' ἐμὲ μέν, ἂν ζῶ, ζῆν ἐᾶθ' ὡς βούλομαι·
τἄλλα πρᾶττ' αὐτὸς παραλαβών· νοῦν ἔχεις σὺν τοῖς
θεοῖς· *by the Grace of the gods*
κηδεμὼν εἶ τῆς ἀδελφῆς εἰκότως. τοῦ κτήματος
(gives dowry) ἐπιδίδου σὺ προῖκα τοὐμοῦ διαμετρήσας θἤμισυ,
τ[ὸ] δ' ἕτερον λαβὼν διοίκει κἀμὲ καὶ τὴν μητέρα.
740 ἀλλὰ κα]τάκλινόν με, θύγατερ. τῶν δ' ἀναγκαίων
λέγειν

725 βοηθήσανθ' ἑαυτῷ Fraenkel: βοηθησαντ'αυτωι B. 727 εἶπ'
Lloyd-Jones: οπερ B. ἄλλος several: αλλως B. 728 χρησμος
B. 729 Corr. several: μειρακιονδ'εανεγω B. 730 οιον B
before, ισως B after correction. 731 περισωθῶ Kassel: περιω
B. τουμαισ'υονατ'εχ εν B. 732 τηνδεσυ B. 733 δ' om. B,
suppl. ed. pr. ὑγιαίνοιμ' Kraus, London seminar: υπαινειν B.
735 ἂν ζῶ om. B, suppl. Zuntz (ἦν ζῶ Handley earlier). 736
ταδ' αλλαπρατ' B. 738 σὺ om. B, suppl. Lloyd-Jones. πρυκα
B. θἤμισυ Maas: ημισυ B. 740 ἀλλὰ suppl. Diano, Fraenkel.

---

[1] The value of Knemon's total estate was estimated by
Gorgias in an earlier scene (lines 328–29) to be about two
talents. A dowry of one talent for Knemon's daughter would
be half the comic norm (see the note at *Aspis* 35) and one third
of the figure offered by the very wealthy Kallippides for
Sostratos' sister (line 824). Menander is always careful to let

DYSKOLOS

Never once assisted him in any way—the man who 725
    didn't
Say ' Good morning ', didn't speak a friendly word,
    and yet he has
Saved my life. Another man might have replied,
    and fairly, too:
' You don't let me come, so I'm not coming. You've
    not been yourself
Any help to us, so now I shan't be to you, either! '

(*Knemon now notices that Gorgias is showing signs of
embarrassment before these words of praise.*)

                                                    But
What's the matter, young man?—Whether I die now 730
    (I feel I may,
Probably I'm badly hurt), or whether I live, either way
I adopt you as my son. Treat all that I possess as
    yours.
I appoint you guardian of my daughter here. And
    find her a
Husband. Even if I did get better, I could never
    track
One down. Nobody will ever satisfy *me*. All the 735
    same,
If I do live,] let me live as *I* like! You take over and
Run the rest. You're sensible, the gods be thanked,
    and you are your
Sister's natural protector. Split my property in two;
Give the girl half for her dowry, with the other half
    provide
For your mother and me.[1]—Help me, daughter, to lie 740
    down.—I don't

the size of his dowries reflect the relative prosperity of the
families who offered them.

303

πλείον'] οὐκ ἀνδρὸς νομίζω· πλὴν ἐκεῖνό γ' ἴσθι, παῖ·
ὑπὲρ ἐ]μοῦ γὰρ βούλομ' εἰπεῖν ὀλίγα σοι καὶ τοῦ
τρόπου.
εἰ τοιοῦτ]οι πάντες ἦσαν, οὔτε τὰ δικαστήρια
ἦν ἄν, ο]ὔθ' αὐτοὺς ἀπῆγον εἰς τὰ δεσμωτήρια,
745 οὔτε π]όλεμος ἦν, ἔχων δ' ἂν μέτρι' ἕκαστος ἠγάπα.
ἀ[λ]λ' ἴσως ταῦτ' ἔστ' ἀρεστὰ μᾶλλον· οὕτω
πράττετε.
ἐκποδὼν ὑμῖν ὁ χαλεπὸς δύσκολός τ' ἔσται γέρων.

ΓΟΡΓΙΑΣ

ἀλλὰ δέχομαι ταῦτα πάντα. δεῖ δὲ μετὰ σοῦ
νυμφίον
ὡς τάχισθ' εὑρεῖν τιν' ἡμᾶς τῇ κόρῃ, σοὶ συνδοκοῦν.

ΚΝΗΜΩΝ

750 οὗτος, εἴρηχ' ὅσ' ἐφρόνουν σοι· μὴ 'νόχλει, πρὸς
τῶν θεῶν.

ΓΟΡΓΙΑΣ

βούλεται γὰρ ἐντυχεῖν σοι—

ΚΝΗΜΩΝ

μηδαμῶς, πρὸς τῶν θεῶν.

741 Suppl. several. εκεινοσιθι B.   742 Suppl. by an unnamed
London scholar (see Quincey and others, *Notes on the Dyskolos
of Menander, AHRC* 2 [1959], 9). σοιολιγα B.   743 Suppl.
Sandbach, Shipp.   744]υτ'αυτος B.   747 ὁ om. B, suppl.
ed. pr.   749 τιν' om. B, suppl. ed. pr.

Think a man should say [more] than he needs to,
  though I want you to
Understand this fact, my child—you see, I'd like to
  tell you one
Or two things [about] me and my ways. If everyone
  behaved
[Like me, we should have] no law-courts, shouldn't
  send each other to
Prison, [and] there'd be [no] wars. Each man would 745
  have enough to live
On, and he'd be satisfied. Perhaps, though, modern
  life is more
To your taste! Well, choose that. This cantanker-
  ous and peevish old
Nuisance won't be in your way.

GORGIAS

        Well, I accept all *that*. But with
Your help, we must find a husband for the girl with-
  out delay,
If that suits you.

KNEMON

  Now look here, I've told you all that I proposed. 750
By the gods, don't bother me!

GORGIAS

      Somebody wants to talk to you . . .

KNEMON

By the gods, no!

ΓΟΡΓΙΑΣ

τὴν κόρην αἰτῶν τις—

ΚΝΗΜΩΝ

οὐδὲν ἔτι τοιούτων μοι μέλει.

ΓΟΡΓΙΑΣ

ὅ σε συνεκσώσας.

ΚΝΗΜΩΝ

ὁ ποῖος;

ΓΟΡΓΙΑΣ

οὑτοσί.

ΚΝΗΜΩΝ

πρόελθε σύ.

ἐπικέκαυται μέν· γεωργός ἐστι;

ΓΟΡΓΙΑΣ

καὶ μάλ', ὦ πάτερ·

755 οὐ τρυφῶν οὐδ' οἷος ἀργὸς περιπατεῖν τὴν ἡμέραν
    ] ... ενοστ . [
    ...] . δίδου· πόει† του[

752 τοιούτων om. B, suppl. Bingen.   753 σε om. B, suppl. ed. pr.
753-54 πρόελθε—ἐστι first assigned to Knemon by Diano (cf.
also Pope, *Acta Classica* 3 [1960], 44; B has paragraphi under-
neath 753 and 754, and dicola after ουτοσι, συ, and εστι).
754-55 καὶ—ἡμέραν assigned to Gorgias by ed. pr. (B appears
to have an additional dicolon after πατερ). 756-57 Part-
assignment and identity of speaker or speakers are uncertain.

DYSKOLOS

GORGIAS

. . . asking for the girl's hand.

KNEMON

[Such details] are no
Longer my concern!

GORGIAS

But it's the man who helped to rescue you!

KNEMON

Who?

GORGIAS (*pointing to Sostratos in the background*)
Him there!

KNEMON

Come forward, you!

(*Sostratos comes forward. Knemon examines him carefully, then addresses Gorgias.*)

He's sun-burnt. Does he farm?

GORGIAS

Yes, sir.
He's not pampered, not the kind to saunter lazily all 755
day

(*Lines 756–60, coming at the top of a new papyrus folio, are severely mutilated. In 756 and 757 the identification of speaker (or speakers) and any divisions between speeches are uncertain. However, the imperatives* give, do *can safely be made out in 757, and here Knemon may have given a laconic assent to Sostratos' suit. 758 begins with Knemon speaking.*)

MENANDER

ΚΝΗΜΩΝ

εἰσκ]υκλεῖτ᾽ εἴσω με.

ΓΟΡΓΙΑΣ

καὶ .[. . . . .] .[.] .[

ἐπιμ]ελοῦ τούτου.

ΣΩΣΤΡΑΤΟΣ

τὸ λο[ιπὸν] ἐγγυᾶν [ἐμοί σε δεῖ
760 τὴν] ἀδελφήν.

ΓΟΡΓΙΑΣ

ἐπανέ[νεγ]κε ταῦτα [γ᾽], ὡς δ[ε]ῖ, [τῷ πατρί.

ΣΩΣΤΡΑΤΟΣ

οὐ[δ]ὲν ὁ πατὴρ ἀντερεῖ [μοι].

ΓΟΡΓΙΑΣ

τοιγαροῦν ἔγωγέ σ[ο]ι
ἐγγυῶ, δίδωμι πάντων [τῶ]ν θεῶν ἐναντίον
ενεγκεινος† δίκαιόν ἐστι π.[.]θη†, Σώστρατε.
οὐ πεπλασμένῳ γὰρ ἤθει πρὸς τὸ πρᾶγμ᾽ ἐλήλυθ[ας,

758–63, 773–77, 805–10 The text, as originally published by
V. Martin, has here been supplemented by two new scraps of
B discovered and first published by R. Kasser and C. Austin,
Papyrus Bodmer XXVI. Ménandre: Le Bouclier, Cologny-
Geneva 1969, 48 f.   758 εἰσκ]υκλεῖτ᾽ suppl. several.   759 ἐμοί
σε δεῖ suppl. Arnott *exempli gratia*.   760 ἐπανέ[νεγ]κε . . . [γ᾽]
suppl. Kasser, Austin.   ὡς δ[ε]ῖ, [τῷ πατρί suppl. Arnott.   762
Suppl. Kasser, Austin.   763 So B, desperately corrupt: could
Menander have written νῦν ἐκείνην, ὡς δίκαιόν ἐστι πεισθείς,
Σώστρατε?

308

DYSKOLOS

KNEMON

Wheel me in!

GORGIAS

[Yes, certainly . . . .] 758
See to all his needs.

*(Knemon's command is obeyed. The old man on his
couch is taken back to his house, by means of the 'ekky-
klema' (see the staging note after 690). Gorgias' words
' See to all his needs' are addressed either to Myrrhine
or, more probably, to Simiche inside Knemon's house.
However, it is likely enough that at this point both
Myrrhine and Knemon's daughter also leave the stage,
entering Knemon's house. The presence of neither of
them is required for the betrothal ceremony that follows.)*

SOSTRATOS

And now [you must (?)] betroth your sister [to (?)]
[Me (?)].

GORGIAS

But that's a matter rightly [for your father (?)] 760
to decide.

SOSTRATOS

Father won't oppose [me].

GORGIAS

Well then, I betroth the girl to you,
And I hand her over, calling all the gods to witness, to
Be your wife.   That's fair and proper, I'm convinced
now, Sostratos.[1]
In approaching this affair you haven't masked your
character,

_____
[1] The Greek text of this line is irremediably corrupt.   Only
a guess may be made at its meaning.

MENANDER

765 ἀλλ' ἁπλῶς, καὶ πάντα ποιεῖν ἠξίωσας τοῦ γάμου
ἕνεκα· τρυφερὸς ὢν δίκελλαν ἔλαβες, ἔσκαψας, πονε[ῖν
ἠθέλησας. ἐν δὲ τούτῳ τῷ γένει μάλιστ' ἀνὴρ
δείκνυτ', ἐξισοῦν ἑαυτὸν ὅστις ὑπομένει τινὶ
εὐπορῶν πένητι· καὶ γὰρ μεταβολὴν οὗτος τύχ[ης
770 ἐγκρατῶς οἴσει. δέδωκας πεῖραν ἱκανὴν τοῦ τρόπ[ου
διαμένοις μόνον τοιοῦτος.

ΣΩΣΤΡΑΤΟΣ

πολὺ μὲν οὖν κρείττω[ν ἔτι.
ἀλλ' ἐπαινεῖν αὐτόν ἐστι φορτικόν τι πρᾶγμ' ἴσως.
εἰς καλὸν δ' ὁρῶ παρόντα τὸν πατέρα.

ΓΟΡΓΙΑΣ

Καλλιππίδης
ἐστὶ σοῦ πατήρ;

ΣΩΣΤΡΑΤΟΣ

πάνυ μὲν οὖν.

ΓΟΡΓΙΑΣ

νὴ Δία, πλούσιός γ' ἀνήρ.

766–73 Portions of these lines (the third quarter, roughly) are preserved in *P. Oslo* 186. 766 Continued to Gorgias by ed. pr. (B has ων:δικελλαν, but no paragraphus below the line). 767]ωιγεν[Oslo, τωμερει B. 768]νοστις Oslo, αιαυτονοτις B. 769 μεταβολὴν Page: μεταβολη[Oslo, μεταβολης B. ουτοστησ τ.χ[(or τησπ.[) B. 771 Suppl. Bingen, Kassel. 772]ορτικοντιπ[Oslo, φορτικοπραγμα B. 773–77 See on 758–63 above. 773 γ'ορων B. 774 Change of speaker after πατήρ indicated by ed. pr. (B omits dicolon).

310

You've been frank, agreed to turn your hand to any- 765
thing for this
Marriage. You love luxury, and yet you took a
mattock, and
Grubbed, and sweated willingly. A true man with
your heritage
Shows up best if he's prepared despite his wealth to
take the poor
As his equals. Such a man will bear with equanimity
Changing fortune. Of your mettle you have given 770
proof enough.
Only see you stay the same!

SOSTRATOS
Oh, I'll improve a good deal [yet (?)].
Self-acclaim, however, is perhaps a vulgar thing.
But look—
Here's my father, coming just on cue!

During Sostratos' speech Kallippides enters from the
left. The length of the ancient stage enables Gorgias
and Sostratos to continue their conversation unnoticed by
Kallippides until 779.)

GORGIAS
Kallippides? Can he
Be your father?

SOSTRATOS
Yes indeed!

GORGIAS
A wealthy man, by Zeus.

MENANDER

ΣΩΣΤΡΑΤΟΣ

775 καὶ δικαίως γ᾽, ὡς γεωργὸς ἄμαχος.

ΚΑΛΛΙΠΠΙΔΗΣ
                  ἀπολέλειμμ᾽ ἴσως
καταβεβρωκότες γὰρ ἤδη τὸ πρόβατον φροῦδα
    πάλαι
εἰσὶν εἰς ἀγρόν.

ΓΟΡΓΙΑΣ
          Πόσειδον, ὀξυπείνως πως ἔχει·
αὐτίκ᾽ αὐτῷ ταῦτ᾽ ἐροῦμεν;

ΣΩΣΤΡΑΤΟΣ
                πρῶτον ἀριστησάτω·
πραότερος ἔσται.

ΚΑΛΛΙΠΠΙΔΗΣ
         τί τοῦτο, Σώστρατ᾽; ἠριστήκατε

ΣΩΣΤΡΑΤΟΣ

780 ἀλλὰ καὶ σοὶ παραλέλειπται· πάραγε.

ΚΑΛΛΙΠΠΙΔΗΣ
                τοῦτο δὴ ποῶ

---

775 καὶ δικαίως γ᾽ ed. pr.: δικαιος B. ὡς om. B, supp.
Eitrem, van Groningen. ἀπολέλειμμ᾽ several: απολειμ᾽ B.
776 καταβεβρωκοτεδη B. 779 πρατερος B. 779–80 Change of
speaker after ἠριστήκατε indicated by ed. pr. (B omits di
colon). 780 ποησω B.

DYSKOLOS

SOSTRATOS

Yes, and
He deserves to be, for he's unrivalled as a farmer!

KALLIPPIDES

I've 775
Missed the lunch, I think—by now they've eaten up
the sheep, and gone
To the farmstead long ago!

GORGIAS

Poseidon, he looks ravenous!
Shall we break the news to him at once?

SOSTRATOS

He'd better have his lunch
First, then he'll be more indulgent.

KALLIPPIDES (*noticing Sostratos for the first time*)
What's this, Sostratos? Is lunch
Finished?

SOSTRATOS
Yes, but your share's been put on one side. Go on in.

KALLIPPIDES

That's 780
What I'm doing!

(*Exit Kallippides into the shrine.*)

MENANDER

ΓΟΡΓΙΑΣ

εἰσιὼν οὕτω λάλει νῦν, εἴ τι βούλει, τῷ πατρὶ
κατὰ μόνας. (by yourself)

ΣΩΣΤΡΑΤΟΣ

ἔνδον περιμενεῖς, οὐ γάρ;

ΓΟΡΓΙΑΣ

οὐκ ἐξέρχο|

ἔνδοθεν.

ΣΩΣΤΡΑΤΟΣ

μικρὸν διαλιπὼν παρακαλῶ τοίνυν σ' ε|

ΧΟ Ρ ΟΥ

ΜΕΡΟΣ Ε΄

ΣΩΣΤΡΑΤΟΣ

οὐχ ὡς ἐβουλόμην ἅπαντά μοι, πάτερ,
785 οὐδ' ὡς προσεδόκων γίνεται παρὰ σοῦ.

ΚΑΛΛΙΠΠΙΔΗΣ

τί δέ;

οὐ συγκεχώρηχ'; ἧς ἐρᾷς σε λαμβάνειν
καὶ βούλομαι καί φημι δεῖν.

781 οὕτω Fraenkel: αυτω B. νῦν om. B, suppl. seve
βουλεις B. 782 εξερχετ[or εξερχει B. 783 σ' om. B, su
ed. pr.

DYSKOLOS

GORGIAS

You go in and have a talk now all alone
With your father, if you like.

SOSTRATOS

You plan to wait inside, do you?

GORGIAS

I shan't leave the house.

SOSTRATOS

In a few minutes then I'll call for you.

(*Sostratos goes off into the shrine, and Gorgias probably
into Knemon's house, where his mother now is. When
the stage is empty, the chorus enter to give their fourth
entr'acte performance.*)

ACT V

(*After the chorus' departure, Sostratos and Kallippides
enter from the shrine, in mid-conversation.*)

SOSTRATOS

But you're not meeting all my wishes, father,
Nor all my expectations.

KALLIPPIDES

What? Haven't I   785
Agreed? I *want* you to get married to
The girl you love, I say you must!

MENANDER

ΣΩΣΤΡΑΤΟΣ

οὔ μοι δοκεῖς.

ΚΑΛΛΙΠΠΙΔΗΣ

νὴ τοὺς θεοὺς ἔγωγε, γινώσκων ὅ[τι
νέῳ γάμος βέβαιος οὕτω γίνετ[αι
790 ἐὰν δι᾽ ἔρωτα τοῦτο συμπεισθῇ ποε[ῖν.

ΣΩΣΤΡΑΤΟΣ

ἔπειτ᾽ ἐγὼ μὲν τὴν ἀδελφὴν λήψ[ομαι
τὴν τοῦ νεανίσκου, νομίζων ἄ[ξιον
ἡμῶν ἐκεῖνον· πῶς δὲ τοῦτο νῦ[ν σὺ φῄς,
οὐκ ἀντιδώσειν τὴν ἐμήν;

ΚΑΛΛΙΠΠΙΔΗΣ

αἰσχρὸν λέγει[ς.
795 νύμφην γὰρ ἅμα καὶ νυμφίον πτωχοὺς λαβεῖν
οὐ βούλομ᾽, ἱκανὸν δ᾽ ἐστὶν ἡμῖν θάτερον.

ΣΩΣΤΡΑΤΟΣ

(KT fr. 116) περὶ χρημάτων λαλεῖς, ἀβεβαίου πράγματος.
εἰ μὲν γὰρ οἶσθα ταῦτα παραμενοῦντά σοι
εἰς πάντα τὸν χρόνον, φύλαττε μηδενὶ
800 τούτων μεταδιδούς· ὧν δὲ μὴ σὺ κύριος
εἶ, μηδὲ σαυτοῦ τῆς τύχης δὲ πάντ᾽ ἔχεις,
τί ἂν φθονοίης, ὦ πάτερ, τούτων τινί;
αὕτη γὰρ ἄλλῳ, τυχὸν ἀναξίῳ τινί,

788 εγωγ‘εγιγινωσκωνο[B, with εγι ruled out and τουτο **written**
above it. ὅ[τι suppl. several. 789 οὕτω J. Martin (οὕτως
θ
Blake, Kassel): ουτος B. 790 τουτος B. πονε[B. 796 **εατε**
ρον:ημιν B. 798 παραμενουντα mss. of Stobaeus, Ecl. 3. 16.
14: περιμενουντα B. 800 τουτων Jacques, Steffen: τουτου B,

DYSKOLOS

SOSTRATOS

That doesn't
Meet everything, I think.

KALLIPPIDES

Yes, by the gods, it does!
I realise that when you're young, it adds
Stability to marriage if it's love   790
That prompts the bridegroom.

SOSTRATOS

So I now can marry
The young man's sister, thinking that *he* won't
Disgrace *us*? Then how can you still refuse
To offer him my sister in return?

KALLIPPIDES

Your plan won't do! I've no wish to acquire   795
Two paupers-in-law at one go—one's quite
Enough for us.

SOSTRATOS

Your theme is money, an
Unstable substance. If you *know* that it
Will stay with you for ever, guard it and
Don't share with anyone. But where your title's   800
Not absolute, and all's on lease from fortune, not
Your own, why grudge a man some share in it,
Father? Fortune might take it all away

ἴλλῳ Stob. ὠνδεμησυ B: αὐτὸς ὢν δὲ Stob. (but ὢν δὲ in margin
of ms. M). 801 εμμηδε B: εἰ δὲ μὴ Stob. 802 τί ἄν Stob.:
ιητε B. 803 αὔτη B: αὐτὴ Stob.

MENANDER

παρελομένη σοῦ πάντα προσθήσει πάλιν.
805 διόπερ ἐγώ σέ φημι δεῖν, ὅσον χρόνον
εἶ κύριος, χρῆσθαί σε γενναίως, πάτερ,
αὐτόν, ἐπικουρεῖν πᾶσιν, εὐπόρους ποεῖν
ὡς ἂν δύνῃ πλείστους διὰ σαυτοῦ. τοῦτο γὰρ
ἀθάνατόν ἐστι· κἄν ποτε πταίσας τύχῃς,
810 ἐκεῖθεν ἔσται ταὐτὸ τοῦτό σοι πάλιν.
πολλῷ δὲ κρεῖττόν ἐστιν ἐμφανὴς φίλος
ἢ πλοῦτος ἀφανής, ὃν σὺ κατορύξας ἔχεις.

ΚΑΛΛΙΠΠΙΔΗΣ

οἶσθ' οἷόν ἐστι, Σώσθραθ'· ἃ συνελεξάμην
οὐ συγκατορύξω ταῦτ' ἐμαυτῷ· πῶς γὰρ ἄν;
815 σὰ δ' ἐστί. βούλει περιποήσασθαί τινα
φίλον δοκιμάσας; πρᾶττε τοῦτ' ἀγαθῇ τύχῃ.
τί μοι λέγεις γνώμας; πόριζε, Σώστρατε·
δίδου, μεταδίδου. συμπέπεισμαι πάντα σοι.

ΣΩΣΤΡΑΤΟΣ

ἑκών;

ΚΑΛΛΙΠΠΙΔΗΣ

ἑκών, εὖ ἴσθι· μηδὲν τοῦτό σε
820 ταραττέτω.

804 παρελομένη Stob.: αφελομένη B.   πάντα Stob.: ταυτ
perhaps B (in 804–10 B is badly torn and defective, but th⟨e⟩
full text is preserved in the Stobaeus quotation).   806 πάτε⟨ρ⟩
Stob.: πατηρ B.   809 ἀθάνατον Stob.: αθανατονποτ' B.   81⟨1⟩
πολλω B: πολλῶν Stob.   κρεῖττον Stob.: κριττων B.   813 οἷο
Mette: οιος B.   814 ταυταυτ' B.   817 πόριζε, Σώστρατ
tentatively Arnott: ποριζεπεριζβαδιζε B, with the secon⟨d⟩
ποριζ scored out.   818 Change of speaker at line-end indicate⟨d⟩
by ed. pr. (B has no dicolon after σοι and no paragraphu⟨s⟩
under line 818).

DYSKOLOS

'rom you, hand it to someone else who doesn't
'erhaps deserve it.   So, as long as you   805
Control it, father, you yourself, I say,
Should use it generously, aid everyone,
And by your acts enrich all whom you can.
Such conduct never dies.   If you by chance
Should ever stumble, it will yield to you a like   810
Repayment.   Better far than hidden wealth
Kept buried is a visible true friend.[1]

KALLIPPIDES

You know the situation, Sostratos.
What I've put by me, I shan't bury in my grave—
How could I?   It's all yours.   You've proved your man 815
And want to clinch his friendship?   Go ahead, good luck
To you.   No need for sermons.   Sostratos (?),
You may dispose, and give, and share.   You've quite
Convinced me.

SOSTRATOS
            Gladly?

KALLIPPIDES
                        Gladly, yes.   Don't let
That worry you at all.

---

[1] Menander plays here on the distinction in Athenian law
between ' hidden ' (ἀφανής) and ' visible ' (ἐμφανής) property.
' Visible ' property was a man's openly acknowledged pos-
sessions, assessable for taxation; ' hidden ' property included
such things as debts owed to the person concerned, claims, and
—because easily concealed—cash.   See A. R. W. Harrison,
The Law of Athens, I, Oxford 1968, 230 f.

MENANDER

ΣΩΣΤΡΑΤΟΣ

τὸν Γοργίαν τοίνυν καλῶ.

ΓΟΡΓΙΑΣ

ἐπακήκο᾽ ὑμῶν ἐξιὼν πρὸς τῇ θύρᾳ
ἅπαντας οὓς εἰρήκατ᾽ ἐξ ἀρχῆς λόγους.
τί οὖν; ἐγώ σε, Σώστρατ᾽, εἶναι μὲν φίλον
ὑπολαμβάνω σπουδαῖον ἀγαπῶ τ᾽ ἐκτόπως,
825 μείζω δ᾽ ἐμαυτοῦ πράγματ᾽ οὔτε βούλομαι
οὔτ᾽ ἂν δυναίμην, μὰ Δία, βουληθεὶς φέρειν.

ΣΩΣΤΡΑΤΟΣ

οὐκ οἶδ᾽ ὅ τι λέγεις.

ΓΟΡΓΙΑΣ

        τὴν ἀδελφὴν τὴν ἐμὴν
δίδωμί σοι γυναῖκα, τὴν δὲ σὴν λαβεῖν—
καλῶς ἔχει μοι.

ΣΩΣΤΡΑΤΟΣ

πῶς καλῶς;

ΓΟΡΓΙΑΣ

           οὐχ ἡδύ μοι
830 εἶναι τρυφᾶν ἐν ἀλλοτρίοις πόνοις δοκεῖ,
συλλεξάμενον δ᾽ αὐτόν.

ΣΩΣΤΡΑΤΟΣ

        φλυαρεῖς, Γοργία.
οὐκ ἄξιον κρίνεις σεαυτὸν τοῦ γάμου;

DYSKOLOS

SOSTRATOS

Then I'll call Gorgias.   820

(Gorgias now enters from Knemon's house.)

GORGIAS

I've overheard you from the doorway on
My way out—all your conversation right
From the beginning. Well then, I admit
That you're a good friend, Sostratos, I like
You very much—but I don't wish to take   825
On things too big for me, and even if I wished,
By Zeus, I couldn't do it.

SOSTRATOS

I don't see your point.

GORGIAS

I'll give my sister to you as your wife, but as
To taking yours—thank you, but . . .

SOSTRATOS

Why the ' but ' ?

GORGIAS

I can't enjoy wealth won by others' labours,   830
But only what I've earned myself.

SOSTRATOS

That, Gorgias,

Is nonsense. Don't you think you're worthy of
This marriage ?

---

822 ου B (for οὖς).   823 σε om. B, suppl. ed. pr.   830 τρυφᾶν ἐν
and δοκεῖ several: τρυφαινειν and δοκω B.

MENANDER

ΓΟΡΓΙΑΣ

ἐμαυτὸν εἶναι κέκρικ' ἐκείνης ἄξιον,
λαβεῖν δε πολλὰ μίκρ' ἔχοντ' οὐκ ἄξιον.

ΚΑΛΛΙΠΠΙΔΗΣ

835 νὴ τὸν Δία τὸν μέγιστον, εὐγενῶς γέ πως
πα[ράλογ]ος εἶ.

ΓΟΡΓΙΑΣ

πῶς;

ΚΑΛΛΙΠΠΙΔΗΣ

οὐκ ἔχων βούλει δοκεῖν
τρυφᾶν·] ἐπειδὴ συμπεπεισμένον μ' ὁρᾷς,
πάρεικ]ε.

ΓΟΡΓΙΑΣ

τούτῳ μ' ἀναπέπεικας· διπλασίως
ἥμαρτον·] ὧν πένης γὰρ ἀπόπληκτός θ' ἅμα
840 τίς ἐλπί]δ' ὑποδείκνυσιν εἰς σωτηρίαν;

ΣΩΣΤΡΑΤΟΣ

ὑπέρευ· τ]ὸ λοιπόν ἐστιν ἡμῖν ἐγγυᾶν.

834 μικραπολλα B. 836–41 An oblong tear has removed the opening 6 to 7 letters of these lines, together with any traces of paragraphi. Plausible supplementation is well-nigh impossible; the text printed here is merely *exempli gratia*. 836, 838 Suppl. Sandbach. 837 Suppl. Arnott. 838 Change of speaker indicated by ed. pr. (B has no dicolon before τουτω). 839 ἥμαρτον suppl. Arnott. γὰρ om. B, suppl. Sandbach. 840 τίς suppl. Arnott, ἐλπί]δ' Barrett. 841 Suppl. Blake (τ]ὸ already ed. pr.). ημινεστιν B: corr. several.

DYSKOLOS

GORGIAS
I believe I'm worthy of
The girl, but not to take so much when I've
So little.

KALLIPPIDES
By almighty Zeus, your pride   835
[Unhinges (?)] you.[1]

GORGIAS
How?

KALLIPPIDES
You desire to act
[Rich (?)], when you're poor. You've seen *me*
swayed by logic,
[Give way yourself (?)], then.

GORGIAS
That's convinced me.   [I (?)]
[Was (?)] doubly [wrong.   Who (?)]'s got [a hope (?)],
if he's
Both poor and senseless, of security?   840

SOSTRATOS
[Splendid!   (?)]   All that remains now is to plight
Our troths.

---

[1] The text of lines 836–41 is defective, and certain restoration of the original Greek impossible. Whether Menander made Gorgias' sudden surrender more plausible than it may appear in the above translation is a question to which we have now no answer.

MENANDER

ΚΑΛΛΙΠΠΙΔΗΣ

ἀλλ' ἐγγυῶ παίδων ἐπ' ἀρότῳ γνησίων
τὴν θυγατέρ' ἤδη, μειράκιον, σοί, προῖκά τε
δίδωμ' ἐπ' αὐτῇ τρία τάλαντ'.

ΓΟΡΓΙΑΣ

ἐγὼ δέ γε
845 ἔχω τάλαντον προῖκα τῆς ἑτέρας.

ΚΑΛΛΙΠΠΙΔΗΣ

ἔχεις;
μὴ δῶς σὺ λίαν.

ΓΟΡΓΙΑΣ
ἀλλ' ἔχω.

ΚΑΛΛΙΠΠΙΔΗΣ

τὸ δὲ χωρίον
κέκτησ' ὅλον σύ, Γοργία. τὴν μητέρα
ἤδη σὺ δεῦρο τήν τ' ἀδελφὴν μετάγαγε
πρὸς τὰς γυναῖκας τὰς παρ' ἡμῖν.

ΓΟΡΓΙΑΣ

(KT fr. 820) ἀλλὰ χρή.

ΣΩΣΤΡΑΤΟΣ

850 τὴν νύκτα [ταύτην κωμάσωμεν ἐνθαδὶ

846 δῶς Arnott, Quincey: δαυ B. Change of speaker after ἔχω
indicated by ed. pr. (εχωτο B). 850–51 Supplementation is
highly speculative, and the text printed is *exempli gratia*. 850
Suppl. Arnott (ταύτην ἐνθάδ' already ed. pr.).

DYSKOLOS

KALLIPPIDES
Well, I betroth my daughter now,
Young man, to you, to harvest lawful children.[1]
I add three talents dowry.

GORGIAS
                Yes, and I've
A talent dowry for the other girl.   845

KALLIPPIDES
Have you?   Don't name too high a figure!

GORGIAS
                      But
I have it.

KALLIPPIDES
Gorgias, you keep the farm
Intact.   Now bring your mother and your sister
Across here to our womenfolk.

(*Kallippides, as he makes this last remark, points to Pan's shrine.*)

GORGIAS
              I must
Do that.

SOSTRATOS
[Let's] stay [and have a party here (?)]   850

---

[1] The formula of betrothal, with its quaintly agricultural wording, seems to correspond with the one in use in contemporary Athens. The announcement about the dowry (whose size here is well above the comic norm: see the notes on *Asp.* 35, *Dysk.* 740) was an integral part of the ceremony. See A. R. W. Harrison, *The Law of Athens*, I, Oxford 1968, 3 ff.

MENANDER

πάντες μέν[οντες· αὔριον δὲ το]ὺς γάμους
ποήσομεν. κ[αὶ τὸν] γέροντα, [Γορ]γία,
κομίσατε δε[ῦ]ρ'· ἕξει τὰ δ[έον]τ' ἐνταῦθ' ἴσω[ς
μ]ᾶλλον παρ' ἡμῖν.

ΓΟΡΓΙΑΣ
οὐκ ἐθ[ελ]ήσει, Σώστρατε.

ΣΩΣΤΡΑΤΟΣ
855 σύμπεισον αὐτόν.

ΓΟΡΓΙΑΣ
ἂν δύνωμ[αι].

ΣΩΣΤΡΑΤΟΣ
δεῖ πότον
ἡμῶν γενέσθαι, παππία, νυνὶ [κ]αλόν,
καὶ τῶν γυναικῶν παννυχίδα.

ΚΑΛΛΙΠΠΙΔΗΣ
τοὐναντίον
πίοντ' ἐκεῖναι, παννυχιοῦμεν, οἶδ' ὅτι,
ἡμεῖς. παράγων δ' ὑμῖν ἑτοιμάσω τι τῶν
860 προὔργου.

ΣΩΣΤΡΑΤΟΣ
(KT fr. 119)   πόει τοῦτ'. οὐδενὸς χρὴ πράγματος

851–56 Suppl. ed. pr.   860 χρὴ πράγματος Stobaeus, Ecl. 3.
29. 45: χρήματος B.

326

DYSKOLOS

Tonight, [and then tomorrow (?)] we can have
The weddings.   Bring the old man, Gorgias,
Too.   Probably he'll find here better service
With us.

GORGIAS

He'll not be willing, Sostratos.

SOSTRATOS

Persuade him!

GORGIAS

If I can.

(*Exit Gorgias into Knemon's house, to attempt to do what
he has been asked.*)

SOSTRATOS

                 We ought to have   855
A glorious party now, dad, and the ladies
Must make a night of it.

KALLIPPIDES

                The other way
Round, rather—it's the ladies who will drink
I'm sure—*we*'ll do the night-work! I'll go now
And get things ready for it.

(*With these words Kallippides goes off into the shrine,
leaving Sostratos alone on stage.*)

SOSTRATOS

               Do!—A wise   860

MENANDER

τὸν εὖ φρονοῦνθ᾽ ὅλως ἀπογνῶναί ποτε·
ἁλωτὰ γίνετ᾽ ἐπιμελείᾳ καὶ πόνῳ
ἅπαντ᾽. ἐγὼ τούτου παράδειγμα νῦν φέρω·
ἐν ἡμέρᾳ μιᾷ κατείργασμαι γάμον
865 ὃν οὐδ᾽ ἂν εἷς ποτ᾽ ᾤετ᾽ ἀνθρώπων ὅλως.

ΓΟΡΓΙΑΣ

προάγετε δὴ θᾶττόν ποθ᾽ ὑμεῖς.

ΣΩΣΤΡΑΤΟΣ

δεῦτε δή·
μῆτερ, δέχου ταύτας. ὁ Κνήμων δ᾽ οὐδέπω;

ΓΟΡΓΙΑΣ

ὃς ἱκέτευεν ἐξαγαγεῖν τὴν γραῦν ἔτι,
ἵν᾽ ᾖ τελέως μόνος καθ᾽ αὑτόν;

ΣΩΣΤΡΑΤΟΣ

ὦ τρόπου
870 ἀμάχου.

ΓΟΡΓΙΑΣ

τοιοῦτος.

861 φρονουνθ᾽ B: ποιοῦνθ᾽ Stob., where Grotius conjectured
πονοῦνθ᾽. 863 τουτο B. 865 ὃν om. B, suppl. ed. pr. 866
προαγεδη B. 867 μητερα B. 870 Change of speaker after
τοιοῦτος indicated by several (B omits the dicolon).

Man never ought entirely to despair
Of any project. Every prize can be
Captured by care and work. Here's an example
To prove it. In one day I have achieved
A marriage no-one in the world would ever have   865
At all thought possible.

(*At this point Gorgias enters from Knemon's house,
shepherding along his mother and his step-sister.*)

GORGIAS

> Do come along

Now, quickly.

(*Sostratos escorts the two women to the shrine. Clearly his
mother receives them, but whether in the original production
this would have been imagined only, as taking place behind
the door of the shrine off stage, or visible to the audience,
with Sostratos' mother standing at the entrance to the
shrine, cannot now be established.*)

SOSTRATOS

> This way.—Mother, you receive

Them. (*To Gorgias*) Isn't Knemon here yet?

GORGIAS

> Why, he begged

And begged me to bring Simiche too, then
He'd be all by himself!

SOSTRATOS

> No fighting him!   870

GORGIAS

That's what he's like.

MENANDER

ΣΩΣΤΡΑΤΟΣ

ἀλλὰ πολλὰ χαιρέτω.

ἡμεῖς δ' ἴωμεν.

ΓΟΡΓΙΑΣ

Σώστραθ', ὑπεραισχύνομαι
γυναιξὶν ἐν ταὐτῷ—

ΣΩΣΤΡΑΤΟΣ

τίς ὁ λῆρος; οὐ πρόει;
οἰκεῖα ταῦτ' ἤδη νομίζειν πάντα δεῖ.

ΣΙΜΙΧΗ

ἄπειμι, νὴ τὴν Ἄρτεμιν, κἀγώ.   μόνος
875 ἐνταῦθα κατακείσει· .τάλας σὺ τοῦ τρόπου.
πρὸς τὸν θεόν σε βουλομένων [τούτων ἄγειν
ἀντεῖπας. ἔσται μέγα κακὸν πάλιν [τί σοι,
νὴ τὼ θεώ, καὶ μεῖζον ἢ νῦν· εὖ πέ[σοι.

ΓΕΤΑΣ

ἐγὼ προελθὼν ὄψομαι δεῦρ' [ὡς ἔχει.

αὐλεῖ

873 ουκ'εια B.   875 ενταυτα B.   877 μεγακον B.   τί σοι suppl.
Page, Webster.   878 καὶ om. B, suppl. Blake, Lloyd-Jones.
πέ[σοι suppl. Kraus.   879 προελθὼν Sandbach: προσελθών B.

---

[1] The goddesses Demeter and Persephone.

DYSKOLOS

SOSTRATOS

Oh well, forget him. Let's

Go.

GORGIAS

Sostratos, I'm shy—with women in
The same room!

SOSTRATOS

Rubbish! Go on. They're all *family*

By now, remember!

(*Sostratos and Gorgias go off into the shrine. Simiche now
enters from Knemon's house. Her little speech is addressed
back through that house's open door to her master, who
must be imagined as lying inside.*)

SIMICHE

Yes, by Artemis,

I *shall* go, too! You'll lie there, all alone.   875
I'm sorry you're like that! [They] wished to [take] you
    to
Pan's shrine, and you refused. [You]'ll come to more
Harm, by the Ladies[1]—even worse than now. May all
[Go] well!

(*Exit Simiche into the shrine. From it, immediately after-
wards, emerges Getas. He walks towards Knemon's
house.*)

GETAS

I'll go and see here [how he is (?)].

(*At this point the papyrus contains the note* αὐλεῖ, '*the
piper pipes*'. *This indicates that the following scene,*

MENANDER

written in iambic tetrameters catalectic [880–958], is performed with musical accompaniment. What effect, however, this piping had on the actual delivery of the words, is now uncertain; cf. Pickard-Cambridge, The Dramatic Festivals of Athens, 2nd edition revised by Gould and Lewis, Oxford 1968, 156 ff.)

880 τί μοι προσαυλεῖς, ἄθλι᾽ οὗτος; οὐδέπω σχολή [μοι.
πρὸς τὸν κακῶς ἔχοντα πέμπουσ᾽ ἐνθαδί μ᾽· ἐπί-
σ[χες.

ΣΙΜΙΧΗ

καὶ παρακαθήσθω γ᾽ εἰσιὼν αὐτῷ τις ἄλλος ὑμῶ[ν.
ἐγὼ δ᾽ ἀποστέλλουσα τροφίμην βούλομαι λαλῆ[σαι
αὐτῇ, προσειπεῖν, ἀσπάσασθαι.

ΓΕΤΑΣ

               νοῦν ἔχεις· βάδ[ιζε.
885 τοῦτον δὲ θεραπεύσω τέως ἐγώ. πάλαι δ[έδοκται
τ[οῦτο]ν λαβε[ῖν] τὸν καιρόν, ἀλλὰ διαπο.[
                ]εσει καὶ τῶν β[
ο]ὔπω δυνησ[   ]ι. μάγειρε
Σίκων, πρόελ[θε δ]εὖρό μοι[κἄκουσο]ν. ὦ Πόσειδον,
890 οἵαν ἔχειν οἶμ[αι δι]ατριβήν.

---

880 Suppl. several.   881 Suppl. Kassel, Sydney seminar.   883 βουλομα B.   884 αὐτῇ Kassel: ταυτη B.   885 Suppl. Richter, Thierfelder.   886 Suppl. several.   889 [κἄκουσο]ν suppl. Post.   890 οἶμ[αι suppl. Barigazzi, Gallavotti.

Why pipe at me, you wretched cur? [I]'ve got no 880
    time for *you* yet!
I'm on a mission to the patient here, so stop your
    piping!

SIMICHE

Yes, someone else can go in there—one of your
    crowd, and sit with
Knemon. I want a chat with mistress now before
    she leaves us,
To talk to her and say good-bye.

GETAS

              That's sensible, be off then.
I'll see to grandad while you're gone.

(*At this point Simiche goes off into the shrine. Getas
continues speaking on the empty stage.*)

              —For ages [I've been planning] 885
To seize this opportunity, and yet [I'm puzzled how
    to (?)]

(*At lines 887–88 the papyrus is so badly mutilated that
plausible supplementation is impossible. Getas may have
peeped through Knemon's door to see if the old man was
in bed and helpless.*)

[. . . . .] and the [. . . . .]
[. . .]'ll not yet be able [. . . . .]. Cook
Sikon, come out here, please, [and pay attention (?)].
    O Poseidon,
What splendid sport I think we've got!

(*Enter Sikon, from the shrine.*)

MENANDER

ΣΙΚΩΝ

σύ μ[ε κα]λεῖς;

ΓΕΤΑΣ

ἔγωγε.

τιμωρίαν [βούλ]ει λαβεῖν ὧν ἀρτίως ἔπασχες;

ΣΙΚΩΝ

ἐγὼ δ' ἔπασχ[ον ἀ]ρτίως; οὐ λαικάσει φλυαρῶν;

ΓΕΤΑΣ

ὁ δύσκολος [γέρ]ων καθεύδει μόνος.

ΣΙΚΩΝ

ἔχει δὲ δὴ πῶς;

ΓΕΤΑΣ

οὐ παντάπ[ασ]ιν ἀθλίως.

ΣΙΚΩΝ

οὐκ ἂν δύναιτό γ' ἡμᾶς

895 τύπτειν ἀναστάς;

ΓΕΤΑΣ

οὐδ' ἀναστῆναι γάρ, ὡς ἐγᾦμαι.

ΣΙΚΩΝ

ὡς ἡδὺ πρᾶγμά μοι λέγεις. αἰτήσομ' εἰσιών τι·
ἔξω γὰρ ἔσται τῶν φρενῶν.

---

893 [γέρ]ων suppl. several. δεπως B. 895 γάρ om. B, suppl.
ed. pr. 896–97 ὡς—φρενῶν assigned to Sikon by ed. pr. (B has
paragraphus under 896 and dicolon after τι).

DYSKOLOS

SIKON

You're calling me?

GETAS

I am, yes. 890

Now [would] you [like] to get revenge for recent gay
  disasters?

SIKON

For recent *gay* disasters? Bugger you, you're talking
  drivel!

GETAS

The peevish old rogue's all alone, asleep.

SIKON

And his condition?

How's that?

GETAS

Not absolutely critical!

SIKON

Could he get up and

Clout us?

GETAS

He couldn't even stand, I don't think, un- 895
supported!

SIKON

How charming your suggestion is! I'll go inside,
  and ask to
Borrow some object. He'll go wild!

MENANDER

ΓΕΤΑΣ

τί δ' ἄν, τὸ δεῖνα, πρῶτον
ἔξω προελκύσωμεν αὐτόν, εἶτα θέντες αὐτοῦ
κόπτωμεν οὕτω τὰς θύρας, αἰτῶμεν, ἐπιφλέγωμεν;
900 ἔσται τις ἡδονή, λέγω.

ΣΙΚΩΝ

τὸν Γοργίαν δέδοικα
μὴ καταλαβὼν ἡμᾶς καθαίρῃ.

ΓΕΤΑΣ

θόρυβός ἐστιν ἔνδον,
πίνουσιν· οὐκ αἰσθήσετ' οὐδείς. τὸ δ' ὅλον ἐστὶν ἡμῖν
ἄνθρωπος ἡμερωτέος· κηδεύομεν γὰρ αὐτῷ,
οἰκεῖος ἡμῖν γίνετ'· εἰ δ' ἔσται τοιοῦτος ἀεί,
905 ἔργον ὑπενεγκεῖν.

ΣΙΚΩΝ

πῶς γὰρ οὔ;

ΓΕΤΑΣ

λαθεῖν μόνον προμηθοῦ
αὐτὸν φέρων δεῦρ' εἰς τὸ πρόσθεν. πρόαγε δὴ σύ.

---

897 τί δ' ἄν om. B, suppl. Handley. 898 Corr. Thierfelder:
προσελκυσωμεν B. θεντεσαυτον B. 903 Corr. Kassel: ημερωτερος
B. 904 Corr. Page: ααιει apparently B. 905–41 The distri-
bution of parts is often unclear in this passage. 905 προμηθοῦ

DYSKOLOS

GETAS

                    I say, here's an idea:
Suppose we drag him out of doors first; then we'll
    dump him down here,
We'll bang on his door, ask for things, and lash him
    into fury!
There'll be some fun, I tell you!

SIKON

                    It's that Gorgias I'm scared of.   900
He'll paste us if he catches us.

GETAS

                    They're making such a racket
In there, carousing—nobody will notice. Top to toe, we
Must civilise the fellow! He's related now by
    marriage,
A member of our family.   If he goes on for ever
Like this, we'll have our job cut out to stomach his   905
    behaviour!

SIKON

You will, for sure!

GETAS

    Just see you're under cover when you bring him
Out here, in front.   Go on, then!

---

allegedly Fraenkel (but not in *CR* 9 [1959], 191): επιθυμου
apparently B.   906 συδη B.   906–07 μικρὸν—ἀπέλθῃς assigned
to Sikon by Diano, Merkelbach (συμικρον:/προσμεινον B).

ΣΙΚΩΝ

μικρὸν

πρόσμεινον, ἱκετεύω σε· μή με καταλιπὼν ἀπέλθῃς.
καὶ μὴ ψόφει, πρὸς τῶν θεῶν.

ΓΕΤΑΣ

ἀλλ᾽ οὐ ψοφῶ, μὰ τὴν Γῆν.

εἰς δεξιάν.

ΣΙΚΩΝ

ἰδού.

ΓΕΤΑΣ

θὲς αὐτοῦ. νῦν ὁ καιρός. εἶέν·
910 ἐγὼ προάξω πρότερος ὤν, καὶ τὸν ῥυθμὸν σὺ τήρει.
παῖ, παιδίον, παῖδες καλοί, παῖ, παιδί᾽.

909 Change of speaker at θὲς αὐτοῦ indicated by ed. pr. (B
has no dicolon after its misspelled ειδου).   910 ὤν Arnott: μη
B.   σὺ ed. pr.: ευ B.   911 παῖ, παιδίον ed. pr.: παιδιον B.
καλοί om. B, suppl. several.   παιδί᾽ Mette: παιδιον B.   911–12
οἴχομ᾽, οἴμοι assigned to Knemon both times by ed. pr. (B has
no paragraphi under 911 or 912, and no dicola before or after
these words).

---

¹ The most plausible interpretation of this command is that
Sikon is requested to carry Knemon from his house on the left
of the stage (see the note on line 5) to a spot in the middle of the
stage. ' To the right ' will accordingly be ' to the audience's
right '. The resulting action will thus be played out most
conveniently for the audience in centre stage, right in front of
the cave of Pan. In real life, no doubt, Getas and Sikon
would have chosen for their villainy a place less vulnerable to
observation from inside the cave, but here dramatic values
take precedence over those of realism. In any case, lines
901–2 may be taken as a dramatic defence not only of Getas'
scheme but also of its location.

DYSKOLOS

SIKON

Wait a bit, please! Don't desert me
And vanish! And don't make a noise, in heaven's
name!

GETAS

In earth's name,
I'm *being* quiet!

(*From line 907 Getas has been urging Sikon in the
direction of Knemon's house. The two have now reached
the old man's door. Sikon quietly pushes it open and dis-
appears inside; Getas probably remains on stage by the
door. A moment later Sikon emerges from Knemon's
house, gently carrying the invalid, who is still asleep.*)

—To the right[1]!

SIKON
There!

GETAS
Lay him here.

(*At this command Sikon lowers the sleeping Knemon gently
to the ground, probably near the front of the stage. See
the note on line 909.*)

—Our moment
Has now come. Well, I'll lead off first, and you[2] 910
must watch the rhythm.

(*Getas now swaggers up to Knemon's door, and bangs on
it loudly and rhythmically, in time with his following
shouts.*)

Ho, boy! Ho, boy there! Lovely boys! Boy! Boys!

[2] The piper. Lines 911 and 912 (see below) are delivered in
a heavily emphasised rhythm, which the piper must follow.

MENANDER

ΚΝΗΜΩΝ

οἴχομ᾽, οἴμοι.

ΓΕΤΑΣ

παῖδες καλοί, παῖ, παιδίον, παῖ, παῖδες.

ΚΝΗΜΩΝ

οἴχομ᾽, οἴμοι.

ΓΕΤΑΣ

τίς οὗτος; ἐντεῦθέν τις εἶ;

ΚΝΗΜΩΝ

δηλονότι. σὺ δὲ τί βούλει;

ΓΕΤΑΣ

λέβητας αἰτοῦμαι παρ᾽ ὑμῶν καὶ σκάφας.

ΚΝΗΜΩΝ

τίς ἄν με

915 στήσειεν ὀρθόν;

ΓΕΤΑΣ

ἔστιν ὑμῖν, ἔστιν ὡς ἀληθῶς.
καὶ τρίποδας ἑπτὰ καὶ τραπέζας δώδεκ᾽. ἀλλά,
παῖδες,
τοῖς ἔνδον εἰσαγγείλατε· σπεύδω γάρ.

ΚΝΗΜΩΝ

οὐδέν ἐστιν.

912 παῖ, παῖδες ed. pr.: παιδες B. 913 τισει: λονοτι B.
913–14 Change of speaker after βούλει indicated by ed. pr. (B
omits the dicolon). 914 σκάφας Handley: σφακον B. 917
Corr. London seminar, Page: αγγειλατε B.

KNEMON (*awakened by the shouts*)
> Oh, this is murder!

GETAS
Ho, lovely boys! Ho, boy! Boy! Boy! Ho, boys!

KNEMON
> Oh, this is murder!

GETAS (*pretending to notice Knemon now for the first time*)
Who's this? Are you from *this* house?

KNEMON
> Obviously. What do *you* want?

GETAS
I want to borrow stewing pans from your house, and
some basins.

KNEMON (*trying in vain to stand up*)
Who'll put me on my feet?

GETAS
> You've got one, yes, you've really got one. 915
And seven stands and twelve small tables. Boys,
pass my request to
The staff inside the house. I'm in a rush.

KNEMON
> I haven't any!

ΓΕΤΑΣ

οὐκ ἔστιν;

ΚΝΗΜΩΝ

οὐκ ἀκήκοας μυριάκις;

ΓΕΤΑΣ

ἀποτρέχω δή.

ΚΝΗΜΩΝ

ὦ δυστυχὴς ἐγώ· τίνα τρόπον ἐνθαδὶ προήχθην;
920 τίς μ᾽ εἰ]ς τὸ πρόσθε κατατέθηκεν;

ΣΙΚΩΝ

ἄπαγε δὴ σύ. καὶ δή·
παῖ, παι]δίον, γυναῖκες, ἄνδρες, παῖ, θυρωρέ.

ΚΝΗΜΩΝ

μαίνει,
ἄνθρ]ωπε; τὴν θύραν κατάξεις.

ΣΙΚΩΝ

δάπιδας ἐννέ᾽ ἡμῖν
χρήσα]τε.

918 οὐκ (before ἀκήκοας) om. B.   920 Suppl. Handley, Page
(τίς εἰ]ς already ed. pr.).   κατατέθηκεν Handley: κατεθηκεν B.
δηκαισυκαιδη B.   923 Suppl. Barrett.

DYSKOLOS

GETAS

You haven't any?

KNEMON

Countless times you've heard me say so!

GETAS

Well then,

I'm off.

(Up to this point Getas has taken the leading role in the victimisation of Knemon, while Sikon looks idly on in the background. But now Getas runs back to join Sikon, leaving Knemon briefly alone at the front of the stage.)

KNEMON

Oh, dear, the misery! However did I come to be brought out here? [Who]'s dumped [me] down before my door?

(Sikon now takes over from Getas the role of Knemon's tormentor. He struts up to the old man's door, and delivers line 921 exactly as Getas did lines 911 and 912, banging loudly on the door in time to the rhythm of his shouts.)

SIKON

(To Getas) Be off, then! 920
And now, [ho, boy!] Boy! Ladies! Gentlemen!
Ho, boy! Ho, porter!

KNEMON

Sir, are you mad? You'll smash the door to pieces!

SIKON

Could your people
[Lend] us nine rugs?

MENANDER

ΚΝΗΜΩΝ

πόθεν;

ΣΙΚΩΝ

καὶ παραπέτασμα βαρβαρικὸν ὑφαντὸ
δίδοτε] ποδῶν τὸ μῆκος ἑκατόν.

ΚΝΗΜΩΝ

εἴθε μοι γένοιτο
925 ἱμάς] π[ο]θεν. γραῦ· ποῦ 'στιν ἡ γραῦς;

ΣΙΚΩΝ

ἐφ' ἑτέραν βαδίζω

θύραν;

ΚΝΗΜΩΝ

ἀπαλλάγητε δή. γραῦ· Σιμίχη. κακόν σε
κακῶς ἅπαντες ἀπολέσειαν οἱ θεοί. τί βούλει;

ΓΕΤΑΣ

κρατῆρα βούλομαι λαβεῖν χαλκοῦν μέγαν.

ΚΝΗΜΩΝ

τίς ἄν με

στήσειεν ὀρθόν;

924-25 Supplementation here is highly speculative. 92
Suppl. tentatively Sandbach. εκαστον B. 925 Suppl. Galla
votti. ἡ om. B, suppl. ed. pr. 926-28 Speech-assignment thu
given by ed. pr. (B has dicola after σιμικη so misspelled and
θεοι). 926 σε Lloyd-Jones: δε B.

---

[1] Such bowls were normally used for mixing wine with
water, in order to provide the weakened drink customary a

344

KNEMON

Impossible!

SIKON

And [let us have (?)] a curtain
Of foreign weave, a hundred feet in length.

KNEMON

If I could only
Find a strap anywhere . . . Old woman! Oh, 925
where *is* the woman?

SIKON (*retreating into the background again*)

Ought I to try another door?

KNEMON

Oh, go away! Old woman,
Ho, Simiche! May all the gods blast *you* for all your
torments!

(*As Knemon curses the retreating Sikon, Getas darts
forward again.*)

And what do *you* want?

GETAS

I should like to get a big bronze wine-bowl.[1]

KNEMON (*trying again to stand, but relapsing to a
sitting position*)

Who'll put me on my feet?

Greek parties. Surviving examples in bronze are illustrated in
W. Lamb, *Greek and Roman Bronzes*, London, 1929, pl. 82,
and G. M. A. Richter, *A Handbook of Greek Art*, London and
New York, 7th edition 1974, figs. 302 and 303.

MENANDER

ΣΙΚΩΝ

ἔστιν ὑμῖν, ἔστιν ὡς ἀληθῶς
930 τὸ παραπέτασμα, παππία.

ΚΝΗΜΩΝ

μὰ τὸν Δί’.

ΓΕΤΑΣ

οὐδ’ ὁ κρατήρ;

ΚΝΗΜΩΝ

τὴν Σιμίχην ἀποκτενῶ.

ΣΙΚΩΝ

κάθου σὺ μηδὲ γρύζων.
φεύγεις ὄχλον, μισεῖς γυναῖκας, οὐκ ἐᾷς κομίζειν
εἰς ταὐτὸ τοῖς θύουσι σαυτόν· πάντα ταῦτ’ ἀνέξει.
οὐδεὶς βοηθός σοι πάρεστι· πρῖε σαυτὸν αὐτοῦ.
935 ἄκουε δ’ ἑξῆς πάντα τἄ[λ]λ’ ..[....]τισ[
          ]αγκας οὐδὲ τὴν [........].[.].[...]ι
ἐπεὶ παρῆλθ]ον αἱ γυναῖκες ἐ[νθάδ’ αἱ] παρ’ ὑμῶν,
τῇ σῇ γυν]αικὶ τῇ τε παιδὶ [περιβ]ολαὶ τὸ πρῶτον

930 μὰ τὸν Δί’ Fraenkel, Quincey: παιδιον B. Change of
speaker before οὐδ’ suggested by ed. pr. (assignment to Getas
first made by Kraus: B has no dicolon before οὐδ’). 931
κάθου Arnott: καθευθε B. σὺ om. B, suppl. Sandbach. μηδὲ
Gallavotti, Lloyd-Jones: μη (followed by a blank space four
letters wide) B. 932 γυναικασμισεις B. 934 Corr. several:
αυτοι B. 937-40 Supplementation here is very uncertain,
and the text offered is merely *exempli gratia*. 937 Suppl.
Arnott (ἐπεὶ), Handley (the rest). 938 τῇ σῇ γυν]αικὶ suppl.
ed. pr., [περιβ]ολαὶ Quincey.

DYSKOLOS

SIKON (*running forward to join Getas*)
　　　You've got the curtain, yes, you really
Do have one, dad!

KNEMON
By Zeus, I don't!

GETAS
And not the wine-bowl, either? 930

KNEMON
I'll murder Simiche!

SIKON (*seriously*)
　　　Sit still, and don't so much as murmur!
You shrink from crowds, you loathe the ladies, you
　　won't let us take you
To join the sacrificers.　You must bear with all these
　　torments—
There's no-one here to help you, so just gnash your
　　teeth there fuming!
And listen to my tale of all the other things (?) [. . .] 935

*(The ending of line 935 and much of 936–37 are so badly
torn in the papyrus that supplementation of 936 is totally
impossible, of 935 and 937 highly speculative.　Sikon,
however, here begins his description of the events at the
party in a flowery and poetic style which may have been
traditional for such passages.)*

[. . . . .] nor the [. . . . .]
[And when (?)] the ladies of your party [made their
　　entrance here (?)], for
[Your] wife and daughter first there were affectionate
　　embraces (?),

347

καὶ δεξιώ]ματ᾽· οὐκ ἀηδὴς διατρ[ι]βή τις αὐτῶν.
940 μικ]ρ[ὸν δ᾽] ἄπωθεν ηὐτρέπιζον συμπόσιον ἐγώ τι
τοῖς ἀνδράσιν τούτοις. ἀκούεις; μὴ κάθευδε.

ΓΕΤΑΣ

μὴ γάρ

ΚΝΗΜΩΝ

οἴμοι.

ΣΙΚΩΝ

τί δ᾽; οὐ βούλει παρεῖναι; πρόσ[εχε] καὶ τὰ λοιπά
σπουδὴ γὰρ ἦν· ἐστρώννυον χ[α]μαὶ στιβάδα τρα-
πέζας
ἔγωγε· τοῦτο γὰρ ποεῖν ἐμοὶ προσῆκ᾽. ἀκούεις;
945 μάγειρος ὢν γὰρ τυγχάνω· μέμνησο.

ΓΕΤΑΣ

μαλακὸς ἀνήρ

ΣΙΚΩΝ

ἄλλος δὲ χερσὶν Εὔιον γέροντα πολιὸν ἤδη
ἔκλινε κοῖλον εἰς κύτος, μειγνύς τε νᾶμα Νυμφῶν

---

939 καὶ δεξιώ]ματ᾽ suppl. Kraus. 940 Suppl. Bingen, Mar
zullo. ἄπωθεν Sandbach: ανωθεν B. 941–42 Change of
speaker after μὴ γάρ suggested by Sandbach (B has no di
colon). 942 τί δ᾽; οὐ om. B, suppl. Kassel. 943 εστρωννυντ[ο
apparently B. στιβάδα Maas: στιβας B. 944 ἐμοὶ ed. pr.: εμ
B. At the end of the line B has τὸν Διόνυσον, clearly a gloss
on Εὔιον in 946. 945 Change of speaker indicated by several
(B has a paragraphus under the line, possibly traces of a
dicolon after ανηρ, and μεμνησοι in mistake for μεμνησο:).

[Hands clasped in greeting (?)]. Their behaviour
  wasn't unattractive.
And there was I [not far (?)] away, arranging for the 940
  men here
A little party—aren't you listening? Don't fall asleep!

GETAS

No,

Not *that*!

(*Here Sikon and Getas shake the weary Knemon, to keep
his attention.*)

KNEMON

Oh, dear!

SIKON

What? Don't you want to be there? Pay attention
To everything that follows. All was bustle. I was
  fixing
A straw couch on the ground, and laying tables.
  That was rightly
My business. Are you listening? I *am* a cook, 945
  remember!

GETAS (*aside, referring to Sikon*)

The man's a sissy[1]!

SIKON

Now a hoary patriarchal vintage[2]
Was tipped into a dimpled urn by hand of one who
  merged it

---

[1] This remark probably refers to Sikon's parodically
effeminate gestures as he prepares to launch into his elabor-
ately poetical description of the party.

[2] Literally, ' a hoary patriarchal Bacchus '.

MENANDER

ἐδεξιοῦτ᾽ αὐτοῖς κύκλῳ, καὶ ταῖς γυναιξὶν ἄλλος.
ἦν δ᾽ ὡσπερεὶ ᾿ς ἄμμον φοροίης· ταῦτα μανθάνεις σύ
950 καί τις βραχεῖσα προσπόλων εὐήλικος προσώπου
ἄνθος κατεσκιασμένη χορεῖον εἰσέβαινε
ῥυθμὸν μετ᾽ αἰσχύνης ὁμοῦ μέλλουσα καὶ τρέμουσα
ἄλλη δὲ συγκαθῆπτε ταύτῃ χεῖρα κἀχόρευεν.

ΓΕΤΑΣ

ὦ πρᾶγμα πάνδεινον παθών—χόρευε, συνεπίβαινε.

ΚΝΗΜΩΝ

955 τί ποτ᾽ ἔτι βούλεσθ᾽, ἄθλιοι;

ΓΕΤΑΣ

μᾶλλον σὺ συνεπίβαινε

ἄγροικος εἶ.

ΚΝΗΜΩΝ

μή, πρὸς θεῶν.

948 εδεξιουν B.   949 ὡσπερεὶ ᾿ς Diano, Sydney seminar: ωσπερει
B.   950 Corr. London seminar: βρεχεισα B.   952 καὶ om. B
suppl. ed. pr.   953 αλλ᾽ηδη B.   954–55 Change of speaker
before τί ποτ᾽ indicated by ed. pr.   (B has no dicolon at the
end of line 954 and no paragraphus under it).   955 τί ποτ᾽ ἔτ
Householder, Marzullo: τυπτετι B.   σὺ om. B, suppl. ed. pr
956 Change of speaker after θεῶν indicated by ed. pr. (B ha
no dicolon).

---

[1] This remark is allusive, but its point seems to be the old
Greek chestnut, so prominent in comedy, about women'

With naiad springs, then pledged the men all round
  the cave.   Another
Man pledged the ladies.   *This* was just like irrigating
  beach sand.[1]
You fathom that?   One of the maids who'd quaffed 950
  too much now shrouded
The bloom of her fair youthful face, and then began
  the rhythmic
Pulse of a dance, demurely though, both hesitant and
  trembling.
A second girl joined hands with her, and shared the
  steps.

GETAS (*to Knemon, as if at first pitying him*)
       Poor victim
Of a quite awful accident—now dance, stand up, we'll
  help you!

Here Getas and Sikon suddenly pull Knemon to his feet,
and try to make him dance with them.)

KNEMON
You pests, what is it *now* you want?

GETAS
        Just try, stand up, we'll help you!   955
You're clumsy.

KNEMON
      By the gods, don't do that!

ibulousness. Women's throats, says Sikon, are like sand:
they can absorb vast quantities of liquid very easily.

ΓΕΤΑΣ

οὐκοῦν φέρωμεν εἴσω

ἤδη σε.

ΚΝΗΜΩΝ

τί ποήσω;

ΓΕΤΑΣ

χόρευε δὴ σύ.

ΚΝΗΜΩΝ

φέρετε· κρεῖττο

ἴσως ὑπομένειν ἐστὶ τἀκεῖ.

ΓΕΤΑΣ

νοῦν ἔχεις. κρατοῦμεν
ὦ καλλίνικοι. παῖ Δόναξ, Σίκων, Σύρε,
960 αἴρεσθε τοῦτον, εἰσφέρετε. φύλαττε δὴ

957 τί ποήσω assigned to Knemon by ed. pr. (B has no dicol
before and after these words). 958 $\overset{\tau\alpha}{\kappa\epsilon\iota\kappa\alpha\kappa\alpha}$ B. κρατοῦμ
several: κρατου B. 959 Σύρε Maas: συγε B.

GETAS

               Let us take you in, then,

ɔw.

KNEMON

Oh, what shall I do?

GETAS (*as if to renew the dance charade*)

            Dance . . .

KNEMON

            Take me in, perhaps it's better
ɔ face the tortures in the cave!

GETAS

You're showing sense. We've triumphed!

*he victory of Getas and Sikon over Knemon virtually
ds the play. All that remains is a brief finale, marked
a reversion of the metre to iambic trimeters, and
cluding at least two features traditional to Greek
medy. These are the procession off the stage of
vellers (κῶμος) wearing garlands and carrying torches
he stage time is now late evening or night, at the end of
is play's long day), and the concluding appeal to the
ɔddess Athena, daughter of Zeus, under her title of Νίκη,
ictory.—Getas continues speaking.)*

urrah, we've won! Hi, boy Donax, Sikon,
nd Syros—lift him up and take him in.   960

*lt Getas' command Donax and Syros, two super-
ɪmerary slaves, emerge from the shrine, and with Sikon's
·lp they lift Knemon up and prepare to carry him into
e cave with them. Getas now turns to address Knemon.)*

353

MENANDER

σεαυτόν, ὡς ἐάν σε παρακινοῦντά τι
λάβωμεν αὖτις, οὐδὲ μετρίως ἴσθ' ὅτι
χρησόμεθά σοι τὸ τηνικαῦτ'. ἀλλ' ἐκδότω
στεφάνους τις ἡμῖν, δᾷδα.

ΣΙΚΩΝ

τουτονὶ λαβέ.

ΓΕΤΑΣ

965 εἶέν· συνησθέντες κατηγωνισμένοις
ἡμῖν τὸν ἐργώδη γέροντα, φιλοφρόνως
μειράκια, παῖδες, ἄνδρες ἐπικροτήσατε.
(= KT *Epit.*
fr. 11) ἡ δ' εὐπάτειρα φιλόγελώς τε παρθένος
Νίκη μεθ' ἡμῶν εὐμενὴς ἕποιτ' ἀεί.

963 τηνικαῦτ'. ἀλλ' London seminar, Thierfelder: τη̣νικαδω̣]
964–5 Change of speaker after λαβέ indicated by several (B ha
no dicolon). 965 ευνησθεντες B.

354

DYSKOLOS

And *you* watch out, for in the future if
We catch you causing any trouble, we'll
Not treat you gently then at all, be sure!
Give us a torch and garlands, someone.

(*Donax and Syros doubtless at their entrance brought
with them a supply of garlands and torches, and now these
are distributed to the characters on stage. Sikon offers
a garland ostentatiously to Knemon.*)

SIKON

You take this.

(*Sikon and the two supernumeraries disappear now with
Knemon into the cave, leaving Getas alone to deliver his
epilogue to the audience.*)

GETAS

Well, if you've all enjoyed our victory   965
With this old nuisance, we request your kind
Applause—youths, boys and men! May Victory,
That merry virgin, born of noble line,
Attend us with her favour all our days!

(*Exit Getas, into the cave.*)

ENCHEIRIDION

(THE DAGGER)

ENCHEIRIDION (The Dagger)

Manuscript[1]

F = *PSI* 99, a small scrap of papyrus roll from Oxyrhynchus written in the second century A.D. It contains the line-endings of one column of text and the left-hand margin (which contains some names of speakers) of the succeeding column. First edition: G. Vitelli, *PSI* 1 (1912), 166 f., identifying it only as a 'fragment of comedy'; the plausible argument for its attribution to the *Encheiridion* was set out by D. Del Corno, *Parola del Passato* 23 (1968), 306 ff. No photograph has been published.

Fragments 1–7 are quotations from a variety of sources. See Introduction, pp. xxiv f.

*   *   *

Pictorial Evidence

A mosaic of the third century A.D. from the ' House of Menander ' at Mytilene in Lesbos. It is inscribed ΕΝΧΕΙΡΙΔΙΟΥ (*sic*, with N for Γ) ΜΕΡΟΣ Δ (*Encheiridion*, Act IV), and portrays a scene involving three men, all dressed alike in tunics and long cloaks. On the left stands an old man (identified on the mosaic

---

[1] On *P. Oxyrhynchus* 2658, see pp. 363 f. below.

358

as ΣΤΡΑΤΩΝ, Straton) turned slightly to the right.
He is clutching a black dagger, point upwards, in his
right hand and holds a long, straight stick in his left.
On the other side of the mosaic stands a second old
man (identified on the mosaic as ΔΕΡΣΙΠΠΟΣ, a
misspelling apparently for Derkippos[1]), whose head is
turned in Straton's direction. Derkippos also holds
a dagger in his right hand and a stick in his left, but
the stick is shaped like a crook. Between them
stands the third figure (identified on the mosaic as
ΚΕΡΔΩΝ, Kerdon), holding in his right hand an
object that most resembles a purse. He is probably a
slave. The interpretation of this picture and its rela-
tion to the literary fragments of the *Encheiridion* are
discussed below. Standard publication of the mosaic:
L. Kahil and others, *Les Mosaïques*, 49 ff. and colour
plate 4.

*   *   *

Plays with the title *Encheiridion* were written also
by two older contemporaries of Menander, Philemon
and Sophilus, and one of this Greek triad doubtless
provided the source for Livius Andronicus' *Gladiolus*,
an early experiment in Roman comedy. Menander's
Encheiridion was well enough known in antiquity to be
included in a tachygraphic list of 16 or 17 plays by

---

[1] In a note in *ZPE* 14 (1974), 240, W. Kraus suggests that
' Dersippos ' may perhaps be the correct spelling, if this old
man came from Macedonia, where ' Dersippos ' would be the
local form of the Attic ' Thersippos '. The idea is most
ingenious, but in fact no instance of the name Dersippos is
known from Macedonia, while Derkippos is attested in Athens
(a syntrierarch, 325–4 B.C., = 3246 Kirchner and Davies, *IG*
ii² 1629, 6. 28. 48).

Menander which probably formed the stock of an
Oxyrhynchus bookseller of the third or fourth
century A.D.,[1] and for a scene from its fourth act to
appear among the Mytilene mosaics, but all that
identifiably survives of its text is one mutilated scrap
of papyrus and a handful of ancient quotations.
Virtually nothing is known of the *Encheiridion*'s plot,
and this makes the interpretation of the scene in the
mosaic a lottery. The other Mytilene mosaics tend
to portray key scenes from their parent plays: the
arbitration in Act II of the *Epitrepontes*, the musicians
in Act II of the *Theophoroumene*, the expulsion of
Chrysis in Act III of the *Samia*, for example: and it is
reasonable to assume that the scene portrayed from
the fourth act of the *Encheiridion* was also pivotal.
Are the daggers held by Straton and Derkippos
recognition tokens, like the sword in Menander's
Misoumenos? If so, how are the two daggers in the
mosaic to be reconciled with the single dagger of
Menander's title? And what is the slave Kerdon
carrying in his pouch? According to one suggestion
the pouch contains money, Kerdon's reward for
services rendered in the identification of the crucial
dagger; another and perhaps likelier possibility is
that the purse contains supplementary recognition
tokens, small ornaments like those in the *Epitrepontes*
(331, 363, 384 ff.). But who is being recognised, and
how are Straton and Derkippos involved? We do not
know.

One further bonus, however, has been provided by

---

[1] *P. London* 2562 (H. J. Milne, *Greek Shorthand Manuals*,
London 1934; J. Stroux, *Philologus* 90 [1935], 88 f.; C.
Corbato, *Studi Menandrei*, Trieste 1965, 52 ff.).

the mosaic. It has enabled a scrap of papyrus in Florence (*PSI* 99) to be identified with some plausibility as a fragment from the *Encheiridion*. The papyrus nowhere overlaps any known quotations from the play, but it identifies three of the characters present as Straton, Doris and Kerd(on). Neither Straton nor Kerdon is a common character name in the remains of Greco-Roman comedy. Straton appeared as an old man in Menander's *Naukleros*[1] (the father of a Theophilos, fr. 286 Körte-Thierfelder), and the name is used to provide plausible detail about the acquaintances of stage characters in Plautus, *Asinaria* 344 and Terence, *Eunuchus* 414.[2] Before the Mytilene mosaics were discovered Kerdon was otherwise unknown as the name of a character with a speaking role in later Greek comedy. A cook in Euphron's *Synepheboi*, a play written in the third century B.C., described Kerdon, Dromon and Soterides as typical names of parvenu trash (fr. 10 Kock, iii p. 322). The name Kerdon was given to slaves in real life ([Dem.] 53.20), to low shoemakers in the mimes of Herodas (6. 48 ff., 7. 1 ff.), and to a

---

[1] Hence Coppola's now rejected suggestion that *PSI* 99 derived from the *Naukleros* (*Aegyptus* 4 [1924], 49 ff.).

[2] In the latter passage ' Strato ' is described as a soldier friend of Thraso's. In later Greek comedy the names given to soldiers (e.g. Polemon in *Pk.*, Thrasonides in *Misoumenos*, Bias in *Kolax*) have a meaning connected with their character or their profession, and it is at least worth considering whether Straton in the *Encheiridion*, with his military name, was not rather a soldier than an old man (cf. the military term in line 22). If he was a soldier, the Mytilene mosaicist would have to be deemed guilty of an inaccuracy in his portrait of Straton for which there is no parallel in this group of mosaics, although the artist does make errors in his labelling.

tradesman in Apuleius (*Met.* 2. 13. 1).[1] Since both
names are unusual in Greek comedy, their close
association first on *PSI* 99 and secondly on the
Mytilene mosaic of the *Encheiridion* is plausible (but
not absolutely watertight) evidence that *PSI* 99 also
derives from the *Encheiridion*.

Unfortunately, this identification helps us very
little towards an interpretation of Menander's plot.
In the papyrus Kerdon converses with Straton, which
may possibly indicate that the former was the latter's
slave. Another character, a female slave called
Doris, is named in the papyrus; there are references
to an inn (line 3), Egyptians (or Egyptian as an
adjective: 6), and Delphi (18); and there appears to
be a lot of movement to and fro (13, 15, 26, ? 29), with
running (21, 27, ? 32) and bustle (32). The reference
to Delphi may imply consultation of the oracle there,[2]
but the mention of Egyptian(s) is more puzzling. An
ancient quotation from the play (here fr. 4) names the
god Sarapis,[3] whose worship was introduced to the
Greeks in Egypt by Ptolemy Soter probably between
323 and 300 B.C., and from there spread throughout

---

[1] Cf. also the anonymous comic fragment 761 Kock (iii p.
542). A slave-boy in Plautus' *Miles Gloriosus* appears to be
called Lucrio (so the mss., but many scholars prefer the
orthography Lurcio: see B. Bader, *Szenentitel und Szenenein-
teilung bei Plautus*, Diss. Tübingen 1970, 158 ff.), and Lucrio is
a Latinisation of Κέρδων.

[2] Unless of course the speaker at this point is telling an
anecdote, using a proverb, or quoting (parodying ?).

[3] See especially T. A. Brady, *The Reception of the Egyptian
Cults by the Greeks, 330–30 B.C.*, University of Missouri Studies,
vol. 10 no. 1, 1935; S. Dow, *Harvard Theological Review* 30
[1937], 183 ff.; P. M. Fraser, (i) *Opuscula Atheniensia*, 3 [1960],
1 ff., and (ii) *Ptolemaic Alexandria*, Oxford 1972, I. 246 ff.; and
W. Hornbostel, *Sarapis*, Leiden 1973, 177 n. 3 and 213 f. n. 3.

the Greek world. It is obviously unwise to use isolated references like these, unrelated to any known dramatic context, as evidence for either the play's dramatic setting[1] or its place of production.

In addition to *PSI* 99 and the six quotations positively assigned to this play by their ancient citers, two further fragments have been tentatively attributed to the *Encheiridion* by modern scholars. An extract from an unnamed play of Menander's preserved by Stobaeus (fr. 639 KT) is a sermon on friendship addressed to two characters named Derkippos and Mnesippos. The name Derkippos is attested for Menander's *Encheiridion* by the Mytilene mosaic, but occurs nowhere else in extant Greek comedy. The attribution of the Stobaeus extract to this play accordingly seems reasonable enough, and it is printed here as fragment 7.

The other attribution is far more dubious. A recently published papyrus from Oxyrhynchus (2658: E. G. Turner, *The Oxyrhynchus Papyri*, 33, 1968, 66 ff.), dating from the second century A.D., contains some tattered remains of two columns of text from a comedy. A woman called Doris is mentioned in it (4, 26, ? 23), there is a reference to an innkeeper (14), and much talk of drink and drinking (6 ff., 15 f., 27 f.). Since *PSI* 99 also mentions a Doris and an inn, the question has been asked whether both papyri may derive from the same play. A completely certain answer is at present impossible. Doris, however, is a standard name for female slaves in later Greek comedy (Menander's *Kolax*, *Peri-*

---

[1] For one theory about this see the notes attached to the translation of fragment 2.

keiromene; *P. Hamburg* 120 [inv. 656] = ? Menander, fr. incert. 951 KT; Diphilus' *Mnemation*, fr. 56 Kock, ii p. 559), and the Oxyrhynchus fragment could be slotted neatly into the gap at the beginning of the third act of the *Perikeiromene* when Polemon and Sosias lead a drunken assault on Pataikos' house, where Glykera is sheltering.[1] Even if this is not the papyrus' home, however, the evidence linking it with *PSI* 99 is too flimsy at present for even a provisional attribution to the *Encheiridion*. It is not printed here. We must wait and see.

No hypothesis, didascalic notice, or cast-list is preserved for this play. Its production date is consequently uncertain. The reference to the new god Sarapis (fr. 4) may have had some topicality, but the precise date when his cult began to be talked about in Athens (if that is where the *Encheiridion* was produced) is unknown.

*   *   *

Dramatis personae, so far as is known:

Doris, a female slave

Kerdon, a male slave perhaps owned by Straton

Straton, probably an elderly man (but just possibly a soldier)

Derkippos, a second elderly man

In the lost portions of the play several other characters presumably had speaking roles. These may have included a man named Mnesippos (unless he was a

---

[1] Glykera's name may even have been mentioned in the Oxyrhynchus fragment, if a plausible supplement at line 18 is accepted (Γλυ]κέρα Turner).

mute; see fr. 7) and a divinity (the ' Corycean god '?
See on fr. 2) who spoke the prologue. There was
presumably also a chorus, possibly of tipsy revellers,
to perform the entr'actes.

ΕΓΧΕΙΡΙΔΙΟΝ

(The Florence papyrus contains the ends of 34 lines of one column of text, and some marginal indications of speakers for the next column. Assignment of individual lines to particular speakers is made only where the papyrus itself supplies the name.)

Column i:]ν [ο]ὗτος· ἤ, καλῶ 1,]τῳ πλησίον 2,] πανδοκ[ε]ίῳ· μανθάνω 3,]μαι. τίς [δ'] ἔστ'; ἰδεῖν 4,] καὶ χορτάζεται 5,]ονειτ' Αἰγυπτίους 6,]αλλ' ἐῶ τοῦ πράγματος 7,] οἶδα πάντα μοι 8,]α πιστεῦσαι δὲ δεῖ 9,] ΔΩΡΙΣ: τάλαν· τοιαῦτα δ' ἂν 10,]ν αὐτὴν εἰδέναι 11,] ἀκριβές. ΚΕΡΔ (ΩΝ): οὐ πάνυ 12,]αδ' ἐγγὺς προσιέναι 13,]ο τὸ πέρας τοῦτ' ἐγὼ 14, τὰς] θύρας εἰσέρχεται 15,]ως νὺξ πάλιν 16,]. ων διενεγκάτω 17,]. ἐκ Δελφῶν

1 Suppl. Arnott. 3 Suppl. Vitelli. 4 Suppl. Edmonds. 6 F has αιγυπτιοις corrected to αιγυπτιους. 8 In the right-hand margin F has the note τὸν Στράτωνα. 9 Or δ' ἔδει. 14 Above the line F has the note].. μεσο .. οι. 15, 19 Suppl. Schroeder.

ENCHEIRIDION
(The Dagger)

(SCENE: A street presumably, but the town is unknown; it may just possibly have been in Pamphylia: see on fr. 2. Unknown also are the occupants of the buildings visible to the audience, although Derkippos may perhaps have been the owner of one, and another may have been an inn.)

(The first column of the Florence papyrus contains only the right-hand third or half of 34 lines. This is not enough to justify the kind of supplementation which would produce a connected text. The identification of a particular speaker is made here only in those cases where the information is supplied by the papyrus itself. The following words and phrases emerge: You! Hi, I'm calling! *1,* neighbouring *2,* [in the (?)] inn, I hear *3,* [But (?)] who is it? To see *4,* and he's eating like an animal *5,* Egyptians, *or* Egyptian *as an adjective 6,* I pass over . . . of the affair *7,* I know . . . everything . . . to me *with an explanatory note ' Straton ' written above the line 8,* but there's (? there was) a need to trust *9,* DORIS: Dear me, such things would (?) *10,* her to know *or* that she knows *11,* precise. KERDON: Certainly not *12,* to approach near *13,* I . . . this conclusion *with an indecipherable note written above it 14,* goes in [the] door *15,* night again *16,* let him (? her) go (? carry) through *17,* from

367

MENANDER

ποτε 18, ελ]θεῖν ἡμερῶν 19,]μοι δ' οὐ δώσετε 20,
]τρεφειδραμετεον 21,]ετη τοὺς συμμάχους 22,
ο]ὐχὶ παίγνιον 23,] . υθ' ημ . [. . .] 24,]ειν
ἀπέχεται 25,] . . υ μεταγαγὼν 26,]η περιδραμὼν
27,]ητας εἴσομαι 28,]ν ἀνάγεται 29,]εὑρηκ'
[ὄν]τα σε 30,]σου· ταῦτα γὰρ 31,]ραμων ὁ
θόρυβος 32, το]ῦτ'· ἰοὺ ἰοὺ 33,]αδ . ην . [. . .]
. . . . . 34.

In column ii the marginal names are Δ[ΩΡΙΣ,
horizontally on a level with line 18 of column i,
Κ[ΕΡΔ(ΩΝ) 19, ΣΤΡ[ΑΤ(ΩΝ) 22, ΣΤΡ[ΑΤ(ΩΝ)
23, ΣΤΡ[ΑΤ(ΩΝ) 24, ΚΕΡΔ(ΩΝ) [26, ΣΤΡΑ-
Τ(ΩΝ) [27, ΣΤΡΑΤ(ΩΝ) [30, ΣΤΡΑΤ(ΩΝ)[
32.

21 Could Menander actually have written]τρέψει δραμετέον?
23 Suppl. Vitelli. 30 Suppl. Schroeder.

Six fragments of Ἐγχειρίδιον, *quoted by ancient
authors*

1 (136 Körte-Thierfelder, 149 Kock)

The whole fragment is cited by Stobaeus, *Eclogae*
4. 40. 7 (περὶ κακοδαιμονίας); the portion from πάντα
to the end by the same anthologist, 4. 47. 8 (περὶ τῶν
παρ' ἐλπίδα). On both occasions the heading is
Μενάνδρου Ἐγχειριδίου·

οὐχ ὅθεν ἂν ὤμην ἠτύχηκα· πάντα δὲ
τὰ μηδὲ προσδοκῶμεν' ἔκστασιν φέρει.

368

Delphi once *18*, to come within . . . days *19*, you'll
(*plural*) not give to me (?) *20*, will turn . . . (?).   I (?)
must run(?) *21*, the allies *22*, not a toy *23*, keeps away
(?) *25*, having conveyed *26*, having run around *27*,[1] I'll
know *28*, puts to sea (?) *29*, I've found that you are
. . . *30*, these things, you see, . . . *31*, having run
(?).   The bustle *32*, it.   Oh dear, oh dear! *or* it.
Hurrah, hurrah! *33*. *These scraps are tantalising; it is
impossible to work out the pattern of what seems to have
been a lively dialogue.*

*No text is preserved from the second column of the
papyrus, but we learn from marginal notes that Doris
spoke at about line 18 of the second column, Kerdon at
about 19 and 26, and Straton at about 22, 23, 24, 27, 30
and 32.*)

Six fragments of Encheiridion, quoted by ancient authors

1

*Stobaeus, Eclogae 4. 40. 7 (the section headed ' On Mis-
fortune '), quoting the whole fragment, and 4. 47. 8 (' On
Baffled Hopes '), quoting only from ' It's all ' to the end.*

This blow's come from an unexpected source.   It's all
The unexpected things that wreck one's poise.

Speaker and context are unknown.

[1] The subjects of the participles in 26 and 27 were male.

Fragment 1, line 1   ἡ τύχη· καὶ mss. of Stobaeus: corr.
Porson.   2 μηδὲ ms. A of Stobaeus, *Ecl.* 4. 40. 7: μηδὲν ms. M
there, μὴ all the mss. at 4. 47. 8.

MENANDER

2 (137 KT, 150 K)

The Byzantine lexica of Photius and the *Suda* introduce Menander's use of this proverb as follows, s.v. Κωρυκαῖος· θεόν τινα παρεισάγουσιν οἱ κωμικοὶ ἐπακροώμενον ἀπὸ παροιμίας τινός. Κώρυκος γὰρ τῆς Παμφυλίας ἀκρωτήριον, παρ' ᾧ πόλις Ἀττάλεια. ἐνταῦθα οἱ ἀπὸ τῆς πόλεως, ἵνα μηδὲν αὐτοὶ κακῶς πάσχωσιν ἀπὸ τῶν ἐφορμούντων τὴν ἄκραν λῃστῶν, ὑπαλλαττόμενοι πρὸς τοὺς ἐν ἄλλοις λιμέσιν ὁρμῶντας κατηκρῶντο, καὶ τοῖς λῃσταῖς ἀπήγγελλον καὶ τίνες εἰσὶ καὶ ποῖ πλέουσιν. ὅθεν καὶ ἡ παροιμία·

τοῦ δ' ἄρ' ὁ Κωρυκαῖος ἠκροάζετο.

οἱ δὲ κωμικοὶ Κωρυκαῖον τὸν θεὸν εἰσάγουσι. Μένανδρος Ἐγχειριδίῳ. The whole trimeter is cited merely as a proverb, with no reference to Menander, also by Strabo, 14. 644; Stephanus of Byzantium, s.v. Κώρυκος; Eustathius, 1534. 54 (commentary on Homer, *Od.* 5. 267); the *Appendix Proverbiorum*, 4. 96 Leutsch-Schneidewin (= 891 in the Bodleian ms., IV. 7 in the Vatican ms.); and the *Suda* again, s.v. τοῦ δ' ἄρα ὁ Κωρυκαῖος ἠκροάζετο. The paroemiographer Zenobius, 4. 75 L.-S. (= I. 51 in the Athos ms.), quotes only the words Κωρυκαῖος ἠκροάζετο with the note ταύτης (sc. τῆς παροιμίας) Μένανδρος μέμνηται ἐν τῷ Ἐγχειριδίῳ; cf. the lexicon of Hesychius, s.v. Κωρυκαῖος ἠκροάζετο· παροιμία παρὰ τοῖς κωμικοῖς.

Fragment 2 The mss. of the various quoters vary between ἄρα and ἄρα. ἠκροάσατο some mss. of Stephanus (VA).

---

[1] The modern Antalya, on the south coast of Turkey.

*Photius' lexicon and the Suda have the following entry:
' Corycean. The comic poets introduce a god eaves-
dropping, from a proverb. Corycus is a headland in
Pamphylia, by the side of which the city of Attaleia[1] is
situated. To avoid themselves becoming the victims of
the pirates who used to anchor by the headland, the
inhabitants of the city would disguise themselves and
eavesdrop on sailors anchoring in other harbours, and
inform the pirates of their identities and also their
destinations. Hence the proverb:*

Aha! The Corycean eavesdropped there!

*The comic poets introduce the god of Corycus. Menander
in the Encheiridion.' Many other writers (they are listed
on the facing page) quote this proverb, sometimes in the
complete form given above and sometimes abbreviated just
to ' Corycean eavesdropped '. The source of the story about
the pirates appears to be the fourth-century historian
Ephorus (F. Gr. Hist. 70, F27 Jacoby). From a drama-
tic point of view, however, the references in Photius
and the Suda to ' the Corycean' as ' a god ' in ' the
comic poets ' are far more interesting. Garbled as they
may be, they seem to imply that a comic poet—most
probably Menander in the Encheiridion—introduced ' the
Corycean god ' into his play as a character, presumably
as a divine prologue. In that case Pamphylia might well
have been the scene of some events mentioned in the plot
(and possibly, but not necessarily, also the scene of the
play itself), and this fragment part of the prologue speech
(where the god was explaining the origin of the proverb,
and its application to any concealed or disguised eaves-
dropper?).*

MENANDER

3 (138 KT, 151 K)

Athenaeus, 10. 446e writes: πίε δὲ δισυλλάβως (?)
Μένανδρος ἐν Ἐγχειριδίῳ·

(A): πίε. (B): πιεῖν ἀναγκάσω
τὴν ἱερόσυλον πρῶτα.

4 (139 KT)

A fragment of an anonymous glossary of Attic terms
in a sixth-century papyrus (P. Oxyrhynchus 1803)
published by A. S. Hunt, The Oxyrhynchus Papyri, 15
(1922), 163 ff., contains the entry (line 8): Σάρᾱπιν
διὰ τοῦ ᾱ, ὡς ἐν Ἐγχειριδίῳ·

ὡς σεμνὸς ὁ Σάραπις θεός.

Fragment 3, lemma   Dobree's conjecture δ' ἀεὶ συνεσταλμένως
for ms. A's banal δὲ δισυλλάβως is attractive.   Line 1 πίε om.
A, suppl. Clericus.

Fragment 4 was assigned to Menander's Encheiridion by Hunt
(the previous entry in the glossary cites Μένανδρος ἐν Συναρισ-
τώσαις, fr. 389 KT).

---

[1] Cf. introductory note to the Encheiridion, p. 362 f.

3

Athenaeus, 10. 446e cites this fragment to illustrate either the banal fact that the aorist imperative form πίε ('drink') has two syllables (so the manuscript at this point), or the more important point that the iota of πίε is always scanned short (so a plausible emendation of the ms.). The fragment runs:

> (A): You drink!   (B): I'll make
> The thieving hag drink first!

This clearly comes from a scene of revelry. The two speakers cannot be identified, but the ' thieving hag ' (where ' thieving ' is merely a general word of abuse: cf. the note on Aspis 226–27) may perhaps be the slave Doris.

4

P. Oxyrhynchus 1803 is a fragment from an ancient glossary of Attic terms which includes the entry "Σάραπιν (= the accusative singular of Σάραπις, Sarapis) with the (sc. second) alpha long, as in the Encheiridion (sc. of Menander):

> How holy the divine Sarāpis!"

This brief quotation is baffling. It is the first known reference in Athenian literature to the new god Sarapis,[1] but we are totally ignorant about its dramatic context. We do not know whether the enthusiastic speaker was imagined to be in Athens, Attaleia, Alexandria, or some other Greek city, whether the cult of this god was an important element in Menander's plot, or whether this mention of Sarapis was only a passing reference.

MENANDER

5 (140 KT, 152 K)

The scholiast on Plato, *Theaetetus* 153d, writes:
παροιμία·

> ἄνω κάτω πάντα.

ἐπὶ τῶν τὴν τάξιν μεταστρεφόντων. Μένανδρος
Ἐγχειριδίῳ. The same note (with the omission of
παροιμία) appears in the paroemiographer Gregory
of Cyprus, I. 61 (Leiden ms.).

6 (141 KT, 153 K)

The paroemiographer Zenobius, 6. 28 Leutsch-
Schneidewin (= I. 69 in the Athos ms.), writes:

> ὑπὲρ ὄνου σκιᾶς.

μέμνηται ταύτης (sc. τῆς παροιμίας) ἐν τῷ Ἐγχειρι-
δίῳ Μένανδρος. The proverb is frequently cited in
the paroemiographers (Diogenian, 7. 1; Gregory of
Cyprus, 3. 81 (= 3. 23 Leiden ms.); Apostolius,
17. 69), the lexica (Hesychius, the *Suda*), and scholi-
asts (e.g. on Aristophanes, *Vespae* 191), but nowhere
else is Menander's name mentioned in connection
with it.

A fragment tentatively attributed to Ἐγχειρίδιον

7 (639 KT, 543 K)

Stobaeus, *Eclogae* 4. 48b. 21 (ὅτι οἱ ἀτυχοῦντες
χρῄζουσι τῶν συμπασχόντων), with the heading
simply Μενάνδρου·

Δέρκιππε καὶ Μνήσιππε, τοῖς εἰρημένοις

5

The scholiast on Plato's Theaetetus 153d and the paroemiographer Gregory of Cyprus, 1. 61 (Leiden ms.), note that Menander used the proverb ' All upside down *' in this play, and that this proverb is applied to things (?) whose arrangement becomes higgedly-piggedly.*

6

The paroemiographer Zenobius, 6. 28 Leutsch-Schneidewin, notes that Menander used the proverb ' For a donkey's shadow *' in this play. This proverb, applied to things not worth fighting for, is frequently found in Attic literature (e.g. Aristophanes, Wasps 191; Plato, Phaedrus 260c; a lost speech of Demosthenes, as recorded by Plutarch, Moralia 848ab).*

A fragment tentatively attributed to Encheiridion

7

Stobaeus, Eclogae 4. 48b. 21 (the section headed ' That Victims of Misfortune need Sympathisers '), cites this fragment without naming the play source (but see the critical apparatus).

Derkippos and Mnesippos, all of us

Fragment 6, lemma   The Athos ms. omits Μένανδρος.

Fragment 7 has been assigned to this play by Del Corno because Derkippos, who is addressed in line 1, is not known to appear as a character in any other play by Menander.   Line 1 Δερκισππε ms. A of Stobaeus.

ἡμῶν ὑπό τινος ἢ πεπονθόσιν κακῶς
ἐστιν καταφυγὴ πᾶσιν, οἱ χρηστοὶ φίλοι.
καὶ γὰρ ἀποδύρασθ’ ἔστι μὴ γελώμενον,
5 καὶ συναγανακτοῦνθ’ ὁπόταν οἰκείως ὁρᾷ
ἕκαστος αὑτῷ τὸν παρόντα, παύεται
τοῦτον μάλιστα τὸν χρόνον τοῦ δυσφορεῖν.

4 Corr. L. Dindorf: ἀποδύρασθαί τι mss.   5 συναγανακτοῦντες A
6 Corr. Meineke: αὐτῶν mss.

ENCHEIRIDION

Enduring injury or slander from
Some source, can find one haven—loyal friends.
The victim then may cry his eyes out free
From ridicule, and when he sees his comrade   5
Stand by and share his anger like a friend,
Then most of all each lulls his rage to rest.

If Derkippos is an old man (see the introduction to this play), then so also will be Mnesippos, a name otherwise unknown to the comic stage.[1] Speaker and context are now unknown, although one of the addressees at this point doubtless considered himself a victim of ' injury or slander '.

[1] A Mnesippos is one of the speakers in the dialogue of Lucian entitled *Toxaris*, but Lucian here in all probability derived his use of the name from Menander's play, since the subject of his own dialogue was friendship.

EPITREPONTES

(MEN AT ARBITRATION)

EPITREPONTES (Men at Arbitration)

Manuscripts

C = *P. Cairensis* 43227, part of a papyrus codex from
Aphroditopolis written in the fifth century A.D.
The codex originally contained at least five plays by
Menander; *Epitrepontes* was third in order (between
Heros and *Perikeiromene*). Extant in C are lines 218–
699, 714–25, 749–59, 853–922, 934–58, 969–89, 1000–
14, 1018–23, 1035–49, 1052–57, 1060–1131. First
edition: G. Lefebvre, *Fragments d'un manuscrit de
Ménandre*, Cairo 1907; the same editor's *Papyrus de
Ménandre*, Cairo 1911, with a revised text, includes
photographs.

O = (i) *P. Oxyrhynchus* 1236, part of a vellum leaf
dating from the fourth century A.D. It contains,
either whole or in part, lines 880–901 and 923–43.
First edition: A. S. Hunt, *The Oxyrhynchus Papyri*,
10 (1914), 88 ff.; no photograph has been published
(but see R. A. Coles, *Location-List of the Oxyrhynchus
Papyri*, London 1974, 28).
(ii) *P. Oxyrhynchus* 2829, ten scraps of papyrus
dating from the third or fourth century A.D. It
contains mutilated portions of lines 218–56, 310–22,
and 347–61, together with six other brief passages
which cannot safely be assigned to a particular con-
text (here printed as fragments 11a to 11f inclusive).

INTRODUCTION

First edition: M. E. Weinstein, *The Oxyrhynchus Papyri*, 38 (1971), 19ff., with photographs.

P = *Membr. Petropolitana* 388, fragments of three leaves from a parchment codex dated to the fourth century A.D. It was originally found in the monastery of St. Catherine on Sinai and was last heard of in Leningrad. One leaf contained lines from the *Phasma*, the other two lines 127–48 and 159–77 from the *Epitrepontes*. First edition of 127–48: C. G. Cobet, *Mnemosyne* 4 (1876), 285 ff.; of 159–77: V. Jernstedt, *Zapiski ist.-fil. S.-Petersburgskago Univ.* 26 (1891), 204 ff. A photograph of 127–48 appears as the frontispiece of E. Capps, *Four Plays of Menander*, Boston, 1910; no photograph of 159–77 has been published, but Jernstedt prints an apparently careful drawing of these lines between pp. 204 and 205 of his paper.

Fragments 1–10 are scraps or quotations from a variety of sources. See Introduction, pp. xxiv f.

Fragment 12 is a scrap of papyrus (Berl. = *P. Berlin* 21142) dating from the second century A.D. and tentatively attributed to one of the missing scenes of the *Epitrepontes*. First edition: C. Austin, *Comicorum Graecorum Fragmenta in Papyris Reperta*, Berlin 1973, 138 f.; no photograph has been published.

*   *   *

Pictorial Evidence

A mosaic of the third century A.D. from the ' House of Menander ' at Mytilene in Lesbos. This mosaic is

inscribed ΕΠΙΤΡΕΠΟΝΤΩΝ ΜΕ(ΡΟΣ) B (*Epi-*
trepontes, Act II) and portrays a moment in the
arbitration scene from which the play takes its title.
In the centre stands Smikrines (his name appears to
his left, ΣΜΕΙΚΡΙΝΗΣ, *sic*), dressed in a white tunic
and a long decorated cloak and carrying a stick in his
right hand (cf. lines 248 f. of the play). To his left
is the shepherd Daos (misidentified on the mosaic as
ΣΥΡΟΣ, Syros), with a black satchel at his left side
suspended from his right shoulder. He holds a
crooked stick. On Smikrines' right is the charcoal-
burner Syros (identified on the mosaic simply as
ΑΝΘΡΑΚΕΥΣ), who also carries a crooked stick.
Both slaves wear costume similar to that of Smikrines.
To the right of Syros, however, stands a woman with
a baby in her arms, evidently Syros' wife. She is
figured on a scale much smaller than that of the three
principal figures, presumably in recognition of the
fact that her role in the play was an insignificant one,
played only by a mute. Standard edition of the
mosaic: S. Charitonidis, L. Kahil, R. Ginouvès, *Les
Mosaïques de la Maison du Ménandre à Mytilène* (*Antike
Kunst*, Beiheft 6, Berne 1970), 44 ff. and colour plate 4.

*   *   *

About half of the *Epitrepontes* is preserved intact,
and a further sixth in what is often a very mutilated
condition. Most of the second act survives, including
the whole of the arbitration scene from which the
play derives its title, and rather more than the first
half of the third act; continuous passages of text,
however, ranging in length from seven to 72 lines, are
extant in each of the other three acts. With the loss

of the opening and closing pages of the play in the Cairo papyrus it is now impossible to calculate the original length of the *Epitrepontes* with any precision, but there is enough evidence at least for a rough estimate. Menander was not apparently in the habit of writing plays with acts seriously disproportionate in length from each other. The length of *Epitrepontes*' third act was 288 + 6 lines, of the fourth 272 + 6 lines, of the second between 232 and 247 lines. The first act, accordingly, is most likely to have been somewhere between 230 and 290 lines in length, and the final act does not appear to have exceeded 230 lines. The total length of the play will thus in all probability have been from 1200 to 1300 lines, considerably greater than the *Aspis*, *Dyskolos*, or *Samia*.

The line-numbering of this edition agrees basically with that of Sandbach's Oxford Text (*Menandri Reliquiae Selectae*, Oxford 1972), although a slight adjustment has been made at one point, where Sandbach's 1003–17 have been renumbered 1000–14 for what seem to be papyrologically justifiable reasons (see *Actes du XVe Congrès International de Papyrologie*, Brussels, III, 31 ff.). On the right-hand margin of the Greek text is added, in brackets, the numbering given in Körte's third Teubner edition (*Menandri quae supersunt*, I, Leipzig 1945).

No hypothesis, didascalic notice, or cast-list is preserved for this play. Its production date is consequently unknown. Many scholars, nevertheless, have assumed that it is a work of Menander's full maturity. They may be correct, but firm evidence for the belief is remarkably absent. The play's text contains no reference to any dated external event. Other dating criteria that have been suggested are dangerously flimsy or subjective. The extant portions of the play are written entirely in iambic trimeters, and some have argued that the avoidance of other metres was a mark of Menander's later work. However, at least a third of this play's text is missing, so that there can be no guarantee that Menander avoided metres such as the trochaic tetrameter entirely in the *Epitrepontes*. In any case, many of Menander's plays are impossible to date, and too little of his work survives for criteria based on his choice of metres to have any validity in the dating of his plays when other kinds of evidence are absent. Other scholars have pointed to the high quality of scenes such as the arbitration scene or the monologues in the fourth act, to the imaginative characterisation of figures like Habrotonon, and to the play's excellent structure, in the belief that these were necessarily marks of full maturity. True: but when was full dramatic maturity a perquisite only of middle age?

*   *   *

Dramatis personae, in order of speaking, so far as is known:

Karion, a cook
Onesimos, the slave of Charisios
An unidentifiable god or goddess, speaker of the (postulated) prologue
Chairestratos, a friend of Charisios
Smikrines, the father of Pamphile
Habrotonon, a harp-girl and *hetaira*, hired by Charisios

INTRODUCTION

Syros, a charcoal-burner, slave of Chairestratos
Daos, a shepherd
Pamphile, the deserted wife of Charisios
Charisios

Mute characters include Syros' wife with a young baby, Simias apparently the cook's assistant, and Sophrone the old slave of Smikrines and formerly Pamphile's nurse. There is a conventional chorus of tipsy revellers, to perform the entr'actes.

ΕΠΙΤΡΕΠΟΝΤΕΣ

(*SCENE: A village street in a well-wooded part of Attica, perhaps about halfway between Athens and Hala Araphenides, a village on the coast eighteen miles east of Athens where the festival of the Tauropolia (see on line 451) took place. The street has two houses visible; one belongs to Charisios, the other to his friend Chairestratos.*)

(*Most of the opening act is lost. Before the first Leningrad fragment, which contains some 35 lines from the end of this act, there appear originally to have been three scenes. The play opened with a dialogue between Charisios' slave Onesimos and the cook Karion, whom Onesimos had been sent into Athens to hire for a luncheon party that day in Chairestratos' house. It is likely that five brief quotations made from this play in antiquity (= frs 1, 2a, 2b, 3, 5) derive from this scene. According to the fourth-century rhetorician Themistius (Or. 21. 262C: the passage is cited at the end of fr. 2b), Karion was characterised by Menander as a gossip, conceited about his own activities and inquisitive about those of others. In fact the play may have opened with the example of Karion's curiosity preserved in fr. 1, where he is questioning Onesimos about Charisios' unusual behaviour in hiring the harp-girl and hetaira Habrotonon for his amusement only a few months after his marriage. Karion's inquisitiveness clearly had the dramatic function of prising out of*)

386

EPITREPONTES
(Men at Arbitration)

Onesimos some of the skeletons in his master's family cupboard, and so of providing the audience with the antecedents of the plot. Onesimos must have described to Karion how he discovered that Pamphile, Charisios' wife, had given birth to a baby during her husband's absence from home just five months after the wedding, and how she had abandoned it with the help of her old nurse Sophrone somewhere in the surrounding countryside. When Charisios arrived back home, Onesimos had immediately blabbed out all he had learnt. Charisios' reaction had been to leave his wife and home, to lodge next door with his friend Chairestratos, and to attempt to deaden his grief over his wife's apparent unchastity by wine parties and the hire of Habrotonon.

After Karion and Onesimos had departed into Chairestratos' house at the end of the opening scene, the stage was almost certainly next occupied by a divinity, delivering a delayed prologue like his (or her) kinsfolk in Aspis, Heros and Perikeiromene. Although not so much as a word is known to survive from this second scene, and the identification of the postulated divinity baffles our ignorance, the play could hardly have been constructed without such a divine prologue. No merely human character was in a position to reveal two key facts which were essential to the audience's appreciation of the plot's irony: first, that the father of Pamphile's baby was Charisios himself, by a drunken act of rape; secondly, that the abandoned baby had been rescued by a slave of Chairestratos completely unaware of its identity. An attractive piquancy is added to the great arbitration scene in Act II, from which the play takes its name, if members of the audience understand that the arbitrator, without knowing it, is deciding the fate of his own grandchild.

The third scene is a puzzle. After the divinity's disappearance at the end of the prologue, Chairestratos entered the stage; but whether he was alone, or whether another character such as, for instance, Habrotonon accompanied him, cannot now be established. If Chairestratos did have a companion, that companion must have left the stage either before or directly after the arrival of a new character: Smikrines, the father of

---

Six fragments of Ἐπιτρέποντες, *quoted by ancient authors*

1 (1 Körte-Thierfelder, 600 Kock)

The whole fragment is cited by an anonymous commentator on Aristotle's *De Interpretatione*, *C.A.G.* IV part 5, p. xxii; line 1 is cited also by Phoebammon, *De Figuris* (*Rhet. Gr.* iii. 45 Spengel), John Doxopater, *In Aphthonium* (*Rhet. Gr.* ii. 289 Walz), and the scholiast on Hermogenes, *De Stat.* (*Proleg. Sylloge: Rhet. Gr.* xiv. 186 Rabe); the first two words of line 3 are quoted by the scholiast on Apollonius of Rhodes, 3. 294.

EPITREPONTES

Pamphile. The entry of Smikrines seems to have occurred shortly before the first Leningrad fragment starts. He has just heard about Charisios' scandalous desertion of Pamphile, and is intending to see his daughter about this. In all probability one ancient quotation (= fr. 6) comes from a remark made by Smikrines directly after his entrance. Smikrines is clearly distressed more by Charisios' prodigality in hiring Habrotonon and giving parties than by his apparent infidelity. At Smikrines' entry Chairestratos withdraws into the background. Smikrines has not yet observed him when the first Leningrad fragment begins. Before giving the text of that fragment, however, I follow the lead of other editors in printing seven ancient quotations which derive from lost portions of the play. Five of these (frs. 1, 2a, 2b, 3, 5) seem to come from the opening scene, and one (fr. 6) from the third, as has been suggested above. The remaining one (fr. 4) introduces a word from the kitchen, and is best assigned to a scene involving Karion the cook, but it is impossible now to be certain whether that scene opened the play or came later.)

Six fragments of Epitrepontes, quoted by ancient authors

1

The whole fragment is cited by an anonymous commentator on Aristotle's De Interpretatione, C.A.G. IV part 5, p. xxii; parts of it are quoted also by other authors, as listed on the facing page.

MENANDER

ΚΑΡΙΩΝ

οὐχ ὁ τρόφιμός σου, πρὸς θεῶν, Ὀνήσιμε,
ὁ νῦν ἔχων τὴν Ἁβρότονον τὴν ψάλτριαν
ἔγημ᾽ ἔναγχος;

ΟΝΗΣΙΜΟΣ
πάνυ μὲν οὖν.

2a, 2b (2 KT, 849 and 850 K)

Both passages are cited by the philosophic com-
mentator Elias, writing on Porphyrius' *Isagoge* and
Aristotle's *Categoriae*, *C.A.G.* XVIII part 1, p. 27;
the second passage is inaccurately quoted also by
Cicero, *Att.* 4. 11. 2, Cyril of Alexandria, *Contra
Iulianum*, 7. 230 (Migne, *P.G.* lxxvi. 852B), and
Themistius, *Or.* 21. 262c.

(2a)   ΚΑΡΙΩΝ
            φιλῶ σ᾽, Ὀνήσιμε·
καὶ σὺ περίεργος εἶ.

(2b)   ΚΑΡΙΩΝ (?)
            οὐδέν ἐστι γὰρ
γλυκύτερον ἢ πάντ᾽ εἰδέναι.

After citing fr. 2b, Themistius twice gives the cook's
name as Καρίων, and adds the following remark: οἷα

Fragment 1 attributed to *Epitrepontes* by Croiset. Line 1
Ὀνήσιμε Phoebammon, J. Doxopater: Ὀνήσιμος apparently
anon. comm. on Aristotle. 2 First τὴν om. anon. comm.,
suppl. Leo and Wilamowitz.

Fragments 2a and 2b attributed to *Epit.* by van Leeuwen.
Lines 3–4 οὐδὲν γὰρ γλυκύτερον Elias, οὐδὲν γλ. Cicero, οὐκ
ἔστι γὰρ γλ. Themistius, ἔστι γλυκὺ (with τὸ π. εἰ.) Cyril.

EPITREPONTES

KARION

Onesimos, in gods' name, isn't it
Your master who's now got Habrotonon,
The harp-girl, and just married, too?

ONESIMOS

                        It's true.

Possibly the opening lines of the play.

2a, 2b

*These two brief quotations were made by the philosophic
commentator Elias, writing on Porphyrius' Isagoge and
Aristotle's Categoriae, C.A.G. XVIII part 1, p. 27; the
second passage, however, is inaccurately quoted by other
authors, who are listed on the facing page.*

(2a)   KARION

                  Onesimos, I like
You—you are nosy, too!

And later on,

(2b)   KARION (?)

                 No, there's nothing I
Love more than knowing all the facts!

*Both these quotations appear to derive from the opening
scene.   When the fourth-century rhetorician Themistius
cites the second passage (Or. 21. 262c), he identifies the
cook's name as Karion, accuses him of gossip, slander,
exaggeration, and petty theft, and makes the following
illuminating comment on one aspect of his characterisation:*

MENANDER

δὲ λέγει ὁ μάγειρος ὁ κωμῳδικὸς οὐδ᾽ ἐκεῖνα πάνυ
ἐλυσιτέλει τῷ πυνθανομένῳ, ἀλλ᾽ ἐπέτριβε τοὺς
δαιτυμόνας, ἐξαλλάττων τὰ ἡδύσματα.

3 (3 KT)

Photius, Berlin manuscript, p. 82 Reitzenstein.
ἀλύειν τὸ μηδὲν πράττειν· Μένανδρος Ἐπιτρέ-
πουσιν·

τί δ᾽ οὐ ποεῖς ἄριστον; ὁ δ᾽ ἀλύει πάλαι
κατακείμενος.

4 (4 KT, 185 K)

Erotian, p. 41 Nachmanson. ἔστιν ἐχῖνος χύτρας
εἶδος μεγαλοστόμου καὶ μεγάλης. μέμνηται τῆς
λέξεως Μένανδρος ἐν Ἐπιτρέπουσιν.

5 (5 KT, 178 K)

Athenaeus, 3. 119 f. Μένανδρος Ἐπιτρέπουσιν·

EPITREPONTES

' *The words of this comic cook did not benefit the enquirer at all, but he irritated the guests by using recherché language to describe his sauces.*' *If Themistius is accurate here in his reference to the play, he must be alluding to a later lost scene and not to the opening one, where his only interlocutor is the slave Onesimos, who could not fitly be described as a ' guest '.*

3

Photius, Berlin manuscript, p. 82 Reitzenstein, says that in this play Menander used the word ἀλύειν *in the sense of ' to achieve nothing ', citing the following fragment:*

Why aren't you cooking lunch?   He's on his couch—
Been there for ages—fretting.

Photius appears to be wrong here in his interpretation; in this context ἀλύει *is better translated ' he's fretting ', not ' he's achieving nothing.'—If this fragment comes from the opening scene, as seems likely, Onesimos will be addressing Karion, and using Charisios' fretful impatience as his excuse to usher the cook off stage into Chairestratos' house.*

4

Erotian, p. 41 Nachmanson, says that in this play Menander used the word ἐχῖνος *to denote ' a type of large jar with a wide mouth '. Such a word is perhaps most likely to have been used in a scene involving Karion, not necessarily the opening one.*

5

Athenaeus, 3. 119 f, cites this fragment with the names of playwright and play; the citation also appears, without the play-title, in two old lexica, listed on the next page:

MENANDER

$$\dot{\epsilon}\pi\dot{\epsilon}\pi\alpha\sigma\alpha$$
$$\dot{\epsilon}\pi\dot{\iota}\ \tau\dot{o}\ \tau\dot{\alpha}\rho\iota\chi\sigma\varsigma\ \ddot{\alpha}\lambda\alpha\varsigma,\ \dot{\epsilon}\dot{\alpha}\nu\ o\ddot{\upsilon}\tau\omega\ \tau\dot{\upsilon}\chi\eta.$$

This fragment is cited also, but without play-title, by Aelius Dionysius, τ 3 (H. Erbse, *Untersuchungen zu den Attizistischen Lexika*, Berlin 1950, 143), and in an anonymous lexicon published by both J. G. J. Hermann, *De emendanda ratione Graecae grammaticae pars prima*, Leipzig 1801, 324 f., and J. A. Cramer, *Anecdota Graeca e codd. MSS. Bibl. Reg. Parisin.*, Oxford 1839–41, iv. 248.

6 (6 KT, 175 K)

Stobaeus, *Eclogae* 3. 30. 7 (περὶ ἀργίας).   Μένανδρος Ἐπιτρέπουσιν·

ΣΜΙΚΡΙΝΗΣ (?)

$$\dot{\alpha}\rho\gamma\dot{o}\varsigma\ \delta'\ \dot{\upsilon}\gamma\iota\alpha\dot{\iota}\nu\omega\nu\ \tau\sigma\hat{\upsilon}\ \pi\upsilon\rho\dot{\epsilon}\tau\tau\sigma\nu\tau\sigma\varsigma\ \pi\sigma\lambda\dot{\upsilon}$$
$$\dot{\epsilon}\sigma\tau'\ \dot{\alpha}\theta\lambda\iota\dot{\omega}\tau\epsilon\rho\sigma\varsigma\cdot\ \mu\dot{\alpha}\tau\eta\nu\ \gamma\sigma\hat{\upsilon}\nu\ \dot{\epsilon}\sigma\theta\dot{\iota}\epsilon\iota$$
$$\delta\iota\pi\lambda\dot{\alpha}\sigma\iota\alpha.$$

(The first Leningrad fragment begins with Smikrines in mid-speech.)

126   [πίνει δὲ πολυτελέστατον

Fragment 5, line 2 ἐὰν Elmsley: ἄν mss. of Ath. and lexica.

Fragment 6, lines 2–3 Corr. Wilamowitz (cf. the paraphrase by Theophylactus, *Epist.* 61): διπλάσια γοῦν (διπλᾶ οἷα γ. S, διπλαοι ἄγουν A) ἐσθίει μάτην mss. of Stobaeus.

If this should happen, I
Have really added fuel to the fire!

*Menander's Greek here is literally rendered '. . . I
have sprinkled salt on salted fish,' and this has led some
scholars to assume that Karion is the speaker and the
context culinary. The words seem better taken, however,
in a proverbial sense, and referred to some situation in the
play where a character has made a bad situation worse by
his interference. One possibility is that Onesimos spoke
these words in the opening scene, when describing the
disastrous consequences of his tale-telling on Charisios'
arrival home. If the suggestion is correct, there would be
an appealing Menandrean irony in having a slave use a
culinary metaphor in conversation with a cook.*

6

*Quoted by Stobaeus, Eclogae 3. 30. 7 (the section headed
'On Idleness').*

SMIKRINES (?)

A healthy idler's far worse than one in
Bed with a fever—he eats twice as much
Without the benefit!

———————————————

(*The first Leningrad fragment begins probably not long
after Smikrines' entry. All of Smikrines' previous
remarks are likely to have been soliloquies, and the
Leningrad fragment begins with part of one, with Smik-
rines in the middle of some tightfisted recriminations
against Charisios, and Chairestratos eavesdropping
unobserved in the background.*)

SMIKRINES

[. . . . .] The fellow [drinks the most (?)]   126

MENANDER

ἄνθρωπος οἶνον. αὐτὸ τοῦτ᾽ ἐκπλήτ[τομαι (1 Körte)
ἔγωγ᾽. ὑπὲρ δὲ τοῦ μεθύσκεσθ᾽ οὐ λέγω.
ἀπιστίᾳ γάρ ἐσθ᾽ ὅμοιον τοῦτό γε,
130 εἰ καὶ βιάζεται κοτύλην τις τοὐβολ[οῦ
ὠνούμενος πίνειν ἑαυτόν.

ΧΑΙΡΕΣΤΡΑΤΟΣ

                                   τοῦτ᾽ ἐγ[ὼ   (5)
προσέμενον· οὗτος ἐμπεσὼν διασκ[εδᾷ
τὸν ἔρωτα. τί δέ μοι τοῦτο; πάλιν οἰμω[ζέτω.

ΣΜΙΚΡΙΝΗΣ

προῖκα δὲ λαβὼν τάλαντα τέτταρ᾽ ἀργύρ[ου
135 οὐ τῆς γυναικὸς νενόμιχ᾽ αὐτὸν οἰκέτ[ην.
ἀπόκοιτός ἐστι. πορνοβοσκῷ δώδεκα   (10)
τῆς ἡμέρας δραχμὰς δίδωσι.

ΧΑΙΡΕΣΤΡΑΤΟΣ

                              δώδεκα·
πέπυσ]τ᾽ ἀκριβῶς οὑτοσὶ τὰ πράγματα.

ΣΜΙΚΡΙΝΗΣ

μηνὸ]ς δια[τ]ροφὴν ἀνδρὶ καὶ πρὸς ἡμερῶν
140 ἕξ.]

127–48 and 159–77 are preserved on two mutilated leaves of
parchment now in Leningrad. 126 Suppl. *exempli gratia* Sud-
haus. 127 Suppl. Cobet. 128 δὲ om. P, suppl. Cobet. μεθυ-
σκεθ᾽ P, corr. Tischendorf. 130 Suppl. Jernstedt. 131, 132
Suppl. Cobet. 133 τί—οἰμω[ζέτω continued to Chairestratos
by several (P has ερωτα· τι, but a single point and a space
do not necessarily indicate a change of speaker: cf. Harsh,
AJP 62 [1941], 103). οἰμω[ζέτω suppl. Körte. 134, 135
Suppl. Cobet. 138 Suppl. van Leeuwen. 139 μηνὸ]ς suppl.
Sudhaus, δια[τ]ροφὴν Cobet. 140 ἕξ suppl. Sudhaus.

[Expensive (?)] wine, that's what amazes me.
About his actual drunkenness, I make
No comment.   What's well-nigh incredible
Is this—how anyone can really bring   130
Himself to drink wine which he buys at one
Obol the half-pint[1]!

CHAIRESTRATOS (*aside*)
                    Just what I expected—he'll
Barge in and wreck the cuddling.   Still, what's that
To me?   Again, to hell with him[2]!

SMIKRINES (*continuing his complaints*)
                              In cash
He took four talents dowry,[3] yet he's not   135
Thought fit to share his wife's house.   He sleeps out,
And gives a pimp twelve drachmas every day.

CHAIRESTRATOS (*aside*)
Twelve, yes!   He's [learnt] the terms.   No error there!

SMIKRINES
That keeps a man for one [month], and [six] days
Besides!

---

[1] Although cheap wines in Menander's time sold normally for
only 1/6th obol a half-pint, those of high quality fetched
prices commensurate with the figure named by Smikrines here.
The old man's indignation is as much an index of his own
parsimoniousness as of his son-in-law's extravagance.
[2] The implication is that Chairestratos had already con-
signed Smikrines to hell in a previous remark now lost.
[3] This was more than the comic norm: see on *Aspis* 35 and
Dyskolos 740.

MENANDER

ΧΑΙΡΕΣΤΡΑΤΟΣ

εὖ] λελ[όγ]ισται· δύ' ὀβολοὺς τῆς ἡμέρας,
ἱκανό]ν τι τῷ πεινῶντι πρὸς πτισ[άνη]ν ποτέ.   (15

ΑΒΡΟΤΟΝΟΝ

Χαρίσι]ός σ[ε] προσμένει, Χαιρέ[στρατε.
τίς ὅδ' ἐσ]τὶ δ[ή], γλυκύταθ';

ΧΑΙΡΕΣΤΡΑΤΟΣ

ὁ τῆς [νύμφης πα]τήρ.

ΑΒΡΟΤΟΝΟΝ

ἀλλὰ τί παθ]ὼν ὡς ἄθλιός τις [φιλόσοφος
145 βλέπει σκύθρωφ' ὁ] τρισκακοδ[αίμων;]

ΧΑΙΡΕΣΤΡΑΤΟΣ (or possibly ΣΜΙΚΡΙΝΗΣ)

[ψάλ]τριαν
146   ]σαν γυναῖκα [. . . . . . .]ι   (20)

(Of the two following lines the endings only are pre-
served:]ιοι 147,]ς 148.   Then there is a lacuna of
between 10 and 30 lines in all probability before the
Leningrad fragment resumes.)

140 εὖ suppl. Sudhaus, λελ[όγ]ισται Cobet.   141 ἱκανό]ν suppl.
Wilamowitz, πτισ[άνη]ν Gomperz. πρὸς om. P, suppl. Sudhaus.
142 The new speaker identified as Habrotonon by Webster.
Χαρίσι]ός σ[ε] suppl. Körte, Χαιρέ[στρατε Capps.   143 τίς ὅδ'
ἐσ]τὶ δ[ή] suppl. Jernstedt, [νύμφης πα]τήρ Kock.   144 ἀλλὰ
τί παθ]ὼν suppl. Körte, after Wilamowitz (τί δὴ παθ]ὼν).
144–45 φιλόσοφος—ὁ suppl. exempli gratia Wilamowitz.   145
τρισκακοδ[αίμων and ψάλ]τριαν suppl. Jernstedt.   Change of
speaker after τρισκακοδ[αίμων suggested by Sudhaus.

398

EPITREPONTES

He's [good] at sums.   Two obols a   140
Day—just [enough] for porridge when you're
  starving[1]!

(*At this point Habrotonon comes out of Chairestratos'
house, and approaches Chairestratos.*)

HABROTONON

Chairestratos, [Charisios] is waiting for
You.   Darling, [who] is [that]?

CHAIRESTRATOS

It's *his* wife's father.[2]

HABROTONON

[What's making] him [look glum (?)], just like
A sad [professor (?)], so pathetic?   145

(*What follows in the manuscript, up to line 148, is too
mutilated for translation, although the ending of line 145
has* harp-girl *and 146* woman *or* wife; *Chairestratos or
Smikrines may here be contrasting the roles of Habrotonon
and Pamphile.   Then there is a gap of between 10 and 30
lines in all probability, during which Smikrines may have
angrily intervened in the conversation between Chaire-
stratos and Habrotonon.   When the Leningrad fragment
resumes, only thirteen lines of the first act remain.   Their*

---

[1] Six obols equalled one drachma, and a month (by Chaire-
stratos' computation) lasted 30 days.   In actual fact Athenian
months varied between 30 and 29 days.

[2] *His* = Charisios'.

399

interpretation is not easy. Lines 166–67, for instance, are mysteriously allusive; the key to them, now only a matter for speculation, may originally have been given in remarks made by Chairestratos and Habrotonon in the lacuna between 148 and 159. And lines 159–60, which directly follow the lacuna, provide three inter-related

---

ΑΒΡΟΤΟΝΟΝ (?)

159 οὕτως ἀγα]θόν τί σοι γένοιτο, μὴ λέγε
160 τοιαῦτά γ'.]

ΣΜΙΚΡΙΝΗΣ

οὐκ ἐς κόρακας; οἰμώξει μακρά.
εἴσειμι ν]ῦν εἴσω, σαφῶς τε πυθόμενος   (25)
ὅπως ἔχει] τὰ τῆς θυγατρός, βουλεύσομαι
ὅντινα τ]ρόπον πρὸς τοῦτον ἤδη προσβαλῶ.

ΑΒΡΟΤΟΝΟΝ

φράσωμ]εν αὐτῷ τοῦτον ἥκοντ' ἐνθάδε;

ΧΑΙΡΕΣΤΡΑΤΟΣ

165 φράσω]μεν. οἷον κίναδος· οἰκίαν ποεῖ
ἀνάστα]τον.

159–60 Supplementation, speech-division, and assignment of parts are all highly speculative, and the text printed is merely *exempli gratia*. 159 Suppl. Kock. 160 Suppl. Arnott, after Sandbach (τοιοῦτον). Speech division before οὐκ and assignment to Smikrines suggested by Hutloff. 161–70 Suppl. Sudhaus (161), Körte (162, 164), van Leeuwen (163), Jernstedt (165, 167–70), and Kock (166).

EPITREPONTES

*problems: how are the initial eight or so letters of each
line, torn off in the manuscript, to be supplemented? Who
are the speakers? Where do the words of the first speaker
end, of the second begin? The solutions offered here are
very tentative. They assume that Smikrines insulted
Habrotonon just before the end of the lacuna.*)

HABROTONON

Bless you, don't speak to me [like that (?)]!

SMIKRINES

To hell   159

With you! You'll suffer loud and long for this!   160
[I'm going] in now. When I've got a clear
Account [of how] my daughter['s fixed], I'll plan
[The] way to tackle *him*[1] accordingly!

(*Smikrines goes angrily off into Charisios' house, to see
Pamphile. Chairestratos and Habrotonon are alone on
stage together.*)

HABROTONON

[Ought] we [to warn] him that this fellow's here?

CHAIRESTRATOS

[Let]'s [warn] him. What a fox[2] he is! He turns   165
A house [all topsy-turvy].

---

[1] In lines 163–65 the personal references, so clearly dis-
tinguishable by gestures on the stage, read confusingly on the
printed page. Smikrines will tackle Charisios; Habrotonon
and Chairestratos agree to warn Charisios; Smikrines is
described as the fox who upsets houses.

[2] The fox was a symbol of shamelessness, as well as of
cunning, in ancient Greece.

MENANDER

ΑΒΡΟΤΟΝΟΝ
πολλὰς ἐβουλόμην ἅμα. (30)

ΧΑΙΡΕΣΤΡΑΤΟΣ
πολλάς;]

ΑΒΡΟΤΟΝΟΝ
μίαν μὲν τὴν ἐφεξῆς.

ΧΑΙΡΕΣΤΡΑΤΟΣ
τὴν ἐμήν;

ΑΒΡΟΤΟΝΟΝ
τὴν σ]ήν γ'. ἴωμεν δεῦρο πρὸς Χαρίσιον.

ΧΑΙΡΕΣΤΡΑΤΟΣ
ἴωμ]εν, ὡς καὶ μειρακυλλίων ὄχλος
170 εἰς τ]ὸν τόπον τις ἔρχεθ' ὑποβεβρεγμένων
οἷς] μὴ 'νοχλεῖν εὔκαιρον εἶν[α]ί μο[ι δοκεῖ. (35)

ΧΟ] Ρ [ΟΥ

---

171 οἷς suppl. Kock, εἶν[α]ί μο[ι δοκεῖ] Jernstedt. ΧΟ]Ρ[ΟΥ
suppl. several.

EPITREPONTES

HABROTONON

Lots of houses ought
To be like that[1]!

CHAIRESTRATOS

[Lots]?

HABROTONON

One—next door, at least!

CHAIRESTRATOS

My house?

HABROTONON

Yes, [yours].   Let's join Charisios
Here.

(*Habrotonon points to Chairestratos' house.*)

CHAIRESTRATOS

[Let]'s, for there's a bunch of teen-age drunks
Just coming, this direction.   I don't [think]   170
This is the time for getting in [their] way!

(*Chairestratos and Habrotonon go off into the former's
house.   The approaching band of drunkards is the
chorus, who now enter after the conventional cue for their
first entr'acte performance.*)

---

[1] Habrotonon *may* imply (the nuances are elusive: see above,
before line 159) that the successful prosecution of her pro-
fession requires husbands in many houses to be unhappy and to
turn to *hetairai* like herself for consolation.   She adds, some-
what inconsequentially, that Chairestratos' house too needs
shaking up: is this because her hirer Charisios has not so far
paid her the attention she expects?

ΜΕΡΟΣ Β΄

ΟΝΗΣΙΜΟΣ (?)

ἐπι[σφαλῆ μὲν] πάντα τἀνθ[ρώπων ἐγὼ
οἰόμ[ενος εἶναι
καὶ τοπ[
175 ὁ δεσπό[της
ὁ γέρω[ν   (40)
οὐδὲ λο[

(Here the Leningrad fragment breaks off, and there
is a lacuna of perhaps between 25 and 40 lines until
the Cairo papyrus begins.)

172–7 Identification of the speaker as Onesimos suggested by
several. The supplementation of 172–73 is purely *exempli
gratia*. ἐπι[σφαλῆ μὲν] and τἀνθ[ρώπων suppl. Jernstedt, [ἐγὼ
and οἰόμ[ενος εἶναι Sudhaus. 175–76 suppl. Jernstedt.

---

*There are mentions of the master in 175, the old man
in 176. Such tantalising scraps derive apparently from a
soliloquy at the beginning of the act, but who was the
speaker? The most plausible guess is that he was One-
simos, entering from Chairestratos' house. Here the
Leningrad fragment breaks off, and there follows a gap of
roughly calculable extent. As a second act of more than
250 lines is doubtful for Menander, the lacuna is unlikely
to have exceeded 40–45 lines; it is equally unlikely to have
contained fewer than 20–25 lines, given the action and
speeches that must be postulated in the gap. Onesimos, if
he was the opening speaker, will have finished his
soliloquy; Smikrines will have entered from Charisios'
house and also have delivered a monologue, probably*

EPITREPONTES

ACT II

(What happens at the beginning of the second act, after the departure of the chorus, is uncertain. The Leningrad fragment has the mutilated remains of the opening six lines, out of which no continuous sense can be made. Lines 172–73 may be supplemented to give something like:

Believ[ing that] all human actions [are]
[Precarious, I] . . . .

---

describing and commenting on the conversation he has just had with Pamphile inside the house. Onesimos will have retired again into Chairestratos' house, either before Smikrines noticed his presence, or, more probably, after an altercation between the slave and the old man. Smikrines is thus left alone, standing in the background doubtless near the door of Charisios' house, when his deliberations are shattered by the entry of two slaves in mid-conversation. The scene from which the play takes its title is about to begin. It is preserved, probably in its entirety, on the Cairo papyrus, together with many of the scenes that follow it.)

(The arbitration scene. Two slaves enter from the left, by the side-entrance which is imagined to lead in from the country. These are the shepherd Daos and the charcoal-burner Syros. Syros is accompanied by his wife, who carries a small baby. Daos clutches a little pouch of trinkets. As they enter, the slaves can be heard in violent argument. Line 218 may be the slaves' first words, or just possibly the opening line or two of the scene came at the bottom of the lost previous page of the Cairo codex. As the slaves talk, they gradually edge nearer to Smikrines.)

MENANDER

ΣΥΡΟΣ

218 φεύγεις τὸ δίκαιον.

ΔΑΟΣ

συκοφαντεῖς δυστυχής.
οὐ δεῖ σ' ἔχειν τὰ μὴ σ'.

ΣΥΡΟΣ

ἐπιτρεπτέον τινί

(Kock fr. 183)

220 ἐστι περὶ τούτων.

ΔΑΟΣ

βούλομαι· κρινώμεθα.

ΣΥΡΟΣ

τίς οὖν;

ΔΑΟΣ

ἐμοὶ μὲν πᾶς ἱκανός. δίκαια δὲ   (45)
πάσχω· τί γάρ σοι μετεδίδουν;

ΣΥΡΟΣ

τοῦτον λαβεῖν
βούλει κριτήν;

218–1131 are preserved on the Cairo papyrus; those corrections and supplements whose author is not named from here to the end of the play were made by the ed. pr. of this papyrus, G. Lefebvre, *Fragments d'un manuscrit de Ménandre*, Cairo 1907, and *Papyrus de Ménandre*, Cairo 1911.   218–56 are partially preserved also on an Oxyrhynchus papyrus (2829: abbreviated in the apparatus to O, like all the other Oxyrhynchus papyri of Menander).   218–19 οὐ δεῖ—μὴ σ' continued to Daos by several (C has a dicolon after δυστυχης).

EPITREPONTES

SYROS
You're deaf to justice!

DAOS
           You low swindler, you've   218
No right to what's not yours!

SYROS
                  This dispute needs
An arbitrator.[1]

DAOS
          I agree, let's have   220
One.

SYROS
    Who then?

DAOS
          Anyone suits *me*. It's just
What I deserve. Why did I offer you
A share?

*(By now the two slaves have reached where Smikrines is
standing.)*

SYROS *(noticing Smikrines, and pointing to him)*
    Will you have *him* as judge?

[1] Private arbitration was commonly used in ancient Athens
to settle disputes of this kind, whose resolution depended on
equity rather than on points of law. The arbitrator's decision
was legally binding, provided that both parties to the dispute
had agreed beforehand on the choice of arbitrator. See further
J. W. Cohoon, 'Rhetorical Studies in the Arbitration Scene of
Menander's *Epitrepontes*', *TAPA* 45 (1914), 141 ff.; and
A. R. W. Harrison, *The Law of Athens*, II, Oxford 1971, 64 ff.

MENANDER

ΔΑΟΣ

ἀγαθῇ τύχῃ.

ΣΥΡΟΣ

πρὸς τῶν θεῶν,
βέλτιστε, μικρὸν ἂν σχολάσαις ἡμῖν χρόνον;

ΣΜΙΚΡΙΝΗΣ

225 ὑμῖν; περὶ τίνος;

ΣΥΡΟΣ

ἀντιλέγομεν πρᾶγμά τι.

ΣΜΙΚΡΙΝΗΣ

τί οὖν ἐμοὶ μέλει;

ΣΥΡΟΣ

κριτὴν τούτου τινὰ   (50)
ζητοῦμεν ἴσον· εἰ δή σε μηδὲν κωλύει,
διάλυσον ἡμᾶς.

ΣΜΙΚΡΙΝΗΣ

ὦ κάκιστ’ ἀπολούμενοι,
δίκας λέγο[ν]τες περιπατεῖτε, διφθέρας
230 ἔχοντες;

ΣΥΡΟΣ

ἀλλ’ ὅμως—τὸ πρᾶγμ’ ἐστὶν βραχὺ
καὶ ῥᾴδιον μαθεῖν. πάτερ, δὸς τὴν χάριν·   (55)
(K fr. 173) μὴ καταφρονήσῃς, πρὸς θεῶν. ἐν παντὶ δεῖ

---

227 Corr. several: δεσε C, δητι[O. 232, 234 Orion, *Anth.*
6. 4, citing these lines (= fr. 173 Kock), omits πρὸς and τοῦ.

EPITREPONTES

DAOS

All right.

SYROS (*addressing Smikrines*)

Sir, could you spare us, in the name of heaven,
A little time?

SMIKRINES

You? Why?

SYROS

We disagree   225
About a point . . .

SMIKRINES

What's that to me?

SYROS

We're looking
For an impartial judge to try it. If
There's nothing to prevent you, settle our
Case.

SMIKRINES (*irritated by their presumption*)

Damn you! Traipsing round in working clothes,
Presenting *cases*?

SYROS

All the same—our problem's   230
A small one, and not hard to grasp. Do us
The favour, sir. In gods' name, don't be snooty!

καιρῷ τὸ δίκαιον ἐπικρατεῖν ἀπανταχοῦ,
καὶ τὸν παρατυγχάνοντα τούτου τοῦ μέρους
235 ἔχειν πρόνοιαν· κοινόν ἐστι τῷ βίῳ
πάντων.

ΔΑΟΣ

μετρίῳ γε συμπέπληγμαι ῥήτορι·   (60)
τί γὰρ μετεδίδουν;

ΣΜΙΚΡΙΝΗΣ

ἐμμενεῖτ᾽ οὖν, εἰπέ μοι,
οἷς ἂν δικάσω;

ΣΥΡΟΣ

πάντως.

ΣΜΙΚΡΙΝΗΣ

ἀκούσομαι· τί γὰρ
τό με κωλύον; σὺ πρότερος ὁ σιωπῶν λέγε.

ΔΑΟΣ

240 μικρόν γ᾽ ἄνωθεν, οὐ τὰ πρὸς τοῦτον μόνον
πραχθένθ᾽, ἵν᾽ ᾖ σοι καὶ σαφῆ τὰ πράγματα.   (65)
ἐν τῷ δασεῖ τῷ πλησίον τῶν χωρίων
τούτων ἐποίμαινον τριακοστὴν ἴσως,
βέλτιστε, ταύτην ἡμέραν αὐτὸς μόνος,
245 κἀκκείμενον παιδάριον εὗρον νήπιον
ἔχον δέραια καὶ τοιουτονί τινα   (70)
κόσμον.

239 τό με κωλύον Eitrem: τοκωλυονμε C, τοκω[λ]υον[O.   246–52
The opening one or two letters of each line, torn off in C, are
supplied by O (252 also by *Etym. Gudianum*, 222. 40, and
other citers of the proverb in this verse).

On all occasions justice *should* prevail,
The whole world over.   Any man should feel
Concerned about it—that's a general   235
Rule of society.

DAOS

A fair tub-thumper I've
Clashed with!   Why *did* I offer shares?

SMIKRINES

Tell me,
Will you abide by my decision?

SYROS

Yes.

SMIKRINES

I'll listen.   What's to stop me?   You speak first—
The quiet one.

DAOS

I'll start a short time back,   240
Not just my dealings with him[1]—that'll make
The facts quite clear to you.   It's thirty days
Or so now since I had my sheep, sir, all
Alone close by this village, in the woods.
And there I found a little baby.   It   245
Had been abandoned, with a necklace and
A few such ornaments.

---

[1] Syros.

MENANDER

ΣΥΡΟΣ

περὶ τούτων ἐστίν.

ΔΑΟΣ

οὐκ ἐᾷ λέγειν.

ΣΜΙΚΡΙΝΗΣ

ἐὰν λαλῇς μεταξύ, τῇ βακτηρίᾳ
καθίξομαί σου.

ΣΥΡΟΣ

καὶ δικαίως.

ΣΜΙΚΡΙΝΗΣ

λέγε.

ΔΑΟΣ

λέγω.

250 ἀνειλόμην, ἀπῆλθον οἴκαδ' αὕτ' ἔχων,
τρέφειν ἔμελλον· ταῦτ' ἔδοξέ μοι τότε.   (75)
(K fr. 733) ἐν νυκτὶ βουλὴν δ', ὅπερ ἅπασι γίνεται,
διδοὺς ἐμαυτῷ διελογιζόμην· ἐμοὶ
τί παιδοτροφίας καὶ κακῶν; πόθεν δ' ἐγὼ
255 τοσαῦτ' ἀναλώσω; τί φροντίδων ἐμοί;   (80)
τοιουτοσί τις ἦν. ἐποίμαινον πάλιν
ἕωθεν. ἦλθεν οὗτος—ἐστὶ δ' ἀνθρακεύς—
εἰς τὸν τόπον τὸν αὐτὸν ἐκπρίσων ἐκεῖ
στελέχη. πρότερον δέ μοι συνήθης ἐγεγόνει·

249 καὶ δικαίως given to Syros by Sandbach, Stoessl (his com-
mentary on *Dysk.* 602). 252 βουληνδ' C: βουλάς *Etym.Gudian.*
(cf. [Men.], *Monost.* 150, ἐν νυκτὶ βουλὴ τοῖς σοφοῖσι γίνεται).
258 εκπρισσων C.

EPITREPONTES

SYROS (*eagerly, and pointing to Daos' bundle*)
                    They're what it's all
About!

DAOS
He won't let me go on!

SMIKRINES (*raising his walking-stick threateningly*)
                    I'll thump
You with my stick, if you butt in!

SYROS (*apologetically*)
                    And serve
Me right!

SMIKRINES
    Go on.

DAOS
            I will.   I picked it up   250
And went off home with it.   I planned to bring
It up.   That made sense at the time.   That night,
Though, I took stock,[1] as all do, and I thought
To myself, raising children and such troubles—
Why me?   Where'll I get all the cash to spend   255
On that?   Anxieties—why me?   That's how
I was.   Next morning I was with my sheep
Again, and *he* came—he's a charcoal-burner—
To that same place, to saw some stumps there.   We'd
    become

[1] A proverbial expression, explained by one of the old paroemiographers (Zenobius, 3. 97) as follows: ' nights are peaceful and offer an opportunity of leisurely reflection to people making decisions on vital issues.'

260 ἐλαλοῦμεν ἀλλήλοις. σκυθρωπὸν ὄντα με
    ἰδών, " τί σύννους, " φησί, " Δᾶος; " " τί γάρ;
    ἐγώ,   (8
    " περίεργός εἰμι, " καὶ τὸ πρᾶγμ' αὐτῷ λέγω,
    ὡς εὗρον, ὡς ἀνειλόμην. ὁ δὲ τότε μὲν
    εὐθὺς πρὶν εἰπεῖν πάντ' ἐδεῖθ', " οὕτω τί σοι
265 ἀγαθὸν γένοιτο, Δᾶε, " παρ' ἕκαστον λέγων,
    " ἐμοὶ τὸ παιδίον δός· οὕτως εὐτυχής,   (9
    οὕτως ἐλεύθερος. γυναῖκα, " φησί, " γὰρ
    ἔχω· τεκούσῃ δ' ἀπέθανεν τὸ παιδίον, "
    ταύτην λέγων, ἣ νῦν ἔχει τὸ παιδίον.

ΣΜΙΚΡΙΝΗΣ

270 ἐδέου σύ γ';

ΔΑΟΣ

        ἱκετεύων ὅλην τὴν ἡμέραν
    κατέτριψε. λιπαροῦντι καὶ πείθοντί με   (9
    ὑπεσχόμην. ἔδωκ'. ἀπῆλθεν μυρία
    εὐχόμενος ἀγαθά. λαμβάνων μου κατεφίλει
    τὰς χεῖρας.

ΣΜΙΚΡΙΝΗΣ
    ἐπόεις ταῦτ';

ΣΥΡΟΣ
    ἐπόουν.

270 ἐδέου σύ γ'; Bodin and Mazon, ἱκετεύων ὅλην κ.τ.λ.
(assigned to Daos) Arnott: εδεουσυρισκ': ολην κ.τ.λ. C (with
σμικ' in left-hand margin).

Acquainted earlier. We talked together.   260
He saw me looking glum. ' Why's Daos fraught? '
He asked. ' Why not? I've been too nosy,' I
Said, telling him the story, how I'd found
The child and picked it up. Then right away,
Before my tale was done, he started pleading,   265
Adding a ' Bless you, Daos ' to each phrase.
He said, ' Give *me* the baby, as you hope
For luck and freedom. I've a wife, you see,
Her baby died at birth.' He meant the woman
Who's got the child now.

> SMIKRINES (*turning to Syros*)
> Did you ask?

> DAOS (*bursting in before Syros can answer*[1])
>   He spent   270
The whole day pleading, begged and tried to win
Me round. I said yes, handed him the child,
And off he went, with blessings on his lips
Galore! He gripped my hands and *kissed* them!

(*Smikrines is surprised that Syros' gratitude should have
been displayed so extravagantly.*)

> SMIKRINES
>   You
> Did *that*?

> SYROS
>   I did.

---

[1] Lines 248–49 provide the most compelling of reasons why
a modern producer at least should present Syros here as rather
hesitant about opening his mouth.

MENANDER

ΔΑΟΣ

ἀπηλλάγη.

275 μετὰ τῆς γυναικὸς περιτυχών μοι νῦν, ἄφνω
τὰ τότε συνεκτεθέντα τούτῳ—μικρὰ δὲ   (100)
ἦν ταῦτα καὶ λῆρός τις, οὐθέν—ἀξιοῖ
ἀπολαμβάνειν καὶ δεινὰ πάσχειν φής᾽, ὅτι
οὐκ ἀποδίδωμ᾽, αὐτὸς δ᾽ ἔχειν ταῦτ᾽ ἀξιῶ.

280 ἐγὼ δέ γ᾽ αὐτόν φημι δεῖν ἔχειν χάριν
οὗ μετέλαβεν δεόμενος· εἰ μὴ πάντα δὲ   (105)
τούτῳ δίδωμ᾽, οὐκ ἐξετασθῆναί με δεῖ.
εἰ καὶ βαδίζων εὗρεν ἅμ᾽ ἐμοὶ ταῦτα κ[αὶ
ἦν κοινὸς Ἑρμῆς, τὸ μὲν ἂν οὗτος ἔλαβ[εν ἄν,

285 τὸ δ᾽ ἐγώ· μόνου δ᾽ εὑρόντος, οὐ παρὼν τ[ότε
ἅπαντ᾽ ἔχειν οἴει σε δεῖν, ἐμὲ δ᾽ οὐδὲ ἕ[ν;   (110)
τὸ πέρας· δέδωκά σοί τι τῶν ἐμῶν ἐ[γώ·
εἰ τοῦτ᾽ ἀρεστόν ἐστί σοι, καὶ νῦν ἔχε·
εἰ δ᾽ οὐκ ἀρέσκει, μετανοεῖς δ᾽, ἀπόδος πά[λιν,

290 καὶ μηδὲν ἀδίκε[ι] μηδ᾽ ἐλαττοῦ. πάντα δέ,
τὰ μὲν παρ᾽ ἑκόντος, τὰ δὲ κατισχύσαντά με,   (115)
οὐ δεῖ σ᾽ ἔχειν. εἴρηκα τόν γ᾽ ἐμὸν λόγον.

ΣΥΡΟΣ

εἴρηκεν;

ΣΜΙΚΡΙΝΗΣ

οὐκ ἤκουσας; εἴρηκεν.

284 Suppl. several.   285 Suppl. Leo, van Leeuwen.   287
Suppl. Ellis.

416

EPITREPONTES

DAOS

He vanished. Now he's turned 275
Up with his wife, and suddenly he's claiming
The things left with the baby—they were small
Things, baubles, worthless—and he says I'm treating
Him wrong because I won't surrender them, but claim
Them for myself. I say he should be grateful for 280
The share he got by pleading. He's no right
To grill me for withholding something. If he'd been
The finder, on a stroll with me—a case
Of ' finding's sharing '[1]—he'[d] have taken half,
And so should I. I found them, though, alone— 285
You weren't there [then]. So how can you demand
The lot, while I'd get nothing? Lastly, I've
Let *you* have one of *my* possessions. If
You like it, keep it. If you don't, or if
You've changed your mind, then hand it back. Don't 290
wrong
Me, or feel thwarted. You've no right to take
The lot—one part by gift, the rest by force!
My speech is finished.

SYROS

Finished?

SMIKRINES

Are you deaf?

He's finished!

---

[1] A proverbial expression: in the Greek literally ' Hermes
shared.' Hermes was the god associated with lucky windfalls,
and it was the ancient Greek custom for everyone present
when something was found to share in the proceeds.

MENANDER

ΣΥΡΟΣ

καλῶς·
οὐκοῦν ἐγὼ μετὰ ταῦτα. μόνος εὗρ' οὑτοσὶ
295 τὸ παιδίον, καὶ πάντα ταῦθ' ἃ ν[ῦ]ν λέγει
ὀρθῶς λέγει, καὶ γέγονεν οὕτως, ὦ πάτερ·   (120)
οὐκ ἀντιλέγω. δεόμενος, ἱκετεύων ἐγὼ
ἔλαβον παρ' αὐτοῦ τοῦτ'· [ἀ]λη[θ]ῆ γὰρ λέγει.
ποιμήν τις ἐξήγγειλέ μοι, πρὸς ὃν οὑτοσὶ
300 ἐλάλησε, τῶν τούτῳ συνέργων, ἅμα τινὰ
κόσμον συνευρεῖν αὐτό[ν· ἐ]πὶ τοῦτον, πάτερ,   (125)
αὐτὸς πάρεστιν οὑτοσί. [τὸ] πα[ιδί]ον
δός μοι, γύναι. τὰ δέραια καὶ γνωρίσματα
οὗτος σ' ἀπαιτεῖ, Δᾶ'· ἑαυτῷ φησι γὰρ
305 ταῦτ' ἐπιτεθῆναι κόσμον, οὐ σοὶ διατροφήν.
κἀγὼ συναπαιτῶ κύριος γεγενημένος   (130)
τούτου· σὺ δ' ἐπόησάς με δούς. νῦν γνωστέον,
βέλτιστε, σοὶ ταῦτ' ἐστίν, ὡς ἐμοὶ δοκεῖ,
τὰ χρυσί' ἢ ταῦθ' ὅ τί ποτ' ἐστὶ πότερα δεῖ
310 κατὰ τὴν δόσιν τῆς μητρός, ἥτις ἦν ποτε,
τῷ παιδίῳ τηρεῖσθ', ἕως ἂν ἐκτραφῇ,   (135)
ἢ τὸν λελωποδυτηκότ' αὐτὸν ταῦτ' ἔχειν,
εἰ πρῶτος εὗρε τἀλλότρια. τί οὖν τότε,

---

302 Suppl. several.   309 Corr. Croiset, Richards: ταυθ'ατι C.
310–22 are partially preserved also on P. Oxy. 2829 (= O).
311 Corr. ed. pr.: εκτριφη or -εφη Ɔ,]αφη O.

---

[1] By the use of gesture the two people referred to as ' he ' in
this speech—Daos and the baby—can easily be distinguished
on the stage. Cf. the note on line 163.

418

EPITREPONTES

SYROS

Thanks! Then *my* turn next! This fellow
Did find the baby on his own, and all   295
His present tale is true. That's how it happened,
Sir, no denial. When I took this child
From him, I begged and pleaded—yes, he speaks
The truth. A shepherd, one he'd talked to and
Who works with him, informed me that he'd found   300
Some jewels with the baby. Sir, he's here[1]
Himself to claim them. Wife, give me the baby.

(*Syros here turns to his wife, who has been holding the
baby throughout the scene. In the lines following he
holds the child in his own arms.*)

This child it is who claims the necklace and
The tokens,[2] Daos. *He* says that they were
Put there for *his* adornment, not your keep!   305
I join him in his claim, since I've become
His legal guardian—your gift has made
Me that.

(*At this point in all probability Syros hands the baby back
to his wife. He then turns again to address Smikrines
directly.*)

In my view, sir, your verdict now
Turns on those golden trinkets—or what else
They're made of. Should the child have these kept   310
    safe
Till manhood, as a gift from his lost mother?
Or should the man who's robbed him keep them, just
Because he found some stranger's trinkets first?

---

[2] In this case pieces of jewellery, which effectively identified
the baby's parentage.

MENANDER

ὅτ' ἐλάμβανον τοῦτ', οὐκ ἀπήτουν ταῦτά σε;
315 οὔπω παρ' ἐμοὶ τοῦτ' ἦν· ὑπὲρ τούτου λέγων
ἥκω δὲ καὶ νῦν, οὐκ ἐμαυτοῦ σ' οὐδὲ ἓν   (140)
ἴδιον ἀπαιτῶν. κοινὸς Ἑρμῆς; μηδὲ ἓν
εὕρισχ', ὅπου πρόσεστι σῶμ' ἀδικούμενον·
(K fr. 180) οὐχ εὕρεσις τοῦτ' ἐστὶν ἀλλ' ἀφαίρεσις.
320 βλέ]ψον δὲ κἀκεῖ, πάτερ· ἴσως ἔσθ' ὁ[ὑτο]σὶ
ὁ πα]ῖς ὑπὲρ ἡμᾶς καὶ τραφεὶς ἐν ἐργάταις   (145)
ὑπ]ερόψεται ταῦτ', εἰς δὲ τὴν αὑτοῦ φύσιν
(K fr. 722) ἄξ]ας ἐλεύθερόν τι τολμήσει πονεῖν,
θηρᾶν λέοντας, ὅπλα βαστάζειν, τρέχειν
325 ἐν ἀ]γῶσι. τεθέασαι τραγῳδούς, οἶδ' ὅτι,
κ]αὶ ταῦτα κατέχεις πάντα. Νηλέα τινὰ   (150)
Π]ελίαν τ' ἐκείνους εὗρε πρεσβύτης ἀνὴρ
αἰπόλος, ἔχων οἵαν ἐγὼ νῦν διφθέραν.
ὡς δ' ᾔσθετ' αὐτοὺς ὄντας αὑτοῦ κρείττονας,
330 λέγει τὸ πρᾶγμ', ὡς εὗρεν, ὡς ἀνείλετο.
ἔδωκε δ' αὐτοῖς πηρίδιον γνωρισμάτων,   (155)
ἐξ οὗ μαθόντες πάντα τὰ καθ' αὑτοὺς σαφῶς
(K anon. fr. 488) ἐγένοντο βασιλεῖς οἱ τότ' ὄντες αἰπόλοι.
εἰ δ' ἐκλαβὼν ἐκεῖνα Δᾶος ἀπέδοτο,
335 αὐτὸς ἵνα κερδάνε[ι]ε δραχμὰς δώδεκα,
ἀγνῶτες ἂν τὸν πάντα διετέλουν χρόνον   (160)
(K fr. 181) οἱ τηλικοῦτοι καὶ τοιοῦτοι τῷ γένει.

316 σ' O, om. C. 319 οὐχ εὕρεσις Choeroboscus on Heph-
aestion, p. 240 Consbruch:]ευρεσις C (O here is defective).
321 Suppl. Jensen, van Leeuwen. 323 Suppl. Leo. πονεῖν
scholia on Homer, *Od.* 2. 10: ποειν C. 324 θηρᾶν scholia:
]ραν C. 333 τοτ' C: πρὶν Dio Cassius 60 (= 61 Boissevain). 29.
334 Corr. Bodin and Mazon: ειδεκελαβων C. 335 Corr.
several: αυτω C. 337 οἱ Choeroboscus on Heph. p. 194
Consbruch: η C.

You'll ask, why didn't I demand them when
I took the child? At that stage I'd no right.   315
But here I am, and *now* I plead for him—
For me, I'm claiming nothing. 'Finding's sharing,'
You said! Don't talk of 'finding' something, where
Wrong to the person is involved. That's not
Discovery, it's robbery! A further point,   320
Sir—just suppose this child's above our class.
Brought up with working folk, he may despise
That, veer to his true nature, steel himself
For high endeavour—big-game hunting, bearing
   arms,
Olympic running! You have been to plays,   325
I'm sure, and know all that—those heroes like
Neleus and Pelias,[1] discovered by
An aged goatherd with a jerkin just
Like mine now. When he noticed that they were
His betters, he revealed their story, how   330
He'd found and picked them up. He handed them
A pouch of keepsakes, and from that these boys,
Then goatherds, truly learnt their history
In full, and so turned into kings. If Daos, though,
Had taken out those tokens, selling them   335
To gain twelve drachmas for himself, men of
Such splendid birth would have remained unknown

---

[1] Syros here takes his example from a lost Greek tragedy.
Neleus and Pelias were the twin sons of the princess Tyro by
the god Poseidon. She abandoned them at birth on a mountain-
side, where they were discovered by a herdsman (actually a
horse-herd, in the most familiar version of the story). Plays
about Tyro are known to have been written by Sophocles and
two later dramatists, Carcinus and Astydamas. It is probably
to one of these that Syros is referring.

MENANDER

οὐ δὴ καλῶ[ς ἔχ]ει τ[ὸ] μὲν σῶμ' ἐκτρέφειν
ἐμὲ τοῦτο, [τὴ]ν [δὲ] τοῦδε τῆς σωτηρίας
340 ἐλπίδα λαβόντα Δᾶον ἀφανίσαι, πάτερ.
γαμῶν ἀδελφήν τις διὰ γνωρίσματα   (165)
ἐπέσχε, μητέρ' ἐντυχὼν ἐρρύσατο,
ἔσωσ' ἀδελφόν. ὄντ' ἐπισφαλῆ φύσει
τὸν βίον ἁπάντων τῇ προνοίᾳ δεῖ, πάτερ,
345 τηρεῖν, πρὸ πολλοῦ ταῦθ' ὁρῶντ' ἐξ ὧν ἔνι.
ἀλλ' " ἀπόδος, εἰ μή, " φήσ', " ἀρέσκει." τοῦτο
   γὰρ   (170)
ἰσχυρὸν οἴεταί τι πρὸς τὸ πρᾶγμ' ἔχειν·
οὐκέτι δίκαιον. εἴ τι τῶν τούτου σε δεῖ
ἀποδιδόναι, καὶ τοῦτο προσζητεῖς λαβεῖν,
350 ἵν' ἀσφαλέστερον πονηρεύσῃ πάλιν,
εἰ νῦν τι τῶν τούτου σέσωκεν ἡ Τύχη;   (175)
εἴρηκα. κρῖνον ὅ τι δίκαιον νενόμικας.

ΣΜΙΚΡΙΝΗΣ

ἀλλ' εὔκριτ' ἐστί· πάντα τὰ συνεκκείμενα
τοῦ παιδίου 'στί· τοῦτο γινώσκω.

ΔΑΟΣ

                        καλῶς·
355 τὸ παιδίον δέ;

---

339 Suppl. von Arnim. 347–61 are partially preserved also on
P. Oxy. 2829 (= O). 348 Corr. Sudhaus: ουκεστι C,].τι[O
with three or four letters torn off at the line's beginning.

---

¹ Once again Syros takes his examples from Greek tragedy,
and perhaps also, with delightful irony, from earlier comedies
by Menander. A brother wished an affair, if not actually

EPITREPONTES

For ever! It's not fair that I should tend
This infant's body, sir, while Daos grabs
His prospect of escape, and smashes it! 340
One man avoided marrying his sister
Through tokens, one man found his mother and
Saved her, a third his brother.[1] Nature, sir,
Makes human life precarious. One must
Guard it with foresight, and forestall events 345
By all means possible. ' If you don't like
It, hand it back,' he says, believing this
Has weight and bearing. That's no longer fair.
If you're required to yield one of his toys,
Will you then try to get the child back, too, 350
To make your crimes less risky next time, now
Chance has preserved some of his things? I've
    finished.
Judge as you think right.

SMIKRINES
                    Well, that's easy. All
The things left with the baby go to it.
So I decree.

DAOS
        Good. And the child?

marriage, with a girl who was proved by recognition tokens to
be his own sister, in Menander's *Perikeiromene* (cf. also
Plautus' *Epidicus*, adapted from an unidentified Greek
comedy); no parallel motif is known from Greek tragedy.
Sons saved mothers, after identifying them by tokens, in the
tragedies about Tyro (see the note on line 327), and in the
partially preserved *Antiope* and *Hypsipyle* by Euripides (cf.
also his lost *Melanippe* and his extant *Ion*). And a brother
was saved by his sister, after recognition, in Euripides'
Iphigenia in Tauris.

MENANDER

ΣΜΙΚΡΙΝΗΣ

οὐ γνώσομ᾿ εἶναι, μὰ Δ[ία, σοῦ
τοῦ νῦν ἀδικοῦντος, τοῦ βοηθοῦντος δ[ὲ καὶ   (180)
ἐπεξιόντος τἀδικεῖν μέλλοντί σο[ι.

ΣΥΡΟΣ

πόλλ᾿ ἀγαθά σοι γένοιτο.

ΔΑΟΣ

               δεινή γ᾿ ἡ [κρίσις,
νὴ τὸν Δία τὸν Σωτῆρ᾿· ἅπανθ᾿ εὑρὼν [ἐγὼ
360 ἅπαντα περιέσπασμ᾿, ὁ δ᾿ οὐχ εὑρὼν ἔχ[ει.
οὐκοῦν ἀποδιδῶ;

ΣΜΙΚΡΙΝΗΣ

φημί.

ΔΑΟΣ

               δεινή γ᾿ ἡ κρ[ίσις,   (185)
ἢ μηθὲν ἀγαθόν μοι γένοιτο.

ΣΥΡΟΣ

               φέρε τ[αχύ.

ΔΑΟΣ

ὦ Ἡράκλεις, ἃ πέπονθα.

356 Suppl. several.   357 i.e. τῷ ἀδικεῖν.   358 γένοιτ᾿: C.
360 Suppl. Headlam, Wilamowitz.   362 Suppl. Leo, Mazon.

424

EPITREPONTES

SMIKRINES

By Zeus,
I'll not decide it's [yours]—you swindled it—
But his—he rescued it, opposing your
Attempts at crime!

SYROS (*to Smikrines*)

May you be richly blest!

DAOS

The [verdict]'s terrible, by Zeus the saviour!
[I] found the lot, I lose the lot.   The one   360
Who didn't find them, gets them.   *Must* I give them
  up?

SMIKRINES

You must.

DAOS

The [verdict]'s terrible, or I'll
Be damned!

SYROS (*to Daos, holding out his hands for the trinkets*)

Here, [hurry]!

DAOS (*ignoring Syros*)

Heracles, what treatment!

MENANDER

ΣΥΡΟΣ

τὴν πήραν χ[άλα
καὶ δεῖξον· ἐν ταύτῃ περιφέρεις γάρ. βρα[χὺ
365 πρόσμεινον, ἱκετεύω σ᾽, ἵν᾽ ἀποδῶ.

ΔΑΟΣ

τί γὰρ ἐγὼ
ἐπέτρεψα τούτῳ;

ΣΜΙΚΡΙΝΗΣ
δός ποτ᾽, ἐργαστήριον.   (190)

ΔΑΟΣ
αἰ]σχρά γ᾽ ἃ πέπονθα.

ΣΜΙΚΡΙΝΗΣ
πάντ᾽ ἔχεις;

ΣΥΡΟΣ

οἶμαί γε δή,
εἰ] μή τι καταπέπωκε τὴν δίκην ἐμοῦ
λέγοντος, ὡς ἡλίσκετ᾽.

ΔΑΟΣ
οὐκ ἂν ᾠόμην.

363 Suppl. Körte.   364–65 βρα[χὺ—ἀποδῶ continued to Syros
by ed. pr. (C has γαρ:βρα[, but no paragraphus under the line).
366 δός ποτ᾽, ἐργαστήριον assigned to Smikrines by Capps, Leo.
367, 370 Suppl. several.   369 οὐκ ἂν ᾠόμην assigned to Daos
by Wilamowitz (C assigns to Syros).

EPITREPONTES

SYROS

Undo] your bag, and show me!   That is where
You've got them!

*At this point Smikrines turns away, intending to leave the
stage by the right side-entrance, which is imagined to lead
in the direction of Athens.   Syros calls him back.)*

        —Wait a bit, please, till he gives   365
Them up!

DAOS (*still ignoring Syros' request*)
    Why did I plump for *him* to judge
Us?

SMIKRINES (*to Daos, threateningly*)
Jail-bird, give them up!

DAOS (*reluctantly handing the trinkets over*)
        My treatment's monstrous!

SMIKRINES (*to Syros*)
Got everything?

SYROS
    I think so, yes—unless
He swallowed something while I made my case—
When he was losing!

DAOS
    It's incredible!   370

MENANDER

ΣΥΡΟΣ

370 ἀλλ᾽ εὐτύχει, βέλτιστε. τοιούτ[ου]ς ἔδ[ει
θᾶτ[τον] δικάζειν πάντας.

ΔΑΟΣ

[ἀδί]κ[ου π]ρ[άγμ]ατος. (195
ὦ Ἡράκλεις, οὐ γέγονε δειν[οτέρα] κρίσ[ι]ς.

ΣΥΡΟΣ

πονηρὸς ἦσθας.

ΔΑΟΣ

ὦ πό[ν]ηρ᾽, ὅ[π]ω[ς σ]ὺ νῦν
τούτῳ φυλάξεις αὖθ᾽, [ἕως ἂν ἐκτραφ]ῇ.
375 εὖ ἴσθι, τηρήσω σε π[ά]ντα [τὸ]ν [χρ]όνον.

ΣΥΡΟΣ

οἴμωζε καὶ βάδιζε. σὺ δὲ ταυτί, γύναι,   (200)
λαβοῦσα πρὸς τὸν τρόφιμον ἐνθάδ᾽ εἴσφερε
Χαιρέστρατον. νῦν γὰρ μενοῦμεν ἐνθάδε,
εἰς αὔριον δ᾽ ἐπ᾽ ἔργον ἐξορμήσομεν
380 τὴν ἀποφορὰν ἀποδόντες. ἀλλὰ ταῦτά μοι

---

371 Daos' words suppl. Croiset. 372 Suppl. Sudhaus. 373
Change of speaker after ἦσθας indicated by several (C has a
paragraphus below the line, no dicolon after ἦσθας, possibly
one after πό[ν]ηρ᾽). End of line suppl. Croiset. 374 Suppl.
exempli gratia Sudhaus, von Arnim.

---

¹ The charcoal-burner Syros is Chairestratos' slave (cf. line
408), but is allowed to live in his own cottage with his wife, and
pays his master a regular sum from his earnings.

EPITREPONTES

SYROS (*to Smikrines, who turns now to go*)
Good-bye, sir!   Every judge should be like you,
These days!

(*Smikrines now finally goes off right, in the direction of Athens.*)

DAOS
    [A shabby] business!   Heracles, [a more]
Outrageous verdict there has never been!

SYROS
                 You were
A villain!

DAOS (*stung by this*)
    Villain, [see] you keep them safe
For him now, [till he's grown (?)].   I'll have my eyes 375
On you, be sure, [the] whole time!

(*Daos now leaves the stage by the left side-entrance, in the direction of the country.   Syros calls after him.*)

SYROS
              Damn you, and
Be off!

(*Syros now turns to his wife.   While he talks to her he examines the trinkets and passes them over to her, one by one.*)

    —Chairestratos, our master, lives
Here, wife.   Takes these inside to him.   We'll stay
The night here.   In the morning we'll go back
To work, when we have paid our dues.[1]   Let's first 380

πρῶτ' ἀπαρίθμησαι καθ' ἕν. ἔχεις κοιτίδα τινά; (205)
βάλλ' εἰς τὸ προκόλπιον.

ΟΝΗΣΙΜΟΣ

                μάγειρον βραδύτερον
οὐδεὶς ἑόρακε· τηνικαῦτ' ἐχθὲς πάλαι
ἔπινον.

ΣΥΡΟΣ

        οὑτοσὶ μὲν εἶναι φαίνεται
385 ἀλεκτρύων τις, καὶ μάλα στριφνός· λαβέ.
τουτὶ δὲ διάλιθόν τι. πέλεκυς οὑτοσί.   210)

ΟΝΗΣΙΜΟΣ

τί ταῦθ';

ΣΥΡΟΣ

      ὑπόχρυσος δακτύλ[ι]ός τις οὑτοσί,
αὐτὸς σιδηροῦς· γλύμμα τ[αῦ]ρος ἢ τράγος·
οὐκ ἂν διαγνοίην· Κλεόστρατος δέ τίς
390 ἐσ]τιν ὁ ποήσας, ὡς λέγει τὰ γράμματα.

ΟΝΗΣΙΜΟΣ

ἐπί]δειξον.

391 Suppl. Sudhaus.

---

    [1] Literally, a fold formed in his wife's dress by drawing up part of it through the belt.   It served as a pocket.
    [2] Free Athenian males normally drank their wine in the dining-room directly after the meal was finished.

Go over these things one by one, though.   Got
A box?

(*Syros' wife shakes her head.*)

—No?   Put them in your pocket.[1]

(*At this point Onesimos emerges from Chairestratos'
house.   He does not notice Syros and his wife until line
387.*)

ONESIMOS

Nobody
Has ever seen a slower cook!   They'd been
Carousing[2] ages yesterday by now!

SYROS

This one looks like a cock, a very scrawny   385
One, too!   Here.—This is set with precious stones.
And here's an axe.

ONESIMOS
What's this?

SYROS

A ring here, gilt
But iron underneath.   The stone's got carved
On it a bull or goat, I can't decide.
It's made by one Kleosιratos, the letters   390
Say.

(*Onesimos pricks up his ears when Syros mentions the
ring.   He now accosts Syros.*)

ONESIMOS

Let me see!

ΣΥΡΟΣ

ἤν. σὺ δ' εἶ τίς;

ΟΝΗΣΙΜΟΣ

οὗτός ἐστι.

ΣΥΡΟΣ

τίς;   (215)

ΟΝΗΣΙΜΟΣ

ὁ δα]κτύλιος.

ΣΥΡΟΣ

ὁ ποῖος; οὐ γὰρ μανθάνω.

ΟΝΗΣΙΜΟΣ

τοῦ] δεσπότου τοὐμοῦ Χαρ[ι]σίου.

ΣΥΡΟΣ

χολᾶς.

ΟΝΗΣΙΜΟΣ

ὃν ἀ]πώλεσεν.

ΣΥΡΟΣ

τὸν δακτύλιον θές, ἄθλιε.

ΟΝΗΣΙΜΟΣ

395 τὸν ἡμ]έτερόν σοι θῶ; πόθεν δ' αὐτὸν λαβὼν
ἔχεις;]

392–97 Suppl. ed. pr.

EPITREPONTES

SYROS (*handing Onesimos the ring, to show its design*)
There.   Who are you?

ONESIMOS (*now very excited*)

It's it!

SYROS

It's what?

ONESIMOS

The ring!

SYROS
Which ring?   I don't know what
You mean!

ONESIMOS
Charisios, my master's!

SYROS

You

Are mad!

ONESIMOS
[The one] he lost!

SYROS
Let go that ring,
You rogue!

ONESIMOS
Let go what's *ours*?   Where did [you] get 395
It from?

MENANDER

ΣΥΡΟΣ

Ἄπολλον καὶ θεοί, δεινοῦ κακοῦ. (220)
οἷον ἀ]π[ο]σῶσαι χρήματ' ἐστὶν ὀρφανοῦ
παι]δός. ὁ προσελθὼν εὐθὺς ἁρπάζειν βλέπει.
τὸν δ]ακτύλιον θές, φημί.

ΟΝΗΣΙΜΟΣ

προσπαίζεις ἐμοί;
400 τοῦ δεσπ[ό]του 'στί, νὴ τὸν Ἀπόλλω καὶ θεούς.

ΣΥΡΟΣ

ἀποσφαγείην [π]ρότερον ἂν δήπουθεν ἢ (225)
τούτῳ τι κ[α]θυφείμην. ἄραρε, δικάσομαι
ἅπασι, κ[α]θ' ἕνα. π[αι]δίου 'στίν, οὐκ ἐμά.
στρεπτόν τι τουτί· λαβὲ σύ. πορφυρᾶ πτέρυξ.
405 εἴσω δὲ πάρ[αγ]ε. σὺ δὲ τί μοι λέγεις;

ΟΝΗΣΙΜΟΣ

ἐγώ;
Χαρισίου 'στὶν οὑτοσί· τοῦτόν ποτε (230)
μεθύ[ων ἀπώλ]εσ', ὡς ἔφη.

ΣΥΡΟΣ

Χαιρεστράτου
εἴμ' οἰκέτης. ἢ σῷζε τοῦτον ἀσφαλῶς,
ἤ μοι δ[ός, ἵν' ἐγ]ώ σ[ο]ι παρέχω σῶν.

398 Suppl. Wilamowitz. 398–99 τὸν δ]ακτύλιον θές, φημί
continued to Syros by ed. pr. (C has a dicolon after βλέπει).
402 Suppl. von Arnim. 409 Suppl. Jensen.

434

EPITREPONTES

SYROS

Apollo and the gods, it's terrible,
This bother! [What a job]—preserving an
Abandoned child's possessions! All at once
Our visitor's got greedy eyes! Let go
[That] ring, I say!

ONESIMOS

Still playing games? It's master's, by 400
Apollo and the gods!

SYROS (*turning away from Onesimos*)

I'd sooner have
My throat slit than concede to *him*, for sure!
My mind's made up. I'll sue the whole world, one
By one. They're baby's, not mine! Here's a torque.
Take it. Some crimson cloth. Go in.

*(From line 401 Syros has been ignoring Onesimos,
examining the few remaining trinkets, and addressing his
wife as he hands them to her one by one. At this point his
wife goes off into Chairestratos' house with the baby, and
Syros turns to face Onesimos again.)*

What's this 405
You're telling me?

ONESIMOS

Me? It's Charisios
Who owns this ring. He [lost] it once when drunk,
He said.

SYROS

My master is Chairestratos.
So either keep it safe, or [give] it me,
[To] keep it snug for you!

435

ΟΝΗΣΙΜΟΣ

βούλομαι

410 αὐτ[ὸ]ς φ[υλάττειν.]

ΣΥΡΟΣ

[ο]ὐδὲ ἕν μοι διαφέρει·
εἰς ταὐτὸ [γ]ὰρ παράγομεν, ὡς ἐμοὶ δοκεῖ,   (235)
δεῦρ᾽ ἀμφότεροι.

ΟΝΗΣΙΜΟΣ

νυνὶ μὲν οὖν συνάγουσι καὶ
οὐκ ἔστιν εὔκαιρον τὸ μηνύειν ἴσως
αὐτῷ περὶ τούτων, αὔριον δέ.

ΣΥΡΟΣ

καταμενῶ,
415 αὔριον ὅτῳ βούλεσθ᾽ ἐπιτρέπειν ἑνὶ λόγῳ
ἕτοιμος. οὐδὲ νῦν κακῶς ἀπήλλαχα.   (240)
πάντων δ᾽ ἀμελήσανθ᾽, ὡς ἔοικε, δεῖ δίκας
μελετᾶν· διὰ τουτὶ πάντα νυνὶ σῴζεται.

ΧΟ Ρ ΟΥ

ΜΕΡΟΣ Γ΄

ΟΝΗΣΙΜΟΣ

τὸν δακτύλιον ὥρμηκα πλεῖν ἢ πεντάκις

410 Suppl. Croiset.

EPITREPONTES

ONESIMOS

      I'd rather [guard] it **410**

Myself.

SYROS

  That doesn't worry me. We're both
Bound for one house here, I believe.

ONESIMOS

       They've company,
Though, now. It may not be the proper time
To break this news to him. I'll try tomorrow.

SYROS

I'll wait. One word: choose anyone you like as judge **415**
Tomorrow, I'll accept!

*(These words are addressed to Onesimos as he turns away
from Syros to make his exit into Chairestratos' house with
the ring. Syros is now alone on the stage.)*

      —I've not done badly, though,
Now, either! Clearly I must quit my job
And practise law—life's modern bastion!

*(With this sally Syros himself withdraws into Chaire-
stratos' house. When the stage is empty, the chorus enter
to give their second entr'acte performance.)*

ACT III

*(After the departure of the chorus, Onesimos comes out
from Chairestratos' house, where the luncheon-party must
be assumed to be in its last stages.)*

ONESIMOS

Five times or more I've started to approach

MENANDER

420 τῷ δεσπότ[ῃ] δεῖξαι προσελθών, καὶ σφόδρα
    ὧν ἐγγὺς ἤ[δ]η καὶ πρὸς αὐτῷ παντελῶς   (245)
    ἀναδύομαι. καὶ τῶν πρότερόν μοι μεταμέλει
    μηνυμάτων. λέγει γὰρ ἐπιεικῶς πυκνὰ
    " ὡς τὸν φράσαντα ταὐτά μοι κακὸν κακ[ῶς
425 ὁ Ζεὺς ἀπολέσαι." μή με δὴ διαλλαγ[εὶς
    πρὸς τὴν γυναῖκα τὸν φράσαντα ταῦ[τα καὶ   (250)
    συνειδότ' ἀφανίσῃ λαβών. καλῶς [ποῶν
    ἕτερόν τι πρὸς τούτοις κυκᾶν ἀπ[οτρέψομαι·
    κἀνταῦθα κακὸν ἔνεστιν ἐπιεικῶς μ[έγα.

ΑΒΡΟΤΟΝΟΝ

430 ἐᾶτέ μ', ἱκετεύω σε, καὶ μή μοι κακὰ
    παρέχετ'. ἐμαυτήν, ὡς ἔοικεν, ἀθλ[ία   (255)
    λέληθα χλευάζουσ'. ἐρᾶσθαι [προσεδόκων,
    θεῖον δὲ μισεῖ μῖσος ἄνθρωπός μέ τι.
    οὐκέτι μ' ἐᾷ γὰρ οὐδὲ κατακεῖσθαι, τάλαν,
435 παρ' αὐτόν, ἀλλὰ χωρίς.

ΟΝΗΣΙΜΟΣ
                          ἀλλ' ἀποδῶ πάλιν
    παρ' οὗ παρέλαβον ἀρτίως; ἄτοπον.

ΑΒΡΟΤΟΝΟΝ
                                        τάλας   (260)
    οὗτος, τί τοσοῦτον ἀργύριον ἀπολλύει;
    ἐπεὶ τό γ' ἐπὶ τούτῳ τὸ τῆς θε[ο]ῦ φέρειν
    κανοῦν ἔμοιγ' οἷόν ʼτε ʼ ν ἐστ', ὦ τάλαν·

425 Suppl. several.   427, 429 Suppl. Wilamowitz.   428 Suppl.
tentatively Arnott.   431 Suppl. van Leeuwen.   432 Suppl.
Capps.   433 μ'ετι C.

438

My master, and show him the ring, but when   420
I'd quite near and reached the very point
Of speech, I blenched.   I've now thought better of
My former revelations.   Time and time
Again, you see, he calls on Zeus ' to smash
To bits that blasted blabbermouth! '   The breach   425
With his wife could be healed.   Then he might seize
That knowledgeable blabbermouth, and end
My life here!   [Better not] to add new troubles
To what we have—the present tangle's [snarled]
Enough!

(*Here Habrotonon bursts out of Chairestratos' house,
addressing impatiently some of the male guests in Chaire-
stratos' house as she enters.   She does not see Onesimos at
first.*)

HABROTONON

    Please, let me go!   Don't badger me!   430
I see I've made a fool—quite blindly—of
Myself, poor thing!   [I thought] he'd *love* me, but
The fellow loathes me with a loathing that's
Uncanny!   Now—dear me!—he won't allow
Me next to him at table even, I'm   435
Some way off!

ONESIMOS (*lost in his own thoughts about the ring*)
    Well, should I return it to the man
I got it from just now?   Absurd!

HABROTONON (*lost in her own thoughts about her
    situation*)
    Poor fellow!
Why is he wasting so much cash?   As far
As he's concerned, I'm qualified to bear—

439

MENANDER

(K fr. 920)   ἀγνὴ γάμων γάρ, φασίν, ἡμ[έ]ρα[ν τρίτ]ην
441   ἤδη κάθημαι.

ΟΝΗΣΙΜΟΣ

πῶς ἂν οὖν, πρὸς τῶν θεῶν,   (265
πῶς ἄν, ἱκετεύω—

ΣΥΡΟΣ

ποῦ 'στ[ιν, ὃν ζη]τῶν ἐγὼ
περιέρχομ' ἔνδον; οὗτος, [ἀπόδος], ὦγαθέ,
τὸν δακτύλιον, ἢ δεῖξον ᾧ μέ[λ]λεις ποτέ.
445   κρινώμεθ'. ἐλθεῖν δεῖ μέ ποι.

ΟΝΗΣΙΜΟΣ

τοιουτονί
ἐστιν τὸ πρᾶγμ', ἄνθρωπε· τοῦ μὲν δεσπότου   (270
ἔστ', οἶδ' ἀκριβῶς, οὑτοσὶ Χαρισίου,
ὀκνῶ δὲ δεῖξαι· πατέρα γὰρ τοῦ παιδίου
αὐτὸν ποῶ σχεδόν τι τοῦτον προσφέρων
450   μεθ' οὗ συνεξέκειτο.

ΣΥΡΟΣ

πῶς;

442 Suppl. several. 443 Corr. and suppl. Wilamowitz: ουτοσενδον[C. 450 Change of speaker after πῶς, not after ἀβέλτερε, suggested by Arnott (πωσαβελτερε./ταυροπωλιοις C, as it seems).

---

[1] In the great procession of the Panathenaic festival, which was held in Athens during the summer in honour of the goddess Athena, the girls chosen to carry the sacred baskets had to be virgins.

440

Dear me!—Athena's basket[1]! I've been left,   440
As men say, *celibate* for two days now!

ONESIMOS (*still lost in his thoughts*)
How could I, by the gods? Please, how?

(*The emergence of yet a third person from Chairestratos'
house interrupts these reveries. Syros enters, in search of
Onesimos.*)

SYROS
                      Where is
The man I'm chasing all around the house?

(*He spots Onesimos. As he begins conversation with him,
Habrotonon retires into the background, where she eaves-
drops unobtrusively.*)

Ho, you, sir! [Give] me [back] the ring, or show
It to the man you mean to! We must settle this.   445
I've got to leave.

ONESIMOS (*irritated by Syros' importunity*)
           It's like this, fellow. It
Belongs, I know for certain, to Charisios,
My master, but I hesitate to show
Him. If I do, I practically make
Him father of the baby it was left   450
With.

SYROS (*somewhat baffled*)
    How?

MENANDER

ΟΝΗΣΙΜΟΣ

ἀβέλτερε,
Ταυροπολίοις ἀπώλεσεν τοῦτόν ποτε   (275)
παννυχίδος οὔσης καὶ γυναικῶν. κατὰ λόγον
ἐστὶν βιασμὸν τοῦτον εἶναι παρθένου·
ἢ δ' ἔτεκε τοῦτο κἀξέθηκε δηλαδή.
455 εἰ μέν τις οὖν εὑρὼν ἐκείνην προσφέροι
τοῦτον, σαφὲς ἄν τι δεικνύ[οι] τεκμήριον·   (280)
νυνὶ δ' ὑπόνοιαν καὶ ταραχὴν ἔχει.

ΣΥΡΟΣ

σκόπει
αὐτὸς περὶ τούτων. εἰ δ' ἀνασείεις, ἀπολαβεῖν
τὸ]ν δακτύλιόν με βουλόμενος δοῦναί τέ σοι
460 μι]κρόν τι, ληρεῖς. οὐκ ἔνεστιν οὐδὲ ε[ἷ]ς
π]αρ' ἐμοὶ μερισμός.

ΟΝΗΣΙΜΟΣ
οὐδὲ δέομαι.

ΣΥΡΟΣ

[τα]ῦτα δή.   (285)
ἥξ]ω διαδραμών—εἰς πόλιν γὰρ ἔρχομαι
νυ]νί—περὶ τούτων εἰσόμενος τί δε[ῖ] ποεῖν.

456 Corr. and suppl. Croiset: ανδεικνυ[..]αντιτεκμηριον C. 462–
63 Suppl. Wilamowitz (but δε[ῖ] ed. pr.).

---

[1] This festival was celebrated in honour of Artemis Tauro-
polos. Its Attic centre was at Halai Araphenides, a coastal
village 18 miles east of Athens. Cf. also the introductory
note on this play's setting, p. 386.

EPITREPONTES

ONESIMOS

You're dim!   The Tauropolia[1] was on
When he mislaid it—a night-festival,
And women.

(*At the mention of the Tauropolia, Habrotonon pricks up
her ears.   She remains in the background, however, taking
no part in the conversation so long as Syros is present.*)

Logical surmise: a girl
Was raped.   She had this baby and abandoned
It, obviously!   Find the girl, show her   455
The ring first—then you'd have clear evidence.
But all we've *now* got is suspicion and
Uncertainty.

SYROS

You see to that.   If your
Game's blackmail, though, and you'd like me to make
A little payment for the ring's return,   460
You're silly.   Sharing's not my style.

ONESIMOS

And not
My wish.

SYROS (*turning to go*)

That's that.   I'm off to town now, but
I'll soon be back.   I've got to learn the next
Move in the game.

(*Exit Syros to the right, in the direction of Athens.   When
he has gone, Habrotonon comes forward and addresses
Onesimos.*)

MENANDER

ABROTONON

τὸ] παιδάριον, ὃ νῦν τιθηνεῖθ᾽ ἡ [γ]υνή,
465 Ὀν]ήσιμ᾽, ἔνδον, οὗτος εὗρεν ἀν[θ]ρακεύς;

ΟΝΗΣΙΜΟΣ

ναί,] φησίν.

ABROTONON

ὡς κομψόν, τάλαν.

ΟΝΗΣΙΜΟΣ

καὶ τουτονὶ   (290)
τὸ]ν δακτύλιον ἐπόντα τοὐμοῦ δεσπότου.

ABROTONON

αἴ, δύσμορ᾽· εἶτ᾽, εἰ τρόφιμος ὄντως ἐστί σου,
τρεφόμενον ὄψει τοῦτον ἐν δούλου μέρει,
470 κοὐκ ἂν δικαίως ἀποθάνοις;

ΟΝΗΣΙΜΟΣ

ὅπερ λέγω,
τὴν μητέρ᾽ οὐδεὶς οἶδεν.

ABROTONON

ἀπέβαλεν δέ, φής,   (295)
Ταυροπολίοις αὐτόν;

ΟΝΗΣΙΜΟΣ

παροινῶν γ᾽, ὡς ἐμοὶ
τὸ παιδάρι[ο]ν εἶφ᾽ ἀκόλουθος.

EPITREPONTES

HABROTONON
Onesimos, this child
The woman's nursing in the house now—did   465
That charcoal-burner find it?

ONESIMOS
              [So] he says.

HABROTONON (*musing about the baby*)
Dear me! So graceful!

ONESIMOS (*showing the ring to Habrotonon*)
            With it, too, he found
My master's ring here.

HABROTONON (*still thinking about the baby*)
            Ah! Poor thing! Well, if
It really is your master's baby, could you see
It brought up as a slave? You'd merit death   470
For that!

ONESIMOS
    As I was saying, no-one knows
The mother.

HABROTONON (*now paying attention to the ring*)
         At the Tauropolia, you claim,
He lost this?

ONESIMOS
      Yes, when drunk. That's what the lad
Who squired him said to me.

MENANDER

ΑΒΡΟΤΟΝΟΝ

δηλαδὴ
εἰς τὰς [γ]υναῖκας παννυχιζούσας μόνος
475 ἐνέ[πεσε· κἀμο]ῦ γὰρ παρούσης ἐγένετο
τοιοῦτον ἕτερον.

ΟΝΗΣΙΜΟΣ

σοῦ παρούσης;

ΑΒΡΟΤΟΝΟΝ

πέρυσι, ναί,   (300)
Ταυροπο[λίοις· π]αισὶν γὰρ ἔψαλλον κόραις,
αὐτ[ή] θ᾽ [ὁμοῦ συ]νέπαιζον· οὐδ᾽ ἐγὼ τότε,
οὔπω γάρ, ἄνδρ᾽ ᾔδειν τί ἐστι.

ΟΝΗΣΙΜΟΣ

καὶ μάλα.

ΑΒΡΟΤΟΝΟΝ

480 μὰ τὴν Ἀφροδίτην.

ΟΝΗΣΙΜΟΣ

τὴν δὲ δὴ παῖδ᾽ ἥτις ἦν
οἶσθας;

---

475 Suppl. several (ἐμο]ῦ already ed. pr.).   477 π]αισὶν suppl.
Capps.   478 Suppl. Headlam, van Leeuwen.   479 καὶ μάλα
assigned to Onesimos by Wilamowitz (εστι·καιμαλα C, with no
paragraphus below the line).   480 δὴ om. C, suppl. Sandbach.

HABROTONON

It's obvious—
He [blundered] on the women at their revels,   475
All by himself.   The same thing happened where
[I] was.

ONESIMOS

Where *you* were?

HABROTONON

Yes, the Tauropolia,
Last year.   I played[1] for some young girls, and [shared]
Their games myself.   I didn't know, not yet,
What men are like.

ONESIMOS (*sarcastically incredulous*)
Oh yes!

HABROTONON

By Aphrodite,   480
I didn't!

ONESIMOS
Do you know the girl's identity?

[1] The night-festival of the Tauropolia (see above, note on line
451) was celebrated with music and dancing, and Habrotonon
would have been hired by the girls' mothers ('the ladies I
obliged' of line 482: more literally, 'the ladies in whose
houses I was') as a professional musician who played the
psaltery, an instrument with strings of unequal length like a
small harp.   At that time she was still a virgin, and it was
presumably this fact that made it possible for her to share in
the free-born girls' amusements, although she was herself a
slave.

MENANDER

ABPOTONON

πυθοίμην ἄν· παρ' αἷς γὰρ ἦν ἐγὼ   (305)
γυναιξί, τούτων ἦν φίλη.

ΟΝΗΣΙΜΟΣ

               πατρὸς τίνος
ἤκουσας;

ABPOTONON

οὐδὲν οἶδα· πλὴν ἰδοῦσά γε
γνοίην ἂν αὐτήν. εὐπρεπής τις, ὦ θεοί·
485 καὶ πλουσίαν ἔφασάν τιν'.

ΟΝΗΣΙΜΟΣ

              αὕτη 'στὶν τυχόν.

ABPOTONON

οὐκ οἶδ'. ἐπλανήθη γὰρ μεθ' ἡμῶν οὖσ' ἐκεῖ, (310)
εἶτ' ἐξαπίνης κλάουσα προστρέχει μόνη,
τίλλουσ' ἑαυτῆς τὰς τρίχας, καλὸν πάνυ
καὶ λεπτόν, ὦ θεοί, ταραντῖνον σφόδρα
490 ἀπολωλεκ[υ]ῖ'· ὅλον γὰρ ἐγεγόνει ῥάκος.

ΟΝΗΣΙΜΟΣ

καὶ τοῦτον ε[ἶχ]εν;

ABPOTONON

         εἶχ' ἴσως, ἀλλ' οὐκ ἐμοὶ   (315)
ἔδειξεν· οὐ γὰρ ψεύσομαι.

490 Suppl. several.

448

EPITREPONTES

HABROTONON

I could enquire.   Those ladies I obliged
Were *her* friends.

ONESIMOS
Heard her father's name?

HABROTONON

I don't

Know anything—except I'd recognise
Her if I saw her.   Gods!   She's pretty, and   485
Rich, too, they said.

ONESIMOS
Perhaps it's *her*!

HABROTONON

I don't

Know.   She was there with us, and wandered off.
Then all at once she ran up by herself,
Tearing her hair and sobbing.   Gods!   Her cloak,
So filmy and so lovely, was quite ruined,   490
All torn to rags.

ONESIMOS
And did she have this ring?

HABROTONON
She may have, but she didn't show it me.
I'll tell no lies.

MENANDER

ΟΝΗΣΙΜΟΣ

τί χρὴ ποεῖν

ἐμὲ νῦν;

ΑΒΡΟΤΟΝΟΝ

ὅρα σὺ τοῦτ'· ἐὰν δὲ νοῦν ἔχῃς
ἐμοί τε πείθῃ, τοῦτο πρὸς τὸν δεσπότ[ην
495 φανερὸν ποήσεις. εἰ γάρ ἐστ' ἐλευθέρα[ς
παιδός, τί τοῦτον λανθάνειν δεῖ τὸ γε[γονός;   (320)

ΟΝΗΣΙΜΟΣ

πρότερον ἐκείνην ἥτις ἐστίν, Ἀβρότονο[ν,
εὕρωμεν. ἐπὶ τούτῳ δ' ἐμοὶ νῦν συ[γγενοῦ.

ΑΒΡΟΤΟΝΟΝ

οὐκ ἂν δυναίμην, τὸν ἀδικοῦντα πρὶν [σαφῶς
500 τίς ἐστιν εἰδέναι. φοβοῦμαι τοῦτ' ἐγώ,
μάτην τι μηνύειν πρὸς ἐκείνας ἃς λ[έγω.   (325)
τίς οἶδεν εἰ καὶ τοῦτον ἐνέχυρον λαβὼ[ν
τότε τις παρ' αὐτοῦ τῶν παρόντων ἀπέβαλεν
ἕτερος; κυβεύων τυχὸν ἴσως εἰς συμβολὰς
505 ὑπόθημ' ἔδωκ', ἢ συντιθέμενος περί τινος
περιείχετ', εἶτ' ἔδωκεν. ἕτερα μυρία   (330)
ἐν τοῖς πότοις τοιαῦτα γίνεσθαι φιλεῖ.
πρὶν εἰδέναι δὲ τὸν ἀδικοῦντ' οὐ βούλομαι
ζητεῖν ἐκείνην οὐδὲ μηνύειν ἐγὼ
510 τοιοῦτον οὐδέν.

ΟΝΗΣΙΜΟΣ

οὐ κακῶ[ς] μέντοι λέγεις.
τί οὖν ποήσῃ τις;

EPITREPONTES

ONESIMOS

What's *my* move now?

HABROTONON

You see
To that.   But if you're wise, and follow my
Advice, you'll bring this to your master's ears.   495
Why should he hide what's happened, if the mother's
Freeborn?

ONESIMOS

Let's first discover who she is,
Habrotonon.   Do [help] me now with this!

HABROTONON

I couldn't—not until I know [for sure]
The culprit's name.   I'm scared of telling tales   500
Without good reason to those ladies whom
I mentioned.   Someone else could have received
It in the group from him as warranty,
Then lost it—who's to know?   Perhaps he put
It in the jackpot as a pledge when gambling, or   505
Was harassed in some deal and let it go.
A million things like that can happen at
These parties.   Till I know the culprit, I
Don't want to look for *her* or blurt one word
Of anything like this.

ONESIMOS

Yes, that makes sense.   510
So what's a man to do?

γϵ
493 νυνϵχης C.   496 Suppl. several: τοσυ.[C.   498 Corr. and
suppl. Headlam: συνυν[.]ϵν[C.

MENANDER

ABROTONON

θέασ᾽, Ὀνήσιμε,   (335)
ἂν συναρέσῃ σοι τοὐμὸν ἐνθύμημ᾽ ἄρα.
ἐμὸν ποήσομαι τὸ πρᾶ[γ]μα τοῦτ᾽ ἐγώ,
τὸν δακτύλιον λαβοῦ[σ]ά τ᾽ εἴσω τουτονὶ

(K fr. 182) εἴσειμι πρὸς ἐκεῖνον.

ΟΝΗΣΙΜΟΣ

λέγ᾽ ὃ λέγεις· ἄρτι γὰρ
516 νοῶ.

ΑΒΡΟΤΟΝΟΝ

κατιδών μ᾽ ἔχουσαν ἀνακρινεῖ πόθεν   (340)
εἴληφα. φήσω " Ταυροπολίοις, παρθένος
ἔτ᾽ οὖσα, " τά τ᾽ ἐκείνῃ γενόμενα πάντ᾽ ἐμὰ
ποουμένη· τὰ πλεῖστα δ᾽ αὐτῶν οἶδ᾽ ἐγώ.

ΟΝΗΣΙΜΟΣ

520 ἄριστά γ᾽ ἀνθρώπων.

ΑΒΡΟΤΟΝΟΝ

ἐὰν οἰκεῖον ᾖ
αὐτῷ τὸ πρᾶγμα δ᾽, εὐθὺς ἥξει φερόμενος   (345)
ἐπὶ τὸν ἔλεγχον καὶ μεθύων γε νῦν ἐρεῖ
πρότερος ἅπαντα καὶ προπετῶς· ἃ δ᾽ ἂν λέγῃ
προσομολογήσω τοῦ διαμαρτεῖν μηδὲ ἓν
525 προτέρα λέγουσ᾽.

ΟΝΗΣΙΜΟΣ

ὑπέρευγε, νὴ τὸν Ἥλιον.

452

EPITREPONTES

HABROTONON

    Onesimos,
See if this scheme of mine appeals at all
To you. I'll make this matter *personal.*
I'll take this ring of yours inside, and go
To him . . .

ONESIMOS

    Explain your point. I've just begun 515
To follow you.

HABROTONON

    He'll spot it on my finger,
And ask me where I got it. I'll reply,
' The Tauropolia. When still a virgin . . . '—I'll
Pass all the girl's adventures off as mine.
The major part I know.

ONESIMOS

    That beats them all! 520

HABROTONON

If he's involved in this affair, he'll dive
Straight in and give himself away. The wine
Will make him blurt it all out fast, ahead
Of me. I'll just back up his statements, to
Avoid mistakes through speaking first.

ONESIMOS

       Yes, by 525
The Sun, that's splendid!

520–21 Corr. Arnott: εανδ'οικειον . . . πραγμ'ευθυς C.

MENANDER

ABPOTONON

τὰ κοινὰ ταυτὶ δ' ἀκκιοῦμαι τῷ λόγῳ   (350)
τοῦ μὴ διαμαρτεῖν· " ὡς ἀναιδὴς ἦσθα καὶ
ἰταμός τις."

ΟΝΗΣΙΜΟΣ

εὖγε.

ABPOTONON

                  " κατέβαλες δέ μ' ὡς σφόδρα·
ἱμάτια δ' οἷ' ἀπώλεσ' ἡ τάλαιν' ἐγώ, "
530 φή]σω. πρὸ τούτου δ' ἔνδον αὐτὸ βούλομαι
λα]βοῦσα κλαῦσαι καὶ φιλῆσαι καὶ πόθεν   (355)
ἔλα]βεν ἐρωτᾶν τὴν ἔχουσαν.

ΟΝΗΣΙΜΟΣ

                    Ἡράκλεις.

ABPOTONON

τὸ] πέρας δὲ πάντων, " παιδίον τοίνυν, " ἐρῶ,
" ἐσ]τὶ γεγονός σοι, " καὶ τὸ νῦν εὑρημένον
535 δε]ίξω.

ΟΝΗΣΙΜΟΣ

πανούργως καὶ κακοήθως, Ἀβρότονον.

ABPOTONON

ἂ]ν δ' ἐξετασθῇ ταῦτα καὶ φανῇ πατὴρ   (360)
ὢ]ν οὗτος αὐτοῦ, τὴν κόρην ζητήσομεν
κατὰ σχολήν.

EPITREPONTES

HABROTONON

To avoid mistakes,
I'll flatter him with platitudes like this:
' You were so bold and brutal! '

ONESIMOS

Good!

HABROTONON

' How roughly
You forced me down! Oh dear, the dress I spoiled! '
I'll say that. In the house, though, first I'll take   530
The baby, cry and kiss it, then I'll ask
Its minder where she got it.

ONESIMOS

Heracles!

HABROTONON

And last of all I'll say, ' So you have got
A baby,' and I'll show the ring that's just
Been found.

ONESIMOS

That's sly, Habrotonon—and naughty!   535

HABROTONON

Then if it's verified, and he is proved
To be its father, we can take our time
Tracing the girl.

---

527 Corr. several: ωσθ' C.   527–28 ησθακαι/καιταμος C.   534
Suppl. Headlam.

MENANDER

ΟΝΗΣΙΜΟΣ

ἐκεῖνο δ' οὐ λέγεις, ὅτι
ἐλευθέρα γίνη σύ· τοῦ γὰρ παιδίου
540 μητέρα σε νομίσας λύσετ' εὐθὺς δηλαδή.

ΑΒΡΟΤΟΝΟΝ

οὐκ οἶδα· βουλοίμην δ' ἄν.

ΟΝΗΣΙΜΟΣ

οὐ γὰρ οἶσθα σύ; (365)
ἀλλ' [ἦ] χάρις τις, Ἁβρότονον, τούτων ἐμοι;

ΑΒΡΟΤΟΝΟΝ

νὴ τὼ θεώ, πάντων γ' ἐμαυτῇ σ' αἴτιον
ἡγήσομαι τούτων.

ΟΝΗΣΙΜΟΣ

ἐὰν δὲ μηκέτι
545 ζητῇς ἐκείνην ἐξεπίτηδες, ἀλλ' ἐᾷς
παρακρουσαμένη με, πῶς τὸ τοιοῦθ' ἕξει;

ΑΒΡΟΤΟΝΟΝ

τάλαν, (370)
τίνος ἔνεκεν; παίδων ἐπιθυμεῖν σοι δοκῶ;
ἐλευθέρα μόνον γενοίμην, ὦ θεοί.
τοῦτον λάβοι[μ]ι [μ]ισθὸν ἐκ τούτων.

ΟΝΗΣΙΜΟΣ

λάβοις.

542 Suppl. Wilamowitz. 544 Corr. several: τουτωνσ' C.

EPITREPONTES

ONESIMOS

You've failed to add one point—
You'll get your freedom.   If he thinks that you're
The mother of his child, he'll buy your freedom[1]   540
At once, that's clear!

HABROTONON

I don't know—though it's what
I'd like!

ONESIMOS

You *don't* know?   Any thanks for me
In this, Habrotonon?

HABROTONON

Yes, by the goddesses—
You'll be the cause of all my bliss, and I'll
Remember that!

ONESIMOS

Suppose you quit, and drop   545
The search for her, on purpose, welshing on
Me, then what?

HABROTONON

Oh, why *should* I?   Do you think
I crave for children?   Freedom's all I want,
Dear gods!   That's the reward I wish to earn
From this!

ONESIMOS

I hope you do!

---

[1] I.e., Charisios will buy the slave Habrotonon from the
pimp who owns her, and then set her free. Cf. A. R. W.
Harrison, *The Law of Athens*, I, Oxford 1968, 182 ff.

MENANDER

550 οὐκοῦν συν[αρ]έ[σκει] σοι;

ΟΝΗΣΙΜΟΣ

συναρέσκει διαφόρως.
ἂν γὰρ κακοηθεύσῃ, μαχοῦμαί σοι τότε.   (375)
δυνήσομαι γάρ. ἐν δὲ τῷ παρόντι νῦν
ἴδωμεν εἰ τοῦτ' ἐστίν.

ΑΒROTONON

οὐκοῦν συνδοκεῖ;

ΟΝΗΣΙΜΟΣ

μάλιστα.

ΑΒROTONON

τὸν δακτύλιον ἀποδίδου ταχύ.

ΟΝΗΣΙΜΟΣ

555 λάμβανε.

ΑΒROTONON

(K fr. 981)   φίλη Πειθοῖ, παροῦσα σύμμαχος
πόει κατορθοῦν τοὺς λόγους οὓς ἂν λέγω.   (380)

550 Suppl. van Leeuwen.

---

[1] The Greek goddess Persuasion exercised her sway over two
fields: rhetorical argument, and (as a companion of Aphrodite

HABROTONON

You like my plan,   550

Then?

ONESIMOS

Yes, I do, immensely!

(*Here Onesimos pauses slightly, and changes his tone.*)

—If you seek
To trick me, then I'll fight you—I shall have
The means.   Let's see right now, though, if the child
Is his.

HABROTONON

Agreed, then?

ONESIMOS

Yes.

HABROTONON

Give me the ring,

Quick!

ONESIMOS (*handing the ring to Habrotonon*)
There.

HABROTONON (*in an attitude of prayer*)
Dear Lady of Persuasion,[1] stand   555
By me, and make the words I speak prevail!

(*With these words Habrotonon goes off into Chairestratos'
house, leaving Onesimos alone on stage.*)

and Eros) love affairs. The hetaira's appeal to her at this
stage of the plot clearly has a double significance.

459

ΟΝΗΣΙΜΟΣ

τοπαστικὸν τὸ γύναιον· ὡς ᾔσθηθ' ὅτι
κατὰ τὸν ἔρωτ' οὐκ ἔστ' ἐλευθερίας τυχεῖν,
ἄλλως δ' ἀλύει, τὴν ἑτέραν πορεύεται
560 ὁδόν. ἀλλ' ἐγὼ τὸν πάντα δουλεύσω χρόνον,
λέμφος, ἀπόπληκτος, οὐδαμῶς προνοητικὸς (385)
τὰ τοιαῦτα. παρὰ ταύτης δ' ἴσως τι λήψομαι,
ἂν ἐπιτύχῃ· καὶ γὰρ δίκαιον. ὡς κενὰ
καὶ διαλογίζομ' ὁ κακοδαίμων, προσδοκῶν
565 χάριν κομεῖσθαι παρὰ γυναικός· μὴ μόνον
κακόν τι προσλάβοιμι. νῦν ἐπισφαλῆ (390)
τὰ πράγματ' ἐστὶ τὰ περὶ τὴν κεκτημέ[νην.
ταχέως ἐὰν γὰρ εὑρεθῇ πατρὸς κόρ[η
ἐλευθέρου μήτηρ τε τοῦ νῦν παιδί[ου
570 γεγονυῖ', ἐκείνην λήψεται, ταύτην [δ' ἀφεὶς
ἐπε]ύξε[ται. τὸ]ν ἔνδον ἀπολείπειν ὄ[χλον.
καὶ νῦν χαριέντως ἐκνενευκέναι δο[κῶ
τῷ μὴ δι' ἐμοῦ ταυτὶ κυκᾶσθαι. χαιρέ[τω
τὸ πολλὰ πράττειν. ἂν δέ τις λάβῃ μ[έ τι
575 περιεργασάμενον ἢ λαλήσαντ', ἐκτεμεῖν
δίδωμ' ἐμαυτοῦ τὰς γονάς. ἀλλ' οὑτοσὶ (400)
τίς ἐσθ' ὁ προσιών; Σμ[ι]κρίνης ἀναστρέφει
ἐξ ἄστεως πάλιν ταρα[κτι]κῶς ἔχων

---

557 Corr. van Leeuwen: ησθεθ' C.   565 μόνον mss. of Stobaeus,
Ecl. 4. 22. 151: μον[C.   569 Suppl. Körte.   570 Suppl.
Sudhaus (ἀφεὶς von Arnim).   571 ἐπε]ύξε[ται suppl. Jensen,
[τὸ]ν . . . ὄ[χλον Arnott (in C the first half of the line is
abraded nearly to vanishing point, and the line-ending torn
off; the printed restoration is merely *exempli gratia*).   572
Suppl. Körte.   574 Suppl. Wilamowitz (μ'[ἔτι ed. pr.).   576
τὰς γονάς Arnott: τουσοδ[ο]ντας C.   578 Suppl. van Herwerden,
Körte.

EPITREPONTES

ONESIMOS (*pensive*)

That girl's a wizard! Realising that
She can't win freedom by the lure of love—
That leads to pointless heart-ache—she now takes
The other route! But as for me, I'll stay   560
A slave for ever—snotty, dumb, incapable
Of plotting schemes like this. I may, though, get
A sop from her if she's successful, that
Is only fair. What idle dreams—poor fool,
Expecting from a woman gratitude!   565
Let me keep clear of further trouble, that's
Enough!—My mistress's position is
At risk now. If some girl is found, who's both
A free man's daughter and the mother of
This present child, he'll marry her, and [by]   570
[Divorcing] mistress [hope] to wriggle free
Of her domestic [contretemps (?)].[1] Today
I feel I've sidestepped neatly—this was not
A stew that *I* stirred up! Good-bye to meddling!
If anybody finds I've interfered   575
Or squealed, I'll let him amputate my—organs!

(*At this point Smikrines enters by the right side-entrance,
which is imagined to lead from Athens. It takes him some
little while to pass through the parodos arch, walk up from
the orchestra onto the stage, and reach Charisios' door.
Onesimos meanwhile continues his monologue, un-
observed by Smikrines.*)

But who's this coming here? It's Smikrines,
On his way back from town. He's bent again

---

[1] The text here is uncertain, but it appears to predict that
Charisios will behave in accordance with normal Athenian
practice.

MENANDER

αὖτις· πέπ[υσ]ται τὰς ἀλ[ηθείας ἴσ]ως
580 παρά τινος οὗτος. ἐκπ[οδὼν δὲ β]ούλομαι
ποιεῖν ἐ[μαυτόν   ] λα[λ]εῖν·   (405)
προ[   ]ν με δεῖ.

ΣΜΙΚΡΙΝΗΣ

ἐξηι[
(K fr. 882) ἄσωτ[[ἡ πόλις]
585 ὅλη γὰ[ρ ᾄδει τὸ κακόν.
εὐθὺς [   ]δη   (410)
σαφῶς [
πίνειν [   ]ιων
τοὔνομ[α   ] ψαλτρίας
590 ζῆν αὐτὸν [   ]ης ἔφη
πλέον ἡμε[ρῶν   (415)
αυτὸν διαλλ[   ]ενον
οἴμοι τάλ[ας   ] . η
κοινωνὸ[   ]λη

579 πέπ[υσ]ται suppl. Wilamowitz, ἀλ[ηθείας ἴσ]ως Jensen.
580–81 Suppl. von Arnim, Wilamowitz (apart from λα[λ]εῖν,
deciphered and suppl. Guéraud). 583–644 The scanty frag-
ments of these lines are put together here on the assumption,
probable but not certain, that frs. M, N and T of the Cairo
papyrus (containing lines 575–82, 609–15, the beginnings of
583–99, ends of 616–33) come from the same leaf as frs. V and
X (containing the ends of 586–608, beginnings of 618–33). V
and X, however, do not cohere at any point with M, N and T,
and it is possible that their placing relative to M, N and T, as
printed here, may be one line too high or too low. See
Robert, *SB Berlin* (1912), 402 ff.; the Gomme-Sandbach
Commentary on 575–644. 584–85 Suppl. Robert from fr. 882
Kock (Orion, *Etym.* 23a 1). 591 Suppl. Robert. 592 Either
αὐτὸν or αὑτὸν.

On mischief.   He may well have learnt the [facts]
From somebody.   I'd like to keep [away (?)]   580
[From him, avoiding (?)] conversation.   [So (?)]
Before (?) [that happens (?)], I had better [fly (?)]!

*(At line 580 the first well-preserved portion of the Cairo
papyrus, extending continuously from the beginning of the
arbitration scene up to just before the end of Onesimos'
present monologue, comes to an end.   From line 581 to
583 the papyrus remains are very lacunose, and neither the
sequence of events nor the interpretation of the remains is
wholly clear.   Onesimos' monologue ends at 582, where-
upon the slave dashes off, presumably into Chairestratos'
house, in order to escape being buttonholed by Smikrines.
Smikrines is now alone on the stage.   On entry he presum-
ably failed to see Onesimos, and now the old man launches
into a long monologue extending at least to line 602.   Of
it only a few disconnected words and letters survive on the
papyrus, but in two places the sense can to some extent be
plausibly supplemented from two ancient quotations of
Menander preserved without play-title, which fit in well
here.   The following words can be made out, with the
supplemented portions indicated by square brackets: 584
proflig[ate] or proflig[acy], 584–85 all [the town],
/You see, [is humming with this scandal], 586 at once,
587 clearly, 588 to drink, 589 the name . . . harp-girl
or harp-girls, 590 that he was living . . . he said,
591 more than . . . days, 592 him or himself recon-
[ciled (?)], 593 oh dear me, 594 sharing, 595 came to
. . . I or I say (?), 596 when . . . the . . . this at
least, 597 finding out . . . me, 598 fond of . . . in
character, 599 opposite . . . simple, 600 and harp-
girls, 601 [never-ending drinking-bouts], gambling
perhaps, 602 but (?) enough of him.   Enough of the*

MENANDER

*monologue survives to show that Smikrines is complaining
again (as he did at the end of the first act) about his son-
in-law Charisios' drunken orgies and the girls he has hired
to entertain his friends and himself. The present
situation, however, seems to be far worse than the one that
formed the subject of Smikrines' previous complaints.*

---

595 προσηλθ[   ]εγω
    ὅτε τὴν [   ]υ τοῦτό γε (420)
    πυνθαν[ομεν   ]τησεμε
    φιλο . [τ]ῷ τρόπῳ
    ἐναντ[ι   ]τατην ἁπλοῦν
600   ] καὶ ψάλτρια[ι
(Ke fr. 659   [πότοι συνεχεῖς,] κύβοι τυχὸν   (425)
= K 914)
                         ἀ]λλὰ χαιρέτω.

ΚΑΡΙΩΝ

                                 ] πολλῶν ἐγὼ
                                 ]ων ἐκτησάμην
605   ] . δ . ινο . . . .
                                 ]η μοι μόνη (430)
                                 ] . εἶναι . . . . .ν
                                 ].........[

    οὐδεὶς . . . . ἕτερος ὑμῖν.

ΣΜΙΚΡΙΝΗΣ

                    ποικίλον

610 ἄριστον ἀρι[σ]τῶσ[ι]ν.

600 Suppl. Sudhaus.   601 Suppl. Robert tentatively from
fr. 659 Körte = 914 Kock (Ammonius, *Diff.* 408 Nickau).   602
Suppl. Robert.   610 Suppl. Körte.

EPITREPONTES

Smikrines appears now to have learnt during his visit to the city centre that Charisios' behaviour is on everybody's lips: what was previously a private misdemeanour has become a public scandal.

Smikrines' monologue appears to end at line 602. At this moment the cook Karion bursts out of Chairestratos' house, probably accompanied by an assistant named Simias. Karion appears to be so excited by what he has lately witnessed in Chairestratos' house that at least until line 623—and perhaps even after that—he fails to notice the presence of Smikrines. Consequently, the cook's words are basically an interrupted monologue, punctuated by asides from the eavesdropping Smikrines. Of Karion's first set of remarks (603–9) only a few uninformative words survive: 603 of many . . . I, 604 I obtained, 606 alone . . . to me, 607 to be [confusion (?)], 609 no other . . . for you or from you. Line 609, however, introduces six lines of text which are better preserved, enabling us to infer that Karion's preceding lines must have commented on the brouhaha caused just now in Chairestratos' house by Habrotonon's exhibition of the ring, and the bad effect this had on the cook's activities.)

(the end of KARION's *speech, reflecting on his hirers)*

> [Such treatment (?)]
> No other [cook would stand (?)] from you.

SMIKRINES *(aside)*

A rich   609

Pot-pourri of a lunch they're having!

465

MENANDER

ΚΑΡΙΩΝ

ὦ τρισάθλιος

ἐγὼ κατὰ πολλά· νῦν μὲν οὖν οὐκ οἶδ᾽ ὅπως   (435)
δ[ια]σκεδάν[νυντ'] ἐκτός· ἀλλ᾽ ἐὰν πάλιν
π . . . [   ] μαγείρου [τι]ς τύχῃ
. . . ν[   ] . ε βαλεῖτ᾽ ἐς μακαρίαν.

ΣΜΙΚΡΙΝΗΣ

615   ]ις τινος

(Of lines 616–17 only the final letters, of 618–20 only
the initial and final letters, are preserved:]ν.. 616,
]κει 617, τα[———]ιν 618, πα[———] ἅ[π]αξ 619,
κα[———]ενον: 620.)

ΣΜΙΚΡΙΝΗΣ

621 Χα[ρισίῳ παῖς γέγονεν ἐκ τῆς ψαλ]τρίας;   (445)

ΚΑΡΙΩΝ

νῦ[ν   ἀριστ]ῶσι καὶ
με[θύουσι

ΣΜΙΚΡΙΝΗΣ

                ] ἆρά γε
. ε[

ΚΑΡΙΩΝ (?)

ἔ]χουσι δή.

612 Deciphered and suppl. Jensen. 613 Suppl. Robert.
614 Corr. Wilamowitz: εισμακαριας C. 615 Or ἐστὶν ὅς.
619 Suppl. Körte. 621 Suppl. Sandbach tentatively (but
Χα[ρισι– already Sudhaus, ψαλ]τρίας Robert). 622–23 Suppl.
tentatively Arnott (νῦ[ν , however, several). 624–36 Division
of parts and identification of speakers are here uncertain. 624
Suppl. Jensen.

EPITREPONTES

KARION

Oh,   610

In many ways I'm out of luck. Somehow
The party's breaking up, they're leaving now.
If [any one of you (?)] should [need (?)] a cook
In future, you may go to blazes [. . . . . .]!   614

*(From line 615 to 654 intelligent appraisal of the scanty
remains is extremely difficult. Line 615, from which only
the expression* of some *survives, probably belongs to
another remark by Smikrines. Then for five lines (616–
20) nothing is preserved but a few unintelligible letters and
the one word* once *(619). At line 621 Smikrines appears
to be speaking again: it may be plausibly guessed—but no
more than guessed—that the old man, excited by the new
information which he has overheard Karion divulging,
responds with an astounded question:*

The harp-girl['s borne] Cha[risios a son]?   621

*The supplements here are uncertain. Nevertheless, even
if they do convey, however imperfectly, something of the
scenic development at this point, it is totally uncertain
whether Smikrines' question is rhetorical and an aside, or
addressed directly to Karion.*
  *The next four lines (622–25) appear originally to have
contained some excited dialogue between Smikrines and the
cook. Karion perhaps first continues with his description
of the events he has just witnessed in Chairestratos'
house; if the words* now *and* on them as they lunched/
And drank *are correctly restored in lines 622–23, Karion
may here have been explaining how Habrotonon suddenly
burst in on Charisios and his fellow-guests at the party.
Smikrines then (623–24) seems to interpose a question of
unknown reference, to which Karion replies with puzzling*

467

MENANDER

ΣΜΙΚΡΙΝΗΣ (?)

625 ο[ἴμοι.

ΚΑΡΙΩΝ

πέ]μπειν ἵνα

.[   ] τὰ χρήματα   (450)

αι[   ]ν ἡλίκη

ει[βού]λομαι·

εἶν[αι   δ]έσποιν' οἰκίας.

630 ὦ Ἡρ[άκλεις,   ] Σιμίας

ἀπίωμ[εν

ΧΑΙΡΕΣΤΡΑΤΟΣ (?)

νὴ τ]ὸν Ἥλιον, (455)

μικροῦ γ[ε   ] ταύτην ἐγώ.

πρώην ἄρ' [νῦν δὲ] τὰς ὀφρῦς

ἐπάνωθ[εν ἕξει τοῦ μετώπου

635 ἔγωγ' ἀπολ[

ὀκνηρο[(460)

ΣΜΙΚΡΙΝΗΣ

637 ἔπειτα δ[

(Of lines 638–42 only the initial letters are preserved:
θυγατέρα [638, τέτοκε κ[639, (Χαιρ. ?) λαβόντ' α[
640, παρακαλ[641, διακονε[642.)

625 ο[ἴμοι suppl. Körte (*exempli gratia*), πέ]μπειν Robert.
628 Suppl. Robert. 629–31, 634 Suppl. ed. pr. (εἶν[αι, how-
ever, Sudhaus). 630 Corr. Wilamowitz: σιμμιας C. 633–34
Suppl. tentatively Arnott (πρώην ἄρ' [εἶχε τοῦ μετώπου] τὰς
ὀφρῦς Sudhaus).

brevity Indeed they have (*624*). *This reply may have caused Smikrines some distress, if his reaction is correctly diagnosed as* O[h dear me] (*625*), *but supplementation here is admittedly very speculative. After this it seems likely that Karion speaks continuously from 625–31, but only a few words from this speech can be made out: 625* to send in order that . . . , *626* the affairs *or perhaps* the money, *627* how great she *or it* . . . , *628* I wish (?), *629* to be . . . lady of the house, *630* O Heracles . . . Simias, *631* let's be off. *The most plausible context for these disconnected tatters would be a speech in which Karion first pictures Habrotonon replacing Pamphile now as the lady in charge of Charisios' household, then turns to see if his assistant Simias is present with him, and finally makes his exit along with Simias, thus leaving Smikrines alone on stage.*

The next scene, which brings the third act to a close at a point somewhere between lines 699 and 714, is veiled in mystery. All that survives from it is a sequence of line beginnings and endings, and a few disconnected fragments. These remains offer some clues to identify the participants in the dialogue and a little of the scenic development, but they provide more problems than solutions. Smikrines evidently remains on stage until the close—or very near the close—of the act; the last attributable words in the scene are spoken by him (691–95). Directly after Karion's departure at line 631, however, another character arrives on stage, engaging at some point probably in conversation with Smikrines, but delivering at least his opening speech without any knowledge of the other's presence. It is reasonable to assume that this character is Chairestratos; the Cairo papyrus seems to identify him as the speaker of some lost words in line 690, and there is no cogent evidence for the appearance on stage during this scene of any other

MENANDER

*character additional to him and Smikrines. But when
does Chairestratos enter? Most plausibly, on the cue
given by Karion's departure. He will then dash onto the
stage from his house at line 631, and deliver a short
monologue (631–36), unaware that Smikrines is already
present and able to eavesdrop on his words. Only a few
scattered words and phrases survive from this monologue:
631–32* Yes, by the Sun,/I almost . . . her (?: =
Habrotonon presumably, if the pronoun here has a
personal reference), 633–34 the other day . . . her (?)
eyebrows high/Above . . . , 635 I've had it *or* I'd
rather die, 636 apprehensive *or* troublesome. *Given
the known dramatic situation at this moment, these frag-
ments would most suitably grace a speech by a man
excited and flustered by the bombshell that Habrotonon has
just dropped in his house. It is most likely she who now,
possibly in contrast to her previously more humble situation,
is described as keeping ' her eyebrows high above ' her fore-
head, a common Athenian phrase expressive of supercilious
behaviour. Habrotonon, as the supposed mother of
Charisios' child, might easily—in Chairestratos' as well as
in Karion's (629) view—aspire to the proud position of
mistress in Charisios' household. Hence Chairestratos'
apprehension.*

ΣΜΙΚΡΙΝΗΣ

643 Χαρ[ισι
τὸ φ[
645 ὑμῶν ἑταῖρος οὗτος, οὐ[δ]’ ᾐσχύνετο
646 παιδάρ[ιο]ν ἐκ πόρνης [ποήσασθαι   (470)

---

643 Suppl. ed. pr.   645 Deciphered and suppl. Sudhaus.
646 παιδάρ[ιο]ν suppl. ed. pr., [ποήσασθαι tentatively Arnott.

EPITREPONTES

At line 637 Smikrines apparently makes a three-line intervention, of which the words then *(637),* daughter *(638), and* she's given birth *(639) alone are preserved. Smikrines here is probably commenting in an aside on what he has just learnt as a result of Karion's and Chairestratos' indiscreet utterances; the ' daughter ' is clearly Pamphile, Charisios' estranged wife, but the reference in ' she's given birth ' is not as obvious as at first sight it might appear. Smikrines could perhaps be repeating what he has just overheard, that Habrotonon apparently has just borne Charisios a son; but it is also possible that Smikrines intended to lament the fact that—so far as he knew—Pamphile had not done likewise. A negative adverb could have been lost before ' she's given birth.' This latter alternative would produce a statement piquant with typically Menandrean irony.*

Of lines 640–42 again only the opening letters survive: 640 taking *(with a masculine subject), 641* summon, *642* serve *or* supply. *Who said what here is impossible to determine. If all three lines belong to Chairestratos, the speaker may have referred to the possibility of Smikrines ' taking ' his daughter Pamphile from Charisios' house and then going on to ' summon ' Charisios' friends as witnesses of the husband's misconduct in an action for divorce before the Athenian archon (cf. A. R. W. Harrison, The Law of Athens, I, Oxford 1968, 40 ff.). But this is pure speculation. At line 643, however, the situation becomes briefly clearer. Smikrines appears to address Chairestratos directly. He names Charisios (643) and goes on to say:*

[Wasn't he (?)]

A crony of your gang ? He felt no shame 645
[At fathering] a baby on a whore! 646

MENANDER

(Of lines 647–54 only a few letters at the beginnings
and/or the ends of the lines are preserved: προσω[
647, _εἰληφ[————]τις 648, παρ..[————]θας 649,
ενη[———— μ]άλα 650,]τεται 651, το]ῦ βίου 652,
_[————το]ῦ δυστυχοῦς: 653, (Χαιρ. ?) .[————]ν
δυστυχῇ: 654.)

ΣΜΙΚΡΙΝΗΣ

655 τοῦτο[   ]ν, ἀλλ' ἴσως ἐγὼ
πολυπραγμ[ονῶ πλεί]ω τε πράττω τῶν ἐμῶν,   (480)
κατὰ λόγον ἐξὸν ἀ[πιέν]αι τὴν θυγατέρα
λαβόντα. τοῦτο μὲ[ν π]οήσω καὶ σχεδὸν
δεδογμένον μ[οι τυγχ]άνει. μαρτύρομαι
660 ὑμᾶς δ' ὁμο[

(Of lines 661–65 only the initial letters are preserved:
μεθ' ὧν σ[661, θυγατέρα[662, ἀνάξι' ὑ[663, (Χαιρ. ?)
μηδεσ[664, καίπερ [665.   After line 665 there is a
lacuna of about 14 lines.)

ΣΜΙΚΡΙΝΗΣ

680 μισεῖ τὸν ἡδὺν λεγόμενον τοῦτον βίον·   (490)
ἔ[π]ινε μ[ε]τὰ [τοῦ] δεῖνος, εἶχεν ἑσπέρας
682 τὴν δεῖν', ἔμελλ]εν αὔριο[ν τὸ] δεῖν'· ἔχει

650 Suppl. von Arnim.   652, 653 Suppl. Körte.   656 πολυπρα-
γμ[ονῶ suppl. ed. pr., πλεί]ω Wilamowitz.   τωνεμωνπραττω C:
corr. Leo.   657, 659 Suppl. Sudhaus.   658 Suppl. Jensen.
681–82 Suppl. Sudhaus (τὸ] δεῖν', however, Arnott).

*Between lines 647 and 654 there is clearly a lively,
probably even angry dialogue between the two, but only a
few identifiable words are preserved. 648 has some (?)
. . has (?) taken, 650 certainly or very, 652 of his
(?) way of life, 653 of the unhappy man (?) or way of
life (?). The last two scraps here may come from
remarks by Smikrines about Charisios' behaviour. At
654 Chairestratos appears to take up Smikrines' last
remark, repeating the word unhappy. Then follows a
better preserved fragment, the opening lines of a speech by
Smikrines:*

[. . . . .] him (?). You may think   655
I'm meddling, trespassing [beyond] my sphere—
And yet I've right and reason on my side,
To take my daughter [right away] from here.
That's what I'll do, my mind's about made up.
Just mark my words—agree (?) [. . . . . .]   660

*Of the following lines only the opening letters survive, but
these are enough at least to show that the subject was still
Charisios' maltreatment of Pamphile. Smikrines' speech
goes on possibly for three lines further (661–63), with
references to his daughter (662) and to improper actions
(663), and a vague with which or whom (661). Chaire-
stratos then apparently makes a deprecatory reply (664
do not . . . , 665 although), the end of which is lost in a
lacuna some fourteen lines in extent. When the text
resumes, at line 680, Smikrines is speaking:*

                    [Are you claiming that (?)]
He loathes this so-called *dolce vita*? He   680
Still drank with *some* man, went to bed (?) last night
[With *some* girl, planned (?)] tomorrow's—*something*
   (?). He's . . .

                                                              473

MENANDER

(Of lines 683–89 only a few letters at the beginnings
and/or endings of the lines are preserved:]ους 683,
αυ[——]εκεν 684, ἀλλ' [——].ει 685, απα[686,
οὐδ' α.[687, μέρος τ[688, ἢ μὴ μετ.[689.)

ΣΜΙΚΡΙΝΗΣ

690   ἡμῖν κεκηδ[ευκ

ΧΑΙΡΕΣΤΡΑΤΟΣ
(His words are lost.)   (500)

ΣΜΙΚΡΙΝΗΣ

(K fr. 177) ὑψηλὸς ὤν τις [οὗτος] οὐκ οἰμώξεται;
κ αταφθαρείς τ' ἐν ματρυλείῳ τὸν βίον
μετὰ τῆς καλῆς [γυν]αικὸς ἦν ἐπεισάγει
βιώσεθ', ἡμᾶς δ[' οὐ]δὲ γινώσκειν δοκῶν
695   εἰ]σάξει λαβὼν   (505)

(Of lines 696–99 only a few final letters are preserved:
δ]ηλαδὴ 696,] ἐμοὶ δοκεῖ 697,]ιν 698, ἐστί μοι 699.
After line 699 there is a lacuna of about 14 lines, in
which Act III ended.)

690 κεκηδ[ευκώς suppl. Wilamowitz. 691 Suppl. von Arnim.
692 καταφθαρειστ'ε[C: καταφθαρεῖσθε ἐν mss. ABC of Harpo-
cration s.v. ματρυλεῖον, καταφθαρεὶς ἐν ms. N; κατὰ τρεῖς ἐν mss.
of Suda, s.v. 693 Suppl. ed. pr. 694 Suppl. Körte. γινώσκειν
Körte: γινωσκων C. 695 Suppl. Sudhaus. 696 Suppl. ed. pr.

474

Further damage to the papyrus cuts off Smikrines' ful-
minations against Charisios in mid-sentence, but clearly
his conversation with Chairestratos continues over the
following seven lines, although here hardly a translatable
word survives (685 but, 687 nor (?), 688 part, 689 or do
not . . .). Smikrines then begins line 690 with the
claim that Charisios by marriage is related to us, *which*
probably implies a previous remark from Chairestratos
challenging Smikrines' right to interfere. Chairestratos
replies to Smikrines at the end of line 690, but his words
are now lost; then Smikrines continues his attack on
Charisios:

[He]'ll pay for being so superior!   691
First, ruin in a brothel, then a life
With this fine girl he's adding to his staff—
That's how he'll live! He thinks we just don't know
[What's going on (?)]. He'll find and introduce   695
[A third girl next (?)]

A few translatable, but dramatically unhelpful, words
survive from lines 696–99 (696 plainly, 697 I think, 699 I
have). Then comes a total lacuna lasting 14 lines, during
which the third act must have ended. The conversation
probably closed with Smikrines disappearing into
Charisios' house, with the aim of persuading Pamphile to
abandon her husband and return to her father's house,
while Chairestratos may have left the stage on some
errand in the city. When the stage is empty, the chorus
enter to give their third entr'acte performance.)

ΜΕΡΟΣ Δ΄

(The opening lines of this act may be lost in the
lacuna that follows line 699.)

ΠΑΜΦΙΛΗ

714 ἀλλ' εἴ με σῴζων τοῦτο μὴ πείσαις ἐμέ,   (510)
715 οὐκέτι πατὴρ κρίνοι' ἄν, ἀλλὰ δεσπότης.

ΣΜΙΚΡΙΝΗΣ

λόγου δὲ δεῖται ταῦτα καὶ συμπείσεως;
οὐκ ἐπι[π]ό[λαιον; α]ὐ[τό, Π]αμφίλη, βοᾷ
φωνὴν ἀφιέν. εἰ δὲ κἀμὲ δεῖ λέγειν,
ἕτοι]μ[ό]ς εἰμι, τρία δέ σοι προθήσομαι.   (515)
720 οὔτ'] ἂν ἔτι σωθείη ποθ' οὗτος, [οὔ]τε σύ.
. . . . .]. ἀμε[λ]ῶς, ἡδέως, σὺ δ[' οὐ] σφόδρα
       ]κουσ' ἐαθείης ἔτ' ἂν
       δια]κονω τούτων τι[
       ]ν ἔχουσ' ἅπαν[(520)
725   ] . [.] ται δ' ο[

(After line 725 there is a lacuna of about 23 lines.)

717 ἐπι[π]ό[λαιον suppl. Jensen, α]ὐ[τό Wilamowitz, Π]αμφίλη
deciphered and suppl. Sudhaus. 718 Corr. van Leeuwen:
αφιει:ει apparently C. 719–21, 723 Suppl. Sudhaus.

EPITREPONTES

ACT IV

(After the departure of the chorus, Smikrines and Pamphile emerge from Charisios' house, deep in conversation. Line 714 may just possibly begin the act, but it is more likely that one or more introductory lines have been lost in the lacuna after line 699.)

PAMPHILE

But if you can't *convince* me here, in your   714
Attempt to save me, you'll no longer seem   715
My father, but my owner.

SMIKRINES

            Does this need
Talk or persuasion?   Isn't it clear-cut?
The act itself speaks, Pamphile, it cries
Out loud.   Still, if I *have* to speak, I'm [ready].
I'll put three points to you.   *He* can'[t] be ' saved '   720
Now—*you* can'[t], either.   [*He*'ll spend (?)] carefree
   [hours (?)]
Of pleasure—*you* wo[n't, not] so much [. . . . . .]

(From lines 722–25 of this speech only broken scraps survive (722 you'd be allowed still, 723 servant (?) . . . of these, 724 they have all or having all).   Clearly Smikrines' imaginative portrayal of Pamphile's fate, should her present ménage be allowed to continue, goes on and on.   After line 725 there is a complete gap of about 23 lines.   When the text resumes at line 749, Smikrines is outlining to Pamphile the financially crippling problems of sharing a husband with another woman (one of Smikrines' ' three points ', possibly).   Did Smikrines' speech continue all through the lacuna?   Or did Pamphile make one or more interventions?   We do not know.)

MENANDER

ΣΜΙΚΡΙΝΗΣ (in mid-speech)

749 τὴν πολυτέλειαν. Θεσμοφόρια δὶς τίθει,
750 Σκίρα δίς· τὸν ὄλεθρον τοῦ βίου καταμάνθανε.
οὔκουν ἀπόλωλεν οὗτος ὁμολογουμένως;
σκόπει τὸ σὸν δή. φησὶ δεῖν εἰς Πειραιᾶ   (525)
αὐτὸν βαδίσαι. καθεδεῖτ᾽ ἐκεῖσ᾽ ἐλθ[ών· σὺ δὲ
τούτοις ὀδυνήσει· περιμενεῖς πάλιν [τρέχειν
755 ἄδει[πν]ος· ὁ δὲ πίνει με[τ᾽ ἐκε]ίνης δη[λαδή
. . . ευ[.] . . . .ς ἐξῆλθε .[
. . . .]κ . . ρευ . . παντ[(530)
. . . . .] . . . σοι βούλομ[
759   ] . . . [. .] . . . λοι[

(After line 759 there is a lacuna in the Cairo papyrus
of about 93 lines. The following fragments may
derive from this missing portion of the play.)

753 ἐλθ[ών suppl. Sudhaus, σὺ δὲ Wilamowitz. 754 πάλιν
[τρέχειν deciphered and suppl. Arnott. 755 ἄδει[πν]ος suppl.
Sudhaus, με[τ᾽ ἐκε]ίνης Jensen, δη[λαδή Körte.

---

[1] Two important Athenian festivals connected with the
worship of Demeter. The Thesmophoria was celebrated by
women over a three-day period in the autumn, and it took its
name from the ' treasures ' (θεσμοί) conferred on mankind by
Demeter Thesmophoros, ritual examples of which were
carried in the procession. The Skira (or Skirophoria) lasted
one day only, in early summer; it also derived its name from
articles carried in its procession, but the identity of these holy
objects is disputed.

[2] The harbour town four miles from Athens, where Smikrines
imagines that Charisios has installed Habrotonon in her own
pied-à-terre.

478

EPITREPONTES

SMIKRINES

[Just reckon up (?)]

The waste!   The Thesmophoria[1]—two bills.   749
The Skira[1]—two bills.   Mark the ruin of   750
His fortunes!   He is finished—there can be
No argument.   Just think of *your* position!
He'll say he's got to walk to the Piraeus.[2]
He'll go and sprawl there.   You'll be hurt by it.
You'll put off dinner, wait for his [return (?)].   755
He'll be with her of course, drinking [. . . . . .]

(*At the end of line 755 the Greek text becomes increasingly
unintelligible.   There are fragmentary remains of four
more lines, in which Smikrines probably continued his lurid
picture of Pamphile's situation and perhaps offered some
advice (756 came out, 757 all, 758 for you I want [?]).
After line 759, the rest of this page and the whole of the
next leaf in the Cairo papyrus have been lost, producing a
gap in the text which can be calculated at about 93 lines in
length.   What can have happened in this gap?   Two
ancient quotations (fragments 7 and 8, printed below)
may derive from the missing text, and afford a partial
answer to the question.   The first (7), if it comes from
the Epitrepontes, seems tailor-made for both the character
and the position of Smikrines; he may have gone on
speaking for a considerable time after line 759 in the
attempt to persuade his daughter to abandon Charisios.
Doubtless Pamphile replied to her father's arguments in a
speech of her own, stressing her decision to stay in
Charisios' house, and in the end Smikrines must have left
for the city again with his mission unsuccessful.   Part of
this scene between Pamphile and her father was over-
heard by Charisios, as later developments reveal (883 ff.,*

479

MENANDER

919 ff.).

The other fragment (8) must come from a monologue
spoken by Pamphile after her father had departed. Its

Two fragments of Ἐπιτρέποντες, quoted by ancient
authors

7 (7 Körte-Thierfelder, 566 Kock)

The whole fragment is cited by Palladius, *Dialogus de
Vita S. Ioannis Chrysostomi*, p. 94 Coleman-Norton;
lines 1–2 are cited also by Cyril of Alexandria, *Contra
Iulianum* 7. 229 (Migne, *P.G.* lxxvi. 849B).

ΣΜΙΚΡΙΝΗΣ
χαλεπόν, Παμφίλη,
ἐλευθέρᾳ γυναικὶ πρὸς πόρνην μάχη·
πλείονα κακουργεῖ, πλείον᾽ οἶδ᾽, αἰσχύνεται
οὐδέν, κολακεύει μᾶλλον.

8 (8 KT, 184 K)

A scholiast on Euripides, *Phoenissae* 1154. τύφεσθαί
ἐστι τὸ τοὺς ὀφθαλμοὺς συγκεχύσθαι. Μένανδρος.

ἐξετύφην μὲν οὖν
κλαίουσ᾽ ὅλως.

After ὅλως the scholiast adds ἐν Ἐπιτρέπουσιν.

Fragment 7 attributed to *Epitrepontes* by Robert. 2 μάχεσθαι
Palladius. 3–4 Corr. Dobree: πλείονα οἶδεν, πλείονα κακουργεῖ
. . . οὐδένα Palladius.

Fragment 8, line 1 ἐξετυφήθην ms. M, ἐξετύφου ms. T of the
scholion.

EPITREPONTES

*length and contents can now only be guessed at; but it may
well have included some description of either her rape or the
events leading up to the abandonment of her baby, for the
passionate metaphor of her words in the fragment testifies
to a magnitude of grief that only these two events could
reasonably justify.)*

Two fragments of Epitrepontes, quoted by ancient authors

7

*The whole fragment is cited by Palladius, Dialogus de
Vita S. Ioannis Chrysostomi, p. 94 Coleman–Norton;
lines 1–2 are cited also by Cyril of Alexandria, Contra
Iulianum 7. 229 (Migne, P.G. lxxvi. 849B). Neither
citer mentions the play-title; this fragment is thus only
conjecturally assigned to the Epitrepontes.*

SMIKRINES
        Pamphile, it's hard, when you're
A lady born, to fight against a whore.
She works more mischief, knows more tricks, she has
No shame, she toadies more.

8

*A scholiast on Euripides, Phoenissae 1154, quotes this
fragment to illustrate the metaphorical application of the
word τύφεσθαι (literally, to smoulder) to eyes blurred
presumably by long and vehement weeping.*

PAMPHILE
        I was all burnt up—
Yes, burnt—with weeping . . .

MENANDER

(The Cairo papyrus resumes with Habrotonon in mid-speech, but the sense at least of her lost opening words can easily be supplied.)

ΑΒΡΟΤΟΝΟΝ

[τὸ παιδίον
853 ἔξειμ᾽ ἔχουσα· κλαυμυρίζεται, τάλαν,
πάλαι γάρ· οὐκ οἶδ᾽ ὅ τι κακὸν πέπονθέ μοι.

ΠΑΜΦΙΛΗ
855 τίς ἂν θεῶν τάλαιναν ἐλεήσειέ με;   (535)

ΑΒΡΟΤΟΝΟΝ
ὦ φίλτατον [τέκνον, πότ᾽] ὄψει μη[τέ]ρα;
καὶ [   ]

ΠΑΜΦΙΛΗ

πορεύσομαι.

ΑΒΡΟΤΟΝΟΝ
μικρόν, γύναι, πρόσμεινον.

ΠΑΜΦΙΛΗ
ἐμὲ καλεῖς;

852 Suppl. tentatively Sudhaus.   856 τέκνον and μη[τέ]ρα
suppl. Jensen, πότ᾽ Fraenkel.

---

[1] The Greek text here, as also at the end of line 863, has been abraded to virtual invisibility. The translations offered are merely tentative attempts to provide linking sense.

EPITREPONTES

(The Cairo papyrus resumes at the point when Habrotonon enters from Chairestratos' house, carrying the baby in her arms. Her main intention is to soothe its fretful whimpers. At first she does not see Pamphile, who is still on the stage. A few words—hardly more than that—of her opening remark have been lost, at the end of the lacuna.)

HABROTONON *(as she enters)*
                  [The baby (?)]—
I'll take it out with me. Poor thing, it's been   853
Crying for ages. Something's wrong with it—
My fault.

PAMPHILE *(unaware of Habrotonon's presence)*
          Which power above will show me some   855
Compassion? I'm so wretched!

HABROTONON *(to the baby)*
                 Darling [child],
[When] will you see your mother?

(Habrotonon suddenly notices Pamphile, and starts.)
                 [Oh, can *that* (?)][1]
[Be her (?)]?[1]

PAMPHILE *(turning to go into Charisios' house)*
          I'll go in.

HABROTONON *(pursuing Pamphile)*
          Madam, wait a moment.

PAMPHILE *(now at her door, and turning only her head)*
                      You
Want *me*?

MENANDER

ABROTONON

ἐγώ.

ἐνα]ντίον [βλέ]π'.

ΠΑΜΦΙΛΗ

[ἦ μ]ε γινώσκεις, γύναι;

ABROTONON

860 αὐτή 'στιν [ἦν] ἑό[ρ]ακα· χαῖρε, φιλτάτη.   (540)

ΠΑΜΦΙΛΗ

τί[ς δ' εἶ] σύ;

ABROTONON

[χε]ῖρα δεῦρό μοι τὴν σὴν δίδου.
λέγε μοι, γλυκεῖα, πέρυσιν ἦ[λθ]ες ἐπὶ θ[έαν
τοῖς Ταυροπολίοις ε[

ΠΑΜΦΙΛΗ

γύναι, πόθεν ἔχεις, εἰπέ μοι, τὸ παιδί[ον
865 λ]αβοῦσ';

ABROTONON

ὁρᾷς τι, φιλτάτη, σοι γνώριμον   (545)
ὧν] τοῦτ' ἔχει; μηδέν με δείσῃς, ὦ γύναι.

ΠΑΜΦΙΛΗ

οὐκ [ἔ]τεκες αὐτὴ τοῦτο;

859-62 Suppl. Sudhaus, except for 859 [ἦ] Merkelbach, 861 [χε]ῖρα Jensen, 862 θ[έαν Wilamowitz.   864 Suppl. Headlam. 865-67 Suppl. ed. pr.

EPITREPONTES

HABROTONON

Yes. [Face me].

PAMPHILE (*turning to face Habrotonon*)
[Do] you know me, lady?

HABROTONON

The very girl I saw! Darling, hello!   860

PAMPHILE (*obviously puzzled*)

Who [are] you?

HABROTONON

Here, give me your hand. Just tell
Me, sweetheart, last year, at the Tauropolia,
Did you go [with some other girls (?)] to see
The sights?

PAMPHILE (*staring at the baby*)

Where did you get that baby? Tell
Me, lady.

HABROTONON

Darling, do you recognise   865
Something it's wearing? You've no need to fear
Me, lady!

PAMPHILE

Aren't *you* its mother?

485

MENANDER

προσεποιησάμην
οὐχ ἵν' ἀδικήσω τὴν τεκοῦσαν, ἀλλ' ἵνα
κατὰ σχολὴν εὕροιμι. νῦν δ' εὕρηκα· σέ·
870 ὁρῶ γὰρ ἦν καὶ τότε.

ΠΑΜΦΙΛΗ
τίνος δ' ἐστὶν πατρός;　(550)

ΑΒΡΟΤΟΝΟΝ
Χαρισίου.

ΠΑΜΦΙΛΗ
τοῦτ' οἶσθ' ἀκριβῶς, φιλτάτη;

ΑΒΡΟΤΟΝΟΝ
εὖ οἶ]δ' ἔ[γωγ'· ἀλ]λ' οὐ σὲ τὴν νύμφην ὁρῶ
τὴν ἔνδον οὖσαν;

ΠΑΜΦΙΛΗ
ναιχί.

ΑΒΡΟΤΟΝΟΝ
μακαρία γύναι,
θεῶν τις ὑμᾶς ἠλέησε. τὴν θύραν
875 τῶν γειτόνων τις ἐψόφηκεν ἐξιών.　(555)
εἴσω λαβοῦσά μ' ὡς σεαυτὴν εἴσαγε,
ἵνα καὶ τὰ λοιπὰ πάντα μου πύθῃ σαφῶς.

872 εὖ οἶ]δ' ἔ[γωγ' suppl. Wilamowitz, ἀλ]λ' Sudhaus.

486

HABROTONON

                              Just a pose.
The object's not to *wrong* the mother, but
To give me time to trace her.   Now I have—
You.   You're the girl I saw before.

PAMPHILE

                              But who's   870
The father?

HABROTONON
It's Charisios.

PAMPHILE

                              My dear,
You're really sure of that?

HABROTONON
                    [I'm certain—but]
Aren't you his wife, from in there?

(*Habrotonon points to Charisios' house.*)

PAMPHILE

                              Yes.

HABROTONON

                              Some power
Above has had compassion on you both!
Oh, happy girl!—A neighbour's door is rattling,   875
He's coming out.   Take me inside with you,
And then I'll tell you clearly all the rest.

(*At line 875 the door of Chairestratos' house begins to rattle as Onesimos unfastens it. Habrotonon and Pamphile hurry off into Charisios' house with the baby before Onesimos emerges onto an empty stage.*)

MENANDER

ΟΝΗΣΙΜΟΣ

ὑπομαίνεθ’ οὗτος, νὴ τὸν Ἀπόλλω, μαίνεται·
μεμάνητ’ ἀλ[η]θῶς· μαίνεται, νὴ τοὺς θεούς·
880 τὸν δεσπότην λέγω Χαρίσιον. χολὴ   (560)
μέλαινα προσπέπτωκεν ἢ τοιοῦτό [τι.
τί γὰρ ἄν τις ε[ἰκ]άσειεν ἄλλο γεγον[έναι;
πρὸς ταῖς θύραις γὰρ ἔνδον ἀρτί[ως πολὺν
χρόνον διακύπτων ἐνδ[ιέτριψεν ἄθλιος.
885 ὁ πατὴρ δὲ τῆς νύμφης τι περὶ [το]ῦ [π]ρ[άγματος (565)
ἐλάλει πρὸς ἐκείνην, ὡς ἔοιχ’, ὁ δ’ οἷα μὲν
ἤλλαττε χρώματ’, ἄνδρες, οὐδ’ εἰπεῖν καλόν.
“ ὦ γλυκυτάτη ” δὲ “ τῶν λόγων οἵους λέγεις ”
ἀνέκραγε, τὴν κεφαλήν τ’ ἀνεπάταξε σφόδρα
890 αὑτοῦ. πάλιν δὲ διαλιπών, “ οἵαν λαβὼν   (570)
γυναῖχ’ ὁ μέλεος ἠτύχηκα.” τὸ δὲ πέρας,
ὡς πάντα διακούσας ἀπῆλθ’ εἴσω ποτέ,
βρυχηθμὸς ἔνδον, τιλμός, ἔκστασις συχνή.
“ ἐγὼ ” γὰρ “ ἀλιτήριος ” πυκνὸν πάνυ
895 ἔλεγεν, “ τοιοῦτον ἔργον ἐξειργασμένος   (575)
αὐτὸς γεγονώς τε παιδίου νόθου πατὴρ
οὐκ ἔσχον οὐδ’ ἔδωκα συγγνώμης μέρος
οὐθὲν ἀτυχούσῃ ταῦτ’ ἐκείνῃ, βάρβαρος
ἀνηλεής τε.” λοιδορεῖτ’ ἐρρωμένως
900 αὑ]τῷ βλέπει θ’ ὕφαιμον ἠρεθισμένος.   (580)
πέφρικ’ ἐγὼ μέν· αὖός εἰμι τῷ δέει.

---

879 Suppl. ed. pr.   880–901 A mutilated text of these lines is
preserved also in *P. Oxy.* 1236 (= O).   881 Suppl. Robert.
882 ε[ἰκ]άσειεν suppl. Croiset, γεγον[έναι Capps, Sudhaus.   883
Suppl. Leo.   884 Suppl. Robert.   885 Suppl. Croiset: περι[C,
]υ[.]ρ[O.   890 δε C: τε O.   899 Corr. several: τ’ελοιδορειτ’
C (words not preserved in O).   900 Suppl. von Arnim,
Wilamowitz.

EPITREPONTES

ONESIMOS

The man's quite mad—yes, by Apollo, mad!
He's really crazy.   Yes, he's mad, by heaven!
I mean Charisios, my master.   He's   880
Got melancholia,[1] or [some] such ailment!
How else could one explain the circumstances?
You see, just now indoors [he spent a long (?)]
Time peeping through that door[2]—[poor fellow (?)]!
     His
Wife's father was discussing [the affair]   885
With her, apparently, and, gentlemen,
I can't with decency describe how he
Kept changing colour.   ' O my love, to speak
Such words,' he cried, and punched himself hard on
His head.   Pause, then resumption: ' What a wife   890
I've married, and I'm in this wretched mess! '
When finally he'd heard the whole tale out,
He fled indoors.   Then—wailing, tearing of
Hair, raging lunacy within.   He went
On saying, ' Look at me, the villain.   I   895
Myself commit a crime like this, and am
The father of a bastard child.   Yet I
Felt not a scrap of mercy, showed none to
That woman in the same sad fortune.   I'm
A heartless brute.'   Fiercely he damns himself,   900
Eyes bloodshot, overwrought.   I'm scared, quite
     numb

---

[1] Literally ' black bile ', which was imagined to cause such
manic-depressive attacks.
[2] The door of Chairestratos' house.   On the implications of
this remark and of the subsequent one by Charisios (919 ff.)
for the staging of the earlier scene between Pamphile and
Smikrines, see pp. 479–80.

οὕτως ἔχων γὰρ αὐτὸν ἂν ἴδῃ μέ που
τὸν διαβαλόντα, τυχὸν ἀποκτείνει[ε]ν ἄν.
διόπερ ὑπεκδέδυκα δεῦρ' ἔξω λάθρᾳ.
905 καὶ ποῖ τράπωμαί γ'· εἰς τί βουλῆς; οἴχομαι. (585)
ἀπόλωλα· τὴν θύραν πέπληχεν ἐξιών.
Ζεῦ σῶτερ, εἴπερ ἐστὶ δυνατόν, σῷζέ με.

ΧΑΡΙΣΙΟΣ

ἐγώ τις ἀναμάρτητος, εἰς δόξαν βλέπων
καὶ τὸ καλὸν ὅ τί ποτ' ἐστι καὶ ταἰσχρὸν σκοπῶν,
910 ἀκέραιος, ἀνεπίπληκτος αὐτὸς τῷ βίῳ— (590)
εὖ μοι κέχρηται καὶ προσηκόντως πάνυ
τὸ δαιμόνιον—ἐνταῦθ' ἔδειξ' ἄνθρωπος ὤν.
" ὦ τρισκακόδαιμον, μεγάλα φυσᾷς καὶ λαλεῖς;
ἀκούσιον γυναικὸς ἀτύχημ' οὐ φέρεις·
915 αὐτὸν δὲ δείξω σ' εἰς ὅμοι' ἐπταικότα. (595)
καὶ χρήσετ' αὐτή σοι τότ' ἠπίως, σὺ δὲ
ταύτην ἀτιμάζεις· ἐπιδειχθήσει θ' ἅμα
ἀ]τυχὴς γεγονὼς καὶ σκαιὸς ἀγνώμων τ' ἀνήρ."
ὅμο]ιά γ' εἶπεν οἷς σὺ διενόου τότε
920 πρὸ]ς τὸν πατέρα; κοινωνὸς ἥκειν τοῦ βίου (600)
φάσκουσα κ]οὐ δεῖν τἀτύχημ' αὐτὴν φυγεῖν
τὸ συμβ]εβηκός. σὺ δέ τις ὑψηλὸς σφόδρα

]ν
] βαρβαρο[
925   ]υν ταύτῃ σοφῶς (605)

913 Corr. ed. pr: καιμεγαλα C. 918, 920 Suppl. ed. pr.
919 Suppl. several. 921 Suppl. Arnott. 923–44 A mutilated
text of these lines is preserved in P. Oxy. 1236 (= O), the sole
witness for lines 923–33, where nothing from C survives; the
text of 934–44, lacunose as it is, is compiled with the help of
both C and O. 924 ? βάρβαρο[ς (so Sudhaus).

With terror. If he sees me while he's in
This frenzy—me, the blabbermouth—he might
Just kill me! So I've slily crept out here.
Yet where to turn? What plan? I'm done for, 905
    finished!
The door is rattling, master's coming out!
O Zeus the Saviour, save me if you can!

(At line 905, Onesimos' paratragic expressions of helpless-
ness turn to genuine alarm when he hears the sound of
Chairestratos' door opening. He rushes off, probably
into Charisios' own house. Charisios now enters, from
Chairestratos' house.)

CHARISIOS

A faultless man, eyes fixed on his good name,
A judge of what is right and what is wrong,
In his own life pure and beyond reproach— 910
My image, which some power above has well
And quite correctly shattered. Here I showed
That I was human. ' Wretched worm,[1] in pose
And talk so bumptious, you won't tolerate
A woman's forced misfortune. I shall show 915
That you have stumbled just the same yourself.
Then *she* will treat you tenderly, while *you*
Insult her. You'll appear unlucky, rude,
A heartless brute, too, all at once.' Did she
Address her father then [as] you'd have done? 920
' I'm here,' [she said (?)], ' to share his life. Mishaps
Occur. I mustn't run away.' You're too 922
Superior [

(Between lines 922 and 1060 the text is fragmentary and

---

[1] Charisios here presumably pictures that ' power above '
(911) addressing him.

491

MENANDER

lacunose. Three passages, each of from seven to nine lines in length (927–35, 952–58, 982–89), are here wholly or supplementably preserved, but these flowers of intelligibility are surrounded by extensive bogs where only one or two words remain from each line of text, or by deserts where for up to 19 lines at a time nothing at all survives.

Even so, enough remains for a reliable reconstruction of the dramatic sequence in at least the first half of this damaged section. Charisios' monologue clearly extends until line 932. From 923 to 926 nothing can be made out

---

　　　　　]ε μέτεισι διὰ τέλους
　　　τῶν δαιμ]όνων τις. ὁ δὲ πατὴρ
χαλε]πώτατ' αὐτῇ χρήσεται. τί δέ μοι πατρός;
ἐρ]ῶ διαρρήδην " ἐμοὶ σύ, Σμικρίνη,
930 μὴ] πάρεχε πράγματ'· οὐκ ἀπολείπει μ' ἡ γυνή.　(610)
τ]ί οὖν ταράττεις καὶ βιάζει Παμφίλην; "
τ]ί σ' αὖ βλέπω 'γώ;

ΟΝΗΣΙΜΟΣ

　　　　　　　πάνυ κακῶς ἔχω σφόδρα·
ο]ἴμοι τάλας. καὶ σο[ῦ δ]έομαι τοῦτ', ὦ γύ[ναι,
μή μ' ἐγκαταλίπῃς.

---

927 τῶν suppl. Hunt, δαιμ]όνων Wilamowitz. 928 Suppl. Arnott. αὐτῇ Hunt: αυτης O. 929 Suppl. Körte, Wilamowitz. 930–33 Suppl. Hunt. 933 τουτο.γυ[apparently O. 934 Change of speaker indicated by Hunt (abrasion has removed any possible traces of dicolon or paragraphus in O;]γκα[C).

EPITREPONTES

except brute *(924) and* her *(?)* wisely *(925).   Was Charisios here continuing to contrast his brutal behaviour with Pamphile's gentle tolerance?   It is interesting to note that in Onesimos' earlier description of Charisios' self-recriminations, the words 'brute' and 'her' are similarly juxtaposed (898).*

At line 926 we are on firmer ground for a short spell. Charisios is coming to the end of his long monologue of self-reproach.   He is now picturing to himself his next confrontation with Smikrines, his father-in-law.)

CHARISIOS

[. . . . .] Heaven's fury will pursue   926
[Me (?)] constantly, [if I reject her now (?)].
She'll find her father very [truculent (?)].
Why worry, though, about *him*?   I'll be blunt
And [say], 'Do[n't] vex me, Smikrines.   My wife's   930
Not leaving me.   So why nag Pamphile
And pressure her?'—What brings *you* here again?

(This last remark is addressed to Onesimos, who rather timidly enters at this point from Charisios' house. Habrotonon either accompanies Onesimos, at first keeping in the background of the doorway, or follows him shortly afterwards.   In the latter eventuality, the remarks addressed to Habrotonon in lines 933–34 would be directed to her by Onesimos back through the open door of Charisios' house.)

ONESIMOS

Oh dear, I'm in the most appalling fix!
Don't leave me, [lady (?)], I beseech you!

MENANDER

ΧΑΡΙΣΙΟΣ

οὗτος, ἐπακροώμε[νος
935 ἕστηκας, ἱερόσυλε, μου;

ΟΝΗΣΙΜΟΣ

[μ]ὰ τοὺς θεούς, (615)
ἀλλ' ἀρτίως ἐξῆλθον. ἀ[λλὰ πῶς] λαθεῖν
ἔσται σ'· ἔπρα[ξ'] ὑμῖν το[σαῦτα], νὴ Δ[ία·
πάντ' ἐπακροάσει.

ΧΑΡΙΣΙΟΣ

ποτ[.....]ουθ[
ἐγώ σε λανθάνειν πον[ηρὸν ὄντα καὶ
940 βροντῶντα;

ΟΝΗΣΙΜΟΣ

δια . ε[(620)

ΑΒΡΟΤΟΝΟΝ

ἀλλ' οὐθὲν ὀφθήσε[ι

ΧΑΡΙΣΙΟΣ

τίς εἰσ[..] . αυ . εισ . [

ΑΒΡΟΤΟΝΟΝ

οὐκ αἰσ[...]ν.

ΧΑΡΙΣΙΟΣ

.[(His words are lost.)

934–35 Suppl. Hunt.   936–37 Suppl. Arnott.   939 Suppl.
tentatively Arnott.   941 Suppl. Hunt.   943 αισ[C.]ν.: or ν..: O.

EPITREPONTES

CHARISIOS

You—
Have you been stood there listening, you crook? 935

ONESIMOS

No, by the gods, I've just come out. [How (?)] can
I keep it from you ?—I've achieved (?) [such things (?)]
For you, by [Zeus (?)]—just listen to it all . . . 938

*(Between lines 938 and 949 the text is again badly
defective, with only the opening letters in each line pre-
served. This makes the general drift and structure of the
dialogue hard to grasp. In lines 938–40 Charisios
appears to be responding to the proud claims of Onesimos'
preceding remarks with an angry question, which may be
speculatively supplemented as follows:)*

When [have (?)] 938
[I (?)] not [been (?)] conscious of your [villainy (?)]
And boastful trumpeting? 940

*(Onesimos' reply to this question cannot be deciphered or
guessed, but directly afterwards Habrotonon seems to
come forward and engage Charisios in conversation for
several lines (941–47). Their opening remarks are too
damaged for much sense to be discernible; Habrotonon
begins 941 with You'll not at all (?) be seen, Charisios
counters in 942 with a question apparently introduced by
the word Who, and Habrotonon then briefly replies to
him (943) with a remark where the only word deci-
pherable is not. Charisios' next remark, in the second
half of line 943, is altogether lost, but then Habrotonon
appears to affirm, in a remark where supplementation
is reasonably easy but uncertain in detail, [The baby
(?)] wasn't [mine] (944). Charisios appears to be*

495

MENANDER

ΑΒΡΟΤΟΝΟΝ

οὐκ ἦν ἐ[μὸν τὸ π]α[ιδίον

ΧΑΡΙΣΙΟΣ

945 οὐκ ἦν σό[ν;   625)

ΑΒΡΟΤΟΝΟΝ

βούλει μ' ἀπ[

ΧΑΡΙΣΙΟΣ

ἀλλ' ἐξαπί[νης

ΑΒΡΟΤΟΝΟΝ
(Her words are lost.)

ΧΑΡΙΣΙΟΣ

ἔμ' ἔπρ[επε

ΟΝΗΣΙΜΟΣ

ἔ[δ]ει σ.[

ΧΑΡΙΣΙΟΣ

950 τ]ί φής, 'Ον[ήσιμ'], ἐξεπειράθη[τέ μου;   630)

ΟΝΗΣΙΜΟΣ

αὔ]τη μ' ἔ[πε]ισε, νὴ τὸν 'Απόλλω [καὶ θε]ούς.

---

944 ἐ[μὸν suppl. Körte, τὸ π]α[ιδίον tentatively Arnott (after
an idea by Sudhaus). 945 Suppl. Körte. 947–48 The identi-
fication of speakers and assignment of parts are here very
speculative. 947 Corr. and suppl. Arnott: εξαπει[C. 948
Suppl. Körte. 949 ἔ[δ]ει σε[tentatively Sandbach. 950 τ]ί
and 'Ον[ήσιμ'] suppl. Sudhaus, ἐξεπειράθη[τέ μου Jensen. 951
αὔ]τη and ἔ[πε]ισε suppl. Sudhaus, [καὶ θε]ούς Jensen.

stunned by this statement, taking it up with It wasn't
yours? *(945). The next four lines are a series of puzzles.
Habrotonon appears to ask* Do you want me to . . . ?
or Do you want to . . . me? *(946), but identification of
the missing infinitive is a matter only for speculation
(' want me to tell you the whole story ' is one possibility).
Charisios may have replied* Yes, *on the instant (947), but
this rendering also is speculative, depending as it does not
only on supplementation but also on a minor correction of
the defective papyrus text. It is possible that Habrotonon
made a brief rejoinder to this, now lost, in the second half
of line 947. Little survives from lines 948 and 949, but
one suggestion is that Charisios first said something
beginning* I ought to have . . . *(948), and that Onesimos
then butted in with* You should have . . . *(949). What-
ever the precise details of these lines of dialogue may
originally have been, however, it is a safe guess that the
core remark was Habrotonon's categorical affirmation
that the baby with which she had earlier created her
sensation at the luncheon party in Chairestratos' house was
not hers. Up to the moment of Habrotonon's affirmation
Charisios apparently had thought that the child was
Habrotonon's and his illegitimate son. Clarification of
the situation follows immediately, in a short passage
(950–58) much better preserved by the Cairo papyrus.)*

CHARISIOS

What's that, On[esimos? The two of you]   950
Were *testing* [me]?

ONESIMOS
She urged me, by Apollo [and]

[The gods]!

MENANDER

καὶ σύ μ]ε περισπᾷς, ἱερόσυλε;

ΑΒΡΟΤΟΝΟΝ

μὴ μάχου,
γλυκύ]τατε· τῆς γαμετῆς γυναικός ἐστί σου
ἴδιον] γ[ά]ρ, οὐκ ἀλλότριον.

ΧΑΡΙΣΙΟΣ

εἰ γὰρ ὤφελεν.

ΑΒΡΟΤΟΝΟΝ

955 νὴ τὴν] φίλην Δήμητρα.

ΧΑΡΙΣΙΟΣ

τίνα λόγον λέγεις; (635)

ΑΒΡΟΤΟΝΟΝ

τίνα; τὸν] ἀληθῆ.

ΧΑΡΙΣΙΟΣ

Παμφίλης τὸ παιδίον;
ἀλλ᾽ ἦν ἐμ]όν.

ΑΒΡΟΤΟΝΟΝ

καὶ σόν γ᾽ ὁμοίως.

ΧΑΡΙΣΙΟΣ

Παμφίλης;
Ἀβρότο]νον, ἱκετεύω σε, μή μ᾽ ἀναπτεροῦ

(After line 958 there is a lacuna of about 10 lines.)

498

CHARISIOS (*to Onesimos*)
　　You in this racket [too], you crook?

HABROTONON
Don't squabble, [darling].　It's your wife's own child,
[*Hers*], not somebody else's!

CHARISIOS
　　　　　How I wish it were!

HABROTONON
[It is, by] dear Demeter!

CHARISIOS (*beginning to realise the implications*)
　　　　　What's this story?　　　955

HABROTONON
[Story?　The] truth!

CHARISIOS
　　　The child is Pamphile's?
[It's mine, though!]

HABROTONON
　Yes, yours equally!

CHARISIOS
　　　　　　It's Pamphile's?
[Habroto]non, please don't build up my hopes　　958
[Too high (?)] . . .

(*The Cairo papyrus breaks off after line 958, and there
is then a complete gap of about ten lines, in which*

---

952 Suppl. Sudhaus.　953 Suppl. Wilamowitz.　954 ἴδιον]
suppl. Arnott (could C have written ειδιον ?), γ[ά]ρ Körte.
955 Suppl. Headlam, Hense.　956 Suppl. Coppola.　957 Suppl.
Sandbach.　958 Suppl. ed. pr.

MENANDER

ΧΑΡΙΣΙΟΣ (?)

969   ]αι γὰρ .[

ΑΒΡΟΤΟΝΟΝ

970   ] πῶς ἐγώ, τάλαν, (640)
πρ]ὶν πάντ᾽ εἰδέναι

ΧΑΡΙΣΙΟΣ

] ὀρθῶς λέγεις

(The speakers in the following 6 lines cannot be
identified.)

]ο μοι:
]τερε
975   ] ὅμως   (645)
]υτο δὴ
] βούλομαι
]ματα.

[ΧΟ Ρ ΟΥ]

971 Suppl. Körte.

EPITREPONTES

Habrotonon must presumably have continued her assur-
ances that the baby was really the son of both Charisios
and Pamphile, and Charisios have come to accept this
startling fact with his brain and with his heart. When
the papyrus resumes at line 969, only the ends of the lines
are at first preserved, and it is difficult to interpret what
was going on. We are only ten lines from the end of the
fourth act. Charisios may perhaps have been asking
Habrotonon why she had not divulged her information
about the baby's parentage before (at that momentous
luncheon?); only the word for (969), *however, survives*
from this conjectured question. Habrotonon appears to
have answered (970–71) How [could] I, dear me,/[—],
before I knew it all? *Charisios may then have spoken*
the words preserved in 972, You're right. *Thereafter*
speakers cannot safely be identified. To me *ends line 973,*
after which there was a change of speaker; from the
ensuing verses only a few words: still (975), *in fact* (976),
I wish (977): *can be made out. One possibility is that*
Charisios and Habrotonon made their exits at line 963 or
thereabouts, the former to effect off-stage in his own house
a full and joyous reconciliation with his wife. They
would thus have left Onesimos alone on stage to deliver a
short monologue which brought the act to its close at 978.
But this is pure speculation.)

ΜΕΡΟΣ Ε′

*(The final act begins with a monologue whose opening
three lines are irremediably defective. The speaker's
identity is merely one of the many puzzles that this act's
first scene, originally some 80 lines or so in length, poses to
the interpreter. Many theories have been advanced; the
most plausible has Chairestratos emerging from his house
at the beginning of the act, as yet unaware of the true
parentage of Pamphile's and Charisios' baby, and still
believing the earlier charade that its mother was Habro-
tonon. If Chairestratos is additionally portrayed as*

―――――

ΧΑΙΡΕΣΤΡΑΤΟΣ (?)

```
                              ]ειμενον
980                           ]υτη[.]επ[        (650)
            ]λω . . . . . . [. .].[. . . .] ἐναντίο[ν,
      Χ[αιρέστρ]ατ', ἤδη τὸ μετὰ τα[ῦτ]α σκεπτέ[ον,
      ὅπως [δια]μενεῖς ὧν Χαρισίῳ [φ]ί[λος,
      οἷός ποτ' ἦσθα, πιστός. οὐ γάρ ἐσ[τι νῦν
985   ἑταιρίδιον τοῦτ' οὐδὲ τὸ τυχὸν [χρῆμ'. ἐρᾷ,   (655)
      σπουδῇ δέ· καὶ παιδάριον ἤδ[η τέτοχ'· ὁ νοῦς
      ἐλεύθερος. πάξ· μὴ βλέπ' εἰς τ[ὴν ψάλτριαν.
      καὶ πρῶτον αὐτὴν κατὰ μόνα[ς Χαρίσιον
989   τὸν φίλτα[το]ν καὶ τὸν γλυκύτατ[ον
```

979 Speaker's identity suggested by Webster. 982 Χ[αι-
ρέστρ]ατ' suppl. Sudhaus, τα[ῦτ]α van Leeuwen, σκεπτέ[ον
Jensen. ἤδη Sudhaus: ηδε C. 983 [δια]μενεῖς suppl. Ellis,
Sudhaus, [φ]ί[λος several. 984–88 The plausible supplemen-
tation of these lines is well-nigh impossible, and the text
printed here is merely *exempli gratia.* 984 ἦσθα von Arnim:
οισθα C. ἐσ[τι νῦν suppl. Arnott (after an idea by
Wilamowitz). 985–86 Suppl. Jensen (apart from χρῆμ',
Arnott). 987 Suppl. Schwartz. 988 Suppl. Wilamowitz.
989 Suppl. ed. pr.

ACT V

having fallen in love with Habrotonon, the complications arising out of (1) his misery at apparently having lost her to Charisios, the father of her putative baby, and (2) his subsequent discovery of the true state of affairs, leading to new hopes or even new despair, would provide material enough for Menander to have composed an effective scene of the required length.

Chairestratos' opening speech—if the speaker is thus correctly identified—yields to translation from the end of its third line.)

Conversely (?), 981
Ch[airestr]atos, its sequel now needs thought—
How best to keep your loyal [friendship] with
Charisios, just as it once was.   She's
No tart, no common [trash (?)] now. [She's in love (?)],
It's serious.   [She's had (?)] a child now, too.   986
[Her mind (?)] is not a slave's [mind (?)].   Stop it,
   don't
Think of [the harp-girl (?)]!   First, those two (?)
   alone :
Her and her darling, dear [Charisios (?)] . . .   989

(*At this point the papyrus breaks off.   If Chairestratos is the speaker, and if the supplements suggested in these lines come at all near to the lost reality (both suppositions are no more than plausible hypotheses), then Chairestratos will have been musing with himself, alone on stage, and expressing his determination not to interfere in the apparent love affair between Habrotonon and Charisios, despite Chairestratos' own infatuation with Habrotonon, which his protestations of loyalty cannot conceal.*

(After line 989 there is a lacuna of between 9 and 11 lines. Then comes a passage, here numbered 1000–14 (= Sandbach 1003–17), where only the initial letters in each line are preserved: (4–5 letters)] . οτρ[1000, (5 letters)]καλ[1001, εἰ τὸ καλὸν . [1002, ὥσπερ λύκ[ος ? 1003, ἀπελήλυ[θ 1004, ἀποστ[1005, ‾ φιλο[1006, δια . [10‾07, οὐ κρι[100‾8, ‾ καιν[1009, ‾ ὅσα μ . [10‾10, ‾ ην μο . [1011, ἔνδον πο . [1012, ἔοικεν : ου[1013, ‾ (4 letters)]οσπ .‾[1014.

After line 1014 a further shred of the Cairo papyrus, containing just the initial letters of each of 6 lines and one indication of a speaker's name, is most plausibly —but not incontrovertibly—inserted. If this placing is correct, the first line of the shred must come at an interval of between 1 and 5 lines after 1014. On this fragment, here given Sandbach's line-numbering, the following is preserved: ἐπ' αὐτὸν [1018, ὄντως . β[1019, ἀλλ' ἐξαπατ [10‾20, ON' ἀπέσωσε‾ συ . [1021, ἐγὼ δὲ‾ προσ[1022, . . αν[1023.

After line 1023 there is a further lacuna of some 10 to 14 lines. Then comes a passage, here numbered 1035–49, where only badly holed and abraded remains

1000–14, 1018–23, 1035–49, 1052–57. The two tattered fragments of the Cairo papyrus that offer these scanty scraps of text are β (1000–14 horizontal fibres, 1035–49 vertical fibres) and U (1018–23 h.f., 1052–57 v.f.). Although the placing of β is assured (another portion of its text overlaps with *P. Oxy.* 1236), the placing of U relative to β is highly controversial. The conjecture adopted here, that U follows soon after β, is tentatively supported by most modern scholars. See the Gomme-Sandbach *Commentary*, pp. 370 f.; Arnott, *Actes du XVe Congrès International de Papyrologie*, (Brussels, III, 31 ff. 1003 Suppl. Sudhaus.

EPITREPONTES

Between line 989, where this fragment breaks off, and line 1060, where a well-preserved leaf of the Cairo papyrus introduces a further 72 lines of virtually complete text, it is very difficult to see what happened. We possess, however, three pieces of evidence which at times raise, at times frustrate our hopes of identifying the speakers and subject-matter of the lost section of text. First, a shred of the Cairo papyrus (fragment β) contains on one side the opening few letters of fifteen lines of text, which seem originally to have come about 9 to 11 lines after line 989. A few translatable words or phrases emerge from the Greek (1002 if the fine thing, 1003 like a wolf, 1004 has or have gone away, 1006 fond of, 1008 not, 1009 all that, 1012 inside, 1013 so it appears), and several indications of change of speaker in what must have been lively dialogue. But who were the speakers? One possibility is that Chairestratos' monologue continued down to line 1006, ending with a remark that the speaker has decided to do ' the fine thing ', going away ' like a wolf' with gaping jaws (1002–4). This simile of the wolf slinking off with gaping jaws was proverbially applied in Menander's Athens (cf. Aspis 372 and note) to those who, like Chairestratos here, had just had their dearest hopes frustrated. At the end of Chairestratos' monologue Charisios and Onesimos may have entered from Charisios' house, and begun to enlighten Chairestratos about the true state of events.

On the other side of this shred of papyrus the endings of a further fifteen lines appear, which must originally have been sited at an interval of about 20 to 24 lines after line 1013. Little can be confidently deciphered on this side of a badly holed and abraded papyrus fragment; a word here and there, however, emerges from the Greek (1035 took, 1038 bad, 1039 not, 1040 Habrotonon,

1047 but you, *1048* this man here). *There is a mark indicating a change of speaker at the end of 1041, but neither this nor the reference to Habrotonon in 1042 gives reliable support to what is nonetheless the plausible hypothesis that Chairestratos, Charisios and Onesimos were still here continuing to discuss the new situation.*

The second piece of evidence is a tiny shred of Cairo papyrus (fragment U), containing on one side the opening letters of six lines of text and the useful information that one of the speakers was Onesimos, and on the other side the final portions of six other lines. The siting of this shred has long exercised papyrologists, but the most plausible

---

of the line-endings are preserved. A few letter sequences can be made out, as follows:]ελαβ[1035,]ουτ[..]ι 1036,]. ου κακὰ 1038,] οὐχ ὅσ[1039, Ἁ]βρότονον 1040,]. ωι: 1041,]τε[1042,]γ[1043,]αν . . . . . σου 1044,]ουτε[1046,]υτ' ἀλλὰ σὺ 1047,] . s τουτ[ο]υὶ 1048.

After line 1049 there is a lacuna of 10 lines before a further well-preserved page of the Cairo papyrus resumes at line 1060. Into this gap the other side of the shred that contained lines 1018–23 may plausibly be slotted. It contains the endings of six lines. Its first line must come at an interval of between one and four lines after 1049. Here Sandbach's line-numbering is adopted: απα]τωμένου: 1052, τὸ]ν Δία 1053,]αυτοῦ τῷ σφόδρα 1054,]ως ὁμολογῶ: 1055, εἰ]s ἐμὲ βλέπει 1056,]αιε[1057.

Three or fewer lines after this last shred of text, a new sheet of the Cairo papyrus begins.)

1040 Deciphered and suppl. Jensen. 1048 Suppl. Arnott. 1052–53, 1056 Suppl. Sudhaus.

home for it is in the gap of about ten lines between the bottom of fragment β and the original end of the page to which fragment β belonged. The side of fragment U that contains the line-beginnings fits in the gap between lines 1014 and 1024, and yields the following words and phrases: 1018 to or against him, 1019 really, 1020 deceive (or some other part of this verb), 1021 he or she rescued (with a marginal note identifying the speaker as Onesimos), 1022 and I. If Charisios and Onesimos had just been talking to each other immediately after their suggested entry at 1007, it is possible that Charisios and Onesimos announced their intention to go up ' to him ' (sc. Chairestratos) in 1018. Words such as ' really ' and ' deceive ' (1019–20) would fit naturally into an animated conversation (fragment U here notes three changes of speaker in its six lines) about Habrotonon's subterfuge with the baby, but the subject of Onesimos' remark in 1021 is uncertain: was it Habrotonon who rescued Charisios from his marital difficulties, or Charisios who rescued Chairestratos from his lovesick despair? The other side of fragment U would consequently slot into the gap between lines 1049 and 1060, where the well-preserved page of the Cairo papyrus begins. This side contains six line-endings, yielding the following sense: 1052 deceived, 1053 Zeus, 1054 by his violent (?), 1055 I agree, 1056 looks to me. Change of speaker is indicated at the ends of lines 1052 and 1055. Who were the speakers? It is at least a reasonable hypothesis that Chairestratos, Charisios and Onesimos were still conversing, although none of the words preserved in 1052–57 can safely be assigned to an identified speaker.

The third and final piece of evidence is the undamaged text of the final two lines of this scene, preserved at the top of the next extant page of the Cairo papyrus (1060–61).

MENANDER

*At first sight these two lines seem puzzling, but if they are
interpreted with due reference to the suggested content and
speakers in the scene whose conclusion this pair of lines
forms, relevant sense emerges. Shortly before line 1060
Chairestratos will have left the stage, doubtless bent on
prosecuting his suit with Habrotonon. Onesimos may
have accompanied him into Charisios' house. That
would have left Charisios alone upon the stage, ready to
deliver an exit monologue concluding with the observation
that it was perhaps just as well that events had so turned
out, for the impetuous Chairestratos could never have kept*

ΧΑΡΙΣΙΟΣ (?)

. . . . . .

1060 σώφρονα· τοιαυτησὶ γὰρ οὐκ ἀπέσχετ' ἂν
ἐκεῖνος, εὖ τοῦτ' οἶδ'· ἐγὼ δ' ἀφέξομαι.

ΣΜΙΚΡΙΝΗΣ

ἂν μὴ κατάξω τὴν κεφαλήν σου, Σωφρόνη,
κάκιστ' ἀπολοίμην. νουθετήσεις καὶ σύ με;   (705)
προπετῶς ἀπάγω τὴν θυγατέρ', ἱερόσυλε γραῦ;
1065 ἀλλ' ἦ περιμένω καταφαγεῖν τὴν προῖκά μου
τὸν χρηστὸν αὐτῆς ἄνδρα, καὶ λόγους λέγω
περὶ τῶν ἐμαυτοῦ; ταῦτα συμπείθεις με σύ;
οὐκ ὀξυλαβῆσαι κρεῖττον; οἰμώξει μακρά,   (710)
ἂν ἔ[τ]ι λαλῇς. τί; κρίνομαι πρὸς Σωφρόνην;

1060–61 Speaker identified by Croiset, van Leeuwen. **1065**
Corr. Körte, Wilamowitz: αλλαπεριμενω C. 1069 ἔ[τ]ι suppl.
von Arnim, Leo. Punctuation (λαλῇς. τί; κρίνομαι) suggested
by Coppola.

his hands off Habrotonon, as Charisios himself would
continue to do. Charisios' self-congratulation has a
delightfully ironic ring. He had, it is true, been able to
resist Habrotonon's allurements. The reason for that
success, however, was not his superior morality, but
rather his prior emotion for Pamphile.)

The closing words of a speech by CHARISIOS (?)

. . . . . .

Controlled. *He'd* not have checked the urge to paw   1060
A girl like her, that's certain—*I* shall, though!

(*Charisios now goes off into his own house, leaving the*
stage temporarily empty. At this point Smikrines
approaches with Pamphile's old nurse Sophrone, entering
from the right. Smikrines will have visited his house in
Athens after leaving Pamphile in the previous act: see the
comment after line 756. He has now brought Sophrone,
who in this scene is apparently played by a mute, with him
to support his final attempt at persuading Pamphile. He
is of course still unaware of the new developments which
have led to the reconciliation of Pamphile and Charisios.
As they enter Smikrines is haranguing Sophrone violently.)

SMIKRINES

If I don't smash your head in, Sophrone,
May I be damned to hell! Rebukes from you
As well? Too hasty am I, fetching home
My girl, you crooked[1] old bitch? Must I wait   1065
Till her fine husband's guzzled all my dowry,
And only *rant* about my property? Is that
What you advise me? Lightning strokes are best!
Say one word more, and you'll be sorry! What?

---

[1] See the note on *Aspis* 227.

1070 μετάπεισον αὐτήν, ὅταν ἴδῃς. οὕτω τί μοι
ἀγαθὸν γένοιτο, Σωφρόνη, γάρ, οἴκαδε
ἀπιών—τὸ τέλμ' εἶδες παριοῦσ';—ἐνταῦθά σε
τὴν νύκτα βαπτίζων ὅλην ἀποκτενῶ,   (715)
κ[ἀ]γώ σε ταῦτ' ἐμοὶ φρονεῖν ἀναγκάσω
1075 καὶ [μ]ὴ στασιάζειν. ἡ θύρα παιητέα·
κεκλειμένη γάρ ἐστι. παῖδες, παιδίον·
ἀνοιξάτω τις. παῖδες· οὐχ ὑμῖν λέγω;

ΟΝΗΣΙΜΟΣ

τίς ἐσθ' ὁ κόπτων τὴν θύραν; ὤ, Σμικρίνης   (720)
ὁ χαλεπός, ἐπὶ τὴν προῖκα καὶ τὴν θυγατέρα
1080 ἥκων.

ΣΜΙΚΡΙΝΗΣ

ἔγωγε, τρισκατάρατε.

ΟΝΗΣΙΜΟΣ

καὶ μάλα
ὀρθῶς· λογιστικοῦ γὰρ ἀνδρὸς καὶ σφόδρα
φρονοῦντος ἡ σπουδή, τό θ' ἅρπασμ', Ἡράκλεις,
θαυμαστὸν οἷον.

ΣΜΙΚΡΙΝΗΣ

πρὸς θεῶν καὶ δαιμόνων—   (725)

1072 ιδες C.   1074 σε several: σοι C. 1074–75 Suppl. ed. pr.
1083 πρὸς θεῶν καὶ δαιμόνων assigned to Smikrines by several
(C has no dicola and no paragraphus under the line).

Is Sophrone my judge? See Pamphile, and make   1070
Her change her mind.   Or else, so help me God, when I
Leave—did you, on your way here, see that pond?—
I'll drown you there, I'll hold you under all
Night long, and force you to agree with me.
I'll stop your wrangling!

(*By now Smikrines and Sophrone have reached Charisios'
door.   Smikrines tries to open it, but finds it locked.*)

                    I must rap the door,   1075
It's bolted.   Slaves there!   Boy there!   Open up,
Someone!   You slaves there, can't you hear me call?

(*Onesimos unhurriedly opens the door, comes out, but
stands directly in front of the doorway, thus blocking all
entry to Smikrines.*)

    ONESIMOS (*as he opens the door*)
Who's knocking at the door?   Oh, Smikrines
The tartar, coming for his dowry and
His daughter—

        SMIKRINES (*intervening*)
          Yes, you blasted scoundrel, *me*!   1080

    ONESIMOS (*ignoring Smikrines' comment*)
—Quite rightly, too!   This keenness suits a smart
And *most* discerning chap.   And, Heracles!
Embezzling dowries—how amazing!

  SMIKRINES (*losing his temper at Onesimos' sarcasm*)
                 Gods
And powers!

MENANDER

ΟΝΗΣΙΜΟΣ

(K. fr. 174) οἴει τοσαύτην τοὺς θεοὺς ἄγειν σχολὴν
1085 ὥστε τὸ κακὸν καὶ τἀγαθὸν καθ᾽ ἡμέραν
νέμειν ἑκάστῳ, Σμικρίνη;

ΣΜΙΚΡΙΝΗΣ
λέγεις δὲ τί;

ΟΝΗΣΙΜΟΣ

σαφῶς διδάξω σ᾽. εἰσὶν αἱ πᾶσαι πόλεις,
ὅμοιον εἰπεῖν, χίλιαι. τρισμύριοι   (730)
οἰκοῦσ᾽ ἑκάστην. καθ᾽ ἕνα τούτων οἱ [θεοὶ
1090 ἕκαστον ἐπιτρίβουσιν ἢ σῴζουσι; πῶς;
λέγεις γὰρ ἐπίπονόν τιν᾽ αὐτοὺς ζῆν [βίον.
(K. fr. 752?) '' οὐκ ἄρα φρον[τί]ζουσιν ἡμῶν [ο]ἱ θεοί; ''
φήσεις. ἑκάστῳ τὸν τρόπον συν[ῴκισαν   (735)
φρούραρχον. οὗτος ἔνδο[ν] ἐπ[ι]τεταγμένος
1095 ἐπέτριψεν, ἂν αὐτῷ κακῶς χρη[σώμεθα,
ἕτερον δ᾽ ἔσωσεν. οὗτός ἐσθ᾽ ἡμῖν θεὸς
ὅ τ᾽ αἴτιος καὶ τοῦ καλῶς καὶ τοῦ κακῶς
πράττειν ἑκάστῳ. τοῦτον ἱλάσκου ποῶν   (740)
μηδὲν ἄτοπον μηδ᾽ ἀμαθές, ἵνα πράττῃς καλῶς.

1090–91 πῶς; —[βίον continued to Onesimos by Richards (C
has a dicolon before πως and a paragraphus under line 1091, but
none under 1090). 1091 Suppl. ed. pr. 1092 φρον[τί]ζουσιν
suppl. ed. pr., [ο]ί [θεοί von Arnim, Richards. 1093 Suppl.
Sudhaus. 1094 ἔνδο[ν] suppl. ed. pr., ἐπ[ι]τεταγμένος ten-
tatively Sandbach. 1095 Suppl. Wilamowitz.

---

[1] Onesimos' sermon is a rigmarole of philosophic ideas
popular at the time, but here comically distorted. When he
estimates 30,000 residents (sc. free adult males) to each city,

EPITREPONTES

ONESIMOS

Do you think the gods have time 1085
To dole out every day to every man
His share of good and evil, Smikrines?

SMIKRINES

What do you mean?

ONESIMOS

I'll make it clear to you.[1]
The world contains about a thousand towns,
Each one with thirty thousand residents.
Can every single man of them be damned 1090
Or guarded by the gods?   Absurd—you'd make
Their [lives] a drudgery.   Then don't [the gods]
Look after us, you'll ask?   They['ve introduced],
As each man's guardian, his character.
Inside us, it's [on duty (?)]—*damns* us if 1095
[We treat] it badly, *guards* the others.   That's
Our god, responsible for failure and
Success in each of us.   To get on well,
You must placate it by avoiding error and
Stupidity!

however, he may well be generalising from the known popula-
tion figures for Attica.   When Demetrius of Phalerum held his
census between 317 and 307 B.C. (cf. W. S. Ferguson, *Hellenistic
Athens*, London 1911, 54 f.; A. W. Gomme, *The Population of
Athens in the Fifth and Fourth Centuries* B.C., Oxford 1933,
18 ff.), it was found that there were in Attica 21,000 citizens and
10,000 foreign residents.   On the relationship between Onesi-
mos' individual points and the philosophic thinking that they
caricature, see particularly the Gomme-Sandbach *Commen-
tary, ad loc.*

MENANDER

ΣΜΙΚΡΙΝΗΣ

1100 εἶθ' οὑμός, ἱερόσυλε, νῦν τρόπος ποεῖ
ἀμαθές τι;

ΟΝΗΣΙΜΟΣ

συντρίβει σε.

ΣΜΙΚΡΙΝΗΣ

τῆς παρρησίας.

ΟΝΗΣΙΜΟΣ

ἀλλ' ἀπαγαγεῖν παρ' ἀνδρὸς αὐτοῦ θυγατέρα
ἀγαθὸν σὺ κρίνεις, Σμικρίνη;

ΣΜΙΚΡΙΝΗΣ

λέγει δὲ τίς   (745)
τοῦτ' ἀγαθόν; ἀλλὰ νῦν ἀναγκαῖον.

ΟΝΗΣΙΜΟΣ

θεᾷ;
1105 τὸ κακὸν ἀναγκαῖον λογίζεθ' οὑ[τ]οσί.
τοῦτόν τις ἄλλος, οὐχ ὁ τρόπος, ἀπολλύει;
καὶ νῦν μὲν ὁρμῶντ' ἐπὶ πονηρὸν πρᾶγμά σε
ταὐτόματον ἀποσέσωκε, καὶ καταλαμβάνεις   (750)
διαλλαγὰς λύσεις τ' ἐκείνων τῶν κακ[ῶ]ν.
1110 αὖθις δ' ὅπως μὴ λήψομαί σε, Σμικρίνη,

1101–02 Change of speaker after παρρησίας indicated by Körte
(the dicolon in C is either omitted or abraded). 1102 Corr.
Leo: ανδροσσαυτου C. 1105, 1109, 1111 Suppl. ed. pr.

EPITREPONTES

SMIKRINES

Then is *my* character   1100
Now acting stupidly, you crook[1]?

ONESIMOS

It grinds you down!

SMIKRINES

The cheek!

ONESIMOS

But do you think it's fair to make
Your daughter leave her husband, Smikrines?

SMIKRINES

Who says it's fair?   It's unavoidable,
Though, now.

ONESIMOS

(turning away from Smikrines to address Sophrone)

You see?   Wrong's ' unavoidable ', the way 1105
He thinks!   It's *character* that's blighting him—
That, nothing else.

(Onesimos turns back to Smikrines again.)

And now, when you were bent
On mischief, chance has intervened to save
You.   Here you'll find those ruptures healed, those knots
Untied.   But, Smikrines, don't let me find   1110

---

[1] See the note on *Aspis* 227.

MENANDER

προπετῆ, λέγω σοι· νῦν δὲ τῶν ἐγκλ[η]μάτων
ἀφεῖσο τούτων, τὸν δὲ θυγατριδοῦν λαβὼν
ἔνδον πρόσειπε.

ΣΜΙΚΡΙΝΗΣ

θυγατριδοῦν, μαστιγία;　　　　　(755)

ΟΝΗΣΙΜΟΣ

παχύδερμος ἦσθα καὶ σύ, νοῦν ἔχειν δοκῶν.
1115 οὕτως ἐτήρεις παῖδ' ἐπίγαμον; τοιγαροῦν
τέρασιν ὅμοια πεντάμηνα παιδία
ἐκτρέφομεν.

ΣΜΙΚΡΙΝΗΣ

οὐκ οἶδ' ὅ τι λέγεις.

ΟΝΗΣΙΜΟΣ

　　　　　　　　　　　ἡ γραῦς δέ γε
οἶδ', ὡς ἐγῷμαι. τότε γὰρ οὑμὸς δεσπότης　(760)
τοῖς Ταυροπολίοις, Σωφρόνη, ταύτην λαβὼν
1120 χορῶν ἀποσπασθεῖσαν—αἰσθάνει γε; νή.
νυνὶ δ' ἀναγνωρισμὸς αὐτοῖς γέγονε καὶ
ἅπαντ' ἀγαθά.

ΣΜΙΚΡΙΝΗΣ

τί φησιν, ἱερόσυλε γραῦ;

1113–14 Change of speaker after μαστιγία indicated by ed. pr.
(C omits the dicolon).　1119–20 The former line is continued
to Onesimos by Kapp, the latter by Legrand (C has para-
graphi under both lines and dicola before and after σωφρονη,
before and after αισθανειγε).

You rushing fences any more—I'm telling you!
Drop those complaints now,

(*Onesimos at last moves aside from the doorway of
Charisios' house.*)

                             enter, take and greet
Your daughter's child.

                SMIKRINES (*in amazement*)
                    My daughter's child, you cur?

                ONESIMOS
You *were* a blockhead, thought you were so smart!
Was that the way to guard a teen-age girl?   1115
That's why we've babies four months premature
To care for—freaks!

                SMIKRINES
                I don't know what you mean.

                ONESIMOS
But this old nurse does, I imagine.   Sophrone,
That Tauropolia . . . my master took the girl,
A good way from the dancing . . . understand?   1120

         (*Sophrone nods agreement.*)

Yes!   Now they've been identified, and it's
All bliss!

                SMIKRINES
      You crooked old bitch,[1] what's this story?

---

[1] See the note on *Aspis* 227.

MENANDER

ΟΝΗΣΙΜΟΣ

" ἡ φύσις ἐβούλεθ᾽, ᾗ νόμων οὐδὲν μέλει· (765)
γυνὴ δ᾽ ἐπ᾽ αὐτῷ τῷδ᾽ ἔφυ." τί μῶρος εἶ;
1125 τραγικὴν ἐρῶ σοι ῥῆσιν ἐξ Αὔγης ὅλην
ἂν μή ποτ᾽ αἴσθῃ, Σμικρίνη.

ΣΜΙΚΡΙΝΗΣ

σύ μοι χολὴν
κ]ινεῖς παθαινομένη· σὺ γὰρ σφόδρ᾽ οἶσθ᾽ ὅ τι
οὗτο]ς λέγει νῦν.

ΟΝΗΣΙΜΟΣ

οἶδε· τοῦτ᾽ εὖ ἴσθ᾽ ὅτι (770)
ἡ γραῦ]ς προτέρα συνῆκε.

ΣΜΙΚΡΙΝΗΣ

πάνδεινον λέγεις.

ΟΝΗΣΙΜΟΣ

1130 οὐ γέγο]νε[ν] εὐτύχημα μεῖζον οὐδὲ ἕν.

ΣΜΙΚΡΙΝΗΣ

εἰ το]ῦτ᾽ ἀληθές ἐσθ᾽ ὃ λέγεις, τὸ παιδίον

1123–26 These lines assigned as one speech to Onesimos by
Sandbach (C has a paragraphus under line 1124 and dicola
before and after τιμωροσει). 1127 Suppl. ed. pr. 1128 οὗτο]ς
suppl. several. οἶδε· τοῦτ᾽ εὖ Sandbach: οιδε.ευ C. 1129
Suppl. Sudhaus. 1130–31 Suppl. Wilamowitz. Change of
speaker at the end of 1130 and assignment of parts in 1130–31
indicated by van Leeuwen (C has no dicolon after ουδεεν).

---

[1] A quotation from a lost tragedy of Euripides, the *Auge*
(fragment 920 Nauck[2]). Onesimos' references to this play
here and again in line 1125 are highly pointed. In Euripides'
play Auge was raped by Heracles at a night-festival, and bore
his child. The father's identity was discovered by means of a

EPITREPONTES

ONESIMOS

' So nature willed, and nature heeds no laws.
Woman was born for that.'[1]   You're so obtuse!
I'll quote you from the *Auge* one whole speech   1125
Of tragedy, if you can't grasp it, Smikrines!

(*Sophrone has now realised in full the implications of
Onesimos' hints, and she dances about the stage for joy, to
the anger of Smikrines, on whom the light of understanding
dawns much more slowly.*)

SMIKRINES (*to Sophrone*)

Your antics make me boil.   You *must* know what
He means!

ONESIMOS

          She does, [the old nurse] cottoned on
To this for sure first!

SMIKRINES (*now understanding*)

          It's a shocking tale!

ONESIMOS (*sententiously*)

No greater blessing['s] ever [come to pass]!   1130

SMIKRINES

[If] what you say is true, this baby then . . .

(*Here the Cairo papyrus breaks off.   The fifth act has
already been in progress for 163 lines; it is unlikely, in
its original extent, to have been longer than any of the
play's three central acts (247, 288 ±6, 272 ±6 lines

ring which he had left with her. By comparing Auge's
experiences with those of his own daughter Smikrines will be
able to come at least part of the way to realising what had
happened to Pamphile and Charisios.

MENANDER

(Lacuna of probably between 20 and 80 lines, up to
the end of the play)

Two fragments of Ἐπιτρέποντες, *quoted by ancient
authors*

9 (9 Körte-Thierfelder, 179 Kock)

This line is cited by the lexicographer Orion, *Antholo-
gnomici* 7. 8 (F. W. Schneidewin, *Conjectanea Critica*,
Göttingen 1839, 51), with its heading first given as ἐκ
τοῦ Γεωργίου (*sic*) but then corrected by the same
hand in the margin to ἐκ τῶν Ἀποτρεπόντων (*sic*:
emended to Ἐπιτρεπόντων by Schneidewin). With-
out the play-title but with the author's name the line
is cited also by Plutarch, *De Tranquillitate Animi* 475b,
and Stobaeus, *Eclogae* 4. 44. 57 (ὅτι δεῖ γενναίως
φέρειν τὰ προσπίπτοντα). Lucian, *Juppiter Tragoe-
dus* 53, in citing it refers to the author vaguely as ὁ
κωμικός. With neither title nor author's name it is
cited by Plutarch, *De Exilio* 599c; John Chrysostom,
In Matthaeum Homiliae 80 (al. 81), 771 (Migne, *P.G.*
lviii. 729); Diogenian, 7. 38; and Macarius, 6. 62.
It appears also in the collection of monostichs culled
from Menander (and other authors), 594 Jäkel.

οὐθὲν πέπονθας δεινόν, ἂν μὴ προσποῇ.

Fragment 9 οὐδὲν δὲ Orion: οὐδὲν or οὐθὲν the other citers (but
John Chrys. misquotes the beginning as οὐδὲν κακὸν πέπονθας).

respectively), and it may well have been a good deal shorter. In all probability, a loss of between 20 and 80 lines ought to be allowed for. How Menander wound up his plot it is now impossible to say in detail. The scene in which Onesimos spells out to the slow-witted Smikrines the facts about the baby born to Pamphile and Charisios and about the parents' happy reconciliation need have continued for only a few more lines after 1131. A new character in all likelihood then joined them (otherwise, why was it necessary in the preceding scene for Sophrone to be played by a mute?), but we can only speculate as to his or her identity. The characters with a potential role still to play in the plot are Habrotonon, Chairestratos, and Charisios. One possibility is that Charisios entered, greeted his father-in-law, and then invited him to an evening party in celebration of the day's events. This would at any rate provide a suitable context for the conventional dramatic coda of promulgated revelry, the request for torch and garlands, and a prayer for Victory, perhaps identical in wording with that preserved in the closing lines of the Dyskolos, 968–69). ————————————

Two fragments of Epitrepontes, quoted by ancient authors

9

A line cited by the lexicographer Orion, Antholognomici 7. 8, and by several other authors (who fail to identify the precise source), as listed on the facing page.

You've met with no reverse if you pretend
[It] never [happened].

These words could have been addressed by Onesimos or Charisios to Smikrines somewhere after line 1131. They would perhaps best suit Onesimos' cocky self-assurance in response to a self-pitying complaint by Smikrines about the disgrace of a grandchild conceived out of wedlock.

MENANDER

10 (10 KT, 176 K)

Stobaeus, *Eclogae* 4. 29. 58 (περὶ εὐγενείας). Μενάνδρου Ἐπιτρέποντος (*sic*: first corrected to -όντων apparently by Meineke).

ἐλευθέρῳ τὸ καταγελᾶσθαι μὲν πολὺ
αἴσχιόν ἐστι, τὸ δ᾽ ὀδυνᾶσθ᾽ ἀνθρώπινον.

Papyrus scraps of Ἐπιτρέποντες *which cannot safely be assigned to a particular context*

11a–11f (frs. 135 V–X Austin, *C.G.F.*)

Fragments 11a to 11f inclusive are six tiny scraps of P. *Oxyrhynchus* 2829 which do not overlap any otherwise known part of the play.

<table>
<tr><td align="center">a</td><td align="center">b</td></tr>
<tr><td>

]εισομαι [
]εισθαικ[
] . ει πάλαι
] . . . λ[

</td><td>

]ξ[
ἀπ]ό[κ]οιτος ἐξ ὅτου[
]ενε . . [. .]τ᾽ ἐξο[
]ων ἐμοί. : τί φησι με[

</td></tr>
<tr><td align="center">c</td><td align="center">d</td></tr>
<tr><td>

] . . [
εἴλ]ηφ᾽ ὅλως
ἐ]βούλετο
] . πεπεισμε . [

</td><td>

] . . . οθ[
]αναξ . [

</td></tr>
<tr><td align="center">e</td><td align="center">f</td></tr>
<tr><td>

] . . . [
]αυτη π[
] . . [

</td><td>

]ε . . νω[
]υδε . [

</td></tr>
</table>

Fragment 10, line 1 μὲν om. Stobaeus, suppl. Heringa.
Fragment 11b, line 2 Suppl. Weinstein.
Fragment 11c, lines 2–3 Suppl. Weinstein.

EPITREPONTES

10

Quoted by Stobaeus, Eclogae 4. 29. 58 (the section headed 'On Nobility ').

It's far more shameful when a free man's held
To scorn—but pain is part of human life.

These lines are hard to place; but if they come from the play's lost ending, they could be spoken either by Smikrines to Onesimos in the same part of the scene from which fr. 9 seems to derive, or by a third character such as Charisios expressing sympathy for Smikrines in his misfortune.

Papyrus scraps of Epitrepontes which cannot safely be assigned to a particular context

11a–11f

P. Oxyrhynchus 2829 consists of ten fragments, four larger ones which duplicate material already known from the Cairo papyrus (lines 218–56, 310–22, 347–61), and six insignificant scraps which, with the possible exception of fragment 11e (but see below), do not. It is a reasonable, but totally unverifiable, hypothesis that these six scraps, here numbered fragments 11a–11f, derive from the same area of the play as the four placed fragments of P. Oxyrhynchus 2829. Frs. 11a–11f, however, yield no single passage of connected sense, and only a word or phrase here and there is conducive to translation (11a, line 3 of old; b, 2 sleeping out since . . . , 4 to me, followed by a different speaker who asks What does he/ she say that I or say that . . . me; c, 1 have/has taken wholly, 2 he/she wished, 3 persuaded; e, 2 it or her). But despite the general insignificance of these shreds of text, two passages call for more detailed comment. First, the sequence of five letters in the Greek of fr. 11e, line 2, matches a sequence in the middle of Epitrepontes 364. However, the traces of three letters in line 1 of fr. 11 e, indistinct as they are, do not at all square with any of the letters in the corresponding portion of Epitr. 363, and so it seems unlikely that this shred of papyrus derives from that preserved section of the play. Secondly, fr. 11b clearly derives from a dialogue (a change of speaker is indicated in its line 4) about Charisios' behaviour subsequent to his separation from Pamphile, for the words

---

A papyrus scrap which is hesitantly assigned to Ἐπιτρέποντες

12 (fr. 138 Austin, *C.G.F.*)

Fragment 12 is a tiny scrap of papyrus (*P. Berlin* 21142), which has been tentatively attributed to this play because its text mentions the name Charisios (line 3), which up to now is not known to occur in any other Greek comedy but this. The scrap contains fragments of two columns of text. From the first only the final letters of lines 1 (ς) and 10 (ν) are preserved; from the second, the following line beginnings: εἰς ἕτερα ν[1, ἤδη 'στὶ πει[2, Χαρισίῳ πρ[3, ἀλλὰ λέλυτα[ι 4, πίνειν μ[5, βινεῖν ε . [6, οὐθείς. : κελ[ευ 7, προστάξατ .[8, ἀγαπα κολα[9, ἐπισταλη .[10, εἰρη .[11.

Fragment 12 was assigned to this play by Maehler. Lines 4, 7 Suppl. Austin.

EPITREPONTES

' sleeping out ([ἀπ]ό[κ]οιτος) since . . .' can refer only
to Charisios. At line 136 Smikrines applies the same
adjective ἀπόκοιτος to the same behaviour of Charisios,
but that fact alone cannot be used as evidence for the
identification of the speakers in fr. 11b. Other characters
than Smikrines could have commented in the lost portions
of the play about Charisios' desertion of his wife.

*A papyrus scrap which is hesitantly assigned to Epitre-
pontes*

12

P. Berlin 21142 is a small scrap containing fragments of
two columns of dramatic text. From the second the
initial letters of 11 lines are preserved. It was originally
a passage of lively dialogue, for paragraphi indicate
changes of speaker in every line except 10, and a dicolon
is preserved in line 7. The following snatches yield to
translation: To other things (1), Is now (2), Charisios
(3), But it/he/she has been solved/released (4), To
drink (5), To make love (6), Nobody.—Order (7),
Command (8), He/she is content *or* Be content (9),
Arranged (10), Peaceful (?) (11). The major reason for
attributing this scrap of papyrus to the Epitrepontes is the
occurrence of the name Charisios in line 3. Unlike those
character names like Smikrines and Moschion which are
repeated in play after play of New Comedy, Charisios so
far is known only from the Epitrepontes. Some weight
must be given also to the fact that the subject-matter of the
scrap—drinking and wenching (lines 5–6)—squares well
with Charisios' alleged behaviour in the early part of the
play. If the attribution is correct, a plausible context for
the scrap would be provided by the conversation between

Karion and Onesimos which is known to have opened the play. βινεῖν (6) *is more likely to have been spoken by a cook or slave than a free man, and it is clear that in their expository opening scene Onesimos and the cook discussed the riotous behaviour of Charisios and his apparent liaison with Habrotonon (see p. 386 f.).*

THE LOEB CLASSICAL LIBRARY

VOLUMES ALREADY PUBLISHED

Latin Authors

1

2

Ovid: Heroides and Amores. Grant Showerman. Revised by G. P. Goold

Ovid: Metamorphoses. F. J. Miller. 2 Vols. Vol. 1 revised by G. P. Goold.

Ovid: Tristia and Ex Ponto. A. L. Wheeler.

Persius. Cf. Juvenal.

Petronius. M. Heseltine; Seneca; Apocolocyntosis. W. H. D. Rouse.

Phaedrus and Babrius (Greek). B. E. Perry.

Plautus. Paul Nixon. 5 Vols.

Pliny: Letters, Panegyricus. Betty Radice. 2 Vols.

Pliny: Natural History. Vols. I.–V. and IX. H. Rackham. VI.–VIII. W. H. S. Jones. X. D. E. Eichholz. 10 Vols.

Propertius. H. E. Butler.

Prudentius. H. J. Thomson. 2 Vols.

Quintilian. H. E. Butler. 4 Vols.

Remains of Old Latin. E. H. Warmington. 4 Vols. Vol. I. (Ennius and Caecilius.) Vol. II. (Livius, Naevius, Pacuvius, Accius.) Vol. III. (Lucilius and Laws of XII Tables.) Vol. IV. (Archaic Inscriptions.)

Sallust. J. C. Rolfe.

Scriptores Historiae Augustae. D. Magie. 3 Vols.

Seneca, The Elder: Controversiae, Suasoriae. M. Winterbottom. 2 Vols.

Seneca: Apocolocyntosis. Cf. Petronius.

Seneca: Epistulae Morales. R. M. Gummere. 3 Vols.

Seneca: Moral Essays. J. W. Basore. 3 Vols.

Seneca: Tragedies. F. J. Miller. 2 Vols.

Seneca: Naturales Quaestiones. T. H. Corcoran. 2 Vols.

Sidonius: Poems and Letters. W. B. Anderson. 2 Vols.

Silius Italicus. J. D. Duff. 2 Vols.

Statius. J. H. Mozley. 2 Vols.

Suetonius. J. C. Rolfe. 2 Vols.

Tacitus: Dialogus. Sir Wm. Peterson. Agricola and Germania. Maurice Hutton. Revised by M. Winterbottom, R. M. Ogilvie, E. H. Warmington.

Tacitus: Histories and Annals. C. H. Moore and J. Jackson. 4 Vols.

Terence. John Sargeaunt. 2 Vols.

Tertullian: Apologia and De Spectaculis. T. R. Glover. Minucius Felix. G. H. Rendall.

Valerius Flaccus. J. H. Mozley.

Varro: De Lingua Latina. R. G. Kent. 2 Vols.

Velleius Paterculus and Res Gestae Divi Augusti. F. W. Shipley.

Virgil. H. R. Fairclough. 2 Vols.

Vitruvius: De Architectura. F. Granger. 2 Vols.

Greek Authors

ACHILLES TATIUS. S. Gaselee.

AELIAN: ON THE NATURE OF ANIMALS. A. F. Scholfield. 3 Vols.

AENEAS TACTICUS, ASCLEPIODOTUS and ONASANDER. The Illinois Greek Club.

AESCHINES. C. D. Adams.

AESCHYLUS. H. Weir Smyth. 2 Vols.

ALCIPHRON, AELIAN, PHILOSTRATUS: LETTERS. A. R. Benner and F. H. Fobes.

ANDOCIDES, ANTIPHON, Cf. MINOR ATTIC ORATORS.

APOLLODORUS. Sir James G. Frazer. 2 Vols.

APOLLONIUS RHODIUS. R. C. Seaton.

THE APOSTOLIC FATHERS. Kirsopp Lake. 2 Vols.

APPIAN: ROMAN HISTORY. Horace White. 4 Vols.

ARATUS. Cf. CALLIMACHUS.

ARISTIDES: ORATIONS. C. A. Behr. Vol. I.

ARISTOPHANES. Benjamin Bickley Rogers. 3 Vols. Verse trans.

ARISTOTLE: ART OF RHETORIC. J. H. Freese.

ARISTOTLE: ATHENIAN CONSTITUTION, EUDEMIAN ETHICS, VICES AND VIRTUES. H. Rackham.

ARISTOTLE: GENERATION OF ANIMALS. A. L. Peck.

ARISTOTLE: HISTORIA ANIMALIUM. A. L. Peck. Vols I.–II.

ARISTOTLE: METAPHYSICS. H. Tredennick. 2 Vols.

ARISTOTLE: METEOROLOGICA. H. D. P. Lee.

ARISTOTLE: MINOR WORKS. W. S. Hett. On Colours, On Things Heard, On Physiognomies, On Plants, On Marvellous Things Heard, Mechanical Problems, On Indivisible Lines, On Situations and Names of Winds, On Melissus, Xenophanes, and Gorgias.

ARISTOTLE: NICOMACHEAN ETHICS. H. Rackham.

ARISTOTLE: OECONOMICA and MAGNA MORALIA. G. C. Armstrong; (with METAPHYSICS, Vol. II.).

ARISTOTLE: ON THE HEAVENS. W. K. C. Guthrie.

ARISTOTLE: ON THE SOUL. PARVA NATURALIA. ON BREATH. W. S. Hett.

ARISTOTLE: CATEGORIES, ON INTERPRETATION, PRIOR ANALYTICS. H. P. Cooke and H. Tredennick.

ARISTOTLE: POSTERIOR ANALYTICS, TOPICS. H. Tredennick and E. S. Forster.

ARISTOTLE: ON SOPHISTICAL REFUTATIONS.
On Coming to be and Passing Away, On the Cosmos. E. S. Forster and D. J. Furley.

ARISTOTLE: PARTS OF ANIMALS. A. L. Peck; MOTION AND PROGRESSION OF ANIMALS. E. S. Forster.

ARISTOTLE: PHYSICS. Rev. P. Wicksteed and F. M. Cornford. 2 Vols.

ARISTOTLE: POETICS and LONGINUS. W. Hamilton Fyfe; DEMETRIUS ON STYLE. W. Rhys Roberts.

ARISTOTLE: POLITICS. H. Rackham.

ARISTOTLE: PROBLEMS. W. S. Hett. 2 Vols.

ARISTOTLE: RHETORICA AD ALEXANDRUM (with PROBLEMS. Vol. II). H. Rackham.

ARRIAN: HISTORY OF ALEXANDER and INDICA. 2 Vols. Vol. I. P. Brunt. Vol. II. Rev. E. Iliffe Robson.

ATHENAEUS: DEIPNOSOPHISTAE. C. B. Gulick. 7 Vols.

BABRIUS AND PHAEDRUS (Latin). B. E. Perry.

ST. BASIL: LETTERS. R. J. Deferrair. 4 Vols.

CALLIMACHUS: FRAGMENTS. C. A. Trypanis. MUSAEUS: HERO AND LEANDER. T. Gelzer and C. Whitman.

CALLIMACHUS, Hymns and Epigrams, and LYCOPHRON. A. W. Mair; ARATUS. G. R. Mair.

CLEMENT OF ALEXANDRIA. Rev. G. W. Butterworth.

COLLUTHUS. Cf. OPPIAN.

DAPHNIS AND CHLOE. Thornley's Translation revised by J. M. Edmonds: and PARTHENIUS. S. Gaselee.

DEMOSTHENES I.: OLYNTHIACS, PHILIPPICS and MINOR ORATIONS. I.–XVII. AND XX. J. H. Vince.

DEMOSTHENES II.: DE CORONA and DE FALSA LEGATIONE. C. A. Vince and J. H. Vince.

DEMOSTHENES III.: MEIDIAS, ANDROTION, ARISTOCRATES, TIMOCRATES and ARISTOGEITON, I. and II. J. H. Vince.

DEMOSTHENES IV.–VI.: PRIVATE ORATIONS and IN NEAERAM. A. T. Murray.

DEMOSTHENES VII: FUNERAL SPEECH, EROTIC ESSAY, EXORDIA and LETTERS. N. W. and N. J. DeWitt.

DIO CASSIUS: ROMAN HISTORY. E. Cary. 9 Vols.

DIO CHRYSOSTOM. J. W. Cohoon and H. Lamar Crosby. 5 Vols.

DIODORUS SICULUS. 12 Vols. Vols. I.–VI. C. H. Oldfather. Vol. VII. C. L. Sherman. Vol. VIII. C. B. Welles. Vols. IX. and X. R. M. Geer. Vol. XI. F. Walton. Vol. XII. F. Walton. General Index. R. M. Geer.

DIOGENES LAERTIUS. R. D. Hicks. 2 Vols. New Introduction by H. S. Long.

DIONYSIUS OF HALICARNASSUS: ROMAN ANTIQUITIES. Spelman's translation revised by E. Cary. 7 Vols.

DIONYSIUS OF HALICARNASSUS: CRITICAL ESSAYS. S. Usher. 2 Vols.

EPICTETUS. W. A. Oldfather. 2 Vols.

EURIPIDES. A. S. Way. 4 Vols. Verse trans.

EUSEBIUS: ECCLESIASTICAL HISTORY. Kirsopp Lake and J. E. L. Oulton. 2 Vols.

GALEN: ON THE NATURAL FACULTIES. A. J. Brock.

THE GREEK ANTHOLOGY. W. R. Paton. 5 Vols.

GREEK ELEGY AND IAMBUS with the ANACREONTEA. J. M. Edmonds. 2 Vols.

THE GREEK BUCOLIC POETS (THEOCRITUS, BION, MOSCHUS). J. M. Edmonds.

GREEK MATHEMATICAL WORKS. Ivor Thomas. 2 Vols.

HERODES. Cf. THEOPHRASTUS: CHARACTERS.

HERODIAN. C. R. Whittaker. 2 Vols.

HERODOTUS. A. D. Godley. 4 Vols.

HESIOD AND THE HOMERIC HYMNS. H. G. Evelyn White.

HIPPOCRATES and the FRAGMENTS OF HERACLEITUS. W. H. S. Jones and E. T. Withington. 4 Vols.

HOMER: ILIAD. A. T. Murray. 2 Vols.

HOMER: ODYSSEY. A. T. Murray. 2 Vols.

ISAEUS. E. W. Forster.

ISOCRATES. George Norlin and LaRue Van Hook. 3 Vols.

[ST. JOHN DAMASCENE]: BARLAAM AND IOASAPH. Rev. G. R. Woodward, Harold Mattingly and D. M. Lang.

JOSEPHUS. 9 Vols. Vols. I.–IV. H. Thackeray. Vol. V. H. Thackeray and R. Marcus. Vols. VI.–VII. R. Marcus. Vol. VIII. R. Marcus and Allen Wikgren. Vol. IX. L. H. Feldman.

JULIAN. Wilmer Cave Wright. 3 Vols.

LIBANIUS. A. F. Norman. Vols. I.–II.

LUCIAN. 8 Vols. Vols. I.–V. A. M. Harmon. Vol. VI. K. Kilburn. Vols. VII.–VIII. M. D. Macleod.

LYCOPHRON. Cf. CALLIMACHUS.

LYRA GRAECA. J. M. Edmonds. 3 Vols.

LYSIAS. W. R. M. Lamb.

MANETHO. W. G. Waddell: PTOLEMY: TETRABIBLOS. F. E. Robbins.

MARCUS AURELIUS. C. R. Haines.

MENANDER. I New edition by W. G. Arnott.

MINOR ATTIC ORATORS (ANTIPHON, ANDOCIDES, LYCURGUS, DEMADES, DINARCHUS, HYPERIDES). K. J. Maidment and J. O. Burtt. 2 Vols.

MUSAEUS: HEOR AND LEANDER. Cf. CALLIMACHUS.

NONNOS: DIONYSIACA. W. H. D. Rouse. 3 Vols.

OPPIAN, COLLUTHUS, TRYPHIODORUS. A. W. Mair.

PAPYRI. NON-LITERARY SELECTIONS. A. S. Hunt and C. C. Edgar. 2 Vols. LITERARY SELECTIONS (Poetry). D. L. Page.

PARTHENIUS. Cf. DAPHNIS and CHLOE.

PAUSANIAS: DESCRIPTION OF GREECE. W. H. S. Jones. 4 Vols. and Companion Vol. arranged by R. E. Wycherley.

PHILO. 10 Vols. Vols. I.–V. F. H. Colson and Rev. G. H. Whitaker. Vols. VI.–IX. F. H. Colson. Vol. X. F. H. Colson and the Rev. J. W. Earp.

PHILO: two supplementary Vols. (*Translation only.*) Ralph Marcus.

PHILOSTRATUS: THE LIFE OF APOLLONIUS OF TYANA. F. C. Conybeare. 2 Vols.

PHILOSTRATUS: IMAGINES; CALLISTRATUS: DESCRIPTIONS. A. Fairbanks.

PHILOSTRATUS and EUNAPIUS: LIVES OF THE SOPHISTS. Wilmer Cave Wright.

PINDAR. Sir J. E. Sandys.

PLATO: CHARMIDES, ALCIBIADES, HIPPARCHUS, THE LOVERS, THEAGES, MINOS and EPINOMIS. W. R. M. Lamb.

PLATO: CRATYLUS, PARMENIDES, GREATER HIPPIAS, LESSER HIPPIAS. H. N. Fowler.

PLATO: EUTHYPHRO, APOLOGY, CRITO, PHAEDO, PHAEDRUS, H. N. Fowler.

PLATO: LACHES, PROTAGORAS, MENO, EUTHYDEMUS. W. R. M. Lamb.

PLATO: LAWS. Rev. R. G. Bury. 2 Vols.

PLATO: LYSIS, SYMPOSIUM, GORGIAS. W. R. M. Lamb.

PLATO: Republic. Paul Shorey. 2 Vols.

PLATO: STATESMAN, PHILEBUS. H. N. Fowler; Ion. W. R. M. Lamb.

PLATO: THEAETETUS and SOPHIST. H. N. Fowler.

PLATO: TIMAEUS, CRITIAS, CLITOPHO, MENEXENUS, EPISTULAE. Rev. R. G. Bury.

PLOTINUS: A. H. Armstrong. Vols. I.–III.

PLUTARCH: MORALIA. 17 Vols. Vols. I.–V. F. C. Babbitt. Vol. VI. W. C. Helmbold. Vols. VII. and XIV. P. H. De Lacy and B. Einarson. Vol. VIII. P. A. Clement and H. B. Hoffleit. Vol. IX. E. L. Minar, Jr., F. H. Sandbach, W. C. Helmbold. Vol. X. H. N. Fowler. Vol. XI. L. Pearson and F. H. Sandbach. Vol. XII. H. Cherniss and W. C. Helmbold. Vol. XIII 1–2. H. Cherniss. Vol. XV. F. H. Sandbach.

PLUTARCH: THE PARALLEL LIVES. B. Perrin. 11 Vols.

POLYBIUS. W. R. Paton. 6 Vols.

PROCOPIUS: HISTORY OF THE WARS. H. B. Dewing. 7 Vols.

PTOLEMY: TETRABIBLOS. Cf. MANETHO.

QUINTUS SMYRNAEUS. A. S. Way. Verse trans.

SEXTUS EMPIRICUS. Rev. R. G. Bury. 4 Vols.

SOPHOCLES. F. Storr. 2 Vols. Verse trans.

STRABO: GEOGRAPHY. Horace L. Jones. 8 Vols.

THEOPHRASTUS: CHARACTERS. J. M. Edmonds. HERODES, etc. A. D. Knox.